"As a professional therapist working with disabled clients, I found *Beyond Victims and Villains* to be an enlightenment. Because we live with these characters, hearing them speak in their own voices, we become more attuned to the voices of those with whom we work. *Beyond Victims and Villains* is a unique and valuable resource for our professional communities."

—CYNTHIA WINEINGER, PROFESSOR,
COMMUNICATIVE DISORDERS, UNIVERSITY OF REDLANDS

BEYOND VICTIMS
AND VILLAINS

BEYOND VICTIMS AND VILLAINS:

Contemporary Plays by Disabled Playwrights

Edited by Victoria Ann Lewis

THEATRE COMMUNICATIONS GROUP
NEW YORK
2006

Beyond Victims and Villains: Contemporary Plays by Disabled Playwrights
is published by Theatre Communications Group, Inc., 520 Eighth Ave.,
24th Floor, New York, NY 10018-4156.

This publication is made possible in part with funds from the New York State
Council on the Arts, a State Agency.

TCG books are exclusively distributed to the book trade by Consortium Book
Sales and Distribution, 1045 Westgate Drive, St. Paul, MN 55114.

LIBRARY OF CONGRESS CATALOGING-IN-PUBLICATION DATA
Beyond victims and villains : contemporary plays by disabled playwrights /
edited by Victoria Ann Lewis.
p. cm.
ISBN-13: 978-1-55936-250-4
ISBN-10: 1-55936-250-2 (pbk. : alk. paper)
1. People with disabilities, Writings of, American. 2. People with disabilities—
Drama. 3. American drama—21st century. I. Lewis, Victoria.
PS628.P46B49   2005
812'.60809207—dc22
2004028026

Cover design by Lisa Govan
Cover image: *Self V, 1999,* (30″ x 40″ oil), Daniel Keplinger; courtesy of
the Phyllis Kind Gallery, New York
Book design and composition by Lisa Govan

First Edition, July 2006

In memory of John Belluso
1969–2006

*"I live my life every day with a great deal
of optimism for our future as a society.
Optimism is a radical weapon."*

Table of Contents

Foreword

By John Hockenberry

When I think about the importance of theater I'm drawn to one of the most dramatic moments in all of Western literature. It is in the Alexandre Dumas novel *The Count of Monte Cristo.* After many months alone in a dark, remote dungeon, prisoner Edmond Dantès hears a faint scratching sound in the stones of his cell and realizes that there is on the other side of the wall another prisoner trying to contact him. For these two entombed men awareness is transformative. For Dantès that contact becomes the basis for restored hope followed by escape from the prison and Dantès's eventual redemption and triumph.

Playwright Susan Nussbaum supplied me with such a transformative moment back in the 1980s. The performance of her play *Staring Back* constituted the scratching on the other side of a wall. I hardly considered myself any kind of a prisoner but the voice of such a strong, sure artist, bringing to the stage the experience of life with a disability, told me I was not alone. To see the effect Nussbaum's words had on a rapt, near hysterical, nondisabled audience was even more powerful. Who were these people, I wondered, who found themselves in this dark room peering through Nussbaum's theatrical window into a new world? I had been raised in the community theater. I thought I understood the power and significance of theater, the connection between audiences and the voices of playwrights seeking the outer edge of life's epic riddles. I can say I had no inkling whatever of the power of theater until that moment when

I saw my own experience up on that stage and realized I was not some walled-off individual but a part of something.

For all time people have used theater as the first tool in articulating a community's life stories and making them a part of the universal human experience. Today the signs of disability culture are everywhere. Disability is an experience that raises deep political and moral questions. It is a narrative that has taken its place as part of the American and global experience. This is the value of these plays. They take us somewhere different and bring us home to a binding universality. These are the precious heirlooms of an emerging culture, the defining manuscripts in the library of some twenty-first-century Alexandria.

Aside from being some of the most talented and inventive playwrights writing today, these authors have also staked out a remote territory and brought audiences into that wilderness to see the world in a new way. Theater can do no better. Writing can be no bolder. The characters in these pages will not go away, they haunt the memory with their voices insisting on living, on being. Life itself can show us no more dramatic birth. It is one of the great ironies of art that these solitary playwrights working alone in their quiet writing places teach us above all through their work that we are not alone. There can be no worthier project than this collection curated by an angel named Vicki Lewis, whose commitment to finding and celebrating emerging voices is lifelong and has already enriched the theater world beyond measure. Because of her, the faint scratching noise behind the wall is no longer faint, and the wall itself is coming down.

Acknowledgments

The bulk of credit for this book goes to the playwrights. I thank them for trusting me with their extraordinary work.

In addition, a few of the many people and programs whose contributions underpin this collection are: Paula Terry, Director of the AccessAbility Office at the National Endowment for the Arts; the California Arts Council Artist in Residency program; Victory Gardens Theater; Barbara Trader and John Kemp, formerly with VSA *arts*; Ensemble Studio Theatre's Youngblood program; New Dramatists; the Non-Traditional Casting Project; Irene Oppenheim of Firehouse Theater Company; and Center Theatre Group/Mark Taper Forum and its Other Voices Project. I am grateful for the role that Gordon Davidson, Terri Jones, Corey Madden, Mara Isaacs, Frank Dwyer, and many, many others at the Taper played in introducing the work of disabled theater artists to the world of not-for-profit theater. My thanks to all those artists and activists who participated in Other Voices over the years. Your talents and ambitions inform this anthology. Special thanks to Robert David Hall, Olivia Raynor and Marty Sweeney.

Important sounding boards for the history and analysis of disability and the performing arts presented in this anthology include Marcy Epstein, Susan Crutchfield, David T. Mitchell, Sharon L. Snyder, Beth Haller, Corinne Kirchner, Teresa A. Meade and David Serlin. In addition, the Society for Disability Studies, The Association for Theatre in Higher Education, the American Society for Theatre Research, and the American Historical Association have all been part of this conversation about disability and drama. Since his first publications on disability and the media, historian Paul K. Longmore has been one of my dramaturgical divining rods. My personal thanks to Paul and to Rosemarie Garland Thomson who opened doors for me and legitimated this work in the academy at several critical junctures. Colleague Carrie Sandahl has produced a powerful body of critical work that has already changed the playing field for disabled theater artists and scholars. Carrie has generously supported and amplified the work of this anthology in countless ways. I am also fortunate to have as friend and advisor Anne Finger whose devotion to the disability community is surpassed only by her gifts as a writer. I am grateful to my colleagues at the University of Redlands for granting me the 2002–2003 Faculty Research/Creative Activity Award and the theater department for encouraging me to finish this work.

Two initiatives of Theatre Communications Group laid the groundwork for this anthology. The first was a TCG Observership I received in 1994. I traveled across the United States meeting with literary and casting departments at major regional theaters and interviewing actors and playwrights from grassroots, disability-identified theater companies in those same cities. The second was the April 2001 issue of *American Theatre*: "Access, Activism and Art." Editor Jim O'Quinn put together one of the first serious discussions in the professional theater about the artistic ramifications of a growing disability culture.

I am grateful to everyone at Theatre Communications Group for shepherding this anthology through the complex process of publication, and especially Terry Nemeth who took the leap and commissioned the work. Editors Kathy Sova and Gretchen Van Lente are responsible for the book you hold in your hands. Every page bears evidence of their attentive and sensitive readings and their insistence that the intentions of the playwrights be meticulously honored. I am especially grateful to Kathy for her faith in and respect for this project and this editor.

To my patient and savvy friends: Doris Baizley, Leslie Brody, Debbie Hoffmann, Lynn Jeffries, Murray Ross, Ann Stocking—and John Belluso. Thanks for the good notes, the good advice, heeded or not, and the good cheer.

Introduction

By Victoria Ann Lewis

> Let me tell you this, when social workers offer you, free, gratis and for nothing, something . . . it is useless to recoil, they will pursue you to the ends of the earth, the vomitory in their hands . . . Against the charitable gesture there is no defense, that I know of. You sink your head, you put out your hands all trembling and twined together and you say, Thank you, thank you lady, thank you kind lady. To him who has nothing it is forbidden not to relish filth.
>
> —Samuel Beckett
> *Molloy*

> People are always saying how great I am and how courageous, and things like that, and I just sit there and say to myself, "Bullshit. This has nothing to do with any of that stuff. It really doesn't." And I try to get that across, but when you say that, people always think you're trying to be self-effacing or humble. I really want them to know it really doesn't have a goddam thing to do with that.
>
> —Paul Ryan
> Sit-down comic; contributing writer of
> *P.H. *reaks: The Hidden History of People with Disabilities*

I have a memory of myself as a nine year old walking down the street outside our apartment building. From an open window, from behind a hedge, from some hidden place, children began to chant, "Cripple! Cripple!" I had never heard the word spoken out loud, polite and protected as I was, but when I heard it, it was all at once familiar to me, as if, like Rumpelstiltskin, I had finally been confronted with my real name. I was no longer a kid in Texas in the 1950s who had a crush on Bob and Christine on *American Bandstand*, who had played one of the Twelve Dancing Princesses in the grade school play and who had happened to get polio at the age of three—I was The Cripple and had been so for centuries. The taunting children came across time and found me out.

"Most of any present is made up of the past," critic Terry Eagleton notes in his discussion of cultural change. Our perception and experience of the present moment is made possible by our considerable inheritance from the past in the form of language and social structures. The young children who taunted me were only exhibiting their successful mastery of a long cultural and linguistic practice of assigning meaning to the impaired body. Possibly, most probably, they had been taught that they shouldn't make fun of people like me, that they should feel sorry for me. But they understood what is clear to any person with a disability—that contempt is the flip side of pity, that "the charitable gesture" can be as cruel as it is kind.

For example, in 1978, I was working on an article about employment opportunities for disabled people in the computer industry. One of my sources, the executive in charge of computer programming for the Bank of America in Northern California, met me outside a downtown San Francisco subway station. He was a well-groomed man wearing an impeccably tailored three-piece suit. He was also significantly disabled by cerebral palsy and drove an electric wheelchair. On the way back to his office for the interview, we paused at an intersection. As we waited for the light to change, a woman dropped some change into the executive's lap. Apparently for this charitable passerby the only explanation for the presence of a significantly disabled person in a public setting was that he must be a beggar. I was stunned by the insult and flushed with anger but my companion remained calm. When the walk sign flashed he pressed on his wheelchair's joy stick and coolly moved into the crosswalk via a curbcut, one of many recently blasted into intersections in San Francisco's downtown business district. Like Beckett's Molloy the bank executive had learned long ago that it "was useless to recoil" from the "charitable gesture." Like sit-down comic, Paul Ryan, he had understood that the myths of disability embedded in our culture would not give way easily. Contesting one's status as a tragic-but-brave object of charity would most likely only result in being labeled as its opposite, the only other role available, that of the bitter cripple, eager to attack and revenge him/herself upon the more fortunate, nondisabled world. The typecasting of the person with a disability has been set for centuries—either "victim" or "villain."

Despite three decades of collective struggle and the passage of several landmark disability civil rights laws, our contemporary streets, our theaters and mass media are still haunted by the ghosts of a disability past. In the 1980s when disabled actors in the performing unions pressured advertisers to include people with disabilities in their spots, the ad executives responded, "But we only have thirty seconds. How could we explain what a guy in a wheelchair is doing in a United ad?" The advertisers' response was not visionary but it was accurate. Using victims and villains to sell airline tickets was counterintuitive.

The playwrights in this collection are highly various and at first glance have more in common with other writers and theatrical movements and impulses than with each other. But they are one in their rejection of the universalizing stories or narratives of disability and in their refusal to accept the subtext of superiority that underlies the charitable gesture. This anthology, the title announces, will take the reader "beyond" the invalidating and infantilizing roles of victim and villain into which the disabled body has been cast in theatrical text and performance. But "beyond" should not be confused with transcendence or an overcoming of the physical body, some sort of cosmic trade-in where one loses one's body but gains a larger intellect or soul. These writers work not so much "beyond" conventional roles as within, beneath, and beside the metaphors and familiar interpretations of the impaired body, giving voice to the moments of silence, shaping the excess of experience that is kept in check by the conventional narratives on the streets, in educational and medical institutions, and on the stage.

THIS ANTHOLOGY

The goal of this anthology is to encourage professional, academic and community-based theaters to produce the plays included, and to search out the work of other talented disabled playwrights, performers and theater artists not out of civic duty but because of the artistic return they will reap from such explorations. The plays in this anthology have all been chosen first for their artistic merit—their language, their staging power, their wit and innovation. Most have been produced by "professional" companies, i.e., theaters that pay artists and technicians and generally only accept scripts from authors represented by literary agents. This does not make these plays better than those that did not make it through the "ring of fire" surrounding the literary departments of the major regional theaters. But it does mean that these plays have had an audience, been critically judged, and benefited from the kind of developmental process that comes with new play development in the American theater—work in the rehearsal room with a director, dramaturg and professional actors. Some have won prestigious awards from the theatrical establishment. Only one has previously been published in its entirety, but several have found their way to multiple productions through the power of word of mouth. This anthology will also give writers and critics in the interdisciplinary fields of disability studies, cultural studies, women's studies and performance studies, whose explorations of disability have of necessity been focused on other literary and performance genres such as the novel and film, an opportunity to investigate playtexts, initially on the page, and most importantly on the stage.

The plays in this anthology are multivoiced dramas, not solo pieces of performance art—even though it is in performance art, and its counterpart in popular culture, stand-up (sit-down) comedy, that disabled actors and writers have been most prolific since the early 1970s. A solo performer can negotiate directly with the audience and win a judgment in favor of a more complex identity. But, practically speaking, solo work is limited—if it is fair to use such a term when referring to such compelling comedy as that of Geri Jewell or Nancy Kennedy or such virtuosic performances and elegantly crafted texts as those of solo artists Cheryl Marie Wade, David Roche and Ann Stocking (and many others I am not mentioning)—because such work must be performed by the individual, unique artist. This anthology presents multivoice-character plays in order to provide playtexts that can be interpreted by many different actors.

Also, with multicharactered drama comes the possibility of a complex presentation of social life. African American playwrights such as Zora Neale Hurston, Lorraine Hansberry, August Wilson, George Wolfe and Suzan-Lori Parks have created dramas with multiple, differentiated characters involved in stories that illuminate the social and political worlds of the African American experience in America. The plays in this anthology are concerned with a similar project—to present disability not as an individual condition, but as part of a social and historical process that takes shape between people and across divisions of race, class and gender.

The writers here, with the exception of Doris Baizley, my co-adapter on *P.H. *reaks: The Hidden History of People with Disabilities,* are all disabled. That doesn't make the plays good or bad but it does make them somewhat unusual. Though disabled characters occur in literally thousands of plays across time in the Western tradition, seldom have the writers of these dramas been disabled themselves. Not discounting recent scholarship in the emerging field of disability studies, which suggests that the role of disability in the lives of literary giants such as Lord Byron, Samuel Johnson and Alexander Pope has been underestimated, the fact remains that the disabled figure continues to be available to all comers in unending supply. The restraints of realism—which have influenced representation of the working class, women, gays and ethnic minorities in the twentieth century—are seldom imposed when it comes to disability. Thus even the progressive American filmmaker John Sayles, capable of nuanced portraits of black/white and class relations, presents a ham-fisted portrayal of an alcoholic, recently disabled woman, in his film *Passion Fish.* In this movie-of-the-week scenario the self-pitying disabled woman is brought to her senses by the intervention and tough love of her paid, personal attendant. Sayles appropriates the disabled figure to tell his story, showing little interest in exploring the material conditions of disabled people, who are in modern societies, "the poorest of the poor."

In this colonial, missionary attitude toward the disabled subject, drama reflects a larger social pattern in which the nondisabled expert, be that a social worker, doctor, nurse, teacher, speech pathologist, psychiatrist, etc., interprets and defines the disability experience and controls the life options of the disabled person. The emphasis of the Disability Civil Rights Movement, also known as the Independent Living Movement, has been the insistence that disabled people are the experts when it comes to disability. A telling motto of the movement has been, "Nothing about us without us," a call for disabled people, including artists, to participate in the decisions that affect their lives and the stories told about them. Though this premise, that the authentic voice can only be found in the person who has experienced the social and economic discrimination, is open to question, in practice this concentrated focus has produced visionary theatrical works. Arguably much of the energy in the legitimate theater in the twentieth century has come from previously marginalized voices. Susan Glaspell's *Trifles,* Lorraine Hansberry's *Raisin in the Sun,* Luis Valdez's *Zoot Suit,* Tony Kushner's *Angels in America*—all have given voice to silenced social groups and by doing so have shaped and revitalized what we call American drama.

Though all the writers in this anthology are disabled, they do not represent all the categories of disability. Writers who define themselves by mental disabilities are not included, nor are deaf or hard-of-hearing writers. This anthology focuses on writers who are physically marked—by the wheelchair, the limp, the scarred face, fits, drooling, spasticity, a white cane, a guide dog. This is not a scientific or theoretical categorization, but rather a recognition of the specifics of theatrical practice surrounding both the representation of the disabled figure and the logistics of pursuing a career either as actor or playwright with a physically marked body. This delimitation is in no way intended to minimize the discrimination and prejudice encountered by artists with mental disabilities or artists who are deaf or hard-of-hearing, though it is not my intention here to speak for these communities. Many deaf and hard-of-hearing theater artists have argued that they are not disabled and, based on the fact that they share a common and separate language, that they constitute a "linguistic minority." Just as Irish, Native Americans and countless other colonized people were stripped of their native languages by colonial forces, the deaf and hard-of-hearing were forbidden use of their language by hearing educators such as Alexander Graham Bell. Because of this particular history, deaf and hard-of-hearing theater should be considered bilingual along with groups such as El Teatro Campesino.

A SECOND GARDEN OF EDEN

Twentieth Century Renaming

> The Lord God formed out of the ground various wild animals and various birds of the air, and he brought them to the man to see what he would call them; whatever the man called each of them would be its name.
>
> —GENESIS 2: 18–20

> The [Oscar] Wilde trials . . . created the modern homosexual as a social subject. Whether Wilde himself thought he was that type of person . . . there's nothing necessarily that Wilde would have read that would have made him construct his identity as a homosexual . . . it was

impossible for men in the Victorian era to think of themselves as gay or homosexual because that construction didn't exist.

—PROFESSOR MARVIN TAYLOR
Gross Indecency: The Three Trials of Oscar Wilde by Moisés Kaufman

As a child growing up in the '30s, I somehow knew never to mention my disability. Saying that I had arthritis would have been like saying that I had syphilis.

—VIRGINIA RUBIN
Visual artist

There was time, and not so long ago, when mentioning disability was taboo. Disabled children, like Virginia Rubin, learned to be silent about their physical impairments. Drawing attention to your disability suggested that you were trying to pull a con of some kind, like the Blind Beggar of Alexandria in George Chapman's play of the same name, the fake crippled mendicants in Bertolt Brecht's *Three-penny Opera*, or *Seinfeld*'s George Costanza who acquires a wheelchair to get a job and a private bathroom. Even if one was legitimately disabled, it was understood that only disreputable failures trying to exploit society's collective guilt would reference their physical conditions. Good disabled people observed a code of silence about their physical needs and conditions and exhibited a cheerful, energetic demeanor in public life. Like Franklin Delano Roosevelt in Vincent Pinto's "changing of the guard" scene in *P.H.*reaks*, the happy handicapped "never let it [the disability] get them down."

All that changed in the early 1970s when a group of significantly disabled young people, calling themselves the "Rolling Quads," decided to throw off the invisibility cloak of shame and reclaim the negative term "disability" as a badge of pride and power. Awareness of this historical event of renaming and redrawing of the social category of disability is essential to understanding the social and cultural changes that disabled people are seeking in the twenty-first century, and to unlocking the plays in this anthology. As cultural critic Stuart Hall reminds us:

Think of how profound it has been in our world to say the word "black" in a new way. In order to say "black" in a new way, we have to fight off everything else that black has meant . . . the entire metaphorical structure of Christian thought, for example.

The first generation of Disability Civil Rights activists hoped for a similar rehabilitation of literary and social identity by self-consciously reclaiming the terms "disability" and "disabled." None of the writers in this anthology identify as "physically challenged," "differently abled," or "handi-capable," the euphemisms for disability so easily satirized in popular culture. All sorts of ingenious, linguistic strategies have been employed by well-intentioned nondisabled people who find the term "disabled" too negative. A "disabled" ship, they reason, is one that can no longer function. One of the most long-lived indicators of sensitive regard is the use of the word "special"— Special Olympics, *Very* Special Arts. But these euphemisms are rejected by disabled leaders who call for the use of "disability" "disabled" and "people with disabilities." Disability oppression, advocates argue, will not be erased by a more sensitive etiquette, but rather by a recognition of the social and economic conditions that characterize life lived with a disability

Indeed, the terms "disabled" and "disability" as used in this anthology have only been in use for about thirty years, and represent a self-conscious effort on the part of disabled activists and thinkers to simultaneously recognize and rehabilitate the social status of people with physical and mental differences. As a baseline of definition we can use the 1990 Americans with Disabilities Act (ADA). A person is considered to have a disability if he or she:

1. has a physical or mental impairment that substantially limits one or more of the major life activities of such an individual;
2. has a record of such an impairment;
3. is regarded as having such an impairment.

The definition has been praised for its breadth and criticized for its vagueness. Its protections extend to physically and mentally disabled people, those with sensory impairments (the blind and visually impaired, the deaf and hard-of-hearing). It covers those disabled at birth (developmental disabilities, such as cerebral palsy, Down's syndrome, spina bifida), those who have acquired disabilities through disease (polio, AIDS, cancer), through accident (spinal cord injuries or burns) or through aging. Invisible disabilities, such as epilepsy and chronic fatigue syndrome are equally protected. The list goes on—obesity, alcoholism. Some feel that the ADA's vast inclusiveness is the reason the conservative courts have been bent on gutting the act, fearful of a rising tide of "victims" claiming discrimination, eager to cash in on their injuries.

But the radical nature of the law is not in the breadth of its definition, but in its acknowledgment in the second and third parts of the definition that discrimination can occur without substantial limitation of major life activities. Discrimination can occur, as disability rights scholar Simi Linton explains, "because someone has a facial disfigurement or has, or is suspected of having, HIV or mental illness. The ADA recognizes that social forces, such as myths and fears regarding disability, function to substantially limit opportunity." This "social model" of disability, which sees identity as constructed through social interaction, is opposed to the "medical model" of disability, which has dominated Western thinking since the Enlightenment. The social model of disability underpins this anthology.

THE OLD STORIES

Moral and Medical

Disabled villains and victims have inhabited the stage for generations, from the stigmatized Oedipus and Richard III to Tiny Tim. These types of characters illustrate what is known as the "moral" or religious model of disability depiction, in which the physically different body is explained by an act of divine or demonic intervention. "Who has sinned, this man or his parents?" the Pharisees asked Christ about the blind man. In the medieval era a spinal deformity was explained by the presence of a devil curled up inside the hump. Choruses of devils babbled in the ears of the deaf. Children born disabled were proof of sinful congress with the devil, and their mothers could be burned at the stake as witches. These images of villain and monster illustrate what sociologists and social psychologists refer to as the *spread* effect of prejudice. A stigmatized trait is perceived to taint the whole person. The disabled person is seen as flawed morally, emotionally and sexually, not just physically. Leslie A. Fiedler contended in his 1979 groundbreaking study of the literary representation of the disabled figure, *Freaks: Myths and Images of the Secret Self* (New York: Simon & Schuster), that such taboos and stigmatization of the disabled person appeared in all cultures across time.

A great sea change occurred with the rise of modern capital and medicine. The "impaired," whether in body or mind, were no longer viewed as supernaturally good or evil, but sick. Under this so-called "medical model" the disabled person must either be charitably removed from society (through institutionalization or in some cases death) or cure themselves (or at least "pass" as cured). The "medical model" of disability added two characters/scenarios to the disabled theatrical repertory: the heroic overcomer and the heroic suicide.

Despite the great changes made in the advancement of the civil rights of persons with disabilities in the latter half of the twentieth century, "moral" and "medical" models of disability continue to dominate theatrical depiction, not only because they fill a deep human need to define ourselves as "normal" against some standard of abnormality, but also, in terms of the theatrical practice, because they are dramaturgically useful. Consider the ease of signaling good vs. evil by the addition of a hook, peg leg or eye patch. Introductory guides to screenwriting actually counsel fledgling authors to give their villain a limp or an amputated limb. This "twisted body, twisted mind" approach to characterization has given us such unforgettable villains as Richard III, Dr. Strangelove in the Stanley Kubrick movie of the same name and Ronald Merrick in the miniseries *The Jewel in the Crown*. Classic melodrama abounds in lame, blind and mute characters whose bodies provide a surface on which to mark the oppression of the pure spirit in an evil universe.

The seductive plot possibilities of the medical model, with its emphasis on a bodily transformation accomplished by an isolated effort of will, are irresistible in creating conventional dramatic structure. The "overcomer" is the protagonist of wheelchair-that-climbed-Mount-Everest scenarios like that of Dore Schary's 1960 drama, *Sunrise at Campobello*, which chronicles Franklin Delano Roosevelt's efforts to "walk." In "overcoming" narratives, disability is a private problem that must be challenged by an act of will on the part of the disabled character. All that prevents the disabled person from a full and meaningful life is an attitude adjustment. The nondisabled characters must often prod the disabled character who is trapped in self-pity and resentment. In these scenarios the perception of societal prejudice and discrimination is dismissed as the paranoia of a maladjusted person who refuses to "accept" his/her disability. As cultural historian Paul K. Longmore notes, the medical model serves as reinforcement for one of the most powerful of all American myths: the rugged individual who pulls himself up by his own bootstraps.

As one of George Bernard Shaw's characters once remarked, the only institution more conservative than the Church is the Theater. The metaphor of disability has been so successful in the imaginative arena that it now functions as real. As a result, the nondisabled theatrical practitioner often feels he/she knows better than the disabled artist what the correct story is to tell about disability—the dramaturgical equivalent of the well-meaning bystander who insists on helping the blind subway traveler by pulling him or her by the cane toward an unwanted destination. A disabled playwright who wants to explore disability in his work is warned against "ghettoizing" himself. Sharp social satire is judged "unlikable" and "too angry." One disabled writer's play was rejected by a regional theater literary department on the grounds that the writer had "denatured and trivialized" the experience of disability. The reader missed the fact that "denaturing" disability was the playwright's intended effect, a desire to destabilize the conventional interpretation of the meaning of the disabled body in civic life and on the stage. Solo artist Cheryl Marie Wade observes that most theater professionals "are still looking at *Whose Life Is It Anyway?* as a valid disability play."

THE FIRST NEW STORIES

Breaking the Medical Model: Deinstitutionalization

> We're modern enlightened and we don't agree
> With locking up patients We prefer therapy
> Through education and especially art our hospital may play its part
> Faithfully following according to our lights
> The Declaration of Human Rights.
>
> —COULMIER
> Director of the mental home
> *Marat/Sade* by Peter Weiss

> I've woven some pretty shitty rugs in my time. But whenever we have visitors, there are always one or two clowns who come over and practically have an orgasm over my rug, no matter how shitty we both know it is.
>
> —PETE
> Worker, sheltered workshop for "victims" of cerebral palsy
> *Creeps* by David Freeman

The earliest play in this collection, David Freeman's *Creeps,* premiered in 1971, winning the prestigious Chalmers Award in Canada. An Off-Broadway production in the U.S. in 1973 won the young writer the New York Drama Critics' Circle Award for Best New Playwright. Set in the men's bathroom of a sheltered workshop for people with cerebral palsy, this play seems to come, like Richard III, before its time, prematurely bearing theatrical witness to wrongs that would not find political analysis and advocacy until later in the decade.

Formally the play has an immediacy and boldness that reminds us again of the coiled energy of Shakespeare's great villain. Freeman's stage world, like Richard's body, is "rudely stamped." The props list calls for urinals, toilet paper, cigarette butts and urine bottles. Bodily function, the need to piss and shit, is the only defense the infantilized young men have against the institutional staff's demand that they constantly perform the role of cheerful, grateful cripples. As Freeman's stage directions clarify, a sheltered workshop is a place where a disabled person goes to work, not for "a living wage," but "to occupy his idle hours." Like Richard, who loathed the "idle pleasures" of the "weak piping time of peace," Pete, Sam and Tom struggle in their various ways against the enforced uselessness of their world, despising the do-gooding Shriners who "molest . . . them in the name of charity" with hot dogs, marching bands, clowns and balloons.

Shakespeare's Richard III "descanted" on his own deformity, that is, played a counterpoint with the social role he had been given. In *Creeps,* Freeman's five voices—Pete, Sam, Tom, Jim and Michael—perform a five-part descant on deformity/disability, with the unseen Thelma's disembodied cry for help providing the opening flourish and the closing coda. Playing off each other's bodies and social roles, the characters engage in an ever-shifting battle for status in the limbo for cripples, which imprisons all of them. Thus, Freeman, by presenting a world populated by many disabled characters, is able to locate the source of his characters' devalued status in a shared social condition, not by an individual failure of character. In the early days of the struggle for the inclusion of African American characters on network television, industry watchdogs at the television networks' Bureau of Standards and Practices observed that if the African American presence in the world of the situation-comedy was limited to one character, that character would be valued by the audience primarily as black. Other character attributes—economic status, gender, age, profession, etc.—would be secondary to the primary identification as African American. In order for other characteristics to register with an audience, more than one African American would need to be depicted (the television phenomenon of Alex Haley's

Roots would prove this thesis). Freeman's solution to use multiple disabled characters allowed him not only to present a variety of disabled character types, but also to theatricalize the lived experience of disability as a collective, social process, not an individual destiny.

Creeps also broke new ground in the gritty realism with which it depicted life for disabled people. Like the first audience of Maxim Gorky's *Lower Depths*, who feared that they would catch fleas from the actors, audiences of *Creeps* found themselves in close proximity to a grubby toilet that you could swear almost smelled. Freeman also allowed his characters rage and anger. The importance of such a permission might be missed by a nondisabled audience of the twenty-first century. Social scientist and disability studies pioneer Irving Zola identified "denial of anger" (along with denial of sexuality) as one of the major contributing factors to the invisibility of disabled identity in the modern era. The dependent status of disabled persons, he explained, required a developmental process in which "we were socialized out of our anger."

Revisiting a Classic

Lynn Manning's one-act *Shoot!* is another first play, and like Freeman's *Creeps* retains a freshness and urgency that speak to a time of beginnings. Manning wrote the one-act in Irene Oppenheim's Available Light Workshop at the Los Angeles Theatre Center. (Oppenheim, a theater critic from the Bay Area, served as dramaturg for an impressive number of disabled, deaf and hard-of-hearing writers during the 1990s.) Oppenheim's project for the workshop of writers with disabilities was an exploration of Shakespeare's *King Lear*. Shakespeare's characters in *Lear* suffer a variety of impairments—blindness, madness, dementia. In Kenneth Branagh's 1990 production in Los Angeles, Emma Thompson played the Fool as a Brueghel-esque, dwarfed, misshapen character, whose legs were bent under her forcing the actor to move in a permanent squat. For Manning, who had already gained a reputation in the Los Angeles poetry scene, *Lear* was a powerful provocation to move from the lyric to the dramatic form and, in his own words, to tell "the story of a black man, once considered a warrior to be feared, now viewed a weak pusillanimous blind man to be pitied, even taunted." The radical shift in status that Lear underwent spoke to the young poet's own experience of acquired disability. Since *Shoot!*, Manning has continued to mine the classics to tell his stories of disability and race in South Central Los Angeles. Other more formal adaptations followed *Shoot!*—Ben Jonson's *Bartholomew Fair*; Georg Büchner's *Woyzeck* (Manning's *Private Battle*); and Brecht's *Caucasian Chalk Circle*, adapted for Cornerstone Theater as *The Central Avenue Chalk Circle*.

Shoot! is not so much an adaptation as an improvisation on Shakespeare's tale of power struggles, family and old age in a mythical Celtic Britain. Manning takes his theme—"unrelenting self-interest to the detriment of all others"—from Shakespeare, but the other parallels are loose and ambiguous. The two half-brothers, Donny and Charles, mirror Edmund and Edgar only in that one is wiser than the other. The revenge-driven, half-brother, Donny, also owes something to the character of Gloucester. Donny has been blinded in an act of violence, the innocent victim of a drive-by shooting some years before the play begins. Another character, a demented, white street person, deliriously channels some of Kent's lines. But what Manning most successfully lifts from *Lear* is an atmosphere of chaos, danger and loss, where struggles for power, status and territory are unavoidable and lethal and family hostilities are fought with the weapons of war. The poet appropriates a mythical Celtic Britain to depict the war zone of South Central Los Angeles at the end of the twentieth century, and Lear's mistreatment at the hands of his family to evoke the disrespect and devaluation that the disabled person experiences in public life.

NEW STORIES

Claiming Community: Disability Civil Rights and the Independent Living Movement

Several of the plays in this anthology theatricalize the historical fact that people with disabilities came together, in the late twentieth century, to effect legislative and social change by claiming a shared identity as a disability community. At first glance, the application of the term "community" to disability, an international demographic category that numbers 45,000,000 in the United States alone, seems highly artificial. What can people not joined by birth, skin color, religion, language or geography, and characterized by vastly different physical and sensory conditions, possibly have in common? And, how has that claim shaped the theatrical imagination of the writers in this anthology? Choreographer Naomi Goldberg voiced her confusion after working with the acting ensemble of *P.H. *reaks*, which included individuals with spinal cord injuries, arthritis, cerebral palsy, people of small stature and wheelchair users, commenting, "The biggest contradiction for me was that we were saying that this was a group and yet everyone was so completely different, more diversified than any other group I had ever worked with."

Social theorist Benedict Anderson has suggested that all collective identities—all communities larger than primordial villages of face-to-face contact (and perhaps even these)—are imagined. As Anderson sees it, the claim of community is not scientific in origin—not identifiable by genetic markers or statistics. It is not even necessarily geographic or language-based. Indonesia, for example, geographically and linguistically fragmented, is a nation. Community, whether that of nation or political movement, is in the end the fragile result of an act of collective imagination, or as Hungarian essayist Paul Ignotus (1901–1978) puts it even more pragmatically, "A nation is born when a few people decide that it should be." Anderson's concept of "imagined community" helps to explain the claiming of community by millions of disabled persons in the twentieth century, a stance which informs many of the plays in this anthology.

The creation of a disability community begins for our purposes here with Ed Roberts, a quadriplegic from polio, enrolling at UC Berkeley in 1962. As none of the dormitory floors could support the weight of his eight-hundred-pound iron lung, which he needed to sleep in every night, Roberts was assigned a room in the student infirmary. Attending classes by day and retreating to the hospital at night, Roberts received a B.A., then an M.A., and started work on his doctorate. By 1967 there were twelve severely disabled students living in the hospital with him. This group of post-polio and spinal cord–injured students came to be known as the "Rolling Quads." Together they would spark a revolution in the life of people with disabilities around the world.

The disabled students rented a vacant car dealership on Telegraph Avenue, a few blocks from UC Berkeley's (in)famous Sather Gate, and started the first Center for Independent Living (CIL). Influenced by other self-help programs of the time, most importantly a peer-mentoring program at San Mateo College designed to correct the high dropout rates for African American and Latino students, and other models such as the Boston Women's

Health Book Collective, the students took control of dispensing the support services necessary to live outside an institution. At CIL you could hire an attendant, rent an apartment, learn how to drive an adapted van, and repair your own wheelchair. Advocates argued then, and continue to argue today, that institutionalization of people who are physically dependent is much more expensive than providing support services so that people can live in their own homes, integrated into society. "Independent Living" came to mean, not physical autonomy, but the ability to make decisions about one's own life.

Several plays in this collection are set in the time after the Independent Living Movement had radically altered living conditions for disabled people. Susan Nussbaum's *No One as Nasty* focuses on the relationship between a disabled woman and her paid personal care assistant/attendant. Mike Ervin's Chuck is attending college and lives in a modified dorm room. In *P.H. *reaks* a split scene compares the struggle of two disabled persons—one the famous artist Henri Matisse and the other a young woman—to negotiate their dependent status with their paid assistants. In *Gretty Good Time* John Belluso employs the beginnings in the 1950s of the Independent Living Movement as a kind of *deus ex machina* to resolve his title character's dilemma.

But Independent Living is a larger concept than providing peer services. What began with the Rolling Quads, a group of people with a specific experience of disability (quadriplegia), became a mass movement embracing a wide array of people with highly various physical and mental differences. So in *The History of Bowling* we find Chuck, a quadriplegic, encouraging his girlfriend, Lou, who has an "invisible" disability (epilepsy) and who can "pass" as normal, to claim her identity as disabled. Ervin's dramaturgical strategy reflects the political philosophy of the Disability Civil Rights Movement, which erased the lines between categories of disability—sensory, mobility, mental. Hierarchies of disabilities that preferred "walkies" to people using wheelchairs, or physical as opposed to mental disabilities were broken down. Conversely, no one was judged for not being disabled "enough." What *was* prized was the decision to "identify" as disabled, which by definition, granted you membership in the "disability community." By joining his two disabled characters at the play's end in a joint recognition of their shared identity as disabled people, Ervin presents the claiming of disabled identity as a regenerating personal and communal act, functioning dramatically in a similar fashion to the wedding that ends a classic comedy.

P.H.*reaks*, though closer to epic theater than Ervin's romantic comedy, is structured around a similar act of communal recognition, and the four "love scenes" in the play track the progress toward fruitful union. At the beginning of the play the disabled "saint" rejects the advances of the disabled "sinner" and opts for the nondisabled caretaker, Father John. Later, "Princess" Angie exposes and rejects the sexual exoticism of the nondisabled country doctor. The penultimate love scene, set in the 1930s during the Washington protest by the League of the Physically Handicapped, depicts a nondisabled woman's flirtation with a handsome, disabled protestor. She ultimately rejects him because of her fear of his disability. The final love scene brings the two disabled lovers from the play's beginning across time to a contemporary motel room where sexual love is finally consummated and arguably publicly celebrated, again, as weddings are in classic comedies. The two young people must be assisted by their personal care attendants to get into bed and undressed. Sexual union becomes public rather than private not only because of the characters' given circumstances and the presence of a theater audience, but because the love between the two disabled people symbolizes an acceptance and claiming of the disabled identity.

WHAT OPPRESSION?

Disability and Economics

> Most people don't know there is a link between poverty and disability
> . . . Most people link disability with tragedy or bravery or gumption.
> —Dr. Douglas Martin
> Disability Civil Rights Movement pioneer

> What any oppressed group has most vitally in common is just the shared fact of their oppression. Their collective identity is in this sense importantly negative . . . bound over a period of time to generate a positive particular culture . . .
> —Terry Eagleton
> *Nationalism, Colonialism and Literature*

Because the old myths of disability have been so successful and provide such comforting fictions, "the shared fact of oppression" (as termed by social critic Terry Eagleton) among disabled people might not be obvious. For many Americans, knowledge of the lived conditions of disability are restricted to soft news stories, such as those about Christopher Reeve or the surgical adventures of conjoined twins. But the realities of life for the majority of the forty-five million disabled Americans have little in common with such inspirational stories. In 1985 a Harris Poll established that disabled people were the poorest, least educated and most underemployed minority in America. Recent studies suggest that these inequities continue to hold as we enter the twenty-first century. In the third world, conditions for people with disabilities are compounded by war and strapped economies. In some "underdeveloped" countries, ninety percent of children with disabilities die before they reach twenty. In India only three percent of boys with disabilities are educated (disabled girls have almost no chance).

Most of the plays in this anthology are informed by the economics of disability. Documentary materials in *P.H.*reaks* track three periods of civil rights actions (1930s, 1970s and 1990s) aimed at dismantling the discrimination in education and employment that traps disabled people in a cycle of poverty. Economic oppression insinuates itself into the theatrical worlds of Freeman, Belluso and Ervin. David Freeman's muted, young disabled men are trapped in a charity-run sheltered workshop without hope of meaningful employment or economic independence. John Belluso's heroine, Gretty, is threatened with a transfer to a state mental institution because she lacks financial resources. Mike Ervin's Chuck narrowly escapes from a life of solitary confinement stuck in front of cable TV in his mother's attic. In the fictional framing story of *P.H.*reaks,* concerned citizens shut down the carnival sideshow on moral grounds, recommending that the freaks be placed in medical institutions for their own protection. The freaks are angered by the loss of their livelihood and are united in their fear of and scorn for medical institutions.

But a deeper fear lies under the freaks' antagonism toward the do-gooding "rubes" who threaten their livelihood. Independent living is more than a "life style" choice over institutionalization. The removal and segregation of physically and mentally impaired people from public life has historically proven to be life-threatening. Early in *P.H.*reaks*, Father John/Freak Show Barker entertains the audience with two rare slides of circus performer Lia Graf, a little person celebrity who toured during the 1920s and 1930s. Commenting on the images, Father John shares the chilling secret of Graf's ultimate fate with his audience: "Lia returned to her homeland [Germany] in 1935. She was arrested as a Useless Person in 1937, sent to Auschwitz in 1944 and never heard from again."

One of the best kept secrets of the hidden history of people with disabilities is the mass euthanasia practiced against them in Nazi Germany where approximately 240,000 disabled persons were the objects of "medical murder." These deaths were justified, not primarily as acts of "mercy," but as an economic necessity. In the 1930s social welfare programs were being eliminated. The Führer of the National Socialist Physician's League, Gerhard Wagner, claimed that "the insane doctrine of equality" which gave social support to the disabled and elderly was worse than communism and contributed to the excesses of the Weimar Republic when "Marxists" built "palaces for the mentally ill," "wonderful parks and gardens." Disabled people were draining national resources, particularly those of the German defense industry. These "useless eaters" had to be eliminated for the economic health of the nation.

Death Wishes

It is hereby prohibited for any person who is diseased, maimed, mutilated, or deformed in any way so as to be an unsightly or disgusting object to expose himself to public view.

—1911 City of Chicago Ordinance

Whoever is not bodily and spiritually healthy and worthy, shall not have the right to pass on his suffering in the body of his children.

—Adolf Hitler
Mein Kampf

We stayed [in America]. Things started to get bad back there [Germany]. Very dark.

—Gretty
Gretty Good Time by John Belluso

It is comforting to isolate the genocidal and inhumane practices of the Holocaust whether directed at people with disabilities, gays, Jews and gypsies to the evil empire of the Third Reich, but the historical record is not so kind. Throughout Western Europe and the United States many icons of social freedom, such as George Bernard Shaw, Margaret Sanger and Emma Goldman, embraced the eugenics solution. According to Robert Proctor in his disturbing study, *Racial Hygiene: Medicine Under the Nazis* (Cambridge, MA: Harvard University Press), even philosopher Bertrand Russell took as a given that "Negroes . . . [were] on average inferior to white men," but since they were so well-adapted to work in the tropics, their extermination "would be highly undesirable." In the 1930s in Pasadena, California, the Human Betterment Foundation, whose members included a "who's who of California (David Starr Jordan, Stanford University's first president; *Los Angeles Times* publisher Harry Chandler; Nobel Prize–winning physicist and Caltech head Robert A. Millikan; USC President Rufus B. von KleinSmid; and Lewis Terman, a Stanford psychologist who develop the IQ test)," pioneered many eugenic practices including mass sterilizations of institutionalized disabled people, which inspired Nazi Germany's eugenicists. The Human Betterment Foundation was not alone in promoting eugenics practices both here and abroad. Until the late 1970s, more than thirty states had laws permitting the sterilizations of "defectives."

Long after the rise and fall of Hitler, the dream of human perfection still tempts humanity. Contemporary discussions of abortion, managed health care and assisted suicide inevitably bring to mind questions of the interpretation of the impaired body as it concerns quality of life, dependency and cost. Interestingly, liberal, progressive theater has functioned as a reactionary force in the evolution of a new construction of the meaning of the disabled body. Two iconic stories of the American stage—John Steinbeck's *Of Mice and Men* (1937) and Brian Clark's *Whose Life Is It Anyway?* (1978)—contain striking depictions of the disability experience that crowd out more nuanced and liberated depictions of the impaired body. John Belluso's *Gretty Good Time* offers a strong counter-narrative to these popular dramas.

Of Mice and Men, Steinbeck's dramatization of the friendship between a nondisabled man, George, and his mentally disabled friend, Lenny, has remained popular since its 1930s debut. The mentally disabled Lenny does not know his own strength and continually kills small animals by petting them too hard, eventually murdering a young woman in a similar fashion. Disability advocates point out that Steinbeck allows the stigma of Lenny's mental disability to spread to his moral life, rendering him incapable of judging his actions as good or bad. Once again, as with Richard III and Dr. Strangelove, the dramatic shorthand of using a mental or physical disability to establish moral deficiency is used to tell a memorable story but a story that finds little support in the actual lived experience of people with mental disabilities. To argue that Lenny has to be killed for his own and society's good, echoes the eugenicist argument for the sterilization and extermination of disabled people.

Brian Clark's play and movie, *Whose Life Is It Anyway?*, has been equally criticized by disabled media watchers. The play's protagonist, Ken Harrison, a quadriplegic due to a car accident, wants to commit suicide after six months in a hospital. As he asserts in his trial: ". . . I'm dead already . . . I cannot accept that this condition constitutes life in any real sense." Disability is equated with death, with a life deprived of sexuality or any meaningful work. The argument of the play clearly points to suicide as the noble course of action for one who is severely disabled.

John Belluso's *Gretty Good Time* cracks the love-equals-death theme of many disability-inspired dramas with a variety of dramatic strategies. Like David Freeman he multiplies his disabled characters: Gretty, Hideko, McCloud. Like the writers of *P.H. *reaks* he employs Brechtian tactics of estrangement. Like Ervin he employs a love story, this time one between a patient and her doctor, but he balances that attraction with two important friendships—one with an elderly inmate in the nursing home and the other with the Hiroshima Maiden, Hideko. But the main wrench he throws into the heroic suicide story is uncovering the true cause of Gretty's suicidal impulse. Slowly as her past unravels we discover that Gretty's brother has committed suicide and that her desire to kill herself is not reducible to her disability but is perhaps an inherited inclination to depression. This scenario bears some similarity with the case of Elizabeth Bouvia, a twenty-six-year-old woman with cerebral palsy in Southern California who, in 1983, sought death because of her disability. When Bouvia's case became a cause célèbre of Right to Die advocates, members of the disability community (most prominently, renowned psychologist Carol Gill) investigated the story. Gill and others found that Bouvia's brother had recently committed suicide, that her marriage had failed, that she had lost her job, dropped out of school and was thwarted in her career goals. Dr. Gill's diagnosis was that the young woman was clinically depressed and, had she not been disabled, no one would have entertained a request to help her die but would have offered community support and counseling to enable her to survive her crisis.

But even uncovering this psychological motivation would not be enough to turn Gretty around. Like many other similarly incarcerated people, she would prefer to die rather than live in a nursing home. Belluso's research into the beginnings of the Independent Living Movement in California allows Gretty a similar turnaround at the end of his poetic and powerful play.

The Freak Show: Ethnicity, Nationalism and Disability

> At some future period, not very distant . . . the civilized races of man will almost certainly exterminate, and replace, the savage races throughout the world.
>
> —DARWIN
> *The Descent of Man*, 1871

> No sound of English, in a single instance, escaped their lips; the greater number spoke a rude form of Italian, the others some outland dialect unknown to me . . . No note of any shade of American speech struck my ear . . . the people before me were gross aliens to a man, and they were in serene and triumphant possession.
>
> —HENRY JAMES
> Commenting on immigrant families in Central Park, 1907

> And he says to me, "You better get right with Jesus, or he ain't never gonna make you walk!" . . . Who the hell does he think he is? So I turned to him and I said, "You better get right with Jesus, or he ain't never gonna make you white!"
>
> —CHUCK
> *The History of Bowling* by Mike Ervin

Some of the most exciting scholarship in the emerging field of disability studies has been in the investigation of the carnival sideshow and the deconstruction of the role of the freak show in establishing our national identity. *P.H.*reaks*, Joseph Chaikin's *Body Songs* and John Belluso's *Traveling Skin* are just a few of the works of modern drama inspired by this new scholarship. Their stories have little in common with past depictions of the sideshow: neither the ominous, vengeful freaks of Todd Browning's 1932 cult classic, *Freaks,* or the refined but tragic fable of John Merrick in Bernard Pomerance's *Elephant Man.* As scholars Robert Bogdan, Rosemarie Garland Thomson and others have demonstrated, the freak show at the end of the nineteenth and the beginning of the twentieth centuries offered a nervous, ever-diversifying America, an entertainment form against which every immigrant could measure himself/herself and establish his/her status as "normal." The two most common forms of exhibit were physically and mentally impaired white men and women and nondisabled persons of color. The most exciting exhibits were those that combined both physical and racial difference, like the first celebrated conjoined twins, Chang and Eng.

This nineteenth century conflation of difference left its mark on the evolution of civil rights in twentieth century America. Proponents of slavery and second-class citizenship for women offered medical evidence that African Americans and women were physically unsuited for freedom, that they were, in fact, disabled. Some medical doctors went so far as to claim that African Americans were born subservient because their knees bent more easily than whites. Freed blacks, the argument continued, became physically disabled in much higher rates than those who remained enslaved. Women were also judged physically inferior by prominent medical authorities and ran a similar risk of illness and insanity if given equality. In the fight for freedom no one questioned that disability was a just basis for discrimination.

The Disability Civil Rights Movement questioned this reading of disability as "naturally inferior," and pressed into law anti-discriminatory protections for disabled people as a class. In order to theatricalize that change in social status, several playwrights in this collection explore the overlap between the stigma of race and the stigma of disability. In Mike Ervin's comedy *The History of Bowling*, Chuck, the disgruntled disabled college student (quoted above), challenges an African American street preacher by drawing a parallel between the condition of disability and that of ethnic identity. John Belluso consciously employs "double and triple identities" in his plays, mixing gender, race and disability so that the audience has a difficult time reducing the story to the dominant narrative of disability—triumph over tragedy. In Belluso's play *Gretty Good Time*, post-polio Gretty, living in a nursing home in the '50s and contemplating suicide, first encounters Hiroshima maiden Hideko, on the television show *This Is Your Life*. Hideko then becomes Gretty's fantasy companion on her journey to escape her "shit body."

Interestingly the Hiroshima maidens have found their way into Susan Nussbaum's dark comedy *No One as Nasty*. She begins by drawing a parallel between her main character, a quadriplegic woman, and the unfortunate, civilian victims of America's first atomic bomb:

> . . . and the Hiroshima maidens got burned and disfigured—there's a word, "disfigured"—because of, why? Because. They were in Hiroshima. They were too close to avoid the fire, too far to be consumed. If I was five seconds earlier or later I wouldn't be this crip now. My life would

be on some different timeline. It was an *accident*; it had nothing to do with whether I was a good or a bad person. We don't live in an ordered universe . . .

The Hiroshima maidens provide both writers with a potent figure to counter the moral and medical construction of disability. Faced with the horror of the external event of the atom bomb, any interpretation which fixes responsibility for disability on the disabled person, or reduces it to an entirely individual tragedy without social resonance—the dominant depiction of disability in the mass media—becomes untenable.

The central conflict in Susan Nussbaum's *No One as Nasty* occurs between a white disabled woman, Janet, and her African American personal assistant, Lois, and offers the beginning of a dramatic dialogue about the nature of oppression in American society. As Lois bathes Janet, she ruminates:

> LOIS: At least you belong to a minority where famous stars can suddenly be members and join your movement. It's not like Christopher Reeve is gonna fall off a horse and be black.
> JANET 2: Although I bet Chris sure wishes he could choose, you know? Between being treated with hatred or pity.
> LOIS: Which would you choose?
> JANET 2: Hatred.
> LOIS: Shows what you know.
> JANET 2: Yeah, it shows what I know.

By linking disability with race, these playwrights encourage audience members to question the fundamental assumptions with which they approach the disability experience, just as they do with race.

COMEDY AND DISABILITY

Since the beginning of a conscious disability drama, the most common strategy used to attack received notions of the physically different body, is laughter. In the 1970s Susan Nussbaum was a student in drama school and acting on the side with a comic street-theater company, Rapid Transit, which specialized in issue-oriented "hit and run performances." After a spinal cord injury that resulted in quadriplegia, Nussbaum was recruited for a disabled role in an "inspirational drama" which fortuitously drove her to write her own plays:

> It gave me the idea that the wrong way to go was sappy shit, and the right way was shoving our differences in people's faces and using humor, the humor in the disability community that had been so much a part of my recovery.

What Nussbaum shares with fellow Chicagoan Mike Ervin, as well as Paul Ryan, Vincent Pinto and Bill Trzeciak of *P.H. *reaks* is a desire to turn the official story upside down, to break open the clichés and seriousness of the common images of disability. These artists assault the power structure, the hierarchy of physical attributes and class, which infantilizes and invalidates them. Their impetus came from the activism of the Disability Civil Rights Movement and their theatrical forms from street theater—people's/political/feminist theater of the 1960s and 1970s. They rely on the comic review—skits, songs, dances, jokes—the choice of political theater artists since at least as far back as the 1920s and Erwin Piscator's R.R.R. (Red Riot Review).

These writers employ time-honored comic strategies of deflation and exaggeration to rout the status quo. In *P.H. *reaks* Vincent Pinto reduces the revered Franklin Roosevelt to an inanimate dummy that gets tossed around by Secret Service officers rehearsing how to make FDR *not* look disabled in front of the public. Ervin's unbridled comic exaggeration leads to the creation of Cornelius, Chuck's blind and deaf college roommate, who communicates with a little finger-spelling in the hand, but mostly by spraying scented room freshener from an aerosol can. Cornelius is a con artist and lady's man who leaves any attempt to pity the handicapped gasping in the dust as his chauffeur-driven limo peals out for the pleasures of Atlantic City. Humorist Paul Ryan jumps into the dark world of the carnival freaks and emerges with an exotic princess of small stature who turns the medical tables on the country doctor who comes to gawk with a bottle in his hand and the privilege of his profession.

These comic writers often run the risk of offending those, who in their understandable desire to correct the damage inflicted by centuries of twisted villains and pure victims, fear any image that can be construed as "negative." But as James Baldwin observed of the early days of black representation on commercial television, the desire to clean up our images can go too far. Commenting on characters, such as Bill Cosby's role as a Shakespeare-cracking Rhodes scholar on *I Spy* and Diahann Carroll's spotless portrayal of a single mother on *Julia*, Baldwin observed: "Aunt Jemima and Uncle Tom are dead, their places taken by a group of amazingly well-adjusted young men and women, almost as dark, but ferociously literate, well-dressed and scrubbed . . ."

Wonders Vs. Normates

> You define something in a certain way
> and poof, there you are.
> And I always think,
> Is that entirely necessary?
>
> —Jorge
> *A Summer Evening in Des Moines* by Charles L. Mee, Jr.

> Sometimes a horse I'll be, sometime a hound,
>   A hog, a headless bear, sometime a fire;
> And neigh, and bark, and grunt, and roar, and burn,
> Like horse, hound, hog, bear, fire, at every turn.
>
> —Puck
> *A Midsummer Night's Dream*

> Frankly there is a thing called normal.
> I didn't make it up.
> I might not like to be normal myself
> but I *have* to be normal, like it or not.
>
> —Morton
> *A Summer Evening in Des Moines* by Charles L. Mee, Jr.

> The implications of the hegemony of normality are profound and extend to the very heart of cultural production . . . one of the tasks for developing consciousness of disability issues is the attempt, then, to reverse the hegemony of the normal and to institute alternative ways of thinking about the abnormal.
>
> —Lennard J. Davis
> *Enforcing Normalcy: Disability, Deafness and the Body*

There are two ways to deal with name-calling and labeling. One is to discredit (eradicate if possible) the label. The other is to claim the label and revalue it as positive. Most of the playwrights in this anthology mix up the two strategies. Belluso, Ervin, Ryan, Pinto and Nussbaum puncture the stereotypes of victim and villain while at the same time arguing for an identity and pride grounded in the specific, lived experience of disability. Of all the writers included here, Chuck Mee has the least patience with labels of any kind. His *Summer Evening in Des Moines* contains no reference to disability as a social identity, no overt reference to disability at all, evidence that Mee, along with his character Jorge (see above), doubts that definitions of things are "entirely necessary." Instead, Mee concentrates on exploding not just conventional plot structure, the "intact" plays he relegates to writers with "intact bodies" as he tells us in his Author's Statement, but the entire construction of the "normal."

Not surprisingly the idea of the "normal" has interested contemporary disabled activists and scholars. The word, in its modern sense of conforming to some agreed-upon standard, only entered the English language in the mid-1800s, as a central term in the emerging science of statistics and its sister "science" eugenics. Thus the concept of the normal was from its beginnings attached to supposedly "natural" hierarchies that placed the white, middle-class, nondisabled heterosexual male as the pinnacle of evolution. What is an alternative to dividing the world between normal and abnormal? One possibility is the theatrical world of Chuck Mee's *Summer Evening in Des Moines*

The play tells of events that happen in an amusement park in a quintessential midwestern town on a summer evening. Benny, a normal young man buys a ticket to the park in hopes of escaping from his daily life. At that moment, a boat (The Ship of Fools) appears, carrying wonders of all kinds: "natives of 'exotic' lands, wookiees [from the *Star Wars* films], holy men, giant puppets, tiny puppets . . ." Captain Vikram wears a mouse suit. A family of three—mother, father and sixteen-year-old daughter—sport fish heads. A ventriloquist operates two talking dummies. Benny climbs aboard the boat and finds himself in a world of folly and transformation, filled with cross-species romances, magic, exploding heads and young women tyrannized by their domineering fathers, recalling the wood outside Athens in Shakespeare's most famous of all plays about midsummer evenings. But there is no patriarchal hero/king at the end of this adventure to restore order to the kingdom. Puck continues his mischievous rule in the dark woods.

Which is not cause for despair, because along the way the fiction of the normal and our deep fear of being judged abnormal, have been exposed as folly. The leading advocate of normality in the play is the patriarch, Morton. Morton justifies his institutionalization of his daughter, Dee Dee, in the Hospital for Hopeless Psychiatric Cases by appealing to the law of the normal: "Frankly there is a thing called normal. / I didn't make it up. / I might not like to be normal myself / but I *have* to be normal, like it or not." But it's been a long time since Morton, his wife, Nancy, and his remaining daughter, Darling, have lived a normal life. Their cruise on The Ship of Fools has lasted for ten years, three months and two days. Their journey, as it is for their fellow passengers, Jorge, Ella and Benny, is both escape and pilgrimage, both a joke about tourism, the world reduced to safe, fabricated adventure parks, such as Londonland, Tuscanyworld and Trigger's Happy Trails, and a pilgrimage that strips away their accustomed identities and social status. So despite strenuous efforts on the part of Morton and Nancy to normalize Darling, efforts that include taking her to see *Cats* twenty-three times and *Phantom of the Opera* seventeen times, Darling falls in love with the cross-dressing Jorge.

Mee taps into an ancient comic tradition to contest "the hegemony of normality," as scholar Lennard J. Davis describes our culture's insistence on dividing the world between normal and abnormal bodies. Comic devices include pratfalls, food fights (The Fruitcake Toss), Apache dance (women and men throwing each other down in dramatic displays of passion), scatological humor, animal disguises and elaborate feasts, all conventions familiar to us not from elite theater but from popular culture—the lazzis of a commedia dell'arte performance, the low comic bits of films such as *Caddyshack* or *Animal House*. Like the medieval monks who wrote ribald joke books, Mee juggles virtuosic erudition with parody and low comedy, moving between high and pop culture with the finesse of a rollerblader in the Louvre—from Dante to Andrew Lloyd Weber; from Desmonema glaciale, a carnivorous jellyfish, to Esther Williams; from mannerist painter Arcimboldo, whose painted portraits were composed of fruits and vegetables, to Donald Duck.

At the center of the play is a presentation of the physical body and life as excessive, fluid, unstable and changeable. Liquids spurt both into and out of bodies. Wooden dummies meditate on death. Gender shifts. Elephants fall in love with human beings. Humans become angels. Knife murderers become pizza boys. Shrinkwrapped corpses resurrect and run down the beach. Jorge tells Darling that while visiting the Duchess of Devonshire, after dining on peacocks, armadillos and dolphin brains seasoned with vanilla, and drinking crushed daffodils and dozens of other exotic and fantastic dishes and beverages, the guests "would blow hot tobacco smoke into their anuses by means of a tube. It was the very pinnacle of civilization!" This sort of representation of the physical body as porous and unstable is part of an ancient tradition of folk humor that enlists the extraordinary, grotesque body, not as evidence of the gods' wrath or as subject of scientific inquiry, but as an antidote against fear and repression. This is not the grotesque body of the Romantic period, the Hunchback of Notre Dame, whose body represents an alien, tragic figure, but the grotesque body of the carnival, whose very degradation promises change and hope.

As the play reels to its end, the question of love and the sins against it, come more clearly into focus. Right before the penultimate scene, a kind of Shakespearean Act Five where all the love plots are untangled and everyone is paired off (except that here the revelations lead to more tangling), Edgar and his two alter egos (the puppets: Charlie and Mortimer) sit on a front porch and talk about love. "Is love the 'ultimate escape' and thus nothing more than an obsession?" they ponder. No, Edgar reasons, love is not just about sexual, individual attraction, though sex is the force that allows "life itself to continue." Instead love is more—it is "social love . . . caring for your neighbors and their neighbors," the "essential glue to hold society together." Edgar explains to his two mouthpieces, "Love is not just the ultimate escape, but also the ultimate reality."

Mee's *Summer Evening in Des Moines* imagines an alternative universe in which the self-enclosed independent body is a distorted, even murderous, variant of human life while the messy, unfinished body—the figure who cannot survive without the care of others—is the opening into the continuation of life. The most viable love on Mee's summer evening is not that of the perfect and noble for one another—of Theseus, Duke of Athens and Hippolyta, the Queen of the Amazons—but instead the union of the creatures of the earth like Bottom with his ass's head and the flawed and fearless Queen of the Night, Titania.

Dinosaurs and Pickles

> The ideology we recognize as modern humanism was inaugurated by a decision not to remain in a home as artificial and stifling as a doll's house.
>
> —Una Chaudhuri
> Professor of English and Drama, New York University

The last play in the anthology, Susan Nussbaum's *No One as Nasty*, has a sampling of many of the dramatic strategies used by her fellow writers. The only play in the anthology that rivals Nussbaum in her attention to the realistic details of living a disabled life is David Freeman's *Creeps*. The only one that equals her embrace of the irrational and disjointed is Mee's *Summer Evening in Des Moines*. Like

John Belluso she investigates double and triple identities involving race, gender and disability. Like Ervin she can set up a joke. Like Manning she can face the tragic without flinching.

The play begins with an opening comic monologue that takes as its subject nothing less than all the previous moral and medical models of disability that have been enlisted historically to assign meaning to the disabled figure. The heroine, Janet, a quadriplegic, refuses to assign meaning to the experience of becoming disabled: "It was an accident like the whole human race is an accident. Like the dinosaurs got blown away by a meteor." Like Sam Shepard's struggle with the myth of the American West, Nussbaum practices a similar distancing, a slight of hand, that allows her to dwell in a location that permits the extremes of immanence—for example railing at her attendant: "You have absolutely no meaning here except to hand the soap to my dead body, get it?"—and yet carry us to a new location. There is a sense of grace, despite Nussbaum's insistence on the messy, uncontained, impaired physical plane.

The play begins and ends with an image of confinement. At the top of the play it is one A.M., and Janet is railing at her absent attendant without whom she cannot get undressed and into bed. The play ends as well with an image of confinement—Janet lies in bed worrying that her new attendant has been eating food from her refrigerator. In between the two poles Nussbaum explores a wildly imagined variety of spatial worlds. Janet dreams of a mystery woman who lures men to Janet's apartment and then sucks the life out of them. Janet shares cocktails with Christopher Reeve, talks to cats and giraffes. Weaving this episodic mosaic of a play together is an ambiguous and difficult relationship between Janet and Lois, her African American attendant, a relationship that ultimately fails them both.

At the play's end, Janet lies in bed worrying about her relationship with her new attendant. Not much has changed. Arguably things are worse. Despite resolutions to the contrary, Janet finds herself being testy with the woman's soporific chat. The new attendant has offensive body odor and a weight problem. Janet suspects that the woman is eating her food, based on a too tightly closed jar of pickles in Janet's refrigerator. Janet doesn't mind her eating the food but she does mind the sneakiness. Lying in her bed, Janet muses:

> I hate myself for even having this discussion. Maybe I'll just forget about the whole thing. Ha ha. No, but maybe I'll let it pass. Unless it gets out of hand. I can't get anything open.

And then the closure, the grace note: "I could be dead wrong about the pickles," Janet tells us. The word "pickles," generations of comics insist, is a "funny" word. "P's" are funny, "K's" are funny and pickles has both consonants. "I could be dead wrong about the pickles," is the punch line of the monologue. "Pickles" is the final word of the play. The last image is of a jar inside a refrigerator in Janet's apartment. The image is fixed, domestic, mundane, insistent in its immanence, underlining the stubborn, antiheroic narrative of the entire play. And yet it makes us laugh. Nothing is containable, the playwright insists, not even a jar of pickles and certainly not the disabled figure.

CONCLUSION

> Two centuries of myth-making about rugged individualism will not yield easily to the painful fact that dependence is the human condition.
> —DEBORAH STONE
> "Why We Need a Care Movement," *Nation*

Implicit in many of the plays in this collection is a questioning of social hierarchy that privileges the intact, male, white body. From Chuck Mee to Susan Nussbaum such a "natural" human cosmology is called into question and found as irrelevant and oppressive as the Great Chain of Being was to the Renaissance readers of Socrates and Vitruvius. Mike Ervin's Chuck fights to keep his bohemian girlfriend arguing for a new model of heroism:

> I think people who have to stick their head in an alligator's mouth just to feel like they're alive are the ones who can't appreciate miracles . . . Well guess what, I'm a daredevil, baby! I'm a daredevil like you never saw! Sometimes just dragging my ass out of bed in the morning is like jumping across the Grand Canyon!

As author Leonard Kriegel has well expressed, the disabled body has no place in a triumphal celebration of America:

> Tiny Tim cannot light out for the Territory as Huck Finn threatens to do. The cripple cannot exist outside the boundaries of a society upon which he is dependent. He cannot claim that he is dependent solely upon his own physical mastery of the universe.

Since the 1980s pop psychology has created a language to convince Americans that we are not our brother's keeper. Language like "co-dependence," "tough love" and "enabling" developed to help families coping with hard-core addiction, is now applied to all situations of human need and misfortune. Our neighbor's unhappiness or poverty is his/her "choice." Your brother lost his job due to the economic downturn, well, "you make your own luck." An elderly neighbor wants you to drop by and help with some chores around the house? She's codependent. The modern sin is dependency, part of a contemporary catechism that allows Congress to abolish Aid to Families with Dependent Children, HMOs to ration health care to our frail, poor and not-so-poor elderly, and our leaders to further diminish health care and Social Security in return for a tax rebate.

The equation of dependency and weakness with pathology is an old story for disabled people and one codified in Western dramatic literature through victims and villains and their more recent relations, "tragic suicides" and "heroic overachievers." Banishing these simplistic figures requires the removal of another cultural icon, one dear to the American heart and mind—the Lone Ranger, the all-powerful hero who triumphs outside of communal support or identity. These plays together offer a reimagining not only of the meaning of the impaired body but also of social life, of how we are connected to one another.

Toward the end of *A Summer Evening in Des Moines*, the ventriloquist Edgar reasons, "if Aristotle was right / that human beings are social animals, / that we create ourselves in relationships to others," then theater, Edgar finds, is the most perfect of art forms to rehearse and discover "what is possible for humans to be." The plays in this anthology make a similar argument for the centrality of disability to our understanding of social and collective life, not because the disabled person instructs us about individual acts of courage in the face of tragic loss, but rather because the impaired body makes manifest the impossibility of living life without community.

A T-shirt graphic created for an ADAPT political action demonstration by disabled activist and artist Anna Stonum echoes this theme. Stonum depicts the familiar visual image for human evolution—an ascending line of figures beginning with an ape walking almost on all fours, progressing to more human-like figures, which gradually unbend to stand straight. Stonum's graphic does not end with Homo erectus. The final figure in her "ascent of man" cartoon is the international figure for disability—the stick figure in a wheelchair outline. The caption reads: "Adapt or Perish. —Charles Darwin." Our survival, Stonum suggests, might just lie in an acceptance of our infinite differences and (inter)dependencies.

SOURCES (BY ORDER OF APPEARANCE)

Beckett, Samuel; Bowles, Patrick, trans. *Molloy*. New York: Grove Press, Inc., 1955, 1956, 1958.

Eagleton, Terry. *Sweet Violence: The Idea of the Tragic*. Oxford: Blackwell Publishing, 2002.

Kaufman, Moisés. *Gross Indecency: The Three Trials of Oscar Wilde*. New York: Vintage Books, a division of Random House, 1998.

Hall, Stuart. "Ethnicity: Identity and Difference." *Radical America,* 23(4), October–December 1989.

Linton, Simi. *Claiming Disability: Knowledge and Identity*. New York: New York University Press, 1998.

Weiss, Peter. *Marat/Sade*. Long Grove, IL: Waveland Press, Inc., 2001.

Martin, Dr. Douglas. Dedication for "Contemporary Chautauqua: Performance and Disability." Los Angeles, Center Theatre Group/Mark Taper Forum, April 16, 2004.

Dr. Douglas Martin (1947–2003) was an influential pioneer of the Disability Civil Rights Movement. Among his many achievements, Dr. Martin is best known for his work in Social Security reform, particularly the removal of work disincentives that discourage disabled people from pursuing employment (see the Afterword on casting).

Eagleton, Terry, Frederic Jameson and Edward Said, *Nationalism, Colonialism and Literature*. Minneapolis: University of Minnesota Press, 1990.

Anton, Mike. "Forced Sterilization Once Seen as Path to a Better World." *Los Angeles Times*, July 16, 2003, Column One: A1–A18

Davis, Lennard J. *Enforcing Normalcy: Disability, Deafness and the Body*. London: Verso, 1995.

Chaudhuri, Una. *Staging Place: The Geography of Modern Drama*. Ann Arbor: University of Michigan Press, 1997.

Stone, Deborah. "Why We Need a Care Movement." *Nation*, March 13, 2000: 13–15.

Deborah Stone is author of *The Disabled State*. Philadelphia: Temple University Press, 1984, an influential history of disability as a social welfare category.

Kriegel, Leonard. *Falling into Life: Essays*. San Francisco: North Point Press, 1991.

Leonard Kriegel is the author of *Edmund Wilson (Crosscurrents/Modern Critiques)*; *Flying Solo: Reimagining Manhood, Courage, and Loss*; *Of Men and Manhood*; *Stories of America* and *Stories of the American Experience*. His essays and stories have been published in the *Nation*, *Harpers* and *American Scholar*.

ADAPT: American Disabled for Attendant Programs Today (formerly American Disabled for Accessible Public Transit).

CREEPS

David Freeman

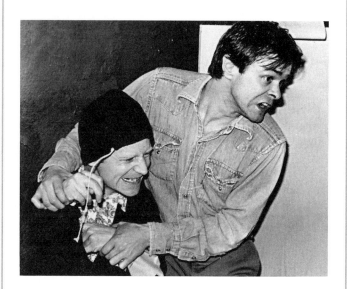

Pete (Jed Mills, left) and Tom (Peter Schreiner) in the Theatre/Theater production, Los Angeles, California, 1982. Photo by Jeff Murray.

To my father

Author's Statement

Creeps was first written as a script for the Canadian Broadcasting Corporation in 1965. It went on to be produced at Tarragon Theatre in Toronto in 1971. It won the first Chalmers Award in Toronto, followed by the Drama Desk Award for best new playwright in 1974.

   Creeps has been produced in Canada, Great Britain and the U.S. *Creeps* was born of my own frustration, working in a Toronto sheltered workshop where I sanded blocks, folded boxes and separated nuts and bolts. It deals with people who have the courage to take their destiny into their own hands.

Production History

Creeps was first presented at the Factory Lab Theatre in Toronto on February 5, 1970. The production was directed by Bill Glassco and designed by Peter Kolisnyk. The cast was as follows:

PETE	Victor Sutton
JIM	Robert Coltri
SAM	Steven Whistance-Smith
TOM	Frank Moore
MICHAEL/CHEF/PUFFO THE CLOWN/	
CARNIVAL BARKER	Len Sedun
SAUNDERS	Kay Griffin
CARSON	Bert Adkins
GIRL	Christina Zorro
SHRINERS	Bernie Bohmers, Mark Freeborn

This revised version of *Creeps* was first presented at Tarragon Theatre in Toronto on October 5, 1971, with the following changes:

SAUNDERS	Josephine Smith
CARSON	Richard Davidson
GIRL	Robin Cameron
SHRINERS	John Candy, Charles Northcote

Creeps was presented at Playhouse 2 in New York City on December 4, 1973. It was produced by Orin Lehman in association with the Folger Theatre (Washington, D.C.). The production was directed by Louis W. Scheeder and designed by David Chapman; the movement consultant was Virginia Freeman and the production stage manager was Bud Coffey. The cast was as follows:

PETE	Steven Gilborn
JIM	Richard DeFabees
SAM	Bruce Weitz
TOM	Mark Metcalf
MICHAEL/TELETHON MC/	
PUFFO THE CLOWN/	
FREAK SHOW BARKER	Philip Charles MacKenzie
SAUNDERS	Robin Nolan
CARSON	Peter Vogt
GIRL	Ronni Richards
SHRINERS	Richard Fancy, Stefan Peters
FOOTBALL PLAYER	Richard Fancy
ASTRONAUT	Stefan Peters
THELMA	Robin Nolan

Characters

Some Notes on the Characters' Movements

Each actor taking on the role of a character with cerebral palsy is faced, as the character, with minor physical problems, the practical solution of which is paramount to a successful rendering of the play. There are many kinds of spasticity, and each actor should base his movements on one of these. There can be no substitute for the first-hand observation of these physical problems. The play should not be attempted if an opportunity for firsthand observation is not available. The following approaches were taken by the actors in the original production:

PETE—the actor in the original production developed a way of speaking that is common to many spastics. The effort required to speak causes a distortion of the facial muscles. The actor was able to achieve this by thrusting the jaw forward and letting the lower jaw hang. The deformed hand was not held rigid in one position. The actor used the hand for many things, keeping the fist clenched and employing the fingers in a clawlike manner.

JIM—the actor walked with his knees almost touching, feet apart, back bent much of the time, using his arms more than any other part of his body for balance.

SAM—Sam is diaplegic, his body dead from the waist down (except for his genitals). He is in a wheelchair. The problem for this actor was to find out how to make the wheelchair an extension of his body.

TOM—the actor walked with one hip thrust out to the side. Forward motion always began with the foot of the other leg, rising up on the toe, and then thrusting downward on the heel. His arms were held in front of him, his fingers splayed, upper arms and shoulders constantly being employed for balance.

MICHAEL—the actor always staggered, his head lolling, his body very loose, constantly on the edge of falling. He fell, or collapsed, rather than sat, and grinned most of the time. He too had a speech problem, very slurred, not employing the facial muscles like Pete.

Setting

The washroom of a sheltered workshop for cerebral palsy victims. A "sheltered workshop" is a place where disabled people go to work at their own pace without the pressure of the competitive outside world. Its aim is not to provide a living wage for the cerebral palsy victim, but rather to occupy his idle hours.

Author's Notes

The actor playing the role of Michael must also play the Chef, Puffo the Clown and the Carnival Barker in the three Shriner sequences.

Thelma is an offstage voice, Thelma is heard. It is important that this voice be spastic, but that what is being said always be clear.

A men's washroom in a sheltered workshop. The hall leading to the wash-
room is visible. In the washroom are two urinals and two stalls. A chair
is set against one of the stalls, which is occupied. There is a bench.

    When the lights come up, Michael, a mentally retarded C.P. of about
eighteen, comes down the hall, enters the washroom and starts flushing
the urinals. Then he moves to the toilets. He comes to the occupied stall
and knocks on the door.

PETE *(From the stall)*: Who is it?
THELMA *(An offstage voice)*: I need a priest!

> *(Michael chuckles to himself; he does not answer. Tom enters, walk-*
> *ing in a sway-and-stagger motion. Having observed the game*
> *Michael is playing, he ushers Michael out, then sits in the chair.*
> *Pete drops his pack of cigarettes.)*

TOM *(Disguising his voice)*: Hey, Pete, you dropped your cigarettes.
    (Pause. A comic book falls) Hey, Pete, you dropped your comic
    book. *(Pete's pants fall; in his own voice)* Hey, Pete, you dropped
    your pants.
PETE: That you, Tom?
TOM: 'Course it's me. Who were you expecting, Woody the Pecker?
PETE: Why didn't you answer?
TOM: When?

PETE: Didn't you knock on the door just now?

TOM: No.

PETE: Must have been Michael flushing toilets.

TOM: Doing his thing.

PETE: He wants to be toilet flushing champion of the world.

TOM: Well, at least he's not like some lazy bastards who sit on their ass all day reading comic books.

PETE: I'm on strike. They only pay me seventy-five cents a week. I'm worth eighty.

TOM: You're always on strike.

PETE: How many boxes did you fold today, smart-ass?

TOM: Oh, about two hundred. How's the rug?

PETE: Fucking rug. I wish to hell she'd put me on something else. At least for a day or two. It's getting to be a real drag.

TOM: Yeah, that's the way I feel about those boxes.

THELMA *(Offstage)*: I need a priest! Get me a priest!

TOM *(Wearily)*: Oh God.

PETE: Old Thelma kind of gets on your nerves, doesn't she?

TOM: Yeah.

THELMA *(Offstage)*: Someone get me a priest!

TOM: Pete, I gotta talk to you about something.

PETE: Okay, shoot.

TOM: No, I'll wait till you're out of the can.

(Knock at the washroom door.)

SAM: Open up! *(Pause)* Who's in there?

(Tom moves to open the door.)

Come on for chrissake.

TOM: All right, hang on.

(Tom gets the door open with difficulty. Sam wheels by him into the washroom.)

Wanna take a leak, Sam?

SAM: No, I wanna join the circle jerk. Where's Pete?

PETE: In here.

SAM: Well, well . . . Pete is actually using the shithouse to take a shit.

PETE: Okay Sam, knock it off.

(Pause.)

TOM *(To Sam)*: How are you making out with the blocks?

SAM: Screw the blocks. You know how many of those fuckin' things I done today? Two. Do you know why? Because that half-ass physical therapist . . .

TOM: Physio.

SAM: Physio, physical, what the fuck's the difference? They're all after my body. She keeps making me do the same damn blocks over again. "That's not good enough," she says. "Get the edges smoother," she says. *(Pointing to his crotch)* Take a bite of this.

PETE *(Flushing the toilet)*: She can be a pretty miserable old cunt at times.

SAM: All the time. How's the rug, Pete?

PETE: That thing.

TOM: I told him, he's never gonna finish it sitting in the john all day.

PETE *(Emerging from the stall)*: I've been weaving that stupid rug beside that hot radiator every day now for three months. And what has it got me? A big fat zero.

SAM: That's because you're a lazy bugger. You know what that stupid idiot who runs this dump says about you.

PETE: Yeah, I know. "Pete, if you worked in my factory, you wouldn't last a day . . ."

TOM: "But since you're a helpless cripple, I'll let you work in my workshop . . ."

SAM: "For free!"

PETE: And the government will give me pension, just for breathing.

TOM: And the rotary and the Shriners will provide hot dogs and ice cream.

SAM: And remember boys, "If they won't do it . . ."

ALL: "Nobody else will!"

(Blackout.

Circus music. Bright lights. Two Shriners enter with a Chef and a Girl in a white bathing suit—"Miss Cerebral Palsy." They dance around the boys, posing for pictures, blowing noisemakers, and generally molesting them in the name of charity. The Chef stuffs hot dogs into their hands. They exit. The music fades. The light returns to normal. The boys throw their hot dogs over the back of the set.)

PETE: Sometimes I wonder how I ever got myself into this.

TOM: Good question, Pete. How did you?

PETE: Another time, Tom, another time.

THELMA (*Offstage*): I need a priest!

PETE: What's the big piece of news you have to tell me?

TOM: It doesn't matter.

PETE: Come on, Tom, crap it out.

TOM: It's okay, forget it.

PETE: I postponed my shit for this.

TOM: That's your problem.

SAM: Hey, I bet he's gonna get laid and he doesn't know what to do.

PETE: Well the first thing he better learn is how to get undressed faster.

TOM: Very funny.

PETE: What's the matter? This place still getting you down?

TOM: Yeah, I can't hack it much longer.

SAM: Can't hack what?

TOM: Everything: folding boxes, the Spastic Club, Thelma, the whole bit.

(*Pause.*)

PETE: How's the art coming?

TOM: Didn't you hear me?

PETE: Sure I heard you. You said you couldn't hack folding boxes. Well, I can't hack weaving that goddamn rug . . . So how's the art?

TOM: Screw the art. I don't want to talk about art.

PETE: Okay.

(*Pause.*)

SAM: Chicken-tracks.

TOM: What's that?

SAM: Chicken-tracks. That's what you paint, Tom. Chicken-tracks.

TOM: I paint abstract. I know to some ignorant assholes it looks like chicken-tracks, but . . .

SAM: Listen, Rembrandt, anything you ever tried to paint always looked like shit warmed over, so you try to cover it up by calling it abstract. But it's chicken-shit and you know it.

TOM: You wouldn't know the difference between a tree and a telephone pole, Sam.

SAM: There isn't any difference. A dog'll piss on both of them.

TOM: And you'll piss on anything, won't you?

PETE: Okay, Tom, cool it.

TOM: Why the fuck should I cool it? This prick's attacking my art.

PETE: You shouldn't take yourself so seriously.

TOM: Oh, do forgive me, gentlemen. I took myself seriously. *(Getting up)* I shall go to Miss Saunders and insist she castrate me.

(He starts for the door.)

SAM: Castrate what?

PETE: Where are you going?

TOM: Where does it look like?

PETE: Damnit, Tom, come on back and stop acting like an idiot.

TOM: Why should I? Whenever anyone tries to talk serious around here, you guys turn it into a joke.

PETE: Nobody's making a joke.

SAM: Look, Tom, even if you do have talent, which I seriously doubt, what good is it to you? You know bloody well they're not going to let you use it.

TOM: Who's "they," Sam?

SAM: The Rotary, the Shriners, the Kiwanis, the creeps who run this dump. In fact, the whole goddamn world. Look, if we start making it, they won't have anyone to be embarrassed about.

PETE: Come on, Sam, there's always the blacks.

TOM: And the Indians.

SAM: Yeah, but we're more of a challenge. You can always throw real shit at a black man or an Indian, but at us you're only allowed to throw pity-shit. And pity-shit ain't visible.

TOM: I think you're stretching it just a bit.

SAM: The only way you're going to get to use that talent of yours, Tom, is to give someone's ass an extra big juicy kiss. And you ought to know by now how brilliantly that works for some people around here.

TOM: You mean Harris?

SAM: If the shoe fits.

TOM: You lay off Jim, 'cause if you'd had the same opportunity you'd have done the same thing.

SAM: So now he licks stamps in the office on a weekly salary, and he's president of the Spastic Club. Whoopee!

TOM *(To Pete)*: Are you going to talk to me or not?

(Jim enters and heads toward the urinal. He is surprised to see Tom. His walk is slow and shaky, almost a drunken stagger.)

SAM: Here's Mommy's boy now.

(Pause.)

PETE: Things slack in the office, Jim?

JIM: Naw, I just thought I might be missing something.

SAM: Oh, you're sweet. Isn't he sweet? I love him.

PETE: Cigarette?

JIM: No thanks, I'm trying to give them up.

(He flushes the urinal.)

SAM: Shouldn't be difficult. Giving up is what you do best.

JIM: Aren't you guys worried about getting caught? *(To Pete)* You know you've been in here for over an hour.

SAM: Shit time. Push me into the crapper, will ya, Pete?

PETE *(Pushing Sam into the stall)*: Saunders won't come in here.

JIM: She might, Pete. Remember Rick and Stanley.

PETE: I do, but I'm not Rick and Stanley.

TOM: Jim, that story's horseshit. Those guys weren't queer.

SAM *(From the stall)*: Sure they were queer. Why do you think they always sat together at lunch, for chrissake?

PETE: I'll never forget the day she caught them in here necking. Screamed her bloody head off. *(To Tom)* Of course the reason she gave for separating them was that they were talking too much and not getting their work done. Right, Jim? *(Jim says nothing)* No, Saunders won't come in here now. Not after a shock like that.

SAM *(From the stall)*: Maybe not, but she might send Cinderella to check up on us. How 'bout it, princess?

JIM: Why would I do a thing like that?

PETE: Then why did you come in?

JIM: Is this washroom exclusive or something?

TOM: It's not that, Jim. It's just that you haven't been to one of our bull sessions for a long time. Not since your promotion.

JIM: I already told you. I just wanted to see if I was missing something.

SAM *(From the stall)*: You are. Your balls.

(Knock at the washroom door.)

SAUNDERS: Jim! What's happening in there? I haven't got all day.

(Silence. Pete and Tom look at Jim.)

JIM: Okay, so she asked me. But I didn't come in here to spy.
SAM *(From the stall)*: Well move your ass, Romeo. You heard what the lady said, she can't wait all day.
SAUNDERS: Jim?
SAM *(From the stall)*: Bye-bye.
SAUNDERS: Jim, are you there?

(Jim moves toward the door.)

TOM: Wait, Jim, you don't have to go.
SAM *(From the stall)*: Damnit, let the fucker go. His mommy wants him.
PETE: Shut up, Sam.
SAM *(From the stall)*: I wasn't talking to you.
TOM: Why don't you stay for a while?
PETE: Yeah, tell old tight-cunt you're on the can or something.

(He grabs Jim and pulls him away from the door.)

SAUNDERS: Jim Harris! Do you hear me?!

(Pete signals for Jim to answer.)

JIM: Yes, Miss Saunders, I hear you. But I'm on the toilet at the moment.
SAUNDERS: What are you doing on the toilet?
PETE *(At the door)*: He's taking a shit. What do you do on the toilet?
SAUNDERS: If you boys aren't back to work in five minutes I'm reporting you to Mr. Carson.

(Footsteps leaving.)

SAM *(From the stall)*: Once upon a time, boys, there was a boudingy bird, and the cry of the boudingy went like this . . .
TOM AND PETE *(In falsetto, forestalling Sam)*: Suck my boudingy!

(Silence while Pete listens at the door.)

JIM: I could use that cigarette now.
PETE *(Bringing him one)*: Thought you were trying to quit.
JIM: I am.

(Pause.)

TOM: Jim, why did you lie?
JIM: I did not lie. Saunders saw me coming in, and she thought I might remind you that you'd been in here a long time. That's all.
TOM: Then why didn't you say so when Sam asked you?
SAM *(From the stall)*: Because he's so used to telling lies, if anyone said he was spastic, he'd deny it.
TOM: Will ya shut up, Sam.
JIM: That's okay. Sam didn't even care for me when I was sanding blocks with him.
SAM *(From the stall)*: Pete, push that chair in here, will you?
JIM: Now that he thinks I've gone over to the other side, he's got even less reason to like me.
SAM *(From the stall)*: Listen, princess, nobody likes a white nigger.
TOM: What's that mean, Sam?
PETE *(As he holds the chair for Sam)*: Why don't you use a bedpan?
SAM: Why do you think, dummy? Because my ass begins to look like the other side of the moon. *(By now he is off the toilet and back in his chair)* All right, all right. *(Wheels backward out of the stall)*
JIM: Well, Sam?
SAM: Well what, stooge?
JIM: What do you mean, "white nigger"?
SAM: Well since you're all so fired fuckin' dyin' to know, I'll tell you. You finished high school, didn't you?
JIM: Yes.
SAM: And you went to university?
JIM: Yes
SAM: And you got a degree?
JIM: So?
SAM: Well, you went to university. You wrote all that crap for the paper about how shitty it was to be handicapped in this country. Then what do you do? You come running down here and kiss the first ass you see. That's what I mean by being a white nigger, and that's what fuckin' well pisses me off.

JIM: All right, Sam, now you listen to me. I still believe everything I wrote, and I intend to act on it. But you can't change things until you're in a position to call the shots. And you don't get there without being nice to people. By the way, what are you doing about it? All I get from you is bitch, bitch, bitch!

SAM: I got every right to bitch. You expect me to sand blocks and put up with the pity-shit routine for ninety-nine years waiting for you to get your ass into a position of power? Fuck you, buddy! You give me a choice and I'll stop bitching.

TOM: Now look who's taking himself seriously.

SAM (*To Tom and Pete*): What do you guys know about the bullshit I put up with? My old lady—now get this—my old lady has devoted her entire life to martyrdom. And my old man, you ever met my old man? Ever seen him give me one of his "where have I failed?" looks? Wait'll ya hear what happened last night. He invited his boss over for dinner, and you know where the old bugger wanted me to eat? In the kitchen. First I told him to go screw the dog—that's about his style—and then, at the height of the festivities, just when everything was going real nice for Daddy, I puked all over the table.

TOM: Charming.

SAM: It was beautiful. Stuck my finger down my throat and out it all came: roast beef, mashed potatoes, peas, olives. There was a *real* abstract painting, Tom. You should have seen the look on his boss's face. Be a long time before he gives at the office again.

(*Michael enters. During the ensuing dialogue he attempts to flush the urinals, but is stopped by signals from Pete.*)

JIM: You know, Sam, you amaze me. You say you don't want to wait ninety-nine years, but you're happy if you can set us back a few. A stunt like that doesn't make Carson's job any easier.

PETE: Okay, Timmy, you're not addressing the Spastic Club.

SAM: Piss on Carson! He doesn't give a shit about us and you know it.

JIM: I don't know it. I don't know what his motives are. But I do know he's trying to help us.

PETE: His motive is to keep the niggers in their place.

SAM: Yeah, by getting Uncle Timmy here to watch over them.

TOM (*To Sam and Pete*): What are you guys, the resident hypocrites? Look, no one twists your arm to go to those Spastic Club meetings. No one forces those hot dogs down your throat.

PETE: Sure, we take them. Why not? They're free. Why look a gift horse in the mouth? But at least we don't kiss ass.

JIM: No, you let me do it for you. *(Slight pause)* But that's beside the point. The point is that Carson does care about what happens to us.

SAM: He does?

JIM: You're darn right he does.

SAM: You ever been over to his house for dinner?

JIM: Yes.

SAM: Ever been back?

JIM: No.

SAM: In other words, you got your token dinner, and now you only see him at Spastic Club meetings and here at the workshop?

JIM: That's not true. He comes to my place sometimes, doesn't he, Tom?

TOM: Yeah, but what about all those times your mother invited him to dinner and he canceled out at the last minute?

JIM: So? That doesn't prove anything.

SAM: Proves a helluva lot to me.

(Michael pokes Pete on the shoulder.)

PETE: What is it, Michael?

MICHAEL: Cigarette, please.

PETE: Okay, Michael, but smoke it this time, don't eat it. Last time everyone accused me of trying to poison you.

(Banging at the door.)

SAUNDERS: Boys! What's going on in there? If you don't come out this minute, I'm coming in.

SAM: We dare you!

TOM: Shut up, Sam.

SAUNDERS: What was that?

PETE: Nothing, Miss Saunders. Sam just said, "We hear you."

SAUNDERS: Oh no he didn't. I know what he said. He said, "We dare you!"

PETE: Well Christ, if you already knew, what the fuck did you ask for? *(To himself)* Stupid bitch!

SAUNDERS: Jim, what's happening in there? Are they doing something they shouldn't?

SAM: Yeah, we're pissing through our noses!

JIM: Cut it out, Sam. No, Tom and Pete are on the toilets, and I'm holding the bottle for Sam.

SAM: Hey, that hurts! Don't pull so hard, you idiot!

SAUNDERS *(Nonplussed)*: Well hurry up, and stop fooling around. I can't wait on you all day.

(She starts down the hallway, stops when she hears:)

SAM *(To the door)*: That's it, Pete, no more blow jobs for cigarettes! Jim, take your hands off me, I've only got one! Michael, don't use your teeth! Christ, I've never seen so many queers in one place. I could open a fruit stand!

(Saunders listens, horrified, then runs off down the hall. Michael sits on the floor and begins to eat the cigarette. The laughter subsides.)

PETE: I think she left.

(Pause.)

TOM: Do I finally get to say something?

PETE: Oh yeah, where were we? You couldn't hack folding boxes.

TOM: Or the Spastic Club.

PETE: Or the Spastic Club.

TOM: Or Thelma.

PETE: Or Thelma.

TOM: Pete.

PETE: What's the matter now?

TOM: Cochran, for once in your life, will you be serious?

PETE: I'm fucking serious.

SAM: It's the only way to fuck.

PETE: If I was any more serious, I'd be dead. I wish to hell you'd get on with it, Tom.

(Pause.)

TOM: You guys ever read a story called "Premature Burial"?

(Sam and Jim shake their heads.)

PETE: What comic was it in?

TOM: Edgar Allen Poe.

PETE: Oh.

TOM: Anyway, it's about this guy who has this sickness that puts him into a coma every so often. And he's scared as hell someone's going to mistake him and bury him alive. Well, that's the way I feel about this workshop. It's like I'm at the bottom of the grave yelling, "I'm alive! I am alive!" But they don't hear me. They just keep shoveling in the dirt.

THELMA *(Offstage)*: I need a priest!

JIM: Tom, if you really feel that way, you ought to talk to Carson.

TOM: Oh, fuck off.

JIM: He's not an idiot, you know.

PETE: Tom, you want to know what I think? I think you should stop reading junk like Edgar Allen Poe. You take that stuff too seriously.

SAM: Pete's right. You should stick to your regular diet.

TOM: What's that crack supposed to mean?

SAM: It's sticking out of your back pocket, sexy.

(Tom reaches around and removes a book from his pocket.)

TOM *(Tossing the book to Sam)*: Here, Sam, why don't you take it for a while? Maybe it'll shut you up.

SAM *(Flips through the book)*: Hey, he's got the dirty parts underlined in red.

PETE: Read some.

SAM *(Reading)*: "'Nothing like a nice yellow banana,' she said aloud. It touched every sensitive area of her pussy. Tears came to her eyes in shots of violent lust. Then her movements began to increase and she spliced herself repeatedly . . ."

TOM: That's enough, Sam.

SAM: "The thick banana swirled in her cunt like a battering ram. She grasped it hard and shoved it faster and faster. Then she sat up, still gorged with the banana . . ."

TOM: I said, that's enough! *(Gets up and moves to take the book away from Sam)*

SAM *(Who has not stopped reading)*: ". . . it hit high up against the walls of her wet cunt. She could move whichever way she liked. 'Oh, shit, this is juicy,' she said aloud. The reflection she saw in the mirror was ludicrous and made her even more hot. 'Oh you big banana, fuck me!'. . ."

(Tom grabs the book.)

PETE: Wait. I want to find out about the banana split.

TOM: If you're so hot about the banana, you can have the goddamn book.

(He gives it to him.)

SAM: It'll only cost you a nickel, Pete, it's underlined.

TOM: Okay. So I get a charge out of dirty books. What does that make me, a creep?

SAM: Well at least I don't pretend to be something I'm not. I don't work myself up during office hours.

TOM: No, you just do it at picnics.

SAM: What about a goddamn picnic?

JIM: Come on, Sam, you remember the Rotarian's daughter.

SAM: So, I remember a Rotarian's daughter. What now?

PETE: She was sitting beside you and you were feeling her up like crazy, that's what now.

SAM: If the silly little fart is stupid enough to let me, why not?

JIM: You were making a bloody spectacle of yourself.

SAM: Love's where you find it.

PETE: Yeah, but with you working her over like that, I could hardly keep my mind on the three-legged race. Didn't she even say anything?

SAM: Nope, she just sat there. Smiled a lot.

THELMA *(Offstage)*: I need a priest!

(Pause.)

JIM: There's a girl who isn't smiling, is she, Sam?

SAM: Shut up, Harris.

THELMA *(Offstage)*: I need a priest!

TOM: Ever since I've been here, Thelma's always calling for a priest. How come?

PETE: Sam knows.

SAM: Yeah, well, mind your own business.

THELMA *(Offstage)*: Someone get me a priest!

SAM *(Screaming, overlapping Thelma)*: Dry up, you stupid fuckin' broad!

PETE: Why don't you go comfort her, Sam? You used to be pretty
    good at comforting old Thelma.

JIM: Yeah, you couldn't keep your hands off her.

SAM: What's the matter, were ya jealous, princess?

TOM: Hey, I'd like to know what the hell's going on.

PETE: This was before your time, Tom. Thelma was all right then.
    Cute kid, as a matter of fact. Until old horny here got his hands
    on her and drove her off her rocker.

SAM: That's a fuckin' lie. The doctors said it wasn't my fault.

JIM: They only told you that to make it easy for you.

SAM: Look, it wasn't my fault.

JIM: What you did sure didn't help any.

SAM: Well why bring it up now?

PETE: Because we're sick and tired of having you put everybody
    down. It's time someone put you down for a change.

TOM: Well, what did he do? Will you please tell me?

PETE: From the day Thelma got here, Sam was after her like a hot
    stud. He was the first being so nice to her, and then coming in
    here and bragging how she was letting him feel her up, and
    bragging how he was gonna fuck the ass off her soon.

THELMA *(Offstage)*: I WANT A PRIEST!

PETE: Maybe you've heard, Tom, that Thelma's parents are religious.
    I don't just mean they're devout, they're real ding-a-lings about
    it. Like, they believe Thelma's the way she is because of some
    great sin they've committed. Like that. Anyway, she was home
    in bed one weekend with a cold, and Sam went over to visit her,
    and her parents weren't out of the room two seconds when Sam
    was into her pants.

SAM: That's another goddamn lie. It didn't happen that way.

PETE: Okay, so it took a full minute. Don't quibble over details.

SAM: Look, I didn't mean for anything to happen that day. What do
    you think I am, stupid? In the first place, she had a cold, and in
    the second place, her parents were out on the goddamn porch.
    I just wanted to talk. She started fooling around, trying to grab
    my cannon and everything. Naturally I get a hard-on. What am
    I supposed to do? Silly little bitch! We were just going real good
    when she changed her mind. That's one helluva time to exercise
    her woman's prerogative, isn't it? Anyway, we . . . she fell out of
    bed. In a few seconds in come Mommy and Daddy. They
    thought I'd fallen out of my chair or something. Well, there I am
    in bed with my joint waving merrily in the breeze, and Thelma's

on the floor minus her pj's, and all hell broke loose. You'd have thought they'd never seen a cock before. The old man, he bounced me out of bed along the floor and into the hallway. The old lady, she dragged Thelma up behind. Then they held us up in front of a little Jesus statue and asked it to forgive us 'cause we didn't know what we were doing. *(Pause)* The doctors said it wasn't my fault.

JIM: They were only feeling sorry for a horny cripple in a wheelchair.

PETE: Yeah, but we all know the truth, don't we Sam?

SAM *(Overlapping)*: Why don't you shut the fuck up, Cochran!

JIM: Hey Pete, remember how Thelma used to dress before Sam put his rod in her? So pretty.

TOM: Okay, guys, knock it off.

PETE: Yeah, but that's all over now. Now she only wears black and brown, and everything's covered, right up to the neck.

JIM: She used to laugh a lot too.

TOM: That's enough!

THELMA *(Offstage)*: I need a priest!

MICHAEL *(Singsong)*: Thelma needs a priest. Thelma needs a priest.

SAM: Fuck off! Piece of shit!

(Sam goes for Michael, who is sitting on the floor, and swings at him. Michael is surprised, but hits back. To stop the fight, Pete grabs Sam's chair from behind. Sam then lashes out at Pete. At the same time, Jim and Tom rescue Michael. Jim falls while Tom tries to get Michael's attention away from Sam. Throughout the commotion, Michael continues to yell, "Thelma needs a priest." Finally, Sam wheels angrily away and Pete helps Jim up.)

TOM *(At one of the urinals)*: Hey, Michael, look—a cockroach. Big fat one.

(Michael sees the cockroach and gets very excited. Pete, Tom and Jim gather around him at the urinal.)

PETE: Hey, Sam, there's livestock in the pisser.

TOM *(To Michael)*: Why don't you use your ray gun and disintegrate it?

MICHAEL: What ray gun? I got no ray gun.

SAM: Yes, you have. That thing between your legs. It's a ray gun.

(Michael looks down and makes the connection.)

MICHAEL *(Delighted)*: I disintegrate it. I disintegrate it all up.

(He turns into the urinal.)

SAM: You do that.

(Saunders returns and knocks at the door.)

SAUNDERS: For the last time, are you boys coming out or not?
SAM: Go away, we're busy.
SAUNDERS: Very well, then, I'm coming in.

(She enters the washroom.)

PETE: Have you no sense of decency?
SAUNDERS: All right, I don't know what you boys have been doing in here, but I want you back to work immediately. Pete, you've still that rug. Tom, there's boxes to be folded. Sam, you'd better get busy and sand down the edges of those blocks if you expect to earn anything this week. As for you, Jim, well, I'm beginning to have second thoughts.
JIM: Yes, ma'am.

(Pause. No one makes a move to go.)

SAUNDERS: Well, get moving!
PETE: I have to take a crap. *(Heads into one of the stalls)*
TOM: Me, too. *(Goes into the other one)*
SAM: I have to use the bottle.
SAUNDERS: And how about you, Jim? Don't you have something to do?
SAM: He has to hold the bottle for me.
SAUNDERS: He has to what, Sam?
SAM: Well, it's like this. I don't have very good aim, so princess here is gonna get down on her hands and knees—
SAUNDERS: All right, that's quite enough. When you're through here, I want you back to work. And fast. Michael, you come with me.

(Michael turns around from the urinal. His pants are open, his penis exposed.)

MICHAEL *(To Saunders)*: I'm gonna disintegrate you.

SAUNDERS *(Screams)*: Michael! Oh, you boys, you put him up to this!
    Didn't you?

PETE: We did not.

SAUNDERS: Right! Mr. Carson will be here any minute. We'll see
    what he has to say.

(She opens the door to leave.)

SAM *(Calling after her)*: Hey, be careful. He's got one, too.

*(More screams. She exits, running down the hall. Pete and Tom
emerge from the stalls laughing. Jim tidies Michael and sends him
out the door.)*

PETE: Sam, you have a warped sense of humor.

SAM: Yeah, just like the rest of me.

JIM: Proud of that, aren't you, Sam? Professional cripple.

SAM: Eat shit, princess.

JIM: And such a sterling vocabulary.

*(Pause. Jim begins to pick up cigarette butts and matches, which by
now litter the floor.)*

TOM: Hadn't you better go before Carson gets back?

JIM: The office can wait.

TOM: What'll you do when he gets here?

JIM: I'll cross that bridge when I come to it.

TOM: Well, we'll all have to cross that bridge soon. We've been in
    here for over half an hour.

SAM: Yeah, we do tend to take long craps.

PETE: I don't care how long it takes me to crap.

(Pause.)

TOM: Did you get your typewriter fixed yet, Jim?

JIM: No, I haven't had time.

TOM: Well, my dad's offer still stands . . . if you'd like him to take a
    look at it.

JIM: Thanks, I would. How is your father?

TOM: He's okay. Why don't you bring it over Sunday?

JIM: I'll have to see. I'm kind of busy at the club. Christmas is coming.

TOM: It will only take an hour.

JIM: You wouldn't like to give us a hand this year, would you?

TOM: What did you have in mind?

JIM: I thought you might like to do our Christmas mural.

TOM: No, I don't think so.

JIM: Spastic Club's not good enough for chicken-tracks, eh? Seriously, Tom, I could use some help. Not just for the mural, but to paint posters, stuff like that.

TOM: How much is the Spastic Club willing to pay for all this?

JIM: Come on, you know there's no payment. All the work for the club is done on a voluntary basis. Carson's never paid anyone before.

SAM: So why should the old fart break his record of stinginess just for you?

JIM: It may interest you to know, Sam, that Carson doesn't get paid for his services either.

SAM: Bwess his wittle heart.

TOM: In that case, the answer's no. If I get paid for folding boxes, why the hell should I paint a lousy mural for free?

JIM: I just thought it might keep you busy.

TOM: I'm busy enough.

(Jim gets up, staggers over to the wastebasket and deposits the litter. Sam applauds.)

PETE: Jim, what's this Spastic Club planning for us boys and girls this year?

JIM: Oh, we've got a few things up our sleeve. Actually, we'd appreciate it if some of the members were a bit more cooperative. So far the response has been practically nil.

TOM: That's horseshit.

PETE: What about my idea of having that psychologist down from the university?

JIM: Well, since you're so interested, Pete, I'll tell you. Carson didn't think too much of it. He was afraid members would be bored. I don't happen to agree with him, but that's the way he feels.

SAM: What about my idea for installing ramps in the subway?

JIM: It's a good idea, Sam, but that sort of thing doesn't come under our jurisdiction.

SAM: Who says so?

JIM: It's up to the city. We're not in a position . . .

TOM: Okay, Jim, what does the Spastic Club have up its sleeve for this year?

JIM: There's a trip to the Science Center. One to the African Lion Safari. We're organizing a finger-painting contest, that sorority is throwing a Valentine's Day party for us . . .

PETE: Wheee! A party!

(Circus music is heard low in the distance.)

TOM: What's the entertainment, Jim?

JIM: Puffo the Clown, Merlin the Magician . . .

PETE: And Cinderella, and Snow White and the Seven Fucking Dwarfs. Jesus Christ, Jim, Puffo the Clown! What do you and Carson think you're dealing with, a bunch of fucking babies?

(Blackout.

Circus music at full volume. Bright lights. Puffo, in clown suit, enters carrying balloons. Girl and the two Shriners enter behind him. Girl is dressed in circus attire, marching and twirling a baton. One of the Shriners is wearing a Mickey Mouse mask and white gloves. He follows her, weaving in and around the boys, dancing in time to the music. The other Shriner is on a tricycle or roller skates, waving to the audience. Puffo presents Sam, Tom and Pete each with a balloon. He exits, followed by Girl and the Shriners. The music fades.)

Who was that masked man, anyway?

(On a signal from Pete, the boys burst their balloons with their lit cigarettes.)

JIM: Wait a minute, Pete, let me finish. We've got other things planned.

PETE: Like what?

JIM: Well, for one, we're planning a trip to the glue factory.

TOM: You're kidding.

JIM: No, I'm not. Carson thinks it might be very educational.

TOM: What do you think, Jim? Do you think it will be very educational?

JIM: I don't know, I've never seen them make glue before.

PETE: Well, you take one old horse, and you stir well . . .

JIM: We're planning other things too, you know?

TOM: What other things?

JIM: Well you know: theater trips, museum trips. These things take time, Tom. We've written letters and . . .

TOM: What letters? To whom?

JIM: Letters. Lots of letters. They're at home in my briefcase. I'll show them to you tomorrow.

TOM: Any replies?

JIM: What?

TOM: How many replies did you get to the letters?

JIM: Look, am I on trial or something?

TOM: I don't know, Jim. Are you?

JIM: Okay, so maybe some of the things we do aren't as exciting as you and I'd like them to be, but I'm doing the job as well as I can, and I can't do it all on my own. You guys bitch about the program, but you won't get off your asses and fight for something better. That idea about the psychologist, I really pushed that idea. Pushed it to the hilt—

PETE: But Carson didn't like it.

JIM: Carson didn't like it, and the more I pushed, the firmer he got.

SAM: Why didn't you push it right up his ass?

JIM *(Ignoring this)*: So I told Pete he should go down and talk to Carson himself. I even made him an appointment. But he never showed up, did you, Pete?

PETE: I was busy.

TOM: Why the hell should you or Pete or anyone else have to beg that prick for anything?

JIM: Tom, that's not fair. So he's a little stuffy, at least he's interested. He does give us more than the passing time of day.

PETE: Sure, he was in for a whole hour this morning.

JIM: Pete, you may not like Carson, but just remember, if he, or the Kiwanis, or any of the other service clubs decide to throw in the towel . . . we're in big trouble.

SAM: "If they won't do it . . ."

JIM: If they won't do it, who will? You?

(A long pause.)

PETE: I've got nothing against the Rotary or the Kiwanis. If they want to give me a free meal just to look good, that's okay with me.

TOM: You're sure of that?

PETE: Tom, the Bible says the Lord provides. Right now He's providing pretty good. Should I get upset if He sends the Kiwanis instead of coming Himself?

JIM: If you feel like getting something, why don't you give something?

PETE: No, sir. I don't jump through hoops for nobody, and certainly not for a bastard like Carson. I might have nothing to say against the groups, but I don't have anything to say for them either.

TOM: You can't stay neutral all the time.

PETE: Tell that to Switzerland. Tom, you're young. You don't realize how tough it is for people like us. Baby, it's cold outside.

SAM *(Under his breath)*: Christ!

PETE: When I came to this dump eleven years ago, I wanted to be a carpenter. That's all I could think about ever since I can remember. But face it, whoever heard of a carpenter with a flipper like that? *(Holds up his deformed hand)* But I had a nice chat with this doc, and he told me I'd find what I'm looking for down here. So I came down here, and one of Saunders' flunkies shoves a bag of blocks in my hand. "What gives?" I said. And then it slowly dawned on me that as far as the doc is concerned, that's the closest I'll ever get to carpentry.

And I was pissed off, sure. But then I think, good old doc, he just doesn't understand me. 'Cause I still have my ideals. So in a few days I bust out of this place and go looking for a job—preferably carpentry. What happens? I get nothing but aching feet and a flat nose from having doors slammed in my face all the fucking time.

And I'm at my wit's end when I get a letter from the Spastic Club. And I said fuck that. I'm about to throw it in the furnace, but I get curious. I've heard of the Spastic Club and I always figured it was a load of shit. But I think one meeting isn't going to kill me.

So I go, and I find out I'm right. It's a load of shit. It's a bunch of fuckheads sitting around saying, "Aren't we just too ducky for these poor unfortunate cripples?" But I got a free turkey dinner.

When I got home I took a good look at myself. I ask myself, What am I supposed to be fighting? What do these jokers want me to do? The answer is they want to make life easier for me. Is that so bad? I mean, they don't expect me to keep you guys in your place or nothing. They just want me to enjoy life. And the government even pays me just for doing that. If I got a job, I'd lose the pension. So why have I been breaking my ass all this time looking for a job? And I got no answers to that. So I take the pension, and come back to the workshop. The only price I gotta pay is listening to old lady Saunders giving me hell for not weaving her goddamn rug.

(Blackout.

Fanfare. Lights up on a far side of the stage. The actor playing Michael enters dressed as a Freak Show Barker. With him is the Girl, his assistant, dressed in similar carnival attire. The following sequence takes place in a stage area independent of the washroom.)

FREAK SHOW BARKER *(To the audience)*: Are you bored with your job? Would you like to break out of the rat race? Does early retirement appeal to you? Well, my friends, you're in luck. The Shriners, the Rotary and the Kiwanis are just begging to wait on you hand and foot . . .

(Charleston music. The Freak Show Barker and the Girl dance. The music continues.)

To throw you parties, picnics . . . To take you on field trips . . . To the flower show, the dog show and the Santa Claus parade.

(More dancing.)

Would you like to learn new skills? Like sanding blocks, folding boxes, separating nuts and bolts? My friends, physiotherapists are standing by eager to teach you.

(The Girl hands him a wooden block and a block covered with sandpaper. More dancing as he sands the block.)

Whoopee, is this ever fun.

(He hands the blocks back to the Girl.)

Now, I suppose you good people would like to know, how do I get this one-way ticket to paradise? My props, please!

(The Girl hands him a life-size model of the human brain, which has the various sections marked off. She also hands him a hammer. The music stops. He walks downstage into a pool of light, directly in front of the audience.)

Now all you do is take a hammer and adjust the motor area of the brain. Like this. Not too hard, now, we wouldn't want to lose you.

(He taps the brain gently.)

Having done that, you will have impaired your muscle coordination, and will suddenly find that you now *(Speaking with the speech defect of Michael)* "talk with an accent." You will then be brought to our attention either by relatives who have no room for you in the attic, or by neighbors who are distressed to see you out in the street, clashing with the landscape.

Now, assuming you are successful in locating the proper point of demolition, we guarantee that this very special euphoria will be yours not for a day, not for a week, but for a lifetime. There's no chance for relapse, regression, or rehabilitation because, my friends, it's as permanent as a hair transplant. It's for keeps. Should you, however, become disenchanted with this state, there is one recourse available to you, which, while we ourselves do not recommend it, is popular with many, and does provide a final solution to a very complex problem. All you do is take the hammer and simply tap a little harder.

(He smashes the brain. At the moment of impact, he becomes spastic, and slowly crumbles to the floor. Blackout.
The lights come up on the four boys.)

SAM: Guys like you really bug me. You got two good legs and one good hand. So the other's deformed. Big fuckin' deal. By the way, who the hell said you couldn't be a carpenter? You had your loom fixed up in five minutes last week while that old fart of a handyman was running around town looking for something to fix it with.

PETE: That was lucky.

TOM: You know what I think, Cochran? I think you're lazy. I think eleven years ago you were looking for a grave to fall into, and you found it in the Spastic Club.

PETE: Don't be self-righteous about things you don't understand.

TOM: I understand laziness.

PETE: You don't understand. I tried.

TOM: Aw, c'mon, Pete, you didn't try very hard.

PETE: There's no place in the outside world for a guy who talks funny.

SAM: Aw, you poor wittle boy. Did the big bad mans hurt your wittle feelings?

(Pete goes for Sam, is about to hit him, but is restrained by Tom.)

TOM: That's not funny, Sam. *(To Pete)* But it is a bit ridiculous. Here you are, you're thirty-seven years old, and you're still worried about something as small as that.

PETE: It may be a small thing to you, Tom. It's not to me.

JIM: Howdya like to have kids following you down the street calling you drunk? I get that all the time, but you learn to live with it.

SAM: Sure you learn to live with it. You learn to rub their noses in it too. Last week I was at this show and I had to be bounced about twenty steps in the chair just to get to the lobby. Well you know what that does to my bladder, eh? So naturally I make for the washroom. The stalls are two inches too narrow, of course. As for the urinals, I never claimed to be Annie Oakley. They don't have urinal bottles 'cause they'd fuck up the interior decoration. But then I did spy this Dixie cup dispenser . . .

JIM: Sam, you didn't!

SAM: Yeah, sweetie, I did. I was just doing up my fly when the usher walked in, saw the cup sitting on the edge of the sink. He thought it was lemonade. Told me patrons weren't allowed to bring refreshments into the washroom. Then he moved closer and got a whiff.

PETE: What happened?

SAM: Another United Appeal supporter had his dreams all crushed to rat-shit.

JIM: And Sam set us back another twenty years.

SAM: What do you expect me to do, Harris? Piss my pants waiting for everything to come under your jurisdiction?

PETE: Sam's right. It's like you said, Jim. You do the best with what you got.

TOM: Come on, Pete, that's a cop-out and you know it. Sam should have got rid of the cup as soon as he took his leak. Putting it on the sink in plain view of everyone, for chrissake!

PETE: Don't be so smug. A guy survives the best way he knows how. You wait, you'll find out. They don't want us creeps messing up their world. They just don't want us.

TOM: Tough! They're going to get me whether they want me or not. I'm a man, and I've got a right to live like other men.

PETE: You're the only man I know who can make a sermon out of saying hello. *(Goes into one of the stalls, slamming the door behind him)*

TOM: Yeah, and pretty soon I'm gonna say good-bye. You expect me to spend the rest of my life folding boxes?

PETE *(Over the top of the stall)*: Look, Rembrandt, we know you're a great artist and all that shit. But if you paint like you fold, forget it.

JIM: Wait a minute, Pete. I've seen some of Tom's paintings. I'm no expert on abstract, but I think they're pretty good. They're colorful and . . .

SAM: Colorful chicken-tracks?

TOM: Fuck off!

JIM: Still, I'm not other people. I might like them, but folks on the outside might not. People get pretty funny when they find out something's been done by a handicapped person. Besides, we both know you can't draw.

TOM: That doesn't make any difference. I paint abstract.

SAM: So you'll win the finger-painting contest.

JIM: Tom, we've been over this I don't know how many times. Name me one good abstract painter who isn't a good draftsman.

SAM: Name me one good writer who'd be caught dead in a glue factory.

JIM: Seriously, can you think of one famous artist who was spastic?

TOM: Jim, if you're sure I can't make it, what about the letter?

PETE: What letter?

JIM *(Shrugs)*: Oh, a letter he got from an art critic.

PETE *(Emerging from the stall)*: What did you say?

TOM: Here, you can read it yourself.

(He hands the letter to Pete, who begins to read it to himself.)

SAM: Out loud.

(Pete starts to read it, gives up, hands the letter to Jim:)

JIM *(Reading)*: "Dear Mr. March, I was fascinated by the portfolio you submitted. I cannot recall an artist in whose work such a strong sense of struggle was manifest. You positively stab the canvas with bold color, and your sure grasp of the palette lends a native primitivism to your work. I am once drawn to the crude simplicity of your figures and repulsed by the naive grotesqueries which grope for recognition in your tortured world. While I cannot hail you as a mature artist, I would be interested in seeing your work in progress this time next year." *(Hands letter back to Pete)*

SAM: Which one of your father's friends wrote it?

TOM: None of them.

SAM: One of your mother's friends?

TOM: The letter's authentic. I'll bring the guy's magazine column if you don't believe me.

PETE: Oh, we believe you, Tom. Critics are so compassionate.

TOM: You shit all over everything, don't you?

PETE *(Handing Tom the letter)*: It's a good letter, I guess.

TOM: You guess?

PETE: Well, what the hell am I supposed to say? You're the artist. I don't even like the Mona Lisa. To me she's just a fat ugly broad. But I can't help wondering, Tom . . .

TOM: What?

PETE: If he wouldn't have said the same thing if you'd sent him one of your boxes. *(Tom starts to protest, but Pete goes on)* Like when I'm weaving that goddamn rug and we have visitors. Now I'm no master weaver. Matter of fact, I've woven some pretty shitty rugs in my time. But whenever we have visitors, there are always one or two clowns who come over and practically have an orgasm over my rug, no matter how shitty we both know it is.

SAM: It's the same with the blocks. They pick one up, tell me how great it is, and then walk away with a handful of splinters.

TOM: It's not the same. This guy happens to be one of the toughest art critics around.

JIM: Even tough art critics give to the United Appeal.

TOM: Yes, and sometimes writers write for it.

JIM: Well, it keeps me off the streets.

SAM: Yeah, Jim peddles his ass indoors where it's warm.

PETE: And Carson has an exclusive contract on it. Right Jim?

JIM: I work because I want to work. It's a challenge, I enjoy it, and I can see the results.

PETE: Sure. So can we: hot dogs, ice cream, balloons, confetti . . .

JIM: Well at least I don't have illusions of grandeur.

TOM: What illusions have you got, Jim?

JIM: Tom, you've got to come down to earth sooner or later. For someone in my situation the workshop makes sense. I can be more useful in a place like this.

TOM: Useful to Carson?

JIM: No, to people like Michael and Thelma.

TOM: What about Carson? Are you going to go on kissing his ass?

JIM: Call it what you like. In dealing with people, I have to be diplomatic.

TOM: Fine, Jim. You be diplomatic for both of us.

(He gets up.)

PETE: Where are you going?

TOM: I'm bored. I'm leaving.

PETE: What's the matter?

TOM: Nothing, Cochran, go back and finish your shit.

JIM: Tom, what is it?

TOM: I'm quitting.

JIM: You're not serious?

TOM: Getting more serious by the minute.

JIM: You're building a lot on a few kind words, aren't you?

TOM: The man doesn't know I'm spastic.

JIM: He's going to find out. And you know what'll happen when he does. You'll be his golden boy for a few weeks, but as soon as the novelty wears off, he'll go out of his way to avoid you.

TOM: What if the novelty doesn't wear off?

JIM: Tom, I don't think you should rush into this.

TOM: How long do I have to stay, Jim?

JIM: Stay until Christmas. Stay and do the mural.

TOM: No.

JIM: But you like painting. It won't hurt you.

TOM: I said no!

JIM: Why not?

(Tom moves toward the door.)

Won't you at least talk about it?

TOM *(Turns and looks at Jim)*: That's all you know how to do now, isn't it? No writing, no thinking, just talking. Well get this straight: I don't want any part of the Spastic Club or the workshop. It's finished, okay?

JIM: Look, I know this place isn't perfect. I agree. It's even pretty rotten at times. But, Tom, out there, you'll be lost. You're not wanted out there, you're not welcome. None of us are. If you stay here we can work together. We can build something.

SAM: Yeah, a monument to Carson. For the pigeons to shit on.

TOM: How long are *you* going to stay here?

JIM: How long?

TOM: Are you going to spend the rest of your life being Carson's private secretary?

JIM: Well, nothing's permanent. Even I know that.

TOM: Stop bullshitting and give me a straight answer.

JIM: Okay, I'll move on. Sure.

TOM: And do what?

JIM: Maybe I'll go back to my writing.

TOM: When? *(No reply)* When was the last time you wrote anything?

JIM: Last month I wrote an article for the *Sunshine Friend.*

PETE AND SAM: "You are my sunshine, my only sunshine . . ."

TOM: Shut up! I mean, when was the last time you wrote something you wanted to write?

JIM: Well, you know, my typewriter's bust—

TOM: Don't give me that crap about your typewriter. You don't want to get it fixed.

JIM: That's not true . . .

TOM: Do you know what you're doing here? You're throwing away your talent for a lousy bit of security.

JIM: Tom, you don't understand—

TOM: You're wasting your time doing a patch-up job at something you don't really believe in. *(Jim does not reply. Tom moves toward him)* Jim, there are stacks of guys in this world who haven't got the intelligence to know where they're at. But you have. You *know.* And if you don't *do* something with that knowledge, you'll end up hating yourself.

JIM: What the hell could I do?

TOM: You could go into journalism, write a book. Listen, in this job, who can you tell it to? Spastics. Now think. Think of all the millions of jerks on the outside who have no idea of what it's really like in here. Hell, you could write a best-seller.

JIM: I've thought about it.

TOM: Well *do* something about it.

JIM: Don't you think I want to?

TOM: Jim, I know you're scared. I'm scared. But if I don't take this chance, I won't have a hope in hell of making it. And if you keep on doing something you don't want to do, soon you won't even have a mind. Do you think if Michael had a mind like yours he'd be content to hang around here all day flushing toilets?

PETE: He's right, Jim. You don't belong here. Why don't you and Tom go together?

TOM: Look, I'll help you. We can go, we can get a place, we can do it together. Come on, what do you say?

(Saunders and Carson are heard in the hallway.)

SAUNDERS: They've been in here all afternoon. I tried to reason with them, but they refused to come out. I know you're busy, and I hate to bring you down here, but I'm really afraid this Rick and Stanley business is repeating itself . . .
CARSON: Miss Saunders.
SAUNDERS: Yes?
CARSON: Thanks, I can take it from here.

(Saunders exits. Carson opens the door and stands in the doorway.)

Okay guys, out.

(Brief pause, then Jim moves to go.)

TOM: Jim, how about it?
JIM: Later, Tom.
CARSON: Much later. It's time to get back to work.
TOM: I'm quitting, Carson.
CARSON: First things first. We can discuss that in the morning. *(He waits)* Let's go.
JIM: I'm quitting, too, sir.
CARSON: Right now I've got a good mind to fire you. Go to my office and wait for me.
SAM: He's making it real easy for you, Jim. He just fired you.
CARSON: You, too, Sam. Out.
SAM: I need the bottle. Hand me the bottle, Carson.
CARSON: You've had all afternoon to use the bottle. Now, out!
SAM: I need the fucking bottle!

(Tom goes to get the bottle, is stopped by Carson.)

CARSON: You leave that bottle alone. I want you all out of here.

(Pete gets the bottle, gives it to Sam.)

Pete! Goddamn it, what's wrong with you guys?

(Sam now has the bottle in his lap.)

Give me that bottle! *(Takes it away from Sam)* Now get out of here, all of you. *(Nothing happens, so he starts to wheel Sam's chair)*

SAM: Take your fuckin' hands off my chair!

JIM: Listen! You never listen to me!

CARSON: For God's sake, Jim, I'll listen, but in my office.

JIM: No, here. Now!

CARSON: What's eating you?

SAM: Give me the goddamn bottle.

(He tries to get it, but Carson holds it out of his reach.)

CARSON: Get out of here, Sam! *(He pushes the chair away)*

SAM: Fucking prick!

CARSON *(Shaken)*: All right, what is it?

TOM: Jim, he's listening.

JIM: I don't want to spend the rest of my life here.

CARSON: Fine. You probably won't. Now can we all get back to work?

SAM: I need the fucking bottle!

TOM: Didn't you hear what he said? He said he doesn't want to spend his whole life in this dump.

CARSON: Look, March, you've been in here all afternoon. You've got Miss Saunders all upset because of Michael, and . . .

SAM: *I need the bottle!*

CARSON: Shut up, Sam!

TOM: Do you know why we've been in here all afternoon? Did you ever think of that?

SAM: Son of a bitch! Do you want me to piss my pants?

(Carson shoves the bottle at him, Sam wheels into the doorway of one of the stalls.)

TOM: Did it ever enter your head that we might think of something besides the workshop, the club, and making you look good?

CARSON: Look, I don't know what you think, and right now I really don't care. All I'm concerned with is that you get out of this washroom. If you've got a complaint, you can come and talk to me.

TOM: I won't be there. Neither will Jim.

CARSON: I said we can discuss that in the morning. *(He turns to Sam and Pete)* Come on Sam, Pete, let's go.

PETE: He can't find it, Carson.

JIM: I want to be a writer.

CARSON *(To Sam and Pete)*: Quit fooling around, and hurry up.

JIM: I want to be a writer!

CARSON: You are a writer.

JIM: You don't understand. I want to make my living from it.

CARSON: Maybe you will, someday. But it's not going to happen overnight, is it?

TOM: If you stay here, Jim, it won't happen at all.

CARSON: It sure as hell won't if he runs off on some half-assed adventure with you.

TOM: Come on, Jim, the man's deaf.

CARSON: And what is it this time, Rembrandt? Poverty in a garret somewhere?

TOM: Better than poverty at the workshop.

CARSON: What are you going to paint, nude women?

TOM: You son of a bitch!

CARSON: Okay, Tom. Let's go. *(Moves to usher Tom out)*

TOM: You fucking son of a bitch! *(In pushing Carson off, he loses his balance and falls. Carson tries to help him up)* Get the fuck off me, Carson! *(Slowly Jim and Pete help him to his feet)* Jim, you can stay and fart around as much as you like, but I'm going. Now are you with me or not?

CARSON: No, he's not. Now beat it.

TOM: Is that your answer, Jim?

JIM: Tom, wait . . .

TOM: I'm tired of waiting.

JIM: Maybe if I had just a little more time.

TOM: There's no time left.

JIM: Couldn't we wait till the end of the week?

CARSON: No, Jim. If you're serious about going, go now.

JIM: What about the Christmas program?

CARSON: I can find someone else.

JIM: But Christmas is the busiest time.

PETE: Go, Jim! Go with Tom.

SAM *(Overlapping)*: Don't let him do it to you, baby. Go!

JIM: But Tom, it's Christmas!

TOM: Jim, please!

JIM: I can't let him down now. Maybe after Christmas . . .

SAM: Fuck Christmas! What about Tom?

JIM: I've written all these letters, made all the arrangements . . .

(Tom turns and moves toward the door.)

SAM: Piss on the arrangements! Are you going to let him walk out that door alone?

PETE: If you don't go now, Tom will be alone, but you'll be more alone. Believe me, I know.

JIM: I can't go! I can't go, Tom, because, if you fall, I'll be the only one there to pick you up. And I can hardly stand up myself.

(Tom has gone.)

SAM: How did you get around on campus, princess? Crawl on your belly? *(He wheels angrily to the door)* Fuckin' door! Hey, Carson, how about one cripple helping another?

CARSON: Get him out, Pete.

(Sam and Pete exit. They wait outside the door, listening. Jim staggers over to the bench and sits.)

CARSON: Why don't we talk about this over dinner? At my place, if you like.

THELMA *(Offstage)*: I need a priest! Get me a priest! Someone get me a priest!

(Lights slowly fade to the sound of Thelma's sobbing. Pete wheels Sam down the hallway. Sam is laughing.)

END OF PLAY

APPENDIX

Interlude

This scene was used in the New York/Washington productions as an alternative to the Shriners sequence on page 11.

(Music plays: "Everything's Coming Up Roses." Lights come up. An Astronaut, Colonel Stardust, enters and poses. A Football Player, Ralph Sonovitch, enters and poses with Stardust. The Girl, Sally Carson, enters and poses between Stardust and Sonovitch, then she poses with Pete, Tom and Sam. Michael, as a Telethon MC, enters.)

TELETHON MC: Marvelous, marvelous. Isn't that fantastic, folks. Come on, let's hear it for our celebrities who've joined us tonight: Colonel Teddy "Ace" Stardust, Crazy Legs Ralph Sonovitch and the loverly Sally Carson. Thank you and I love you all, as we come to the end of our annual fifty-three-hour telethon for cerebral palsy. You know, folks (are we on?), they're recycling old newspapers, old beer cans and other rubbish. So tonight, with your help—and remember, I love you all, each and every one of you—so help us to recycle these poor, unfortunate cripples, or at least help us to get them off the streets!

Now, seriously, folks, we don't like to parade these people in front of you, but we *do* want to allow you to meet them; to get to know them and love them as *I* have. The *real* celebrities! First there's Bob here . . .

TOM: Tom . . .

TELETHON MC: Bob here folds boxes. You know, those little boxes
you take your chop suey home in. Keep up the good work, Bob.

Now we come to old Pete. Don't be afraid, Pete. Pete weaves
rugs. Do you know, and I think that's incredible, that is, folks . . .
that he can weave rugs with . . . *(Holds up Pete's deformed hand)*

And last, but certainly not least, we come to the big fellow,
my pal, Sammy. Sammy sands blocks. In *this* wheelchair!
Sammy, I love you!

Come on, folks, send us a check—one dollar, five dollars,
ten dollars, anything. But please help us to help these poor
blunders of God. Wwgghh! Wwggh!

(Blackout.)

Alternative Dialogue

This dialogue was used in the New York/Washington productions as
an alternative to the text found on pages 20–21.

SAM *(Reading)*: "As the biggest zeppelin took his place on the bed
with the helpless Miss Collins, Milton stood beside her, slipping
out of his clothes. He quickly stripped to the nude and tossed
his clothes aside. His male member stood hard, erect and ready
for action . . ."

TOM: That's enough, Sam.

SAM *(Ignoring him)*: "She reached down and cradled it, bouncing it
gently, rubbing the delicate underside. Basil swung around
behind her, his trousers bulging with passion. He pressed her
body against his. Even through . . ."

TOM: That's enough, for chrissake! *(Gets up and moves to grab the
book away from Sam)*

SAM: " . . . two layers of clothing, she could feel the hardness of his
prick pressing into the crack of her ass."

(He hands the book to Tom.)

PETE: Wait! I want to find out where she gets the zeppelin.

TOM: If you're so hot about her, here read the goddamn book.

(He throws it across to Pete.)

DAVID FREEMAN was born in Toronto, Canada, on January 7, 1945. At the age of six, he entered Sunnyview School, a school for the handicapped. From school, he was sent to a sheltered workshop. This experience led to the article "The World of Can't," published in *Maclean's* magazine (July 4, 1964). It signaled the beginning of a series of articles in other magazines and newspapers. He graduated from McMaster University in Hamilton, Ontario, Canada, in 1971. His involvement in theater began with the production of his play *Creeps*. Other plays include *The Battering Ram, You're Gonna Be All Right, Jamie Boy, Flytrap* and the radio play *Year of the Soul* (broadcast by CBC Radio, 1982). He lives in Montreal and continues to write daily.

SHOOT!

Lynn Manning

Donny (Lynn Manning) in the Hudson Theater production, Hollywood, California, 1992. Photo by Carol Petersen.

Shoot! is the very first play I ever wrote. It was born out of Irene Oppenheim's Available Light Workshop. Prior to being invited into Available Light, I was a poet splashing alone in the shallow end of playwriting for the Braille Institute's drama class. All of us student actors, as well as the lead instructor, Ethel Winant, were either blind or visually impaired. Even so, the scenes and monologues that Ethel encouraged us to bring to life were exclusively peopled by sighted characters: *Streamers, Days of Wine and Roses, A Streetcar Named Desire*, etc. It was challenging work, made even more gratifying by the occasional opportunity to prove to sighted audiences that blind actors could convincingly portray sighted characters.

When Irene Oppenheim contacted me about joining her playwriting workshop, I'd already begun exploring the form. She asked to see samples of all my writing. After silently reading through my earliest attempt at a play, she said, "You have a good facility for dialogue." I lit up. Then she went on, "It still surprises me how even disabled writers buy into these movie-of-the-week plots. The disabled characters always need able-bodied people to convince them that life is worth living. It's insidious. Judging from your other writing, this isn't your story, is it?"

It wasn't. The depressed and self-pitying blind man I'd created didn't resemble anyone in my life. Not me. Not my fiercely independent, highly motivated blind friends. That stereotypical character had slithered into my play from a dank dungeon crammed with cliché cripples and inspirational invalids. Sighted for twenty-three years and blind for twelve, I'd been bombarded with such disabled stereotypes, and that had left me brainwashed—so much so that I'd been unwittingly poised to perpetuate the fraud.

Irene's observation embarrassed me to the core. I'm a black man. I should have known better. I had made it my life's mission to shatter the stereotypes and the lowered expectations of mainstream America regarding "young black males." I now vowed to be as diligent about crushing the myths and assumptions held about the blind and disabled:

The Magic Wand

Quick-change artist extraordinaire,
I whip out my folded cane
and change from black man to blind man
with a flick of the wrist.
It is a profound metamorphosis—
From God-gifted wizard of roundball
dominating backboards across America
to God-gifted idiot savant
pounding out chart-busters on a cockeyed whim;
From sociopathic gangbanger with death for eyes
to all-seeing soul with saintly spirit;
From rape-deranged misogynist
to poor motherless child;
From welfare-rich pimp
to disability-rich gimp;
And from "white man's burden"
to every man's burden.
It is always a profound metamorphosis.
Whether from cursed by man to cursed by God
or from scripture-condemned to God-ordained,
my final form is never of my choosing.
I only wield the wand;
you are the magician.

Production History

Shoot! was originally developed in the Available Light Workshop in Los Angeles, 1990–91, with Irene Oppenheim as dramaturg. The play was first produced in the summer of 1992 at the Hudson Theater in Hollywood, California. The production was directed by Roxanne Rogers. The cast was as follows:

DONNY	Lynn Manning
CHARLES	John Freeland, Jr.
BROWN	John Nesci

Characters

DONNY—blind black man in his thirties. Athletic in appearance, at least six feet tall. He is dressed in a sport coat (cloth or leather) and uses a straight, noncollapsible white cane. No sunglasses.

CHARLES—Donny's sighted younger half-brother. Similar size and build, more casually attired.

BROWN—white pawnbroker. At least fifty years old. Rough around the edges, shabby dresser.

NEWS ANCHOR'S VOICE—female, unavoidably sexy.

Set

The stage is empty, save for the suggestion of a pawnbroker's counter, which can be brought downstage by Brown as needed.

Time

The present.

Place

Los Angeles, California.

The stage is black. We hear static and the garbled voices of a radio being tuned in. It settles on a newscast. Donny appears and taps his way downstage.

NEWS ANCHOR'S VOICE: Now for the lead story on K-I-L-R News this Monday morning. County law enforcement agencies report thirteen shooting deaths this past weekend—a near record number. Eight of the deaths are believed to be gang-related. Thirty-one people in all fell victim to shootings since Friday, making this one of the most violent weekends in Los Angeles County history. A police department spokesman said, "This willful violence runs deeper than turf wars and drug rip-offs." He compared it to "a malignant cancer devouring civilized society."

DONNY *(Now center stage)*: It went down like this: I walk right up to the counter of Brown's Collateral Loan Company—that's what they're calling pawnshops these days—and I say, "I'd like to see what you have in handguns for sale." So, there's this long silence.

(Lights up on Brown, behind pawnshop counter.)

BROWN: You won't believe what happened at the shop today. This blind guy comes into the store. Big, black, cane as long as I am tall. And he wants to buy a gun.

DONNY: Now I know the man's giving me this "you must be kidding" look. So I say, "You do sell handguns here, don't you?" The man stutters a bit, says, "Ah ah ah, yeah." So I say, "That's what I thought. I'm in the market for a pistol. Something reliable, preferably automatic. I'd like to see what you have."

BROWN: An automatic! I figure the guy's gotta be puttin' me on, right? What's a blind man want with a gun? Besides, except for the white cane, the guy don't look all that blind. I figure he must be fakin'. Next thing you know, the guy from that hidden video show will come crawlin' out of the woodwork. I kinda look around just to be sure he ain't hidin' in the store somewhere.

(Brown does this, initially oblivious to Donny approaching the counter. He then turns and tentatively wiggles his fingers in front of Donny's eyes.)

I also kinda wiggle my fingers in front of this big guy's face. Believe it or not, he's as blind as a May Company mannequin. And serious about the gun.

DONNY: The man tries to play me off at first, so I whip out my wallet. And the dude leaps into action. Abracadabra, zip, zap, bam! Three pieces on the counter in front of me. Like they say, "Money talks and bullshit walks."

BROWN: The fella lays out the cash to prove he means business. So, *(Snaps fingers)* business we do. After all, there ain't no law against a blind man ownin' a gun. He might even sue if I don't sell him one. I show him what we have. *(Places three pistols on the counter. Speaking loudly, as if Donny is hard of hearing)* Okay, let's see now. Here you are, sir. How's that baby feel? *(Sticks the largest gun in Donny's hands. Donny scrutinizes it, frowning. Aside to audience)* Just to make sure he's not jerkin' my chain, I flip him off a few times while I show him the merchandise.

(Brown does so, blatantly at first, then with creative selectivity throughout the rest of the scene.)

DONNY: What is this?

(Donny inadvertently points the pistol in Brown's face and Brown gingerly moves the barrel aside.)

BROWN (*With reverence, and still too loudly*): That there is a Desert Eagle .44-Magnum automatic!

DONNY (*Recoiling from Brown's volume*): You hard of hearin' or somethin'?

BROWN: No. I thought . . .

DONNY: Me neither. Not yet anyway. (*Quickly moving on*) You say this is a .44-Magnum automatic? I didn't even know there was such a thing. (*Hefts it*) This baby's heavy too.

BROWN (*Softer*): Weighs two and a half pounds, without the nine-cartridge clip.

DONNY: Damn. A serious piece of business. How much?

BROWN: For you? Seven hundred. Comes with a lifetime guarantee.

DONNY: I'll bet. Must come with homing-device bullets too. (*Hands it back to him*) Too serious for my taste. I'm looking for something a little cheaper and handier.

BROWN: Okay. Try this one on for size—a chrome-plated .22. (*Hands Donny the smallest pistol*)

DONNY (*Turning to audience with a look of disgust on his face*): Now I'm startin' to feel like Goldilocks or some-damn-body. (*Puts on effeminate voice*) Oh, that one's too big, oh, this one's too small. (*In own voice*) It's too feminine for a man my size. The mugger's liable to bust out laughin', I flash somethin' this small. I mean, the white cane's bad enough. The low-life mothahfuckah already thinks he's got an easy mark. No need to add insult to injury. What I need is something that's gonna put the fear of God in his heart (*Taps his chest with a fist*) and the fear of lead in his ass. (*Mimes pulling trigger; to Brown*) You got somethin' like that?

BROWN (*Chuckles*): Why didn't you say so. I've got just the thing. (*Hands Donny the third gun*) Try this beauty. (*Seductive*) It's a sweet, nickel-plated, .9-millimeter semiautomatic. It's got the look, and it's got the power.

DONNY (*Pleased with the feel of it*): I'll take it. (*Lays pistol on counter*)

BROWN: It's yours. (*Puts other two guns away; to audience*) Blind or not, he knows what he likes. (*Places forms on counter and hands Donny a pen*) Now, if you sign on the dotted line, we got a done deal. (*Brown busies himself putting away the guns*)

DONNY (*After a moment*): Ah, you have to show me where to sign.

BROWN: Oh, yeah, right there.

(*Uses his middle finger to tap a spot on the paper, then takes Donny's finger and places it at the same spot. Donny signs.*)

(To audience) After seein' his ID I know for sure he's blind, so I say, *(To Donny, once again too loudly)* "Ah, screw the coolin' off period. You can take it with you today."

(Brown shoves the gun into Donny's hands. Donny takes it, turns downstage and freezes.)

(To audience) You get a hunch about these things. Besides, who ever heard of a blind felon?

(Brown exits with counter.)

DONNY *(Becoming animated)*: This is it! Ready to wage war. Dropped by Big-5, got me some ammo. *(Cocks pistol)* Now I'm ready for Freddy and his whole fuckin' family. This baby holds thirteen rounds! That's lead for a mothahfuckah's ass! *(Holds the pistol up for audience to admire)* Doesn't look like it, does it? No, never have to worry about missin' with this baby. If the first one doesn't get him, the next twelve will. *(He tucks pistol away in lower back, then draws it out quickly and brandishes it beneath the nose of an imaginary assailant; grins and imitates Gomer Pyle)* "Surprise! Surprise! Surprise!" *(In own voice)* Guess who's rippin' who, mothahfuckah? *(Laughs maliciously)* Yeah, best believe he'll think twice before he tries to jack another blind man.

(Blackout.
    Muted city night sounds; lights come up on Charles, making his way downstage center.)

CHARLES *(Highly agitated)*: Donny must be out of his fuckin' mind—the stunt he pulled tonight. I'm beginning to doubt we're related at all, let alone half-brothers. Check this out. We dropped by the Juicy Jungle after work, like we usually do on payday. You know, kick it over a couple of boilermakers while I describe for Donny the bumps and grinds of the bikini dance girls. *(Imitates girls)* Not that he gives a damn for my play-by-play. I think he digs the joint 'cause the girls eventually let him check out the merchandise for himself. *(Aside)* We should all be so blessed. *(Back to audience)* Anyway, we fall out of there after a couple of rounds and a little friendly touchy-feely, and we're both feelin' good!

   Now, out in the parkin' lot, we get approached by this freaky-lookin' white boy. The dude is barefooted, dreadlocked and raggedy. Nasty-lookin'.

He says to me, *(Imitating weird white boy)* "Yo, bro, can you spare some change for a man on a mission?"

I ain't carryin' nothin' smaller than a twenty, besides, he don't look like his mission is anything I care to contribute to. So, I say, "Sorry, man. Out of pocket." Donny mutters something, too, and we keep steppin'.

The dude follows us, sayin', "That ain't cool, bro. That ain't no way to be. I know you got some money!"

He says it with this threatening tone in his voice and Donny and I both turn to check him out.

(Donny enters, cane in hand, making his way toward Charles.)

The dude's all wide-eyed and crazy-lookin', like he's trippin' on somethin'. I want to tell Donny, but the dude is too close. *(Takes a couple of steps backward)*

DONNY *(With hand on Charles's shoulder)*: There was somethin' menacin' about the dude's voice—like he was hintin' he might have to hurt somebody if he didn't get some change pretty damn quick.

CHARLES: I tell the dude, "Hey, man, I don't know what your problem or your mission is, but don't sweat me. I told you, I'm out of pocket."

DONNY *(Using exaggerated "surfer dude" voice)*: You need a translator, dude? The brother said he didn't have any change to spare. Now, fuck off, dude-ski!

CHARLES: I knew that was a bad move right off. The dude kind of went into shock, like Donny's voice had blindsided him. His face started twitchin' somethin' serious.

DONNY: All of a sudden the dude starts talkin' like Shakespeare or some-damn-body. Sayin' . . .

CHARLES *(Using Shakespearean voice while striking a fencer's pose)*: "What say you, knave? Whoreson rascal! Disinherited slave and heir of a mongrel bitch; I'll beat you into clamorous whining."

DONNY: I ain't no brainiac, but I catch his drift. *(To imaginary man)* I got you, homeboy. You wanna throw down. I'm game. Let's get it on.

CHARLES: I'm wonderin' why Donny wants to jump bad so quick. *(To Donny)* Squash it, man. This dude's wigged-out. *(Takes Donny by the arm)*

DONNY *(Pulling free)*: He ain't that wigged out.

CHARLES: Then the raggedy mothah says, "How now, you dog! A blind nigger stand up thus?! By God, I'll smite thee!"

CHARLES AND DONNY *(After a shocked pause)*: Now I know the dude is crazy.

DONNY: You must be out of your fuckin' mind. *(He moves toward imaginary man and Charles attempts to pull him back)* Screw you and the God you rode in on, mothahfuckah! This "blind nigger" is more than you bargained for.

CHARLES: I haven't seen Donny this pissed in years. He's twitchin' bad as the white boy.

DONNY: You want some of me, punk? Come get some. *(Donny invites him forward with one hand and tosses his cane to the ground with the other)*

CHARLES *(To imaginary man)*: Look, man, go on about your business. *(Picks up cane and gives it to Donny)* Squash it, Donny. Take your cane and let's go.

DONNY: Nah, man. This punk needs to be taught a lesson. *(Throws the cane down to the opposite side)* Come on, patty boy. Come get some of this blind niggah. Let's get it on!

CHARLES: Next thing I know, the freak is growlin' and rushin' Donny like a linebacker. *(Shouts)* Look out! *(Shoves Donny upstage)* I have to tackle the mothah to stop him.

(Charles goes down on his knees and mimes the struggle he describes upstage; Donny looks around in a panic.)

We get to squabblin' right there on the spot. The dude smells like who did it and why. He's tryin' to bite me; tryin' to scratch my eyes out.

DONNY *(Recovered)*: Let the mothahfuckah go! Turn him loose. I got somethin' for his ass. *(Reaches around his back and brings out pistol)*

CHARLES *(Still struggling)*: He's got that crazy-man strength too. I'm thinkin', Holy shit! What have I gotten myself . . .

(Donny fires the gun in the air. The report is thunderous. Charles instinctively drops to all fours, taking cover, then whirls around to look on the gun in frozen horror. Donny points gun in Charles's direction with trembling two-handed grip.)

DONNY: Now what you got to say, mothahfuckah? Who's smitin' who?

CHARLES: The freak was outta there in a flash.

(Charles watches the imaginary man run off as Donny tracks the man's receding footsteps with the pistol.)

DONNY: Yeah, buster, you better run. *(Lets out a triumphant howl)* Wooooooo!

(Donny hears Charles get to his feet, realizes he's not sure who ran away, and quickly turns the gun on Charles.)

CHARLES: No, Donny! Don't shoot! *(Shields himself)* It's me. Don't shoot.

(Donny recoils, shocked. The two men freeze, their horror palpable.
    Light goes out save for a single spot on Donny. Charles exits. There is a weighty pause, then Donny lowers the pistol and laughs long and hard.)

DONNY: It was too cool the way that freak jetted out of there. Dude coulda outrun Ben Johnson on steroids. I don't know what Charles got all bent out of shape about. *(He feels around on the ground with his feet, searching for his cane as he speaks)* He oughta know I got more sense than to shoot when he's mixin' it up with somebody. That would be stone crazy. 'Bout as crazy as that patty musta been—frontin' off a couple of brothahs with that "nigger" shit. *(Picks up cane)* Musta been mad-dog crazy. *(Moves toward downstage center)* Lucky for him Charles was there, or I'd have put some lead in his ass right off. Nothin' to do but shoot a mad dog. *(Puts pistol in front waistband)*
    You know what really pissed me off about the dude, though, was he acted like I wasn't even there at first—like I was a big zero. I get that kind of shit all the time; can't stand it. It's like they be sayin' a blind man, no matter how big or buffed he is, don't count for shit when it comes to throwin' down. *(He sneers)* It's like you ain't a man in that way anymore.

(Light shifts as sounds of morning birds rise.
    Donny listens to the birds a moment, his mood lightening.)

It's like what went down the day I decided to cop this piece. I was catchin' the bus to work. Since I have a ways to go, I gotta head out early. There are usually just a couple of people at the stop. *(Stands as if waiting for bus)* On this particular morning, a group of young dudes are waiting, too.

They're shootin' the shit—talkin' the same trash we used to talk when we were that age—early high school. *(With exaggerated cool)* All about gettin' laid *(Clutches his crotch)* and gettin' high. *(Mimes hitting a joint, coughs, then laughs)* And every other word a cuss word.

(Sounds of city traffic begin to rise.)

I figure there's five of them—two brothahs, three Chicanos. I think, There's some progress, anyway.

So, after a while they start trippin' on me—wonderin' out loud if I'm really blind or *(Immitates teen)* "fuckin' fakin' to ride the fuckin' bus for free." *(Imitates second teen)* "Yeah, dog, the mothahfuckah don't look blind to me." I overhear this kind of shit all the time, so I ignore it. Then one of them decides to test me.

(Traffic noise rises with increasing tension of Donny's tale.)

He walks up and asks, "Hey man, you really blind?"

And I say, *(Bored)* "Yeah man, I'm really blind."

"Then how come you don't look blind?"

I can tell he's wavin' his fingers in my face *(Waves fingers in front of his face)* and I say, "What am I supposed to look like? This?" *(Throws his head back, grins and rocks, then stops abruptly)* "Is that blind enough for you?"

"You tryna be fuckin' funny or somethin'?"

"No. Just get the fuck out my face!"

He says, "Fuck you!" And spits in my face! *(Recoils, wiping at face and clothes)* It's tobacco juice or snuff or some shit. I'm drippin' with it. *(Shaking with anger)* I go after the mothahfuckah, but he jumps back. I try to hit him with my cane. *(Lashes out with cane)* But he stays out of reach, laughin'! His fuckin' friends are laughin', too. *(Swings after friends)*

You gon' remember this one day when you get yours, mothahfuckah! You bad, now. Spit on a blind man and run. Real bad. Let me get my hands on you; I'll show you bad. *(Stops swinging)* Just fight me like a mothahfuckin' man!

(Traffic noise ceases. Donny's words hang in the silence.)

(Struggling to compose himself) I woulda given my life on the spot to be able to run that mothahfuckah down like back in the old days; show him what kind of damage an "All City" linebacker can do. *(Places his hand on butt of pistol and regains composure)* Best believe I'll catch his ass next time. *(Smiles, slow and malicious)* Then we'll see who's really bad.

(Blackout.
    Lights come up on Charles.)

CHARLES: Donny's lost it for real. A blind man with a gun. *(Shakes his head)* It's bad enough when somebody who can see packs a piece on the street. Self-defense or not, sighted or not, the shit's crazy! Folks start bustin' caps, no tellin' who gets hit. It's like sayin', "Fuck everybody else, I got mine covered." You got to go for yourself. Fuck the little kids watchin' TV in the front room across the street. Screw the family eatin' dinner down the block. And to hell with that old couple struggling to get their groceries out of that cab.

    It ain't cool, not cool at all. The way I see it, it's better to lose hand-to-hand or blade-to-blade rather than endanger all those people. Give up the cash, the ass, whatever. If dyin's what I gotta do, fuck it. You gotta go sometime.

    I told Donny that. Put it in terms I thought he'd understand. "Defendin' yourself with that thing ain't no different than one of these gangbangers pullin' a drive-by, man!" *(Guilt shades his tone)* But he had nerve enough to get pissed at me. Said I was takin' a cheap shot, since that's what happened to him.

    See, back in high school, some gangbangers from a rival school rolled up and opened fire on the football practice field. *(Voice cracks)* Donny's helmet was full of blood. He's lucky his sight was all he lost. And he didn't have nothin' to do with gangs. Nothin' at all. *(Pauses)* Now he says he can't see how this amounts to the same thing. *(With resignation)* Blind in more ways than one.

    I told him, "Fuck the world then, Donny. Just stay the hell away from me. I'm not gon' be one of your accidents. I hope you aren't either." *(Turns and exits)*

(Lights come up on pawnshop counter.)

BROWN: I gotta tell you, looks are deceivin' things. You wouldn't believe the guy that cleared for a gun license today. Wild-lookin' young guy. A white kid, but he's got his hair all matted up in that African style. His clothes are filthy and he stinks to high heaven. You wouldn't think he's got the price of a cup of coffee, to look at him, but he does. Sure as I'm standin' here, he lays seven brand-new hundred dollar bills on the counter. Wants the best gun I got: .44-Magnum, Desert Eagle. I gotta take this one through the rigmarole, though—lookin' the way he's lookin'. Besides, the guy mutters this old-sounding English to himself when my back is turned. Stuff like, *(Shakespearean voice)* "To face the dark night, take up a cudgel of like kind." *(Whistles and waggles hand)* I think, Maybe he's a mental case. But I ain't worried. I keep a loaded Magnum underneath the counter at all times. *(Nonchalantly reveals revolver)*

But that was a week ago. The paperwork cleared this morning and he picked up the weapon this afternoon. *(Slightly defensive)* No law sayin' he can't own a gun if he don't take a bath. I guess he's got the right to stink if he wants. And the right to protect himself. Who am I to judge? Hunh?

(Lights out on counter.
Lights up on Donny, confidently tapping his way to downstage center.)

DONNY: Yeah, the next punk that steps to this blind man better be able to outrun a bullet, and do it without touchin' the ground. 'Cause if I hear him, I can hit him. *(Chuckles softly, savoring the idea. Handles his cane as if tracking a moving target through the audience with a rifle)* Yeah, if I hear him, I can hit him. If I hear him, *(Sights down the cane)* I can hit him. *(Freezes)*

(Sound of thunderous shotgun blast.
Donny recoils as if he fired the shot, then freezes.
Blackout.)

END OF PLAY

LYNN MANNING is an award-winning playwright, poet, actor, former world champion judo competitor and paralympic silver medalist. He accomplished all of this after being shot and blinded at the age of twenty-three. Mr. Manning's autobiographical one-man play *Weights* won three NAACP Theater Awards in 2001, including Best Actor for Manning. His other critically acclaimed plays include *The Last Outpost, Private Battle, The Convert, Object Lesson, Colorized Version* and *Before the Drive to Oakwood Station*. Mr. Manning wrote and stars in the independent short film *Shoot!*, inspired by his one-act play of the same name. The film premiered at the 2001 Sundance Film Festival and debuted on HBO/Cinemax later that year. He has several plays and screenplays in the works. He is cofounder of the not-for-profit Watts Village Theater Company in Los Angeles.

P.H.*REAKS:

THE HIDDEN HISTORY OF
PEOPLE WITH DISABILITIES

*A collaborative project developed and adapted by
Doris Baizley and Victoria Ann Lewis from the
writing of Isaac Agnew, Doris Baizley, Victoria
Ann Lewis, Mary Martz, Ben Mattlin, Peggy
Oliveri, Steve Pailet, Vincent Pinto, John Pixley,
Paul Ryan, Leslye Sneider, Bill Trzeciak and
Tamara Turner*

From left to right: the Angel Golf Caddie (Shari Weiser), Beth (Tamara Turner) and Mother Nature (Lisa Dinkins) in an Other Voices' History Project production at Mark Taper Forum's New Work Festival, Los Angeles, California, 1994. Photo by Jay Thompson.

In memory of two fierce comic spirits—
Vincent Pinto (1951–2006) and
Paul Ryan (1955–1998)

Author's Statement

By Vincent Pinto, a collaborative writer, *P.H.*reaks*

Before this workshop (through Other Voices' History Project) you couldn't get me in a room of disabled people. My first inclination was to blow it off as yet another pathetic attempt to "help the handicapped deal with their issues" by some grant-grabbing academic who was at best a do-gooder. I cringed as I imagined myself in a room full of other people with disabilities, sitting in a circle baring our hearts and scars to each other, while the able-bodied handlers took notes. And then they'd put us in matching windbreakers or something while we "put on a show" somewhere. But fate (or more probably circumstance) stepped in and I joined the Tuesday night sessions. I had just moved in with the love of my life and she thought it was way cool that I got picked for the writing workshop and pointed out that Tuesday was a lousy night for TV. I preferred to think of it as yet another way to impress myself into her pants.

So I signed up for the workshop, and well that I did. The Other Voices' History Project turned out to be a catalyst, changing this person from being someone who always wanted to write into someone who actually writes. The nurturing effect of collectively writing *P.H.*reaks* showed me a process which took my inner dialogue out into the real world. Finally, the best thing about Other Voices were the other voices. I became fast friends with several of those in the group, particularly Paul Ryan. He was a funny guy even when he wasn't trying to be, with a dry wit that left you parched. He had a way of stinging you with his irony even as he made you laugh. Ultimately I believe I got more from the workshops than I gave.

We never did get those matching windbreakers . . .

Production History

*P.H.*reaks: The Hidden History of People with Disabilities* was presented through the Other Voices' History Project as part of Mark Taper Forum's New Work Festival (Center Theatre Group, Los Angeles) in 1994. The production was directed by Victoria Ann Lewis, with set and costumes designed by Lynn Jeffries. The cast was as follows:

WOMAN IN WHEELCHAIR	Tamara Turner
YOUNG MAN IN WHEELCHAIR	John Pixley
WOMAN OF SMALL STATURE	Shari Weiser
MAN IN WHEELCHAIR	Richard Redlin
OLDER MAN	Bill Trzeciak
YOUNGER MAN	Barry Schwartz
YOUNG WOMAN	Lisa Dinkins

Characters

The following roles must be played by actors with disabilities and should be double-cast as follows:

WOMAN IN WHEELCHAIR (Sister Elizabeth, Elizabeth the Half-Lady, Telethon Guest and Beth).

YOUNG MAN IN WHEELCHAIR, WITH SPEECH IMPAIRMENT (A Wild Man, Zoltan the Wild Man and Joey).

WOMAN OF SMALL STATURE (Eugenia, Little Princess Angie and Angel Golf Caddie).

MAN IN WHEELCHAIR (Andreos the Legless Wonder, Telethon Star and Vendor).

The remaining characters need not be played by actors with disabilities, but should be double-cast as follows:

OLDER MAN (Father John, Freak Show Barker, God, Male Doctor, Matisse and Priest).

YOUNGER MAN (Joshua, Telethon Director, Louis-Michel, Old Bodyguard and Male Sports Reporter).

YOUNG WOMAN (Mother Nature, Female Doctor, New Bodyguard, Unemployment Clerk, Traffic Cop and Female Sports Reporter).

The company plays various other Voices, Attendants, Demonstrators, Hecklers and others.

Note on Casting

In the initial productions of *P.H. *reaks*, Woman in Wheelchair was a quadriplegic, Man in Wheelchair was a paraplegic and Young Man in Wheelchair had cerebral palsy with a speech impairment. In addition, Man in Wheelchair used a variety of mobility aids: a sports wheelchair, crutches and a cart on wheels for Andreos. While innovative casting is encouraged, the script will resist too much variation from these descriptions.

Setting

The action of *P.H. *reaks* moves back and forth across time and place, between documentary materials and fantasy. Slide projections are useful but not necessary; the characters in the ensemble create the time and place.

Authors' Note

"P.H." stands for "physically handicapped," the civil service classification used in 1937 to exclude people with disabilities from federal work programs.

Part One: Magic

SLIDE: A STAINED-GLASS WINDOW

We are in a side chapel of a medieval cathedral. An altar or shrine. Sister Elizabeth sits in some facsimile of a medieval wheelchair, or perhaps strapped to a reclining board, which is propped up. Crude wooden crutches are attached to her display. Sister Elizabeth should be obviously disabled, with no movement in her legs and very limited arm movement. She is enshrined as if she were the central religious icon of this altar. She is holy-card beautiful in her flowing white robes, and the entire tableau is illuminated by the glow from a bank of votive lights in front of her. Hanging on the bank of lights are luxury items: gold goblets, silver plates, crowns and jewels, offerings left by worshippers. In front of these items is a brass bowl of coins on the floor.

A penitent in rich, medieval clothing enters, bows toward Sister Elizabeth and empties a sack of shimmering gold coins into the brass bowl. He stands a few feet from Sister Elizabeth's altar.

SISTER ELIZABETH: Look at me. Look. Look. I see you. I know you. Your sufferings, your hopes, your fears. I know your longings. Come, come here.

(The penitent approaches slowly, as if hypnotized, and kneels.)

Yes. Don't be afraid. Look at me. Look at my poor withered limbs. You want to touch me, don't you? Come. Come closer and the Light will come to you.

(The penitent reaches up to touch the hand or foot of Sister Elizabeth. The exposed flesh should appear almost lifeless, like one of the wax body parts left as offerings at saints' shrines in Roman Catholic cathedrals. As he touches her, the penitent lets out a cry of relief, somewhere between a nervous giggle and a shout of release.)

Good. Take strength from my weakness. Take comfort from my tears. Give me your pain and rejoice in the Spirit. Now you can light the candle.

(The penitent begins to light one of the votive candles, but is interrupted by the sound of a shouting mob. Barking dogs. The cathedral doors slamming shut. A Wild Man enters, roaring. He wears beggar's rags and a wild wig. The penitent runs out in fear.

Wild Man circles Sister Elizabeth. His attempts at speech seem like meaningless roars.)

What is it? What dogs of hell are trapped in your body?

(Wild Man approaches and attempts to speak, but only succeeds in blowing out some of the votive lights.)

Take care. These are God's candles. These are the hopes and fears of human souls.

(Wild Man, still vocalizing, blows out more candles.)

The devil has your throat. Let me help you. Let the Light come. Let it come . . .

(Wild Man accidentally overturns the bowl of money.)

You want the money? Go ahead. I don't need the money. You need it, take it. It means nothing to me. People leave it because they think it saves them. It protects them. But it's the Light in their faces. That's what's so beautiful. They leave their guilt and fear with me. I burn through their guilt and fear. And the Light comes.

(Wild Man stares at Sister Elizabeth.)

Come, wretch, closer. Come out of the darkness. Look at me. Look at me. You want to touch me, don't you? *(Wild Man looks at her, calm now)* I know you. You want some sweetness. You want someone to touch you . . . You're hungry . . . I know. I feel with your skin. Don't despair. There is hope. Come here.

(He touches her awkwardly.)

Light a candle—one candle and the Light will come to you . . . and you will know comfort and peace . . . Just light the candle. *(Wild Man tries to light a candle)* Light it. Go ahead. That's it. Can you light the candle? Good. Light it. Light the candle . . . *(He struggles with the candle)* LIGHT THE FUCKING CANDLE!

(Wild Man backs away from her.)

Go away. The devil still controls you.

(She rings a bell. Father John enters.)

FATHER JOHN: Yes, Sister Elizabeth Beloved of the Lord.

(Wild Man attempts to vocalize.)

What is this thing? What horrible perversity has brought forth this beast?

SISTER ELIZABETH: Who sinned, this man or his parents, that he is so cruelly formed? . . .

FATHER JOHN: This has not happened to him because he has sinned, or his parents . . .

SISTER ELIZABETH: But that in him God's work should be displayed.

(Wild Man moves toward her.)

FATHER JOHN: Back to the streets, you monster. Filthy thing. You dirty this place. Back to the streets. You won't last long.

SISTER ELIZABETH *(To Wild Man)*: You must understand. I need someone to light the candles.

(Wild Man exits. Another penitent comes in.)

Yes. Don't be afraid. Look at me. I can see you. I know you. I know your hopes and fears. You want to touch me, don't you? Come. Light a candle. Come closer and the Light will come to you . . .

FATHER JOHN: Beware, careless souls: I saw with mine own eyes the marks of their tongs upon his mangled tongue. The devil's slaves had silenced the beast so he would not reveal their master's secrets. These are the same devils that roar in the deaf man's ears so he cannot hear the words of Light. These are the same darknesses that curl inside the hunchback's burden. Have you not smelled the sulfur as these monsters pass?

SLIDE: OLD WOODCUTS OF ANCIENT GODS; ACTS OF BESTIALITY

Beware: the devil grew bold in the old days. He came as a swan or a bull. He called himself Zeus or Pan and he made men hungry for the dark. "Roman women often bare their buttocks to donkeys, inducing the beasts to mount them," Juvenal the Pagan Historian tells us.

SLIDE: SATYRS; FAUNS; DEVILS

Beware, careless souls: satyrs, fauns, the devil still comes to tempt. Some weak souls fall. Pretending to sleep, they invite Lucifer himself into their beds and find him beautiful. But when the woman sees the repulsive issue of that union, when the monster claws out between her legs, she is grateful for the kindness that ties her filthy body to the stake and burns it clean.

SLIDE: GIANTS; DWARVES; GNOMES; MERMAIDS; HUNCHBACKS; DANNY DEVITO AS THE PENGUIN IN *BATMAN RETURNS*

Wise men of old times have condemned these offspring of the devil. "Deformed and infirm children should be hidden away in a secret place," Plato tells us. Aristotle advises they should not be fed.

SLIDE: THE PENGUIN BEING THROWN TO HIS DEATH

Some monsters remain to warn us: if the soul is fouled, the body cannot escape. The monsters warn us. "There is no injustice in the universe," Eileen Gardner, assistant in the Department of

Education under Ronald Reagan, tells us. "The handicapped assume the lottery of life has penalized them at random. This is not so. Nothing comes to an individual that he has not summoned."

SLIDE: BEGGARS ON THE STREET, 1940s

Beware careless souls: mark the devil's easy entry into the world. This is why our earthly kings protect monsters at their feet.

SLIDE: SEVENTEENTH-CENTURY COURT DWARFS

The great are tempted greatly, and so in their courts keep a grotesque reminder of the fate of those who, opening a door on darkness, carelessly pass through.

SLIDE: PAINTING OF EUGENIA IN COURT DRESS

(We hear the sound of seventeenth-century court music. Eugenia enters in court dress. She performs a slow, formal court dance over the following. Her lines are heard via voice-over.)

Imagine if you will . . . early morning in Madrid, 1686. The sun is beginning to rise. Eugenia Martinez Vallejo—"La Monstrua"—awakens from her tiny wooden bed, couched among the beds of the court attendants in a small dusky room in the castle of the King of Spain.

EUGENIA *(Voice-over)*: I must rise and prepare for my posing. It is better to be in the court than on the streets begging for food scraps. I am not as feeble-minded as they make me out to be.

FATHER JOHN: Today she will pose for the great painter, Carreno. And what a pose it will be!

EUGENIA *(Voice-over)*: Today I become Bacchus, the god of wine, the god of inspiration, the god of fertility.

FATHER JOHN: And well-known god of the drunken orgy. What better model could Carreno find? From the pharaohs of Ancient Egypt, every court had its dwarf—jester and adviser—beauty and beast—infernal and divine.

SLIDE: DWARFS REPRESENTED IN ARTWORK

EUGENIA *(Voice-over)*: I am not Bacchus. I am a woman.

FATHER JOHN: But Carreno will paint her as a young boy. Men and women alike will take her on their laps. The erotic cult of the dwarf flourishes in seventeenth-century Spain—France—Poland. And *what's this?*

SLIDE: LIA GRAF ON J. P. MORGAN'S LAP

Little Lia Graf sitting on J. P. Morgan's lap at the Senate banking hearings in 1933? Did she represent the shrinking dollar? Or was she the good luck token J. P. needed? Lia returned to her homeland in 1935. She was arrested as a Useless Person in 1937, sent to Auschwitz in 1944 and never heard from again. *(A beat)* But let us return to a happier time.

SLIDE: EUGENIA IN COURT DRESS

Smile, poquita. Your portrait will live forever.

EUGENIA *(Voice-over):* For a meal, a bed and free-flowing wine I will be Bacchus for you.

FATHER JOHN: She takes off her robe of heavy brocade and steps out of her wooden sandals. Carreno gives her a crown of grape leaves for her head and a rose for her modesty.

SLIDE: THE NUDE EUGENIA AS BACCHUS, BY CARRENO

EUGENIA *(Voice-over):* Look at me as long as you like. You won't see me smile.

(Lights out on everything but the slide.
Lights up on Father John, who discards his monk's robe and puts on a sweat-stained, wrinkled jacket and an old straw hat to become the Freak Show Barker. He stands next to Eugenia, who is now Angie.)

FREAK SHOW BARKER *(Speaking into a little megaphone):* Oh yeah. Let's give a big hand to Little Princess Angie. Highest paid little lady on the midway. Just a sample of what we got here.

Come and see 'em folks, come on and see. Strangest human beings in the world today. We got 'em all here. And they're all alive. Keep your eyes up here, and we'll bring 'em out to give you a sample. No laughter or rude remarks. Try not to be shocked at what—here they come, here they come now—

(Sister Elizabeth, Andreos and Wild Man enter, wearing faded, turn-of-the-century circus garb. They line up next to Angie.)

Here's Elizabeth—America's Only Living Half-Lady. Can't use her arms, can't use her legs. Why? Only God knows, folks. She was born that way! Next you have Andreos the Legless Acrobat. How does he do it? Come and see. Come and see—and special tonight—we've got Zoltan the Wild Man: Half-Man, Half-Beast.

WILD MAN *(Unintelligibly)*: I'm hungry. Where's lunch?

FREAK SHOW BARKER: Hear those sounds? That's animal language. That's right. Don't be scared. That's animal talk—straight outta the jungle—

WILD MAN: When's lunch???

FREAK SHOW BARKER: BACK, WILD MAN! BACK! You'll get your live chickens later. *(To audience)* Two dollars extra to see him at feeding time. No pregnant women or children under twelve allowed. Come and see 'em. We got 'em all here . . .

(Andreos takes the stage, striking a big, presentational pose and displaying his well-developed upper torso.)

ANDREOS *(Announcing himself theatrically)*: Hey!

FREAK SHOW BARKER: Ladies and gentlemen—before your very eyes—Mighty Andreos! The World's Eighth Wonder and greatest legless acrobat—captured by pirates in the Gulf of Persia, thrown into the shark-infested Caribbean and raised by reptiles in the Everglades. You've read his inspiring True Life Story, now see the Human Wonder Himself!

(Andreos performs an acrobatic trick: he stands on his head with his legs still strapped to a beggar board.)

ANDREOS: Hey!

FREAK SHOW BARKER: Just a sample of what we've got here. Ask questions. Go ahead. Look as long as you want. Ask about anything. Let your mind wander. Don't feel guilty. You paid for the privilege. Wanna peek backstage for a closer look? . . .

(Lights change to backstage. Angie is in a bathrobe, taking off her makeup. Joshua, a freak show spectator, sneaks in, holding a bottle of bourbon.)

JOSHUA: Angie . . . Angie? . . .

ANGIE: Who's there?

JOSHUA: It's me, Joshua. Haven't you seen me around? I've been here every night this week. *(Holds up the bottle)* I thought you might like to have a drink with me.

ANGIE: Looks like you've had a few without me.

JOSHUA: Yeah, I guess I have. I've been waiting a while. It's good stuff, my grandpa made it. Here, try some.

(Moving toward her, he trips and falls. Holds the bottle up.)

Didn't spill a drop. Maybe you could use me in the show.

ANGIE: We're all pros here. You're out of your league.

JOSHUA: I'm a professional, too.

ANGIE: Yeah, what do you do?

JOSHUA: I'm a doctor.

ANGIE: I haven't met many doctors who operate out of a bottle. Where's your little black bag?

JOSHUA: I left it in my office. This wasn't an official visit.

ANGIE: So, you've been coming around every day since we opened. Why?

JOSHUA: Curious, just like everyone else I guess.

ANGIE: Curious people come once and then talk about us for a month at dinner. You've got other reasons. Talk.

JOSHUA: Sure, I've got more than a passing interest. I'm interested for medical reasons—what can be done to help prevent or cure these sorts of things.

ANGIE: You gonna put me on a rack and stretch me?

JOSHUA: Sure, after I soak you in alcohol to loosen you up.

ANGIE *(Taking the bottle)*: So that's what this is for?

JOSHUA: Just to loosen your tongue, for now.

ANGIE: What do you want to know?

JOSHUA: Why you put yourself on display, allow yourself to be exploited like this.

ANGIE: I don't believe it, another bleeding-heart idiot. I was just starting to like you too. Maybe you should go.

JOSHUA: I'm sorry if I offended you. Maybe I'm just a stupid hick from a small town, but I really don't understand.

ANGIE: Listen, smart boy, it's easy—we're always on display. You think that if I walked down the street of your stinking little nowhere town, people wouldn't stare at me? Damn right they would, and tell their neighbors and friends and talk about me over dinners and picnics and PTA meetings. Well, if they want to do that, they're going to have to pay me for that privilege. You want to stare at me, fine, it's twenty-five cents, cash on the barrel. You want a picture, that's another quarter. My life story? Pay me. You think I'm being exploited? You pay to go to a baseball game, don't you? What's the difference if you watch some big oaf hitting a ball with a stick or me pretending to be a princess?

JOSHUA: You mean you're not?

(She looks at him to see if he's serious. They both burst out laughing. He leans over and kisses her.)

ANGIE: You always get fresh with your medical specimens?
JOSHUA: You're not just any specimen.

(He leans over to kiss her again. She ducks away.)

ANGIE: You know, you're a pretty interesting specimen, too. Mind if I examine you?
JOSHUA: Go right ahead.
ANGIE: Stand up. Close your eyes.

(He complies, and she kicks him in the shin.)

JOSHUA: Ow!
ANGIE: Just checking your reflexes. Now close your eyes again. Don't worry, I'm not going to kick you. *(Takes a pin out of her hair and starts poking him in the legs and buttocks)* Can you feel this? How about this? Stand still, this is important. Does this feel sharp?
JOSHUA: Yes, yes, ow, that's enough!
ANGIE: Not so much fun being on the receiving end, is it?
JOSHUA: No, I guess not.
ANGIE: Come over here, I'm not finished yet.
JOSHUA: I think I am.
ANGIE: Oh, don't be such a baby. I won't hurt you anymore, I promise. Come over and sit down. Please. *(Rubs his shoulders and neck)* Just relax, there, isn't that better?
JOSHUA: Yes, much better.
ANGIE: You're a fascinating case, I want to examine you further . . . Don't worry, no more tricks. Here, have some medicine.

(She tips the bottle to his mouth. She slowly unbuttons his shirt. He tries to reach for her, but she pushes his hands down.)

Uh-uh. I'm the doctor. I'll do the examining. I think you need more anesthesia.

(She tips the bottle to his mouth. She puts her arms around him from behind and starts rubbing his chest.)

Oh yes . . . This is more serious than I thought . . .

(She has him mesmerized. She reaches down and slips his wallet out of his pocket.)

Yes, I'm afraid it's hopeless.

(She gives him a long kiss, then runs off. He lies there for a second, then sits up. He sees that she's gone, then he exits.)

SLIDE: "TELETHON REHEARSAL"

(Woman in Wheelchair enters as Telethon Guest, wearing a contemporary jacket, with a Telethon Director, wearing a headset.)

TELETHON DIRECTOR: He's gonna love this. A few little touches and you're done. *(Puts a bow in her hair)*

(Man in Wheelchair enters as the Telethon Star.)

(To Telethon Star) Okay, it'll begin something like this: music starts, then lights come up on the girl—
TELETHON STAR: On *me* and the girl.
TELETHON DIRECTOR: Exactly. Then you say— *(Telethon Guest starts to speak)* Not you. He says . . . *(Reading from script)* "Look at this, folks. *Can* you look at this? . . ." *(Points to Telethon Guest)* "Imagine what their daughter's disease has done to a wonderful, happy family. Please. Don't let this happen to any more children—"
TELETHON STAR: Where's the family?
TELETHON DIRECTOR: What?
TELETHON STAR: HER FAMILY! Mother. Father. You know. A nice-looking, normal mom and dad standing there crying, "How

could this happen to people like us?" She can't just sit there looking like she got here on her own.

(Telethon Guest starts to speak again, but—)

TELETHON DIRECTOR: She did. She flew out here yesterday—
TELETHON STAR: She doesn't even look like a kid.
TELETHON DIRECTOR: Well . . . she's not actually—
TELETHON STAR: I WANT A FAMILY! GET A FAMILY HERE NOW!
TELETHON DIRECTOR: They're in Cincinnati. That could get expensive. We've got a budget.
TELETHON STAR: A family, or you're fired!

(Telethon Star exits.)

MOTHER NATURE *(Offstage)*: Excuse me. Playing through.

(A golf ball rolls onto the stage. Mother Nature enters with Woman of Small Stature as her Angel Caddie, carrying a golf bag.)

Don't mind me, children. Carry on. Mother Nature's got a wicked lie here.
TELETHON DIRECTOR: *Mother* Nature? Did you say "Mother"? This is perfect! You're just who we're looking for, we need a mother—
MOTHER NATURE: Of course. Who doesn't?
TELETHON DIRECTOR: There won't be any salary, you understand, but it is for a wonderful cause—heartbreaking, really, when you look at something like this . . . *(Indicating Telethon Guest)*
MOTHER NATURE: Yes, Las Vegas, jeez . . . What was I thinking when I made it like this? It's one big sand trap. *(To Angel Caddie)* Hand me the seven iron.
TELETHON DIRECTOR: I don't think you understand the tragedy that's going on here.
MOTHER NATURE: What tragedy? What's wrong with you?
TELETHON DIRECTOR: Nothing's wrong with *me*— *(Pointing to Telethon Guest)*
MOTHER NATURE: What's happened to her?
TELETHON DIRECTOR: Can't you tell?
MOTHER NATURE: Lovely girl. Give her a kiss.

(Telethon Director gives Telethon Guest a peck on the cheek.)

TELETHON DIRECTOR: Don't you get it? We're trying to give her *life*!

MOTHER NATURE: She has life. Give her another kiss.

(Another peck.)

TELETHON DIRECTOR: We are trying to save her from her fate. She doesn't deserve to be punished like this.

MOTHER NATURE: Have you been punishing her more than she deserves?

TELETHON DIRECTOR: Not me, *you*. You're Mother Nature. Why did you make her like this?

MOTHER NATURE: I make them all kinds of ways. *(Pointing to audience)* One's this way, another one's that way. And you're— *(Looking at him)* —the way you are. Everybody's different.

TELETHON DIRECTOR: But she'll never fit in like normal kids.

MOTHER NATURE: Fit into what? And what do you mean by normal?

TELETHON DIRECTOR: Oh come on. You think she'd choose to be that way?

MOTHER NATURE: Nobody has that choice.

TELETHON DIRECTOR: She'll go through life scorned by others.

MOTHER NATURE: Whose fault is that? Not mine. No one is outside of Nature. I have a really wide vocabulary, you know. I love variety in people like I love the variety of colors in flowers and shapes in species. Don't insult my creativity by limiting your acceptance of Human Form. *(To Telethon Guest)* I bet they've been listening to the Old Boy, haven't they? That's where they get all this crap about people not meeting minimum requirements. That egomaniacal son of a bitch thinks everyone's supposed to be made in His image. Well, I'll show you "image"!

(She raises her arms to reveal four more arms: a Hindu goddess.)

GOD *(Offstage)*: Are you going to hit the ball or what?

MOTHER NATURE: Oh boy, here we go! *(Drops the pose)*

TELETHON DIRECTOR: Look here. This is enough. I'm going to have to call security, here.

(God enters. He has a beard, wears a gold crown and carries a golf bag. The Telethon Director stands back in awe, falls to his knees.)

Oh—my God!!!

GOD: Thanks, my boy. And keep up the good work. I love what you're doing here. Nice suit, by the way. *(Picks lint off Telethon Director's jacket)* Oh. *(Looking at Telethon Guest)* Poor thing . . . *(Turns to Mother Nature)* Nasty lie, Mother N. I'd use a wedge.

MOTHER NATURE *(To Telethon Director)*: Give me the six iron. *(Makes a lousy shot)*

GOD: Should have used the wedge.

MOTHER NATURE: I wanted it to go there. I love to explore the rough.

GOD: It's out of bounds.

MOTHER NATURE: There is no out of bounds.

GOD: Typical female. Always insisting they know better.

MOTHER NATURE *(Raising her club)*: Why you imperious, left-brained, power-hungry son of a—

GOD *(Taking the club away)*: Come on now, Mother. We haven't got all day.

MOTHER NATURE: Yes, we have, dear boy. We most certainly have . . .

(Mother Nature and Angel Caddie exit.)

GOD *(To Telethon Director)*: Good work, son. Great work you're doing here. You're a real saint. *(He starts out)* Oh—bring my bag, would you . . . *(Exits)*

TELETHON DIRECTOR: A saint. He said I'm a saint . . .

GOD *(Offstage)*: Did you hear me, son? Are you DEAF?

TELETHON DIRECTOR: Yes sir! I mean—no, sir. *(A beat, in awe)* I'm a saint. *(Falls to his knees, kisses the hand of Telethon Guest)* Thank you. Thank you. Thank you. *(Picks up God's golf bag and starts out)* I'm a saint! *(Exits)*

TELETHON GUEST: Hey—what about me?

(Female Doctor enters and puts hospital gown on Woman in Wheelchair.)

FEMALE DOCTOR: You'll be in examination room 115.

(Wild Man enters with newspaper.)

WILD MAN: ANGIE! Angie? Did you read this?

ANGIE *(Entering)*: Did I read what?

SLIDE: "SAD NEWS FOR CIRCUS FREAKS—NO MORE HUMAN WONDERS FOR THE BIG SHOW THIS YEAR"

FEMALE DOCTOR *(To Woman in Wheelchair)*: The nurse will help you
   take off all your clothes—and leave the gown open in front.
ANGIE: Oh my God—Andreos!

(Blackout.)

Part Two: Medical

Hospital sounds. Woman in Wheelchair moves to center spotlight. All freaks now stand on the side of the stage, reading newspapers.

FEMALE DOCTOR: Lie on the table, please.

ANDREOS: "The Hall of Human Curiosities has been canceled from the Ringling Brothers circuit indefinitely."

FEMALE DOCTOR: I'm just going to measure you now.

ANDREOS: "The cruel exhibition of these poor unfortunates is distasteful to an increasingly refined and educated public."

FEMALE DOCTOR: Okay. Good. Now turn over.

ANDREOS: "Most of these individuals, whose sole means of livelihood is the exhibition of their physical infirmities to a gaping crowd, are pathological rarities: the Giant presents a severe case of acromegaly. The Half Woman—Quadriplegia. The Princess Angie—acromesomilia. The Wild Man—cerebral palsy."

WILD MAN *(Snarling)*: Fuck 'em.

FEMALE DOCTOR: Try not to move, please! Let's get rid of this gown.

ANDREOS: Bastards!

FEMALE DOCTOR: Okay. That's better. Hmmm.

ANDREOS: They didn't even mention me.

FEMALE DOCTOR: Good. Now. I'm just going to ask a few of my colleagues to observe here.

(Male Doctor enters wearing a stethoscope, with an examining light on his forehead.)

Okay, this is what I told you about. Interesting, isn't it? It's three quarters of an inch.

MALE DOCTOR: I'd say half an inch.

FEMALE DOCTOR: Measure, you'll see.

MALE DOCTOR: You're right. Just like that case in Detroit.

FEMALE DOCTOR: Yes, but here it's more severe.

MALE DOCTOR: But the muscle tone is better.

FEMALE DOCTOR: Okay, turn over. Now, you see?

MALE DOCTOR: Yes, it's clearer from the front. What is this, a tenodesis?

FEMALE DOCTOR: Yes, two years ago.

MALE DOCTOR: Not bad. Graft?

FEMALE DOCTOR: No, repair.

MALE DOCTOR: And now?

FEMALE DOCTOR: I think a laminectomy.

MALE DOCTOR: Fenestration?

FEMALE DOCTOR: No, decompression. Okay, turn again, please. Good.

MALE DOCTOR: Interesting.

FEMALE DOCTOR: You can see it better here.

MALE DOCTOR: Like the case in Detroit.

FEMALE DOCTOR: More severe.

MALE DOCTOR: But the muscle tone is better.

BOTH DOCTORS: Good.

MALE DOCTOR: Thank you.

FEMALE DOCTOR: That will be all.

(Doctors exit.)

ANDREOS: "Curiosities they may be. What they are more certainly is sick."

(The Male Doctor comes back to the Woman in Wheelchair.)

MALE DOCTOR: You may get dressed now.

(The Woman in Wheelchair exits as we see:)

SLIDE: "1911—CITY OF CHICAGO ORDINANCE PROHIBITS ANY PERSON WHO IS DISEASED, MAIMED, MUTILATED OR DEFORMED

IN ANY WAY, SO AS TO BE AN UNSIGHTLY OR DISGUSTING OBJECT, FROM EXPOSING HIMSELF TO PUBLIC VIEW."

(Andreos exits.)

SLIDE: "1919—WISCONSIN SCHOOL BOARD EXPELS AN ELEVEN-YEAR-OLD BOY WITH CEREBRAL PALSY BECAUSE HIS TEACHERS AND OTHER STUDENTS FIND HIM DEPRESSING AND NAUSEATING. THE WISCONSIN SUPREME COURT UPHOLDS THE EXPULSION."

(Wild Man exits.)

SLIDE: "1927—THE U.S. SUPREME COURT UPHOLDS STATE STERILIZATION LAWS 'TO PREVENT THOSE WHO ARE MANIFESTLY UNFIT FROM CONTINUING THEIR KIND.'"

(Angie exits.)

SLIDE: FDR AT THE WHEEL OF HIS CAR; FDR AT THE TILLER OF HIS SAILBOAT; FDR STANDING AT A PODIUM, WAVING TO THE CROWD

FDR *(Voice-over)*: . . . I speak, therefore, tonight, to and of the American people as a whole. My most immediate concern is in carrying out the purposes of the great work program just enacted by the Congress. Its first objective is to put men and women now on the relief rolls to work . . .

(The White House. A life-sized dummy sits in a wheelchair. New Bodyguard does jumping jacks, as Old Bodyguard takes notes on a clipboard.)

NEW BODYGUARD: Seventy-three, -four, -five—
OLD BODYGUARD: Your dad got hurt in a crash or something, right?
NEW BODYGUARD *(As he jumps)*: Yes sir. He got crippled in a combine accident. Seventy-eight, -nine, eighty. *(Stops jumping)* There.
OLD BODYGUARD: Give me ten more.

(New Bodyguard starts more jumping jacks.)

Used a wheelchair?
NEW BODYGUARD: Huh?

OLD BODYGUARD: Your father.

NEW BODYGUARD: Yeah.

OLD BODYGUARD: You helped him get up and around and all?

NEW BODYGUARD: Yes sir. *(Stops jumping)* Okay, what now?

OLD BODYGUARD *(Checking the clipboard)*: Says here you're left-handed.

NEW BODYGUARD: That's right. What gives? Why all this?

OLD BODYGUARD: Security. You're replacing the president's right-hand man. We lost our right-hand man in the incident. We need a strong left-hander.

NEW BODYGUARD: Right. So when do we go to the firing range?

OLD BODYGUARD: After the wheelchair.

NEW BODYGUARD: The wheelchair???

OLD BODYGUARD *(Checking clipboard)*: Okay, you got clearance. Guess it's okay to tell you. *(Lowering his voice)* There's a lot more to being FDR's bodyguard than providing security.

NEW BODYGUARD: Okay . . .

OLD BODYGUARD: You know the president got polio.

NEW BODYGUARD: Right. So?

OLD BODYGUARD: I mean—he *really got polio.*

NEW BODYGUARD: So what? He never lets it get him down.

OLD BODYGUARD: Well, it got him down more than anyone knows. Crippled him up considerably.

NEW BODYGUARD: You're sayin' the president's *a cripple?*

OLD BODYGUARD: I'm not sayin' he *is* a cripple, it just affected his body.

NEW BODYGUARD: Whatta you mean? Either he is or ain't a cripple—

OLD BODYGUARD: Okay, it's this way: what do you think when you see someone with polio?

NEW BODYGUARD: I dunno.

OLD BODYGUARD: Well, you never admired 'em, did you?

NEW BODYGUARD: No—I feel sorry for them.

OLD BODYGUARD: Now how about the president? Feel sorry for him, do you?

NEW BODYGUARD: No sir.

OLD BODYGUARD: Right. Probably admire him, too. Probably wouldn't mind being more like him, either.

NEW BODYGUARD: I never thought of him as a cripple.

OLD BODYGUARD: Now you got it! We go to a lot of trouble to see that no one does. Now we do the stand-and-walk. *(He goes to the wheelchair)* You take the right side, I take the left. Get him up and out of the chair.

(New Bodyguard starts to lift the dummy.)

NOT LIKE THAT! You look like you're lifting.

NEW BODYGUARD: You said get him up—

OLD BODYGUARD: But you can't look like it. *(Demonstrates)* You're just a guy talking to him, see? You bend down. Look like you're whispering something in his ear. You take his right elbow. Weight on your left arm. Slowly rise. He'll be with you.

(They stand the dummy.)

Don't lift—just support. He's got great upper-body strength. That's it. Stay in close for the walk.

(They walk the dummy.)

Keep the conversation going. Blah blah blah—up to the podium. Blah blah blah—away from the podium.

NEW BODYGUARD: I don't believe it. I'da sworn I seen him walk in the newsreels.

OLD BODYGUARD: All part of our job. Around here we perform magic. He's only as helpless as people think he is.

NEW BODYGUARD: Press much of a problem?

OLD BODYGUARD: Nah. Occasional new guy. Rule is: no pictures of him in the chair or below the waist. And never of him being helped. By anyone. Be nice, but firm.

NEW BODYGUARD: And if they persist?

OLD BODYGUARD: I make sure they don't. *(Lowers the dummy into wheelchair)*

NEW BODYGUARD: So, are you gonna tell me?

OLD BODYGUARD: About what?

NEW BODYGUARD: The "incident." Was it really an assassination attempt?

OLD BODYGUARD: So, they're buying it, huh? That's good.

NEW BODYGUARD: What really happened? How come I'm replacing the other guy.

OLD BODYGUARD: It was a fund-raising dinner at the Mayflower. Joe and I were walking him out the side door when we run into the DuPonts. The president tells us to leave him on his crutches while he talks. Then outta nowhere comes this bellhop walking six or seven dogs on their nightly constitutional. There we are—

dogs milling everywhere. I'm thinking any minute one of these mutts is gonna cut a crutch out from under him. They finally move on. He's finished talking and we head for the car. Then we spot it—a steaming pile of dog shit near his left crutch tip. He don't see it—plants his crutch and turns. He slips—but before he can fall, Joe lunges under him yelling, "HEY—OUT THERE! HE'S GOT A GUN!" As everybody looks out, Joe falls onto the dog pile, passes me the crutch and I prop him back up. Joe threw his back out. Not to mention the mess with the suit. He won't be back on the job for a while.

NEW BODYGUARD: What a yarn. Wait'll Sally hears about this—

OLD BODYGUARD: Hey. That's classified.

FDR *(Voice-over):* . . . Never since my inauguration in March 1933 . . .

OLD BODYGUARD: Okay. He's almost finished. We'll walk him out after the radio crew leaves. Oh yeah. Keep this with you at all times. *(Hands New Bodyguard a small can and brush)* Black paint for his braces and crutches. Can't have them drawing attention in the photographs. Come on. It's time for you to meet the President of the United States.

(They exit as FDR's speech comes to an end.)

FDR *(Voice-over):* . . . We have survived all of the arduous burdens and the threatening dangers of a great economic calamity. We have, in the darkest moments of our national trials, retained our faith in our own ability to master our destiny. Fear is vanishing and confidence is growing . . .

SLIDE: "UNEMPLOYMENT OFFICE"

(A Clerk enters. Freaks enter and form a line.)

CLERK: May I help you?

SISTER ELIZABETH: Yes, we're here to get jobs.

CLERK: Name please.

SISTER ELIZABETH: I'm the Half-Lady.

CLERK: Name.

SISTER ELIZABETH: I'm Elizabeth, America's Only Living Half-Lady, and this is Princess Angelica—

CLERK: I said *name*!

ANGIE: Sure, how many you want? Countess Angela, Queen Angelina, Empress Angelissima—

ANDREOS: Andreos the Legless Wonder.

SISTER ELIZABETH: And this is Zoltan the Wild Man—

WILD MAN *(Unintelligibly)*: Joey—

CLERK: I beg your pardon?

WILD MAN *(Struggling to be understood)*: My name is Joey.

CLERK *(Loud and slow)*: Would somebody tell him, I ASKED FOR YOUR *NAMES.*

SISTER ELIZABETH: He heard you.

WILD MAN: My name is Joey.

CLERK: Back in line, please. Let's try that again. Your names as they appear on your birth certificates.

SISTER ELIZABETH: My mother burned mine.

ANDREOS: I was raised by reptiles in the Everglades.

ANGIE: You can read about me all the way back to my great-great-great—

WILD MAN: My name is—

ANDREOS: Forget it, Joey, you're better off as the Wild Man.

CLERK: We will have to have some official identification before we can process you. *(Wild Man lunges at the Clerk, who ignores him and continues)* Now—job desired.

ANGIE: What's wrong with my old job?

SISTER ELIZABETH: I'll take whatever pays the rent.

ANDREOS: What have you got for a "Wonder"?

CLERK: Before we go any further with this, you're all going to have to have a complete physical examination. Medical history and description . . .

SISTER ELIZABETH: Spinal cord injury, C5-6. Quadriplegia.

ANGIE: Acromesomilia dysplasia.

ANDREOS: Spinal cord injury, t(12;21). Partial paraplegia. Hey!

WILD MAN: What about jobs?

CLERK: Oh, that's a shame.

SISTER ELIZABETH: He said, what about jobs?

CLERK: Restricted activities?

ANDREOS: I use this board—I've also got crutches—

CLERK: So that would mean limited ambulation?

ANDREOS: I'll get to work on time if that's your question.

CLERK: Do you require any assistance in your daily living?

SISTER ELIZABETH: Hold on a minute. This isn't anybody's business. We're here to find jobs.

ANGIE: Yeah. When do we hear about our jobs?

CLERK: Classification: P.H.—"physically handicapped." "Substandard Unemployable." Your relief checks will be mailed to your home or institutional addresses.

(Blackout.)

Part Three: Movement

SLIDE: 1936 HEADLINES; PHOTOS OF THE LEAGUE OF THE PHYSICALLY HANDICAPPED PICKETING

(Company enters in 1930s street clothes. The company will switch roles, alternating between Demonstrators and Hecklers. Man in Wheelchair, as a Demonstrator, uses crutches if possible.)

FREAK SHOW BARKER *(Voice-over)*: Now, ladies and gentlemen, I will show you something so astounding you'll wonder how it ever came to pass: in 1936, in Washington, D.C., these odd remnants of human miscellanea lumbered out onto public streets and uttered their strange, chilling cry—

DEMONSTRATORS *(Together)*: WE WANT JOBS! NOT TIN CUPS! WE WANT JOBS! NOT TIN CUPS!

FREAK SHOW BARKER *(Voice-over)*: Ladies and gentlemen, look if you dare at the ragtag battalion of despair—the League of the Physically Handicapped.

DEMONSTRATORS *(Together)*: We want jobs! Not tin cups!

DEMONSTRATOR 1: The WPA promised jobs for everybody! Why not us?

DEMONSTRATOR 2: P.H. doesn't stand for Put at Bottom of Stack.

DEMONSTRATORS *(Together)*: WE WANT JOBS! NOT TIN CUPS!

DEMONSTRATOR 3: We won't leave Washington till we talk to Harry Hopkins.

DEMONSTRATOR 4: We demand satisfaction from the WPA.

DEMONSTRATOR 5: We'll stay in the street! We'll sleep in his office if we have to!

DEMONSTRATOR 6: *Fight* injustice against the handicapped.

DEMONSTRATOR 1: We don't need relief, we're trained to work. WE WANT JOBS!

DEMONSTRATORS *(Together)*: NOT TIN CUPS!

HECKLER 1: Communist cripples!

HECKLERS *(Together)*: Freaks!

HECKLER 2: You oughta be ashamed—

HECKLER 3: Using your crutches to get sympathy.

HECKLER 4: Shame!

DEMONSTRATOR 2: We don't want sympathy—we want jobs!

DEMONSTRATORS *(Together)*: WE WANT JOBS, NOT TIN CUPS!

DEMONSTRATOR 3: A group of us went to the commissioner in charge of the civil service examinations. He told us one of his reasons for keeping us out of civil service was that he disliked the sight of an employee who limped through the halls.

HECKLERS *(Together)*: Freaks!

HECKLER 5: They oughta string up the whole bunch on telegraph poles.

HECKLERS *(Together)*: Shame!

DEMONSTRATOR 4: *We demand* a job for every unemployed person.

DEMONSTRATOR 5: You think they put "P.H." on Mr. Roosevelt's job file? You think they made him take a physical exam?

DEMONSTRATORS *(Together)*: We want jobs!

HECKLERS *(Together)*: TWISTED BODIES! TWISTED MINDS!

DEMONSTRATOR 6: Fight injustice against the handicapped!

DEMONSTRATOR 1: We demand satisfaction from the WPA. We want jobs!

DEMONSTRATORS *(Together)*: *WE WANT JOBS! NOT TIN CUPS! WE WANT—*

DEMONSTRATOR 2: Go ahead and stare. We're staring back.

(All freeze.

Man in Wheelchair, as Demonstrator on crutches, moves out of the demonstration as Young Woman, in a soft, flowery dress, enters with a pitcher of lemonade. The demonstration scene fades out as she leads him to her kitchen: a small table and two chairs.)

DEMONSTRATOR: A hard chair would be good. With a straight back.

YOUNG WOMAN: How's this?

DEMONSTRATOR: Good. *(Sits in the chair)*

YOUNG WOMAN: I hope you don't think I'm being too forward.

DEMONSTRATOR: You don't have to apologize—

YOUNG WOMAN: You looked so hot—

DEMONSTRATOR: Nothing wrong with forward in my book.

YOUNG WOMAN: Oh—well—

DEMONSTRATOR: Beats backward any day.

YOUNG WOMAN: That's true.

DEMONSTRATOR: That lemonade looks good.

YOUNG WOMAN: Oh. Sorry—what was I thinking? *(Pours him a glass of lemonade)* Are you comfortable?

DEMONSTRATOR: Are you?

YOUNG WOMAN: Me?

DEMONSTRATOR: Yeah. Do I make you uneasy? You heard what they were calling us—"communist cripples," "twisted bodies, twisted minds"—right here in your kitchen—

YOUNG WOMAN: Are you really a communist? I've read so much about it, but I've never actually met one—

DEMONSTRATOR: That's not what I meant—

YOUNG WOMAN: I know. *(A beat)* You're from New York, aren't you? I saw the sign on your truck. Are you familiar with Greenwich Village? I'm hoping to live there one day.

DEMONSTRATOR: No kidding.

YOUNG WOMAN: Nope. Back home I'm considered pretty progressive.

DEMONSTRATOR: Where's that?

YOUNG WOMAN: Ohio.

DEMONSTRATOR: You're a college girl?

YOUNG WOMAN: For two years. My folks couldn't afford any more than that. Now the WPA's got me working here.

DEMONSTRATOR: Yeah, the WPA's got us here, too. I guess we've got that in common.

YOUNG WOMAN: I bet you don't even know it, but I saw you first thing this morning. You were the second one out of the truck. I watched you set up three tables out there.

DEMONSTRATOR: No kidding.

(A beat.)

YOUNG WOMAN: What is it you have? . . .

DEMONSTRATOR: Well . . . I wouldn't call it communism, exactly, more like a mild case of socialism, but it's terrible what it can do to a person—and it's mighty contagious too, given the right circumstances—

YOUNG WOMAN: You know what I meant.

DEMONSTRATOR: I know. *(A beat, disappointed)* You're curious.

YOUNG WOMAN: What's wrong with that?

DEMONSTRATOR: I liked forward better.

YOUNG WOMAN: Okay. I'm forward. *(A beat)* What is it?

DEMONSTRATOR: It *was* polio.

YOUNG WOMAN: Oh Lord. I've read about that.

DEMONSTRATOR: Communism's a lot more interesting.

YOUNG WOMAN: Can you feel anything?

DEMONSTRATOR: Hm. Let's see . . . *(Pinches his leg, a series of comic grimaces)* Ow—ow—ow—ouch! Yeah—and here—

YOUNG WOMAN: Okay, okay, stop that.

DEMONSTRATOR: What about you?

YOUNG WOMAN: What?

DEMONSTRATOR: You have any conditions that might be of interest? You know, a mole, a birthmark? Medically speaking, of course . . .

YOUNG WOMAN: Of course. *(A beat)* Well, how about this? *(Lifts her hair to show the nape of her neck)* Mother said if there was one more little mole right there it would be just like the Little Dipper. See, there?

(He holds her hair, traces the pattern.)

DEMONSTRATOR: And this would be the North Star . . .

YOUNG WOMAN: Yes.

DEMONSTRATOR: Very nice.

(Neither one moves. He lets her hair go.)

YOUNG WOMAN: You know . . . I really admire what you're doing— out there, speaking up for yourselves like that. It must take a lot of nerve to go up against everybody and say, "This is who I am and this is what I want." *(Pause)* I don't think, I mean, I wish I could, but I know—well, I wouldn't be able to do it.

DEMONSTRATOR: Well. The lemonade was a good start.

*(He picks up crutches and exits as their scene fades.
Freak Show Barker brings on an antique wheelchair.)*

FREAK SHOW BARKER: Fame, fortune, beauty, talent—the grace of God—the hand of fate, or a good doctor? What fine line separates us from them, my friends? Witness the heartbreaking story of Henri M. . . . *(Slowly collapses into the chair)* A brilliant artist, at the height of his career, on intimate terms with the Muse herself—struck down to the basest level of human capacity, from the Olympian heights of productive imagination, to this!

SLIDE: MATISSE IN WHEELCHAIR

(On one side of the stage, an Attendant joins Woman in Wheelchair. On the other side, the Freak Show Barker becomes Matisse, in his wheelchair. He is joined by his assistant, Louis-Michel. The two scenes play simultaneously.)

LOUIS-MICHEL: Monsieur Matisse, is this the right color? *(Matisse nods)* I'm finished with the blues. Do you want me to start on the reds?

MATISSE: I have a piece for the cutout. Place it like this, below the oval. This is her torso.

WOMAN IN WHEELCHAIR: Well, are you ready to start?

ATTENDANT: Yes. Okay, I turn on the water and, while it is warming up, rinse out your cup, put toothpaste on the toothbrush, and then fill your cup up with warm water.

WOMAN IN WHEELCHAIR: Great. Okay, give me the roll of toilet paper. *(Pause)* No, don't unroll it. I'll do it myself.

ATTENDANT: I'm sorry. I can pull some off for you. I think I can handle that.

WOMAN IN WHEELCHAIR: Oh, I know. But if I do it, then I can fold it the way it's easiest for me.

ATTENDANT: Now what?

WOMAN IN WHEELCHAIR: Vitamins, and then go fix the bed.

LOUIS-MICHEL: I am so amazed by the difference in style between your paintings and these cutouts. Is there a reason for your change?

MATISSE: The scissors, please, Louis-Michel.

ATTENDANT: Are you sure you don't want me to brush your teeth for you?

WOMAN IN WHEELCHAIR: No thanks.

LOUIS-MICHEL *(Holding on to the scissors)*: Let me help. If you draw your shapes on the paper, I'll cut them out for you. Then you won't need to hold the heavy scissors.

MATISSE: Louis-Michel, give me back the scissors.

LOUIS-MICHEL: I was only trying to help. I want to save your energy.

MATISSE: Yes, that is most understandable. Take the shape and place it on the cutout.

ATTENDANT: I happened to see you brushing your teeth and it looked so difficult and uncomfortable. That's what I'm here for: to help you with anything you can't do.

WOMAN IN WHEELCHAIR: Oh, well, thank you. But I can brush my teeth. I just don't do it the same way you do.

ATTENDANT: Okay. There are your vitamins. Now your pajama top?

WOMAN IN WHEELCHAIR: Yes. Pull my shirt up in the back and then over my elbow.

MATISSE: Move it a little to the right . . . No. That's a little too far . . . Back to the left a little . . .

WOMAN IN WHEELCHAIR: No—wait—just over my elbow. I'll get the rest.

LOUIS-MICHEL: That's just where I had it.

MATISSE: More to the right . . . Tip the bottom to the right a little bit.

LOUIS-MICHEL: It doesn't look any different from the way I first had it.

MATISSE: It is different. Where you have it now is fine. Please come and get these pieces.

ATTENDANT: I didn't mean to offend you.

WOMAN IN WHEELCHAIR: That's okay. Now let me pull my shirt over my head myself. I will take it off completely and then put it on the bed.

LOUIS-MICHEL: Here, let me clean up the scraps around your chair. This mess must bother you.

MATISSE: No, don't touch them! I will tell you when I want my papers cleaned up.

LOUIS-MICHEL: Ahh, forgive me . . .

ATTENDANT: My grandpa—

WOMAN IN WHEELCHAIR: Now open up my pajama top—

ATTENDANT: He feels sorry for you people.

WOMAN IN WHEELCHAIR: I will slide my arms in—

ATTENDANT: He says he can't understand how you do it—

WOMAN IN WHEELCHAIR: And pull it over my head myself—

ATTENDANT: Having people dress you, feed you—

WOMAN IN WHEELCHAIR: Pull it down in the back—

ATTENDANT: Helping you go to the bathroom . . .

WOMAN IN WHEELCHAIR: You can put the shirt in the dirty clothes.

ATTENDANT: What a struggle to live.

MATISSE: When I cut into a color, it has a certain effect on me. A certain blue enters my soul; a certain red affects my blood pressure and another color wakes me up. I do not cut the oranges and reds the same way I cut the greens and blues. Here, this is ready. Place it above the torso, so it looks as if soon it will touch, but for now it floats.

WOMAN IN WHEELCHAIR: My wristbands go in the middle drawer on the right.

LOUIS-MICHEL: How's that?

MATISSE: No. That's not it. That's a collision. Much higher and on a slight diagonal. No, higher. *(A beat)* Not on the ceiling!

ATTENDANT: He says if it was him—

WOMAN IN WHEELCHAIR: I need some lotion.

ATTENDANT: He couldn't do it.

WOMAN IN WHEELCHAIR: Squirt one drop on my palm. I'll rub it in myself.

ATTENDANT: He says he'd want to kill himself.

WOMAN IN WHEELCHAIR: Okay, we're ready to transfer. Slide one arm underneath my knees to your elbow, push against the cushion with your other hand. Now pull me out a little—

LOUIS-MICHEL: Is this how you want it? . . . Am I doing it right? . . . Is this EXACTLY how you want it?

ATTENDANT: How is this?

MATISSE: That is fine.

WOMAN IN WHEELCHAIR: Good.

LOUIS-MICHEL: Are you sure?

MATISSE: Fine.

WOMAN IN WHEELCHAIR: Sit me up.

MATISSE: Only a few more pieces are needed.

WOMAN IN WHEELCHAIR: Grip one arm around my lower back and cup your other hand underneath my butt. Use your knees and stand up. *(A beat)* Whoa—whoa! Wait—wait! We need to stand and wait, so the spasms don't throw us off—and so I can have weight bearing on my legs.

ATTENDANT: The physical therapist I worked for said it's bad to do that because your legs are so brittle, and I shouldn't take the chance of breaking them.

WOMAN IN WHEELCHAIR: It's called osteoporosis. It will get worse if I can't get weight bearing—and then you *will* break my leg—ask *my* therapist.

LOUIS-MICHEL: Monsieur Matisse . . . this work is so tranquil . . . why don't we try more tension?

ATTENDANT: You're telling me to throw my knowledge out the door?

MATISSE: There are sufficient bothersome things in the world. I do not wish to add to them. I want my art to be like a good armchair.

LOUIS-MICHEL: An armchair?

WOMAN IN WHEELCHAIR: Now we need to swing my legs onto the bed. Support under my knees and ankles, please.

MATISSE: A place to rest from physical fatigue.

LOUIS-MICHEL: But Monsieur Matisse, truly great work must be dangerous, disturbing.

ATTENDANT: You are so stubborn. Why can't you take any suggestions?

MATISSE: Louis-Michel, I need your help because I can no longer stand, but my art must still be my creation.

WOMAN IN WHEELCHAIR: I'm not stubborn. I've been in a chair twelve years. I've learned what works best for me.

LOUIS-MICHEL: Why have you never done a piece about your illness, your pain? We could create one. That would be a great work.

MATISSE: To express my pain for others to see? . . . No . . . That is not my art. My art is light. It is open, free, bright. Pain is heavy, like a blanket of dark lead. It has taken away my freedom, robbed me of vitality. But I will not let it rob me of my creativity.

WOMAN IN WHEELCHAIR: And as far as your grandpa is concerned, I think I have a pretty incredible life.

MATISSE: I have created a little garden on the wall around my bed, where I can walk. In this garden I have put familiar things: leaves, fruit, a bird, a nude figure. Surrounded by my cutouts, I am never alone.

WOMAN IN WHEELCHAIR: I like my adventures. I have plenty to live for. It's too bad your grandpa would want to kill himself. I feel sorry for him.

MATISSE: Take this. Above the blue and a little to the left. And swivel it to the right. Back a fraction. Fine. Good.

ATTENDANT: Okay, I think that's it for tonight.

LOUIS-MICHEL: Is this piece finished . . . Is it finally finished?

WOMAN IN WHEELCHAIR: Thanks. See you tomorrow.

MATISSE: Ah, Louis-Michel, you are so young. One has only one life, and one is never finished.

SLIDE: MATISSE COLLAGE, "THE NEGRESS," 1953

(Blackout.)

SLIDE: 1970S DEMONSTRATIONS; THE HEW (HEALTH, EDUCATION AND WELFARE) SIT-IN IN SAN FRANCISCO

(Lights up on 1970s demonstrators, at the sit-in.)

DEMONSTRATOR 1: These are the facts. In 1972, Congress passed the Rehabilitation Act, which was our first civil rights act, eighteen years before the ADA. Any program with federal funding could no longer discriminate against people with disabilities. By 1977 the regulations were drawn up, but Carter's HEW chairman, Califano, still hadn't signed them. April fourth was our deadline. When nothing happened, we moved into ten federal buildings across the U.S. In most places the sit-ins lasted only a few hours, but in San Francisco we stayed for twenty-eight days!

DEMONSTRATOR 2: Nobody expected it to last that long. I mean, some of us had sleeping bags, but even that wasn't official because we couldn't let anyone know we were planning to stay. But twenty-eight days!

DEMONSTRATOR 3: It was a lot of work. Everyone was on a committee: security, press, food, medical. Big strategy meetings every night. Democracy at work. Ten to three in the morning. Every night. And then up at six to let the cleaning people in.

DEMONSTRATOR 4: We had our hands full with the press. They were there all the time. They loved this story. At the beginning we had to steer them away from those "brave, sweet cripple" stories to hard facts about civil rights. And try to clean up their language: "deaf and dumb," "polio victim," "wheelchair bound," "confined to a wheelchair" . . . The same old litany.

DEMONSTRATOR 5: I'd been active in a lot of political stuff—the war, the black movement, abortion rights—but nothing like this, ever . . . this direct effect. I mean—we won! After twenty-eight days, we get those regs signed.

DEMONSTRATOR 6: But the most wonderful thing about that time was that I knew there'd be someone there for me every morning and every night. Someone to get me out and then into bed. No attendant flake-out. And I'd be fed.

DEMONSTRATOR 1: We'd all be fed. Quite a list of contributors: Glide Memorial Church, McDonald's—

DEMONSTRATOR 2: And the Black Panther Party.

DEMONSTRATOR 3: When it was the Black Panthers, the food was wonderful. And every day we were doing this work that was changing the world.

DEMONSTRATOR 4: I'd wake up on the floor—me, who *had* to use a hospital bed at home—I'd wake up on this skimpy mattress on the floor with my two cups of coffee in front of my nose. And then my attendant would move on to help four other people. Everyone was acting as an attendant: sign language interpreters, deaf people, blind people.

DEMONSTRATOR 5: I'd never felt so safe and powerful in my life. It was so, well—PEOPLE FELL IN LOVE! I'm not kidding. I could name quite a few couples who met there.

DEMONSTRATOR 6: Some of them are still together.

DEMONSTRATOR 1: I hated being dirty. There was no shower. Toward the end, Mayor Moscone sent in a portable shower gizmo—the joy of it!

DEMONSTRATOR 2: The bathrooms weren't accessible. It took great ingenuity to go to the john. There were long lines for the one stall we had removed the door from.

DEMONSTRATOR 3: And no privacy. People would be lying a foot away from you, naked, getting a sponge bath, but nobody cared.

DEMONSTRATOR 4: Lining up with our dimes to use the one accessible phone, nobody cared.

DEMONSTRATOR 5: There were two hundred of us, and we were there for ourselves and about thirty-five million other disabled people—

DEMONSTRATOR 6: And that's not an exaggeration. For many of us it was, and is, the most important thing we'd ever done with our lives. I mean, so much so that our final political crisis, after we won, was that a whole group refused to leave the building. They didn't want to go back to the real world, even if there were regs now.

DEMONSTRATOR 1: We fiddled with the media, told them we had to clean up the building like the good citizens we were—

DEMONSTRATOR 2: And gently we coaxed our comrades through the doors with us and out to the waiting crowd.

SLIDE: DEMONSTRATORS LEAVING THE BUILDING

(The Demonstrators exit. Man in Wheelchair and Joey and Beth, also in wheelchairs, remain behind. Man in Wheelchair wears a placard that reads: FREE OUR PEOPLE! DOWN WITH NURSING HOMES!)

MAN IN WHEELCHAIR: Since 1983 Joey and I—between the two of us—have been arrested forty-three times doing civil disobedience for disability rights. Joey lived in a nursing home for the first twenty-five years of his life. He had to sue the state to get out. The only difference between a jail and a nursing home is the color of the uniform. They use a nightstick in jail, medication in a nursing home.

(Beth moves to Joey. The scene shifts focus to them.)

JOEY: My words twirl . . .

BETH:

> My words twirl
> Play fifty-two-card pickup
> On my tongue.

JOEY: This tongue . . .

BETH:

> This tongue fights
> My careful control,
> Lashing out against
> An unfriendly palate.
> A beating lips curling,
> Twisting into tantrum.

JOEY: My words dance . . .

BETH:

> My words dance
> Wait to come
> How they can.

MAN IN WHEELCHAIR: June 15, 1989. It was very hot. I was wearing a T-shirt and jeans. I had to be careful the catheter didn't get ripped away. It took a long time—twenty minutes that seemed like forever. Seventy of us got out of our wheelchairs and crawled up the Capitol steps. We took a lot of flak for it, but I've thought a lot about crawling. First, people like me in most of the world—if they're not dead—they have to crawl to get around. There's no wheelchairs, no access. Do I think I'm better than them? Second, the media responds. I wouldn't crawl to see a movie, but I'd do it to get the Americans with Disabilities Act passed. *(Exits)*

SLIDE: OUTSIDE OF A MOTEL; THEN A MOTEL ROOM WITH RUMPLED BED

(An Attendant helps Joey into bed, next to Beth.)

ATTENDANT: Okay, let's go . . . easy . . . relax . . . easy does it . . . Oh sure, like now is the time to relax. *(Joey laughs)* God, you would have to laugh now. Get those spasms going, that's the last thing we need now . . . we have to work on our foreplay—

BETH: You shut up about foreplay!

JOEY: Foreplay? You ain't seen nothing yet!

ATTENDANT: Yeah, buddy! You tell Beth she ain't seen nothing yet. That's my bud! Go for it!

BETH: You guys shut up—both of you!

ATTENDANT: Okay, if you two are all set . . . I'll be right outside, so just call if, you know, you need something.

BETH: Sure. Thanks.

JOEY: Yeah. Hey, thanks a lot, Mike.

ATTENDANT: Sure thing. I'll leave you two . . . have at it!

JOEY: Fuck off, Mike!

ATTENDANT: What?

BETH: He said fuck off, Mike. He'll see you later.

ATTENDANT: Okay, okay, okay, Beth. Okay, Joey. I'm outta here. See ya! *(Exits)*

BETH: Not bad. Not bad. I knew we could pull it off. Now if one of us could get a double bed at home we wouldn't be stuck with this thirty-five dollar a night scene—

JOEY: I know. I know. But this is just the beginning.

BETH: Yeah, it is the beginning . . . We'll have plenty of time to work out stuff later. *(Sighs, shifting focus)* You can come closer, you know. I won't bite. Maybe nibble a bit. Love bites. *(Suddenly serious)* Oh, Joey, easy!

JOEY: What? You all right?

BETH: I'm all right. Just take it easy. Like we talked about.

JOEY: Sure?

BETH: Sure. Easy. Nice and slow. Nice. More like it. Mmmmm . . . I feel you.

JOEY: Yeah . . . you . . . you're warm.

BETH: You're warm, too. *(Suddenly panicky)* Joey! Joey! Your foot—you're kicking me!

JOEY: Shit. Sorry.

BETH: No, come back. No, you're doing fine. We can work it out. And besides, this is your first time.

JOEY: Yeah, but shit . . .

BETH: You're doing fine. Just nice and easy . . .

(Joey breathes hard, grins. Beth smiles.)

It's tickling me, you know. I feel you.

JOEY: Yeah . . .

BETH: Mmmmm . . . amazing . . . just a little . . .

JOEY: Right . . .

BETH: LET GO! Joey! Damn it! Let go!

JOEY: Beth? . . . Beth? You okay?

BETH: I'm . . . I'll be fine . . .

JOEY: I'm sorry, I didn't mean—

BETH: I know. I know you didn't mean to, Joey. We just have to learn . . . explore . . . how to be . . . enjoy each other . . .

JOEY: Sure, but . . . it's hard. I want to . . .

BETH: What?

JOEY: I . . . want . . . I want to . . .

BETH: Do you want to be with me? . . .

JOEY: Yeah. I want to be with you.

BETH: Then why don't you scoot that bod of yours on over here. You know . . . the way you scoot—it's so sexy, it's a real turn-on . . .

(Joey moves closer, facing Beth.)

That's it. This is where it's at. There you are. You're tickling me again.

JOEY: Yeah . . .

(Lights fade on them.)

SLIDE: A HOT DOG IN VARIOUS STAGES OF BEING EATEN

FREAK SHOW BARKER: Today we are far too sophisticated to engage in anything as debasing as a freak show. We see everyone as a fellow human being and take great care to afford them their privacy and dignity. What you are about to see is a dramatization of a real event.

(Beth wheels up to hot dog Vendor.)

BETH: One chili dog, please.
VENDOR: You want ketchup and mustard on that?
BETH: Sure, why not.
VENDOR: That'll be one dollar.

(Beth hands him the dollar and starts to eat the hot dog. The Vendor watches.)

Hey, you can do that all by yourself.
BETH: Of course I can. Did you think I bought this for you to eat?

(She takes another bite of the hot dog.)

VENDOR: I think it's great. *(Traffic Cop enters)* Hey, Sergeant, come over and check this out.
TRAFFIC COP: Way to go, hon. It's amazing what you people can do when you put your mind to it.
BETH: It's just a hot dog, for heaven's sake.
TRAFFIC COP: Hey, Padre, come over here for a minute. *(A Priest enters)* Look, she did this all by herself. *(Priest takes hot dog)*
BETH: Hey, give me my hot dog back.
PRIEST: It's truly a miracle.
BETH: Can I have my hot dog back?
PRIEST: Praise God for the miracle that lets this poor soul eat her food. And let us pray to God Almighty for the power to heal this tortured soul, to cast out the demons that oppress her and confine her to this mechanical device.
BETH: I'm not oppressed, I'm hungry. *(Grabs the hot dog)* Hey, I'm outta here . . .

(Beth tries to escape, but a crowd enters, cheering her, and she's surrounded. A Female Sports Reporter enters.)

FEMALE SPORTS REPORTER: Good evening, ladies and gentlemen, and thank you for joining us at this historic event. Beth Pinto, a tragically injured quadriplegic, is at this very moment eating a hot dog completely under her own power, with no assistance whatsoever. If she completes this task, this will indeed be one for the record books. Bob, what's the latest report?

(Male Sports Reporter emerges from the crowd.)

MALE SPORTS REPORTER: I'm hearing that she's losing steam. Apparently, she got off to a very fast start, and now she hasn't had a bite in more than five minutes.

FEMALE SPORTS REPORTER: Could just be heartburn.

MALE SPORTS REPORTER: Could be, but the reports I'm getting say that it appears as though she's lost her will to continue, that she's given up the fight.

FEMALE SPORTS REPORTER: That would be a shame, especially when she's come so far. But she is a very courageous young woman, so we shouldn't count her out yet—

MALE SPORTS REPORTER: Good news, Jane, she's taken another bite. She's only a couple of mouthfuls from the finish line.

FEMALE SPORTS REPORTER: I hope she can go the distance, Bob. Do you know if this was a regulation-size hot dog, or a foot-long?

MALE SPORTS REPORTER: That's a good question, Jane. If it is one of the foot-long variety, this will be a record that could stand for a long time.

(Cheers from the crowd.)

She's got the last of it in her mouth, Jane. She's chewing it. She's swallowed it, Jane! She swallowed it!

FEMALE SPORTS REPORTER: Listen to that crowd, Bob. I haven't seen an outpouring of emotion like this since Joe Willy Namath led the Jets over the Colts in the '69 Super Bowl. See if you can get in for a word with Beth—

MALE SPORTS REPORTER: Here she comes now. Beth! Beth!

BETH: OUTTA MY WAY!!!

(Beth breaks out of the crowd and escapes, with everyone in full pursuit.)

MALE SPORTS REPORTER: Apparently she has some pressing engagement.

FEMALE SPORTS REPORTER: We'll bring that to you live, as soon as we catch up to her. Let's break for a commercial and we'll be right back.

(Beth starts to exit, with the crowd in pursuit. They freeze as Joey and the Woman of Small Stature enter.)

WOMAN OF SMALL STATURE: Where's Beth? . . . I don't believe it. Is she late again?

JOEY: Yeah . . .

WOMAN OF SMALL STATURE: She's always late. *(A beat)* Hey, you wanna hot dog?

JOEY: Yeah.

WOMAN OF SMALL STATURE: Me, too. Come on.

(They cross to the Vendor and order hot dogs. The full company turns to stare at them and freezes. Woman in Wheelchair moves out of the crowd.)

WOMAN IN WHEELCHAIR: November 20, 1992. We're barricading McDonald's, and this disabled guy yells at me from down the street, "BEHAVE YOURSELF! You make a bad name for us."

This one woman in a chair told me she wished I was dead because I was fighting Special Transit to get all the city buses accessible. She likes Special Transit the way it is because she doesn't know the names of the streets—and she doesn't want to learn them.

We've made a lot of progress in Denver. See, in Denver I'm part of the picture for the bus driver: a *regular* pain in the ass, not a *special* pain in the ass. Just another pain in the ass . . .

(Lights fade to black.)

END OF PLAY

Doris Baizley lives in Los Angeles, where she is a founding member of L.A. Theatre Works (originally Artists in Prisons and Other Places). For seven years she was resident playwright for Mark Taper Forum's Improvisational Theater Project for young audiences. Her latest play, *Sexsting*, written in collaboration with defense attorney Susan Raffanti, won The Playwrights' Center/Guthrie Theater's "Two-Headed Challenge" in 2004. Her other plays, *Shiloh Rules, Mrs. California, Tears of Rage, Catholic Girls, Daniel in Babylon, Agnes Smedley: Our American Friend* and her adaptation of *A Christmas Carol* have been produced by U.S. regional theaters, including ACT Theatre, Alabama Shakespeare Festival, Capital Repertory Theatre, Center Theatre Group/Mark Taper Forum, The Cleveland Play House, People's Light and Theatre Company and the National Theater of the Deaf, and internationally at the Semafor Theatre in Prague and the Icon Theater at the National Theater of Taiwan. *Mimi's Guide, Tears of Rage* and *Guns* have been recorded for L.A. Theatre Works' "The Play's the Thing" radio series.

As founding director of Mark Taper Forum's Other Voices Project, Victoria Ann Lewis created and directed a series of documentary, community-based plays with a variety of communities, including two television specials for Norman Lear, *Tell Them I'm a Mermaid* in 1983 and *Who Parks in Those Spaces?* in 1985; as well as the stage plays *The Greatest Story Never Told* in 1987 for the AFL-CIO, and *Teenage Ninja Mothers* in 1991, with African American and Latina teen mothers. Ms. Lewis's critical writing has been published in *American Theatre, Radical History Review, Michigan Quarterly Review* and various collections and anthologies. Ms. Lewis's credits as an actress include The Old Globe, Center Theatre Group/Mark Taper Forum, the Los Angeles Theatre Center, the Eugene O'Neill Theater Center and Ensemble Studio Theatre. She was an ensemble member of San Francisco's Lilith Theater, and Family Circus Theater in Portland, Oregon. In 2000, Ms. Lewis received a Ph.D. in theater from UCLA, and she is now an associate professor of theater at the University of Redlands.

THE HISTORY
OF BOWLING

Mike Ervin

Chuck (Robert Ness) in the Victory Gardens Theater production, Chicago, Illinois, 1999. Photo by Liz Lauren.

Author's Statement

The History of Bowling germinated from a tale of discrimination told to me by a friend with epilepsy. When she was in high school, the physical education teacher would not let her participate, but he did require her to suit up and watch from the side. She had to write reports on the activities. He said that it was for her own safety. So while everyone else swam, she sat by the pool in her bathing suit and wrote about swimming. This struck me as a hilariously grotesque caricature of the subtle sadism found in the worst disability bigotry.

Bowling is about the power and glory of rejecting shame. The characters Chuck and Lou are desperate not to be forced into that tiny, claustrophobic box labeled "invalid." (It doesn't matter if you put the accent on the first or second syllable. It means the same thing.) It takes an awful lot of shame to make someone believe they deserve to be banished into such insignificance. This is the central battle of living with a disability, and those who win it are those who laugh in the face of shame.

To me, the disability experience is mostly comical. It brightly illuminates the absurdity of many human priorities and pop culture values. The job I feel privileged to take on as an artist and an activist is to illustrate and challenge this farce. I don't think I'll ever write anything for the stage that doesn't revolve around someone with a disability. Our daily lives make for great drama and high comedy. You don't have to reach far for rich stories. There are enough man-made obstacles out there to turn a trip to the drugstore into a harrowing journey.

I take pride in being a part of disability culture the way some take pride in their ethnic culture. If we had a flag, I'd fly it. If we had an anthem, I'd sing it.

Production History

The History of Bowling was developed through the Other Voices' History Project at Mark Taper Forum (Center Theatre Group, Los Angeles) in 1997, where the author was mentored by playwright Murray Mednik. Through this program, the play was subsequently given a workshop production at the Falcon Theatre in Burbank. It was directed by Joan Mankin. The cast was as follows:

LOU	Kara Zediker
CHUCK	Jim Troesch
BARNES	Robert David Hall
CORNELIUS	Lynn Manning

The History of Bowling premiered at Victory Gardens Theater in Chicago in the spring of 1999. The production was directed by Susan Nussbaum. The cast was as follows:

LOU	Doran Schrantz
CHUCK	Robert Ness
BARNES	Jeffrey Rogers
CORNELIUS	James Joseph

The History of Bowling was then produced in 2001 with the Know Theater Tribe in Cincinnati; in 2002 at Mixed Blood Theater in Minneapolis; in 2004 at Circle Theater in Omaha, Nebraska; and in 2005 at Hot City Theatre in St. Louis, Missouri.

Characters

LOU—a woman with epilepsy, college student, twenty-two.

CHUCK—a man in a motorized wheelchair, college student, thirty-two.

BARNES—the gym teacher, forties.

CORNELIUS—blind and deaf, Chuck's roommate, twenty-five or so.

Time

Late in the twentieth century.

Place

An urban, American college campus.

Author's Note

Chuck's disability is such that he can't move anything but his head and shoulders. He moves his chair either by a sip-and-puff mechanism or with the drive box mounted high so he can he can operate it with his head or chin.

Act One

Scene 1

Lou and Chuck are on opposite sides of the stage.

LOU *(To audience)*: I finally broke down and got a doctor's note. I hated to do it, but I had to. It was the only way I could get out of that stupid mandatory PE credit. I had the doctor at the student infirmary write me a note saying it was unsafe for me to take PE, because it could set off a seizure if I got hit in the head with a ball. Of course it was bullshit. But the doctors at the student infirmary are like retired podiatrists. They don't know any better.

   I felt cheap and sleazy after I did it. Not because it was a lie, but because I played the cripple game. I only played the cripple game once before in my whole life. I could have played it a thousand times. But the only time I ever did, I stood up and said, "Well, Your Honor, sir, it's just that I have epilepsy. And if I were to have a seizure in the jury box . . ."

CHUCK *(To audience)*: I, on the other hand, am the king of the doctor's notes. I could fill a gymnasium with all the doctor's notes I've had to get. When I got the license plates with the little wheelchair hieroglyphic, I had to get a doctor's note. When I got this wheelchair—doctor's note. When I applied to this university—doctor's note again. One time I was in a shoe store and the manager rushed up and he said that before he would let any of his salespeople touch my feet, I would have to bring a doctor's note.

LOU *(To audience)*: I know, I know, I should have stood up and said, "I have epilepsy, Your Honor, but it will in no way interfere with my ability to do the job!" But I didn't have time for jury duty.

CHUCK *(To audience)*: The shoe store manager was so uptight. He said, "I'm sorry, sir, but I don't want them to be responsible if something should happen." I said, "What, you had a cripple come in here once and his feet exploded?" And he said, "It's not that I don't have empathy for your situation." That really made me laugh. I said, "How can *you* feel sorry for *me*? You manage a shoe store!"

LOU *(To audience)*: My mother would hate it if she knew I got a doctor's note. The one thing she has no patience for is "those people who use their handicap as a weapon."

CHUCK *(To audience)*: Beggars on the street are like that, too. They try to hit up everyone who comes by, but never me. It's an insult. They're wearing shoes they found in the dumpster, but they think they're better off than me. I wish I could afford to flash five hundred bucks at one of them! I'd show them, boy!

LOU *(To audience)*: I should have known it wouldn't be that easy. I delivered my doctor's note to Mr. Barnes, the PE teacher. I tried to act like I was really broken up about not being able to take PE.

(Mr. Barnes enters, perusing the note. He's the devil wearing gym teacher's clothes, complete with whistle around his neck.)

BARNES: Oh dear, epilepsy, huh?

LOU: Yes. And I really can't take the risk.

BARNES: Oh, mercy no. Most certainly not.

LOU: I'm really sorry. I'll have to get an exemption, I guess.

BARNES: We'll have to put you in the special section.

LOU: What!

BARNES: Oh yes, the special section. For the people with handicaps. Maybe you can't literally participate in athletic activities, but you surely can write term papers about them. You and your partner.

LOU: Partner?

BARNES: But of course. Another handicapped person.

LOU: You mean, someone who's blind, or in a wheelchair?

BARNES: Could be a hemophiliac. *(Laughs a diabolical laugh; exits)*

CHUCK *(To audience)*: The street preachers are the worst. I try my best to ignore them, until they start with that, "Pray to Jesus and he'll make you walk!" One day I passed that one who's always in front of the drugstore with the bullhorn shouting, "Jesus! Jesus! Jesus!" And he says to me, "You better get right with Jesus, or he ain't never gonna make you walk!"

LOU *(To audience)*: Oh God! A partner! My mother would say, "Serves you right! You can either use your handicap to make excuses or you can stand on your own two feet."

CHUCK *(To audience)*: "You better get right with Jesus or he ain't never gonna make you walk!" Who the hell does he think he is? So I turned to him and I said, "You better get right with Jesus, or he ain't never gonna make you white!"

LOU *(To audience)*: I had to meet my partner at the cafeteria. Two o'clock, Tuesday. All I knew was his name was Chuck. That's all I knew. Oh God. I don't belong here.

CHUCK *(To audience)*: He told me, don't think my wheelchair will keep me from going to hell! I said I hope not. One time I made airplane reservations and they told me before I could board I'd have to have a doctor's note. I just bet you if I did go to hell, Satan would hit me up for a doctor's note.

LOU *(To audience)*: There was this black boy named Terry. His face was hideously burned. It was like his face was made of wax and big wax tears dripped down and solidified. His face was smeared, like someone tried to put it back in place with a putty knife.

(Lou sees Chuck sitting at a cafeteria table and walks toward him.)

Chuck?

CHUCK: Yeah.

LOU: I'm Lou.

CHUCK: My partner?

LOU: Yes.

CHUCK: What are you? Hemophiliac?

LOU: Epilepsy.

CHUCK: Epilepsy people can't take PE?

LOU: There's been a mistake. I was supposed to get an exemption.

CHUCK *(Laughing)*: An exemption from Barnes? That sadistic bastard? They say he wouldn't let his dead grandma off the hook for PE. We're lucky he's not making us run laps.

LOU: I wish he was.

CHUCK: Thanks.

LOU: I didn't mean it like that.

CHUCK: Right.

LOU: I didn't.

(Pause.)

CHUCK: You a freshman?

LOU: No. A senior. It's my last semester.

CHUCK: A senior? And just taking PE now?

LOU: I put it off until the last minute. And now I can't avoid it anymore. What are you?

CHUCK: A freshman.

LOU: How old are you?

CHUCK: Thirty-two.

LOU: And you're a freshman?

CHUCK: It's a long story.

(Pause.)

LOU: I didn't mean anything by what I said. It's just that I hate writing term papers. And especially about sports. I don't know anything about sports. I hate sports. I have no idea what to write about.

CHUCK: Yeah, well, that's okay. I know a lot about sports. That's all I did for the last fucking fifteen years, watch sports on cable: stock car racing, water polo, the world table tennis championships. But I was about to tell Barnes he could shove his busywork, then I got to thinking about it and pretty soon I got real excited. So don't worry. I know exactly what we're gonna write about!

LOU: Oh good. What?

CHUCK *(Bitterly)*: Bowling!

LOU: Bowling?

CHUCK: Bowling.

LOU: I hate bowling.

CHUCK: So do I.

LOU: I don't know anything about bowling. I've never set foot in a bowling alley.

CHUCK: That's all right. I know all about bowling. I did it enough times.

LOU: You? Bowling?

CHUCK: Yep: Bowling Buddies. Crippled kids bowling club, every third Saturday. The bastards. I think they were Christian kids. Real clean rah-rah types. I think maybe we were extra credit. They'd close down Rainbow Lanes for the afternoon and bring the cripples in. Sons of bitches.

LOU: My God.

CHUCK: I know. And the Bowling Buddies motto was "anybody can bowl a strike." They had this ramp. It looked like a miniature playground slide. They'd put the ball on top and you'd push it and it would roll down the ramp and head down the lane. Anybody could do it. There was this kid with no arms. He pushed the ball with his head.

LOU: Please. I don't want to hear any more.

CHUCK: He was a maniac. He'd get a running start and butt heads with the bowling ball. They made him wear a leather helmet. We called him kamikaze. And in Bowling Buddies, no one ever threw a gutter ball. You know why?

LOU: Don't tell me.

CHUCK: Because the Christians ran alongside the lane and if the ball headed for the gutter, they'd kick it back on course.

LOU: All right! All right! We'll do bowling!

CHUCK: It's all true. Every word.

LOU *(To audience)*: He made me feel how I felt when my friend Amy told me about the bastard she was married to who beat her up for years. The Amy I knew was the head of an agency, served on several boards. She was an activist. If any man tried that with the Amy I knew, she'd break his neck. Same way with Chuck. I couldn't believe he let them do that to him. Somewhere along the line, he'd completely transformed.

(Lou approaches Chuck.)

CHUCK: Still exists, Bowling Buddies. Chapters all over the country.

(Lou crawls up onto Chuck's lap and kisses him long and hard. Barnes runs out frantically blowing his whistle and throws a penalty flag.)

Scene 2

The cafeteria. Lou and Chuck sit at a table with food trays on it. Lou has a pen and writing pad.

CHUCK: Okay. Read that back.

LOU: Again?

CHUCK: Yes. Again. Got to get it right. You know what a fucker Barnes is.

LOU: All right, all right! *(Reading)* "The history of bowling . . ."

CHUCK: Not from the top. Start from the part about Old Lady McDonald.

LOU *(Reading)*: "Bowling Buddies was founded in 1962 by Mrs. Roger McDonald as a monument to her late husband. She wanted to combine his two great passions in life: service to the less fortunate and bowling."

CHUCK: Okay. Great. Now skip down to the part about the blind kids.

LOU: This is depressing.

CHUCK: I know. Keep reading.

LOU: Blind kids . . . blind kids . . . okay. *(Reading)* "The blind kids were the worst bowlers in the world. Everybody ran for cover. But even the blind kids never threw a gutter ball. No one ever threw a gutter ball in Bowling Buddies. That was another one of our proud mottoes. But why not? What's wrong with throwing a gutter ball? What were they afraid of? And we all accepted it. No one questioned it. Not one of us ever demanded our inalienable right to throw a gutter ball!"

CHUCK: Okay. Good. Now add, "In life, there's gutter balls. It's a fact. Better learn how to deal with it."

LOU: This is bullshit. You don't have any respect for me. We're supposed to be partners! I'm just a fucking secretary!

CHUCK: No. I just think better out loud.

LOU: And this whole paper is all about you.

CHUCK: No way. It's more about you than me. It's your worst nightmare.

LOU: What the hell is that supposed to mean?

CHUCK: They're gonna kidnap you and make you a Bowling Buddy!

LOU: Write your own fucking paper!

CHUCK *(Mocking Lou)*: Help! Help! Zombies! Hey, you think I don't have respect for you? You get the toughest job of all. You get to do the oral presentation.

LOU: Presentation? To whom?

CHUCK: To Barnes. He didn't tell you that part?

LOU: No!

CHUCK: Oh yeah, oral presentation. To the whole gym class. It's our final. At the end of the semester he parades all the cripples into the gym and they present their papers to all the jocks.

LOU: That's sick!

CHUCK: I know. I told you he's a sadist. That's how he gets his jollies. Him and the jocks. But we're gonna get the last laugh.

LOU: Oh God. Why did I try to get an exemption.

CHUCK: Oral presentation's a tough job. Takes a tough woman. So see, I have respect for you.

LOU: No way! Why don't you do it?

CHUCK: Oh don't worry. I'll be there. I just haven't figured out in what capacity.

LOU: No way am I doing any oral presentations!

CHUCK: We need to finish this.

LOU: I'm serious.

CHUCK: We'll discuss it later. Now what did I say before? Life is full of gutter balls.

LOU *(Reluctantly picking up the pad)*: Oh screw it. I don't care. Write about whatever you want. I just want to get this over with so I can graduate.

CHUCK: Good. Okay, so write that down about gutter balls.

LOU: The minute I get out of here, I've already decided what I'm gonna do. You know what I'm gonna do?

CHUCK: I'd love to hear every detail, really I would. But let's do the gutter balls first.

LOU: I'm gonna hop a boxcar. I don't care which one. Just pick one and go. I did it once before. All by myself. Rode all the way across Indiana. Changed my life. I know it's hard to believe riding across Indiana could change your life. But it's the boxcar. It's magic . . . the moonlight . . .

CHUCK: Even Indiana.

LOU: Yes! Even Indiana! Exactly. That's the beauty of it. I'm glad I wasn't in West Virginia or someplace that really is beautiful or I wouldn't have gotten the full impact. It was the only time I rode. It scares me when I think back . . . not because I was alone . . .

I'm glad I was alone. I wouldn't have gotten the full impact if I wasn't alone. But when I think back, I'm lucky I didn't kill myself when I jumped off. I could've broken both legs. Then what? In the middle of a prairie. I could've died out there. I could've been eaten by wolves. People hop moving boxcars and they get sucked under the train and killed. That's the thing. I was so depressed and I did it all with such a sudden rush of abandon— almost suicidal . . . not completely suicidal. It wasn't guaranteed death, like jumping off a cliff. There was just a chance. But I didn't care. But I trust my motivations now. They're positive. I'm doing it to reward myself. And I'll wait until the train is stopped from now on before I hop on and off. But God, it's so amazing out in a boxcar. I was howling at the moon like a coyote.

CHUCK: Yeah well, I wouldn't know. I don't do boxcars.

LOU: Oh. Sorry. Where were we?

CHUCK: Gutter balls. Ever since the dawn of time there have been gutter balls.

LOU: I want to tell you something.

CHUCK *(Irritated)*: Can we write that down first?

LOU: I want to tell you now before we go any further.

CHUCK: Okay! What?

LOU: Because it may make a difference.

CHUCK: In what?

LOU: In general.

CHUCK: It won't. What?

LOU: This is my third college.

CHUCK: Uh-huh?

LOU: And I'm only twenty-two.

CHUCK: Okay?

LOU: I started college when I just turned seventeen. I was double-promoted twice. I was honor society.

CHUCK: Congratulations.

LOU: So, I dropped out of two colleges in two years. I was running from lovers.

CHUCK: So?

LOU: So, the second one was a woman.

CHUCK: Was it fun?

LOU: Fun? I don't know. I guess. Mostly. Until the end.

CHUCK: Well, good. Can we finish with the gutter balls?

LOU: Will you pose for me?

CHUCK: What?

LOU: I'm a photographer too. I want you to pose for me. Please?

CHUCK: Okay, sure. Now, please—

LOU: Nude.

(Pause.)

CHUCK: You're kidding, right?

LOU: No. It's an ongoing series I'm doing. People I know. I don't ask everybody I know to pose. Very few, actually. They have to have a certain charisma . . . not really charisma . . . more like audacity . . . audacity and a certain playfulness . . . the audacity to be playful. But I guess that's charisma. I've only asked four or five of my friends. And my aunt.

CHUCK: You took naked pictures of your aunt?

LOU: She's not like most aunts. She's real cool. What I do is I take their picture in their natural habitat—doing something they do every day, except nude. And they do it like they don't even realize they're nude. Just go about their business. Except nude. Like the one I took of my aunt, she was vacuuming. And my friend Gordon, the thing he does every day is wait for the stupid subway. So we went down to the subway late at night when no one was around. And he stood there naked waiting for the train. So with you, I'd probably do it in your dorm room working on your bowling paper. Except nude.

It's the juxtaposition of the mundane and the extraordinary. A statement about freedom. So will you do it?

CHUCK: I don't know.

LOU: Why not? Can't you handle it?

CHUCK: I can handle it!

LOU: Then you'll do it?

CHUCK: Maybe.

Scene 3

Chuck's dorm room. There are two beds, two desks, two dressers. Chuck and Lou enter.

CHUCK: Okay. You can sit on my lap again.

LOU: What?

CHUCK: The door's locked. Nobody's watching.

LOU *(Defensively)*: Why should I care about that?

(Lou sits on Chuck's lap.)

I smell cigars.
CHUCK: That's Cornelius. My roommate.
LOU: Your roommate!

(Lou jumps off Chuck's lap. A toilet flushes.)

CHUCK: Relax. Corny's deaf and blind.

(Cornelius enters from the bathroom tapping a white cane and smoking a cigar.)

Corny's the perfect roommate. If I blast my stereo, he doesn't care. We could do it in the next bed till we wake the dead and he won't care. Won't that be cool?

(Cornelius taps toward his bed.)

I guess they put him in here because this is the cripple room and all cripples go in the cripple room. Big bathroom and bars around the toilets. See that aerosol can? Spray it in the air.
LOU: What for?
CHUCK: That's how I get his attention. You can't just run up and grab him. He knows judo.
LOU: Does he really? No he doesn't.
CHUCK: Yes he does.
LOU: No he doesn't. Did you ever see him do it?
CHUCK: No. Do you want to grab him and find out?
LOU: How do you know he knows judo?
CHUCK: That's what he says to everybody. He says, "I have to warn you, don't just run up and grab me, because I know judo!"
LOU: He's just saying that.
CHUCK: Okay. Whatever. Spray the can.
LOU: I mean, he has to say something. He's totally defenseless.
CHUCK: Defenseless? Corny? Boy, he'd get a big laugh if he heard you say that.
LOU: You know what I mean.
CHUCK: He has a judo robe.

LOU: No he doesn't.

CHUCK: Right there in the closet.

LOU: He probably got it at a thrift store.

CHUCK: Forget it. Spray the can.

LOU: Pretty smart idea though.

CHUCK: Please spray the can!

(Lou sprays the aerosol.)

(Really loud) Honey, I'm home!

(Cornelius sniffs, stops, turns toward Chuck.)

CORNELIUS: Chuck?

(Cornelius reaches out for Chuck and discovers Lou.)

Oh. Excuse me. What's your name?

(Cornelius holds out his hand.)

CHUCK: Do you know how to finger spell?

LOU: You mean like the Miracle Worker?

CHUCK: Yes.

LOU: No.

CHUCK: Then write your name on his palm. With your finger. That's how the rookies do it.

(Lou writes her name.)

CORNELIUS: L-o-u. Lou. I see. You're a girl?

CHUCK: Tap his wrist once, that's "Yes."

(Lou taps his wrist. Cornelius drops to one knee, kisses her hand and stands.)

CORNELIUS: Charmed.

CHUCK: He's such a bullshitter.

CORNELIUS: But I have to warn you. Don't just run up and grab me because I know judo.

CHUCK: See! You know what else is real cool? Pull his shirttail.

LOU: Why?

CHUCK: You'll see. It's really cool. Pull it.

(Lou pulls Cornelius's shirttail.)

CORNELIUS: Philosophy.

CHUCK: You just asked his major.

CORNELIUS: And classic lit. You?

LOU *(To Chuck)*: Chemical engineering?

CHUCK: Oh God. It'll take you six weeks to spell that one. Just tap his wrist three times, that's "Don't know."

(Lou taps Cornelius's wrist.)

CORNELIUS: I see. Well, Godspeed. I'm off to do yoga.

(Cornelius kisses her hand again and taps over to his bed. He sits rigid on the bed and takes deep breaths. He strikes a yoga pose.)

CHUCK: That's the only time he gets pissed about the stereo. When he's doing yoga. I guess the vibrations fuck up his karma or something.

LOU: Was he born like that?

CHUCK: No. Brain damage. He took a brick in the head.

LOU: Oh God! How'd that happen?

CHUCK: Don't know. That's all he ever says. Brick in the head. Corny is so cool. He's a real salty dog! The first time I saw him and I said, "Where the hell am I?" I was about ready to repack all my shit and leave. But he's about my best friend now.

LOU: Really? Why?

CHUCK: He just is.

LOU: Why? How do you communicate with him?

CHUCK: We don't, really. I mean we do. We communicate a lot. We just sort of communicate by who we are. Who he is and who I am. It's just a thing. A weird thing. It's hard to explain. He's the one who gave me the idea to write about bowling. He's my role model in a lot of ways. I feel like an ass when I say that. I think role models are bullshit. But Corny's sort of one for me. Closest thing anyway. You gotta watch out for him, though. He's a bull-shitter. He only acts like that around women.

LOU: Like what?

CHUCK: All sophisticated. And Corny's a gambler too. Big time. He's got this bookie named Leo. Corny calls him his "broker." He takes Corny's money and bets it for him. He calls and says, "Tell Cornelius he hit on the trifecta." Corny's always a wreck on Sundays. At night I spell him all the football scores. If he wins big, he's like Scrooge on Christmas morning: dancing a jig and throwing money around. But if he loses, he's a wreck, like he's gonna die or something. You should see his killer crap games.

LOU: God! He sounds like an addict.

CHUCK: I think it's a survival thing. That's the only way he can get these dorm boys to do stuff for him: he flashes his wad. "Who wants twenty bucks to take me to the liquor store?" "Who wants twenty bucks to help me make a phone call?" And they all jump up and down: "Pick me! Pick me!"

LOU: That's terrible. I would never do that.

CHUCK: Me either. Well, okay, I did at first. He'd give me a ten spot if I'd let him hold on to my chair and walk him around. But I never charge him a cent anymore. That's another way you can tell if Corny's in the money. If he's broke, you see him going around campus holding on to my chair. But if he's got cash, he has me hire him a limo. He goes to classes in a limo. Or sometimes you'll see one of those dorm boys walking him around or toting his laundry. Because sometimes if he whips their asses in craps or poker, he takes it out in personal services. These are the Cornelius leading economic indicators.

LOU: That was my favorite movie when I was little. *The Miracle Worker.* I wanted to be Annie Sullivan.

Scene 4

Chuck's dorm room, a week later. Lou sits on Chuck's lap. Lou flips a coin.

LOU: Tails. Okay, you go first.

CHUCK: This is dumb.

LOU: Come on! Ask me a question.

CHUCK: I hate this true confessions crap.

LOU: Come on, Mr. Poop.

CHUCK: All right. So, when's the last time you had a seizure?

LOU: Come on!

CHUCK: I'm serious.

LOU: It's supposed to be something intimate and revealing. Something you really want to know.

CHUCK: I really want to know.

LOU *(Exasperated)*: Okay. Seven years ago.

CHUCK: Figures.

LOU: What do you mean, "figures"?

CHUCK: Where'd it happen?

LOU: What do you mean by "figures"?

CHUCK: By "figures," I mean figures. Where'd it happen?

LOU: None of your damn business.

CHUCK: Why not? Were you embarrassed?

LOU: Of course.

CHUCK: Why? Where'd it happen?

LOU: At a pep rally, okay!

CHUCK *(Laughing)*: A pep rally?

LOU: Yes! I was a cheerleader.

CHUCK *(Laughing)*: A cheerleader?

LOU: Yes.

CHUCK: You?

LOU: Yes!

CHUCK: Wait a minute. Why would big-brains, honor-society woman want to be a cheerleader?

LOU: I know. I hated it. But I see now I was trying to prove something. It was the last place someone with epilepsy belonged. That's why I wanted it real bad.

CHUCK: Figures.

LOU: Stop saying "figures"!

CHUCK: I'm surprised they let you try out.

LOU: They didn't know. God, are you kidding? Nobody knew. I knew they wouldn't let me if they knew. I was taking a lot of medication and I thought I had it under control. And then one day we were having a pep rally. And when I came to, there was a panic going on, like the gym was on fire.

(Chuck laughs hard.)

Shut up! It's not funny! The cheerleading coach humiliated me! She made me apologize to the whole squad! Right in front of all of them she says to me, "Imagine the destruction your deceitfulness would have caused, young lady, had you been in the middle of a human pyramid!"

CHUCK *(Still laughing hard)*: A pep rally! Oh God! Perfect!

LOU: I was embarrassed!

CHUCK: Why?

LOU: Because, damnit! It always happened to me that way. I'd never had a seizure when I was in my room by myself. I had one at Girl Scouts. I prayed to God I'd get through prom without having one.

CHUCK *(Laughing)*: Oh God! That would've really blew their minds!

LOU: It's not funny!

CHUCK: I'm jealous.

LOU: Shut up!

CHUCK: I am! It's not a curse. It's a gift.

LOU: Maybe to you.

CHUCK: So ever since then you take lots of medication.

LOU: They make them a lot better now.

CHUCK: Because you don't want to be embarrassed.

LOU: Are you saying I should stop taking medication?

CHUCK: I would.

LOU: Oh bullshit. You would not.

CHUCK: Sure I would. It's like wearing a toupee. What have I got to hide?

LOU: You are so full of shit! I can't believe how full of shit you are!

CHUCK: Who took you to the prom?

LOU: What if I had cancer?

CHUCK: What about it?

LOU: If I get chemo, am I a big sellout?

CHUCK: I'm surprised they didn't ban you from the prom.

LOU: Answer me. Do I just suffer to prove a point?

CHUCK: Who says you're suffering?

LOU: Answer me!

CHUCK: I did. Who says you're suffering? Are you suffering?

LOU: Yes.

CHUCK: How?

LOU: Everybody suffers.

CHUCK: Not me.

LOU: God, are you full of shit!

CHUCK: Suffering is, like, burning to death. That's about it. I've never been anywhere near suffering.

LOU: Well, I have.

CHUCK: Well, I'm happy for you. Who took you to the prom?

LOU: Nobody, okay! I went with some girlfriends.

CHUCK: Well, if I would've been there, I would've asked you. The minute I saw you lurching around on the gym floor in your little cheerleader outfit, I would've been in love.

LOU: Really?

CHUCK: Absolutely.

LOU: Bullshit.

CHUCK: I'm serious.

(They kiss.)

Would you kiss me if I was a drooler?

LOU: What!

CHUCK: Would you kiss me if I was a drooler?

LOU: Why do you always ask me stupid shit like this?

CHUCK: Ever kiss a drooler?

LOU: No. Have you?

CHUCK: No. But I would, if I met one that turned me on.

Scene 5

Chuck's dorm room, a few days later.

Cornelius sits on his bed. Chuck sits in his chair beside the bed. They're playing poker and smoking cigars. Chuck drinks Jack Daniel's straight from the bottle with a long straw. He wears headgear with a dowel rod protruding from it, which he uses to tap Cornelius's hand by nodding his head. They both have a pile of money beside them. Cornelius deals. He puts Chuck's cards in his card holder, which is a slotted block of wood. Chuck is pretty drunk. He plays along, but he's not interested in the card game.

CORNELIUS: Five card draw. Nothing wild. No sissy stuff.

CHUCK: Boxcars, man! Fucking boxcars!

(Cornelius feels the braille bumps on the top of his cards.)

CORNELIUS: Dealer takes two.

CHUCK: You know what she said about you? She said you were polite . . . gentle . . . no, genteel. That's what she said. Genteel.

(Cornelius discards.)

CORNELIUS: You? *(Chuck taps Cornelius's palm four times)* Four! Show me an ace! *(Chuck finally looks at his cards and taps Cornelius's leg three times)* I knew you didn't have an ace. Cheater.

(Cornelius takes three cards from Chuck's holder and replaces them with three more.)

CHUCK: Genteel. And I laughed. I said, "Are we talking about the same deaf and blind Cornelius? That ornery old fart!"

(Cornelius examines his cards.)

CORNELIUS: Oooh baby. Okay. Fifty cents. *(Throws money into the pot)* In or out?

CHUCK: She said she'd not seen your ornery side. And I said, "How can you help but see it? It's right there. Plain as—"

CORNELIUS: In or out, man? *(Chuck taps him on the shoulder)* See and raise! Oooh! Big man! Is he bluffing? *(He examines his cards and thinks)*

CHUCK: I said, "He just walks in the room and he's ornery."

CORNELIUS: Poker face.

CHUCK: Just when they think they got it all figured out, in walks Corny!

CORNELIUS: All right! He's bluffing! See it and raise! *(Throws in more money)*

CHUCK: That's why you're beautiful, man.

CORNELIUS: Come on! Are you in? *(Chuck taps his hand. Cornelius takes money from Chuck's pile and throws it in the pot)* He's in! Okay, I call! Flush! *(Takes Chuck's cards and feels the bumps)* Pair of jacks? Woo hoo! Dealer wins again! *(Scoops up the pot of money)*

CHUCK: Ornery Cornery!

(Cornelius shuffles the cards.)

CORNELIUS: Okay. Winner deals. And dealer's game is one-card gut. All you get is one card. Play what you got.

CHUCK: Corny the human monkey wrench! Corny the trump card! I roll in a great big cake and out pops Corny!

(Cornelius deals.)

CORNELIUS: Down and dirty.

CHUCK *(Continuing)*: Surpriiiiise! Take that, you high-and-mighty shitheads!

CORNELIUS *(Examines his card)*: All right. What's the bet? *(Holds out his hand)*

CHUCK: But you know what? She—

CORNELIUS: Come on. Just one card. *(Wiggles his hand impatiently)*

CHUCK: She's only twenty-two years old and she knows the names of all the Supreme Court Justices. I don't—I don't even know how many Supreme Court Justices there are. Six?

CORNELIUS: Hey! Did you pass out? *(Knocks on the table)*

CHUCK: She knows the names of all the seven dwarfs too. Miss Fucking Honor Society.

(Chuck doesn't even look at his card. He taps Cornelius on top of his head.)

CORNELIUS: A buck! Shit! *(Rubs his card and thinks)*

CHUCK: I know how many fucking seven dwarfs there are!

CORNELIUS: A buck. Shit.

CHUCK: Seven!

CORNELIUS: Chuck bets a buck.

CHUCK: I can't believe what she asked me the other day. She asked me if I'd ever been to Africa! Africa? And I'm—

CORNELIUS: What the hell! A buck! Call! *(Throws in a dollar and snaps down his card)* Red hot queen! Whadaya got? *(Grabs Chuck's card and feels the bumps)*

CHUCK: And I'm thinking, who the hell does she think I am? I've been to Jersey once. That's about it. You know what she says?

CORNELIUS: Whadaya got?

CHUCK: She says I'm very worldly.

CORNELIUS: Nine of spades? Ha! *(Scoops up the money)*

CHUCK: "Worldly"? Nobody ever called me that before.

CORNELIUS: Pizza break! *(Eats pizza)*

CHUCK: But later I'm thinking, hey, she's right. I guess I am worldly, man! I mean, I always thought I'm the opposite: social retard. Fifteen years behind on everything. Like I've been in a coma. But she's right. She's pretty damn sharp! I am worldly! Damn right I am! So what if I've never been past New Jersey! I've still been around! Yeah! I'm worldly, goddamnit! And you know what else she—

CORNELIUS: Ever eat possum?

CHUCK: What?

CORNELIUS: I did once. I ran it over with my car and I was curious.

CHUCK: You're a salty dog, Corny man!

(Cornelius eats pizza.)

Maybe that's why she asked me to pose naked for her, man. Because I'm worldly.

CORNELIUS: Possum meat's tough and dry.

CHUCK: Naked, Corny man! Can you believe that! Naked? Me? And I felt proud when she asked me, prouder than I ever felt before. This woman wants a naked picture of me. Scarred-up, crippled-up, dented-up me! This is one helluva sharp woman.

CORNELIUS: Hot sauce. Lots of hot sauce.

CHUCK: But then she's going on and on again about this boxcar. And I'm sitting there thinking, Oh sure. There's something we can run off and do together. No problemo! All we got to do is wait till a boxcar rolls by, door wide open—then shoot me out of a cannon!

CORNELIUS: Buddy of mine ate a raccoon. Shot it and ate it. Said it tastes like pork.

CHUCK: So you know what that means, don't you—all that boxcar crap? Soon as the semester's over it's, "See ya later, Chuck ol' pal. Sayonara."

CORNELIUS: People always ask me what I miss most. They think I'm gonna say music or the sunset or bullshit like that. I tell them I miss feeding my snake. I had a python. Esther. She looked like an Esther. I fed her a whole live chicken. Something brutally fascinating about watching her eat it. *(Eats pizza)*

CHUCK: You know what else I hate! I really hate that daredevil crap!

CORNELIUS: Possum on a pizza! Ha!

CHUCK: But that's what it takes to hit the mark with her, boy! That's the kind of man that gets her all juiced up! A boxcar-jumping maniac! Nothing sexier than a mummy in traction. Well, I'm sorry, darlin', but I don't need to break my neck to have a good time.

(Cornelius shuffles the cards.)

CORNELIUS: New game: Mexican Sweat.

CHUCK: Fucking boxcars!

Scene 6

Chuck's dorm room, a week later. Chuck sits in his wheelchair, naked, drinking beer, smoking a cigar and reading the term paper aloud. Lou circles around him, snapping his picture with a camera. Cornelius sits on his bed in a yoga pose.

CHUCK *(Reading)*: "Everybody envied my bowling ball. Custom-made. Urethane. A giant, translucent marble. Fire-engine red. Lightning bolts. And emblazoned across it in fiery letters, our Bowling Buddies team name: The Thunderbolts. Everybody envied it. I'm sure that's why they always elected me team captain."

LOU: Wait. You were team captain?

CHUCK: Yep. Six fucking seasons straight. Unanimous. And I wanted to get a black light bowling ball—glow in the dark. But the guy at the bowling ball store said he couldn't do that. And I had a cape. My mother made it. It was red, like my bowling ball, and it had lightning bolts. I looked like some flaming Zorro.

LOU: Do you still have it?

CHUCK: The cape? I don't know.

LOU: That would be the perfect picture: you wearing nothing but that cape. I could take it in a bowling alley.

CHUCK: Hey, I was a maniac. I kept statistics. I was such a maniac, I got in a big fight with a guy on another team. He was captain of the mongoloid team.

LOU: You're not supposed to call them that anymore.

CHUCK: That's what they called them back then. His name was Wilbur. He was big as a damn truck. And hey, he was asking for it. He really pissed me off! He rolled a strike every damn time! But big deal, he didn't even use a bowling ball. You know what he bowled with? A basketball! That's how they were at Bowling Buddies: whatever it takes to bowl a strike. I mean, hell, a guy in a coma could bowl 600, too, if they let him use a damn basketball! And whenever Wilbur bowled a strike he'd whoop it up like a drunken hillbilly. So finally, I got so damn pissed, I rammed him with my chair. And he went berserk and tried to strangle me! So that's when I bit his nose off.

LOU *(Stops taking pictures)*: You what!

CHUCK: Wait. Hold on. He was trying to strangle me. It was self-defense. I didn't bite the whole thing off, just the tip . . .

not even the whole tip, just a bunch of skin. But it bled like a bastard!

LOU: My God.

CHUCK: Hey, if he was an innocent little retard, my ass is a ginger-bread man.

LOU: But still—

CHUCK: And that's another thing about Bowling Buddies. They never kept score. That way, see, nobody gets hurt. Everything in life is one big happy-ass freakin' tie!

(Lou resumes taking pictures.)

Okay now, here's the part where it really gets ironic. *(Reading)* "It was the same thing with the satellite dish. My mother paid a fortune for the satellite dish, just like for my custom-made bowling ball. But if it hadn't been for the satellite dish, I would never have seen that guy who weighed nine hundred pounds. And if I hadn't seen the guy who weighed nine hundred pounds, I would never have woke up."

LOU: I remember that. Didn't he live in New Jersey?

CHUCK: Who knows. The point is, when I saw the guy who weighed nine hundred pounds, that's what made me go to college.

LOU: An epiphany.

CHUCK: Yeah. I guess so.

LOU: I have a lot of those.

CHUCK: Yeah, well, this guy weighed nine hundred pounds. He had big sagging tits like an orangutan. He had to wear a hospital gown. I guess they didn't make clothes that fit him. And when he died, they took him out of the house with a crane. And all the people were watching and they interviewed his mother and she was all distraught. And I remember thinking, "Damn, woman. Who the hell's been feeding him?" He couldn't even fit through the door. He pissed and shit in a bucket. So she must've spent all day just baking him pies and shit.

LOU: Yes. I definitely remember that. That's what I thought too: she was an enabler.

CHUCK: And then I got a chill because I thought, "Whoa! Wait a minute! That's me!" My mom spent all that money on that custom-made bowling ball and that satellite dish. And why? So she could feed me. Not food, but sports. To keep me fat and sedated. I was so stuffed and useless, pretty soon the only way you'd get me out of my room up in that attic would've been with a god-damn piece of heavy machinery . . . it's a cripple thing . . . it's like quarantine . . . it's like a lobotomy . . . it's like you're full of nitroglycerin and everybody's afraid one little shift of the wind and you'll explode.

LOU: See, that's why I hate sports: the opiate of the masses.

CHUCK: And that's the way they give us a lobotomy without us even knowing it: bowling! Pump us full of painkillers. And I never would've realized it if I didn't see them swinging that fat guy around with a crane like a grand piano. And I would've never saw it if I didn't have the satellite dish.

LOU *(Stops taking pictures)*: See! I told you you've suffered!

CHUCK: Think so, huh?

LOU: Oh yes! Absolutely. You don't think that's suffering?

CHUCK: No.

LOU: You just don't want to admit it.

CHUCK: So what if I don't?

LOU: So what if you don't.

(Lou resumes taking pictures.)

CHUCK: But my point is, I had to get the hell out of my mother's attic fast. So I went to college.

LOU: Please come see the comet with me! *(Stops taking pictures)*

CHUCK: Oh Lord, don't start on the comet again.

LOU: Please.

CHUCK: It's cold as hell.

LOU: So dress warm. It comes around every ten thousand years!

CHUCK: This comet shit always ends up in a damn argument.

LOU: Come on.

CHUCK: It's just like when I was a kid, about ten. There was this big hype about comet Kahoutek. It was the biggest bust of all time. My dad and mom got me out of bed. We went out in the yard . . . didn't see a damn thing. I saw a jet and I thought that was it.

LOU: This one's supposed to be as big as the moon.

CHUCK: There'll be ten thousand drunk frat boys up on Harper's Point having a comet party, blasting their boom boxes.

LOU: I don't want to go there. I've got a spot where no one will be. It's a clearing in the woods. No one's ever there. It's my secret spot.

CHUCK: It'll be cloudy.

LOU: How do you know? Jesus!

CHUCK: You can still go. You don't need me.

LOU: That's stupid. It's not the kind of thing you want to do alone.

CHUCK: Why not? I would.

LOU: It comes around every ten thousand years, Chuck! Don't you want to see a miracle?

CHUCK: I see miracles every day.

LOU: You know what I mean.

CHUCK: I do. I see miracles every day. I'm a miracle, you're a miracle. Corny's definitely a miracle. That camera is a miracle. This beer can's a miracle. Out of that great big bang we got me and you and this beer can. Everything's a miracle, considering the odds against it.

LOU: But this is the miracle of miracles.

CHUCK: It's cold as hell. I'll catch pneumonia if I stay up all night. I'll get a sore on my ass.

LOU: I know what you're really afraid of.

CHUCK: Oh really!

LOU: You're afraid to realize that you can't appreciate beauty. Because a miracle is the essence of beauty. So if you can't appreciate a miracle, you can't appreciate beauty. And so you avoid beauty and make fun of it. And I know, because I was the exact same way. Except I was the opposite. I was afraid I'd appreciate beauty too much. And that can get you in a lot of trouble. So I avoided it, too. It's a terrible thing.

CHUCK: Nice try, Freud. But you know what I think? I think people who have to stick their head in an alligator's mouth just to feel like they're alive are the ones who can't appreciate miracles. And I think the ones who really can't appreciate beauty are people who think suffering is cool!

LOU: I suppose that's supposed to mean me!

CHUCK: Anyone who's ever had third-degree burns all over their body, anyone who's ever been tortured, the last thing that they want is for anything like it to ever happen again.

LOU: I suppose you know! I suppose you've been tortured!

CHUCK: Without suffering, life would sure be empty, wouldn't it?

LOU: Oooh, look who's talking about empty lives—the boy who's never been past New Jersey.

CHUCK: Hey, I never—

LOU: It's just a comet, Chuck! Jesus, would it kill you? What are you so afraid of?

CHUCK: What am I afraid of? You think you know all about what a daredevil is. Well guess what, I'm a daredevil, baby! I'm a daredevil like you never saw! Sometimes just dragging my ass out of bed in the morning is like jumping across the Grand Canyon! Who the hell needs comets and boxcars?

LOU: I have no idea what you're talking about. It's just a comet.

CHUCK: It's not the comet! It's the principle!

LOU: Look, I'll never intrude on you again, Chuck, okay? I'll go see the comet, and you stay home and watch arm wrestling! And I promise I will never again try to take away your precious little excuses for inaction!

CHUCK: Look who's talking about excuses for inaction! Nobody loves those more than those pseudo-sufferers. They wallow in it. Emotional hypochondriacs!

LOU: Look, I'm not afraid to take my suffering and name it!

CHUCK: Name it? It's not a fucking pet!

LOU: Just shove it, okay?

CHUCK: What did you name it? Spot? . . . Princess?

(Lou opens the camera, rips the film out, exposing it, and throws it on the ground.)

LOU: Thank you, Chuck, for putting me so in touch with how stupid I am. I can't believe I was stupid enough to think you might be someone who would find some significance in a cosmic phenomenon! And I really can't believe I was stupid enough to think you had the fortitude to pose for me!

CHUCK: Okay, I changed my mind, I'll go see the comet.

LOU: Don't patronize me!

CHUCK: I'm not.

LOU: How dare you call me an emotional hypochondriac! You might as well spit on me than call me something like that!

CHUCK: I'm sorry. I didn't mean it.

LOU: Yes you did!

CHUCK: Okay, I did. But so what, nobody's perfect.

LOU: See what I mean?

CHUCK: What about me? You said I don't have fortitude. That's a cruel thing to say, too.

LOU: Well you don't.

CHUCK: I got fortitude. I got fortitude coming out of my ass. I'll prove it: take my picture.

LOU: Forget it.

CHUCK: Come on. I'll make you a deal. You take my picture and I'll go see the comet.

LOU: Gee, thanks. There's nothing I enjoy more than watching comets with people who couldn't care less.

CHUCK: I'll care. I'll care because it's real important to you. And you'll take my picture because it's real important to me. Fair deal, right? Come on.

LOU: You don't give a damn about anything.

CHUCK: Yes I do! This picture. I don't want to blow it. Hell, posing like this is the highlight of my year. I don't know why, I just really want this picture. For a souvenir, I guess. I don't know. So, come on. Please.

LOU: Is this really the highlight of your year?

CHUCK: Year? Hell, decade. Pretty pathetic, huh?

LOU: But I don't have to put up with this! And I won't!

CHUCK: I'm serious. I promise. I'm so damn serious that if it's cold when we go see the comet I'll wear long underwear. That's pretty damn serious for me because I don't even wear regular underwear. So come on, take my picture.

LOU: Well, I've lost the inspiration now. I can't just turn it on and off like a switch.

CHUCK: Well, try maybe warming up some. Take some pictures without any film in the camera until you get the muse back.

(Lou takes pictures with the empty camera.)

A big retarded guy bowling with a basketball. You don't think that's a miracle?

LOU: But I'm keeping the negatives! And I swear to God if you start up with me one more time, I'll flush them down the fucking toilet!

CHUCK: I won't.

(Lou takes pictures.)

Scene 7

Chuck's dorm room. Chuck and Lou are in bed. Chuck is sound asleep. Lou is sitting up, wide awake, smoking, looking like she's been thinking hard. She nudges Chuck.

LOU: Hey! Wake up!

CHUCK: What?

LOU: Wake up!

CHUCK: I'm awake! What?

LOU: What if I want to drive a car?

CHUCK: Huh?

LOU: What if I want to drive a car?

CHUCK: What about it?

LOU: If I don't take my medication, I could have a seizure behind the wheel.

CHUCK: Uh-huh.

LOU: So, I could kill myself. And maybe somebody else. Maybe a little baby! Am I supposed to kill myself and maybe a little baby, just to prove a political point?

CHUCK: So take your medication.

LOU *(Victoriously)*: I will!

(Pause.)

CHUCK: What the hell were you doing in Indiana?

LOU: On the boxcar? That's where I'm from.

CHUCK: Really? Damn.

(Chuck goes back to sleep. Lou rises from the bed. A throne rolls in with Barnes the devil sitting on it. Lou reads from the bowling paper:)

LOU *(Melodramatic reading)*: "Brutality? Some may say I use too strong a word. But in the final analysis, I think not. For oppression in any form is brutality—be it blatant, be it subtle, be it wrapped like smug nobility in the insidious cloak of benevolence . . . The end."

BARNES: Fascinating approach to the subject matter.

LOU: Really?

BARNES: Oh my word, yes.

LOU: Great! I wrote the ending myself.

BARNES: It has your imprimaturs.

LOU: You really like our paper?

BARNES: It's not about bowling at all, is it?

LOU: No, exactly! It's about discrimination, and pain!

BARNES: Man's inhumanity to man.

LOU: Yes—oppression! Like I said, oppression, and paternalism, humiliation.

BARNES: Teeming with righteous anger.

LOU: Yes! And it's the kind of dehumanization thousands of us endure every day.

BARNES: Shameful.

LOU: I myself have endured it in many forms. I never realized it before, but I have.

BARNES: Oh, I'm sure.

LOU: Like when I was in junior high, my family took a vacation to Iowa. We wouldn't be caught dead in Iowa, but there was this shrine there. It was a weather-beaten Virgin Mary statue in the middle of a farmer's field. They said if people kissed her forehead, miracles would happen.

(Barnes rises from his throne and approaches Lou.)

BARNES: Amazing.

LOU: Blind people would see.

BARNES: Really? May I?

LOU: Of course. *(Hands him the paper; he flips through it)* We waited in a long line of blind people, hunchbacks, thalidomide babies, dwarfs. My brothers and sisters were mad that we had to take this kind of stupid vacation because of me. *(Barnes pulls a cigarette lighter out of his pocket)* And then I had to get up on this stepladder, right in front of everybody, and kiss her forehead.

BARNES: You must have felt so—violated! *(Flicks the lighter on)*

LOU: Yes! And my mother took my picture and she made copies and sent it to the whole family!

(Barnes sets the paper on fire.)

What the hell are you doing?!

BARNES: Do go on, please.

LOU: Sonuvabitch! What are you doing?!

BARNES: It's not about bowling at all, is it?

(Lou grabs the burning paper from Barnes, drops it on the floor and stomps on it.)

LOU: You bastard!

(Barnes slowly exits into smoke, laughing. Light comes up on Chuck in bed. He wakes up and sees Lou stomping the floor.)

CHUCK: What the hell are you doing?!

(Lou looks around, groggy and confused.)

Act Two

Scene 1

The cafeteria. Chuck sits at the table, alone and anxious. Lou enters quickly.

CHUCK: Where the hell have you been?

LOU: I was up all night. I had another epiphany. Here, I took notes.

CHUCK: Oh God.

LOU *(Flipping through a notebook)*: Yeah. And the best thing is, it's really good stuff for the bowling paper! It's all about Ken. Thinking about this paper brought me to a realization about him. And all this time I've been punishing myself.

CHUCK: Excuse me—Ken?

LOU: Okay. Sorry. Let me back up. Remember I told you I dropped out of college because I was running from a lover? Well, that was Ken.

CHUCK: The guy one.

LOU: The guy one. Right.

CHUCK: The first one.

LOU: Yes. The way we met was kind of strange. We met when I called a suicide hotline. Yes, I know it's weird and sick, but it seemed romantic at the time. I wasn't really going to kill myself. I could never do that.

CHUCK: Good.

LOU: I just wanted to be pampered.

CHUCK: So you called the suicide hotline.

LOU: Yes. I was feeling overwhelmed! And he was so kind and sweet and funny. I remember somehow we got to talking about square dancing. Somehow it went from this obsession I have with getting straight As to square dancing. I think his parents were square dance callers. That's what it was! And we laughed about that. And then he says, "You know this is one hundred and ten percent against the rules, but . . ." And he asked me out for pizza. And he was so sweet and so funny. And we made love. And he was so kind and he called me angel. And when he reached climax he had tears in his eyes. And I remember what he said . . . I'll never forget it. He said, "I don't know how anyone can just fall asleep after making love. I feel so alive! I feel like writing a symphony!" And then, the next morning, while I was in the shower, he left. And I left messages for him at the suicide hotline and he never called back. I left messages like, "Tell him LuLu called and I'm going to kill myself!"

CHUCK: LuLu?

LOU: And then one day when I called they said he didn't work there anymore. But here's where the epiphany part comes in.

CHUCK: Good.

LOU: I went around for weeks just wrecked. I get like that. Because he was my first lover. I'd just turned seventeen. I'm wondering, How could he do something like that? And then it hit me: he's a pharmacist!

(Pause.)

CHUCK: A pharmacist.

LOU: Yes!

CHUCK: Okay?

LOU: Or studying to be one. And I realized that while I was in the shower, he probably saw my medication. That explained it! To anyone else it wouldn't mean a thing, but he put it all together and figured out I had epilepsy. But here's the epiphany part: I realize now he didn't screw me like that because he was a pharmacist. You know why he did?

CHUCK: Why?

LOU: Not because he was a pharmacist. He screwed me like that because he was a prick!

CHUCK: Definitely!

LOU: I mean, maybe he did see my medication, but that's not why he screwed me over. He screwed me over because he was a prick! Pure and simple!

CHUCK: And an idiot too.

LOU: So I want to write this up and put it in the paper. It fits right in with the Bowling Buddies.

CHUCK: And I bet his name wasn't even Ken. A lot of times on those hotlines they use an alias.

LOU: Wow. Maybe.

CHUCK: And I bet the reason he signed up for the suicide hotline was because he wanted to get laid. I know guys that would do that. And I bet that stuff about his parents calling square dance—I bet he made that up too, just to get laid. I know guys that would do that too.

LOU: Well, I want to write all this up and put it in the paper. Don't you think it's a great epiphany?

CHUCK: Definitely. And I figured out something about the paper, too. While you read it, I'm gonna sit right next to you holding my bowling trophy—

LOU: You still have that thing?

CHUCK: Yep. And I found my cape too. It's got the chapter sponsor's name on the back: Conroy Funeral Home.

LOU: I can't believe you still have those things.

CHUCK: I started to throw it all into an incinerator once, but I told myself that was the chicken-shit way out. Gotta come to terms with it. Now I'm glad I didn't. Because now I've got the perfect answer. While you read the paper, I'm gonna sit right next to you in the whole get-up. And I'm gonna just stare at Barnes hard the whole time. And every once in a while I'm gonna shout out, "Look at me, damnit! Look at me!"

LOU: Oh God!

CHUCK: You think that'll blow his mind?

LOU: I think he'll call the campus police.

CHUCK: You think so? God, that would be perfect!

Scene 2

Chuck's dorm room. Lou enters, all bundled up in winter clothes. She has a blanket and a picnic basket. Cornelius stands on his bed doing martial arts motions.

LOU: Chuck? *(Knocks on the bathroom door)* Chuck? *(Still no response, so she sprays the aerosol)*

CORNELIUS: Chuck? *(Lou takes his hand and spells)* Lou! *(Kisses her hand)*

LOU *(Spelling)*: Where's . . . Chuck?

CORNELIUS: Sorry, my dear. Haven't seen him.

LOU: Damnit! You're kidding!

CORNELIUS: Haven't seen him all day.

LOU: Damnit! This is such bullshit! *(Spelling)* We . . . had . . . a date . . . to . . . see . . . the . . . comet.

CORNELIUS: Really. And he's not here?

LOU: Christ, I can't believe what an idiot I am! I can't believe I fell for all his bullshit about—

CORNELIUS: I apologize for his rudeness.

LOU: Nothing pisses me off more than being stood up! Especially this! It's once every ten thousand years! God, I hate him!

CORNELIUS: I bet you're angry.

LOU: Furious! God, what a manipulator!

CORNELIUS: Are you angry?

LOU *(Spelling)*: Fuck . . . him!

CORNELIUS: Whoa! You are mad! Well, you certainly have every right.

LOU: Hell yes! I just knew it. I'm such an idiot! Why does he love making me feel like an idiot? I've never been screwed like this before. Am I supposed to go alone now?!

Scene 3

Lou's secret spot. Lou and Cornelius are sitting on the ground bundled in winter clothes. Cornelius has a blanket wrapped around him. There are two wine glasses and a wine bottle next to the picnic basket. Cornelius is smoking a joint.

LOU: So I guess, technically, I'd have to say I'm a bisexual. I mean, if I'm really being honest. It was just the one time, but I kind of hope it's not the last . . . if I'm being really honest.

(Cornelius offers the joint to Lou. Lou guides his hand toward her mouth and takes a hit.)

CORNELIUS: Jamaican.

LOU: Very good . . . very mellow. *(Takes another hit)* But anyway, her name was Lucy and she was a grad student. And she dumped me just before spring break. And I was so full of anger. I felt as if I gave up my religion for her . . . and as soon as I did, boom! I felt like I'd renounced my rights to the throne just for her. And there was no way I could say to my parents . . .

CORNELIUS: Still cloudy?

LOU *(Taps his wrist)*: Yes. Damnit.

CORNELIUS: I see. Describe me.

LOU *(Spelling)*: What?

CORNELIUS: Describe me. In one word. My essence.

LOU: Your essence? *(Thinks about it for a while, then spells in his hand)*

CORNELIUS: M-y-p-

LOU: No. Wait. *(Spells again)*

CORNELIUS: M-y-s-t-i-c-a-l. Mystical. I see. I'll accept that. And my word for your essence is . . . vibrant.

LOU: Vibrant. *(Tugs on his thumb)*

CORNELIUS: You're welcome.

LOU: Vibrant.

CORNELIUS: Chuck's not mystical.

LOU *(Spelling)*: Fuck . . . him.

CORNELIUS: Chuck doesn't have an essence.

LOU *(Spelling)*: Fuck . . . him!

(Long pause. Lou takes a drink from her wine glass and hands it to Cornelius.)

But it was clearly my own damn fault with Lucy. I can see that now. I got too clingy, like I always do. When I fall, I fall hard. My problem is . . .

CORNELIUS: Good wine. Very dry. Very bold. French? *(Lou spells in his hand)* Domestic? Really?

LOU *(Spelling)*: Napa . . . Valley.

CORNELIUS: Incredible. Chablis?

LOU *(Taps his wrist)*: Yes.

CORNELIUS: You seem like a Chablis girl. *(As Lou spells in his hand, he clutches her hand with both of his)* Goodness. Your hands are ice. *(He puts his arm around her, pulls her close to him, and wraps the blanket around both of them. Lou goes along with it, a little apprehensively)* Better?

LOU: Yes.

(Long pause.)

Everything is so vast. My dad's best friend is an orthodontist and he takes vacations in Egypt. He takes a boat deep into the river Nile. He says there's butterflies with two-foot wing spans. And if—

CORNELIUS *(Reciting poetry)*:
> The moon more indolently dreams tonight
> Than a fair woman on her couch at rest,
> Caressing, with a hand distraught and light,
> Before she sleeps, the contour of her breast.
> And when at times, wrapped in her languor deep,
> Earthward she lets a furtive tear-drop flow,
> Some pious poet, enemy of sleep,
> Takes in his hollow hand the tear of snow.
> Whence gleams of iris and of opal start,
> Hides it from the sun, deep in his heart.

LOU *(Spelling)*: That's . . . beautiful.
CORNELIUS: Baudelaire. "The Sorrow of the Moon."

(Cornelius attempts to stick his tongue in Lou's ear, but she's looking skyward and doesn't notice. Lou stands up suddenly.)

LOU: Oh my God! Oh my God! *(Shakes Cornelius vigorously)*
CORNELIUS: I'm sorry!
LOU: Oh my God! It's incredible! Oh my God! *(She spells in his hand)*
CORNELIUS: The comet! Oh!

(Lou taps his wrist and spells in his hand.)

It's . . . organic?
LOU: No! *(Tries again)*
CORNELIUS: It's . . . or-gas-mic.
LOU: Yes!
CORNELIUS: Oooh!

(Cornelius kneels beside Lou, hugging her waist.)

LOU: Oh my God! Big as the moon! At least! I can't believe—

CORNELIUS: Describe it.

LOU: Oh my God! It's a ball of fire! With a tapering tail! *(Spells in his hand)*

CORNELIUS: A . . . blazing . . . sperm?

LOU: Yes!

CORNELIUS: I see.

LOU: Oh my God! It's so amazing!

CORNELIUS: Fuck Chuck.

LOU: It's a miracle! I will never be the same!

CORNELIUS: This is the perfect moment.

LOU: I'm just a speck. Less than a speck. In the whole universe, I'm just . . . a blink of the eye. And yet, somehow, realizing that brings me great peace . . . Oh shit! Damn clouds! Damnit! No!

(Lou kneels next to Cornelius.)

CORNELIUS: It's incredible!

LOU *(Spelling)*: It's gone.

(Cornelius slowly sits down on the blanket next to Lou. They kiss.)

Scene 4

The cafeteria. Lou reads the bowling paper with a disturbed look on her face. Chuck sits next to her, scowling, waiting for her to finish. Lou pushes it aside.

LOU: I don't want to do this anymore.

CHUCK: What?

LOU: You know what . . . all this stuff about the Bowling Buddy kid with the colostomy bag.

CHUCK: Hey, it's real!

LOU: It's way too graphic.

CHUCK: So?

LOU: It goes on for five pages!

CHUCK: Yeah, so?

LOU: And you want me to stand up there and read this to Barnes and all those sniggering jocks?

CHUCK: Why not?

LOU: This is a paper for a gym class, Chuck. A gym class, remember?

CHUCK: I knew I'd lose you when it got real.

LOU: You're a creep.

CHUCK: Can't take it, huh? How're you ever gonna be Annie Sullivan? *(Lou stands and collects her things)* I would never have gotten to first base with you if I was a drooler, would I! You're too high-and-mighty.

LOU: Go fuck yourself.

CHUCK: I wouldn't have even got out of the dugout if I had a colostomy bag!

LOU: Good-bye, Chuck.

CHUCK: I wrote this stuff last night, you know.

LOU: What a surprise! You were buried in your precious paper.

CHUCK: And you were out looking at the comet.

LOU: Damn right I was!

CHUCK: I bet it was goddamn breathtaking.

LOU: Oh yes, it was. An incredible miracle! Sorry to disappoint you. I know you were doing your fucking rain dance and all. And you know what was even more incredible? I found someone to go with me. And we got stoned and drunk. And we went back to my room and humped our brains out, mister! And I came so hard—oh my God—I thought I would never stop. Way better than I ever did with you. And not only was he a drooler, Mister Superior, he was way worse than a drooler!

CHUCK: Cornelius!

LOU: You got it! It was the night of his life. And it could have been you, but you stood me up, motherfucker!

CHUCK: Holy shit!

LOU: And I'm going to see him later. And you know where he's taking me?

CHUCK: Coney Island.

LOU: What? How did you know?

CHUCK: He didn't give you my note, did he?

LOU: What?

CHUCK: My note. I knew it! That slimy sonuvabitch! He set us up.

LOU: What!

CHUCK: Jesus Christ, I'll kill that bastard! I didn't stand you up. I was just late. I got a flat tire on my chair and I had to get it fixed. I tried to get a hold of you, but I couldn't. So I told him we were going to see the comet and to tell you I'd be back. I gave him a note explaining it all and I told him to give it to you.

LOU: You're a liar! Cornelius wouldn't do that to me.

CHUCK: What, you think you're the first one? You think you're Florence Nightingale? Big old martyr giving it up for poor Corny? He's got a harem! He gets them with that routine: "Oh poor me. Ever since I took a brick in the head, no one understands me." Or he gets them with the charmer thing: Corny the hand-kisser. That sensitive deaf and blind poet crap. Or he rents a limo. That's how you're going to Coney Island, right? In a limo. A white one, right?

LOU: Yes.

CHUCK: With red interior and a wet bar. He had me call to set it up this morning. That was the sonuvabitch's little subtle way of gloating about it. Remember I said he was an inspiration? My role model? That's why. Here he is, deaf and blind, and somehow the women eat it up. He's got a harem. How the hell does he do it? Where I come from, cripples just sit in the attic and jerk off all day.

LOU: Jesus, I've never been screwed like this before!

CHUCK: Guess what? He's renting a tuxedo to wear to Coney Island. He had me set that up too.

LOU: Oh my God!

CHUCK: Next time I ought to walk his blind ass out in front of a truck!

LOU: Shut up!

CHUCK: You think I'm a liar? I still got my long johns on. I'll prove it. Unzip my pants.

LOU: Stop it!

CHUCK: I dare you! Unzip my pants!

LOU: Stop it! I can't hear you! I can't hear you! *(Singing loudly)* "Deck the halls with boughs of holly!" *(Sticks her fingers in her ears)* "Fa la la la la la la la la. Fa la la la la la la la la."

(Long pause.)

Damnit! I asked him what he misses most, and he said riding the roller coaster. So we decided to go to Coney Island. The roller coaster was supposed to be a compromise. He wanted me to elope! And I might've done it, if it wasn't for finals. But when he asked me to elope, I almost did it. But now I can see what made me so excited—the same reason my orgasm was so powerful.

CHUCK: Yeah. You were bombed.

LOU: No, please! When he asked me to elope, I pictured bringing him home to meet my parents. "Mom, Dad, this is my husband,

Cornelius!" Oh God, they'd have coronaries! And that's what excited me. I've got millions of things I want to say to them, so many things I've been feeling lately. But I'm too much of a coward to say it. But Cornelius is worth a thousand words. He says it all. I was using him to show them how much I've changed. And not just show them but really rub their noses in it! Damnit, none of this would've ever happened if I wasn't so fucking selfish all the time. But all I ever think about is me, myself and me. I'm a user. I used him, I used you. I'm so sorry. I'm really really really really really really sorry. And now I've wounded you. And I should go. I should just go, because the only decent thing for me to do is just go, because I did it again and I wounded you, and the longer I stay here, the longer it just festers and grows and . . . But we have to do the mature thing, Chuck. And the mature thing is to somehow find it within ourselves to just put everything aside and finish this paper and do our presentation, and then I can graduate and then I'll leave you alone forever, Chuck, and hope that somehow, somewhere, you'll heal from all the wounds I've caused you.

CHUCK: Wait a minute! What the hell are you—

LOU: But let me just say this one last thing. I don't care, Chuck, if I'm eighty years old. Whenever I pass a bowling alley, I'll never look at it in the same way ever again.

CHUCK: Jesus! I knew this was coming. Well guess what, I don't want your goddamn Purple Heart. I quit.

LOU: You can't quit now!

CHUCK: Fuck maturity! I quit!

LOU: You've got a lot of nerve talking about Barnes being a sadistic bastard.

CHUCK: I don't care! Who the hell needs you to write about cripple bowling. You're just dead weight.

LOU: See what I mean! If you weren't such a— No wonder I believed Cornelius. As soon as I saw you weren't even in your room, after I spent all afternoon buying wine and brie and biscotti and hot cider—of course I believed it! It made perfect sense. Of course you'd screw me like that to get off the hook. You'd screw your own grandmother!

CHUCK: Well at least my grandmother would have the sense not to let Corny—

LOU: And the way you pump him up, it's sick! "Oh Corny, oh Corny. He's so cool. He's just God!" No wonder I believed it.

CHUCK: Look, what do you want me to say? You win, all right? You kissed a drooler first. You win the bet. You win the Nobel cripple-fucking prize, all right! So fine, so who needs me? So do your own paper. I wouldn't write about cripple bowling with you if I was on my deathbed!

LOU: Okay, well, screw you too then. I'll do my own paper.

CHUCK: Oh you will, huh? All by yourself?

LOU: Watch me.

CHUCK: What do you know about cripple bowling?

LOU: A lot. More than you think.

CHUCK: You're gonna get up in front of all those jocks, all by yourself, and talk about cripple bowling?

LOU: Why not?

CHUCK: Lotsa luck, sweetheart.

Scene 5

The gymnasium. Barnes enters, sarcastically wiping tears from his eyes and blowing his nose with his penalty flag. He plays canned applause on a boom box.

BARNES: What a breathtaking exposé. Thank you so much, Stanley and Esther. Never has anyone so eloquently captured the subtle poetry of badminton. And now we have what promises to be a very special event. We have Chuck, a quadriplegic, and Lou, WHO'S AN EPILEPTIC! And their report is entitled "The History of Bowling."

(Barnes exits, playing more canned applause. Chuck and Lou enter from opposite sides. Chuck wears his Bowling Buddies cape. Chuck comes forward. Sound fades.)

CHUCK: The history of bowling. So, I'm sitting there naked as the emperor, right? And this woman I just met a month ago is taking my picture. How the hell did this happen, I'm saying to myself? What does this have to do with bowling? But all the while that I'm sitting there naked, I can't stop thinking about Wilbur. I'm thinking about the mongoloid bus. They brought all the mongoloids to Bowling Buddies in a big yellow bus. And on the side it said "St. Mary's Home for Mongoloids." And you never knew what that Wilbur might do if he bowled a strike. He was dangerous. One time he got so excited he whipped off his clothes and sprinted through Rainbow Lanes. And he got all the way to the snack bar before the Bowling Buddies tackled him. And I'm sitting there naked, and I'm thinking that maybe the reason I bit Wilbur's nose off was because I was jealous. Can you imagine, me, jealous of a mongoloid? But maybe I was jealous because he was so much more dangerous than me. And I'm sitting there naked, and suddenly I'm feeling like this is sweet revenge. I'm getting revenge for Wilbur. I'm getting revenge for the fat guy. I'm getting revenge for Little Miss Honor Society and I'm getting revenge for me. Because I'll tell you what it's all about: shame. Stupid, worthless shame. That's what makes us kiss the Virgin's forehead: shame. And that's why they locked the mongoloids up in a home, because they felt no shame. And when they felt no shame, they were dangerous. So I guess that's what it is, I say to my naked self. I want to take this picture and blow it up fifty by fifty. And I want to put it up on a big old billboard, right along the interstate. Me and my bare crippled ass! Praise the Lord! At long, long last, I am officially shameless!

(Barnes plays cricket sounds on his boom box. Chuck recedes, and Lou steps forward and stands on a chair.)

LOU: The history of bowling. For the first time in my life Gary, Indiana, was beautiful! "Hello, you big, beautiful smokestack! Mmm, take a big bite of that delicious smog." The rusty moan of the slowing train wheels . . . the surging determination . . . the moonlight . . . a prairie. Impenetrable darkness . . . only cool moonlight. What made me jump? I was suddenly sane. A searing slap in the face. "Oh dear God, I have epilepsy. I could have a seizure! Out here! In this boxcar! They'll find me dead. Get me out of here!" I leaped.

(Lou jumps down from the chair.)

A prairie, pitch black. Thank God for the moonlight. A prairie, a mine field. Each step could be my last. I could be eaten by wolves. Run! Rattlesnakes. Run or die! Run! Light, man-made light. Civilization! A train depot. Run! Civilization. Kiss the earth!

(Lou kisses the earth.)

Meanwhile, in tiny Hendersonville, Indiana—it's two A.M. at the train depot. All is calm. Suddenly, in the thick darkness, a commotion. And then this creature, this alien being, pulls herself onto the platform, like an amphibian from the lagoon. She's vaguely humanoid. She's covered with mud. Her clothes are shreds. She's panting. Her eyes are wild. And when she tries to speak—a giant, invisible fist seizes her and spins her around and slams her to the platform! The creature convulses—like a corpse with a thousand volts shooting through it—like a screeching, writhing mule attacked by a swarm of bees!

And when I came to, an old woman had fainted. Children were crying. A man in a black overcoat hovered above, gulping with fear, his arms extended, his sheriff's badge in one hand, a gun in the other. Sirens blaring, tornado sirens. "Now you just keep still right there. I called the volunteer fire department."

They rushed me to the hospital. And they gave me eight stitches—right here. *(Lifts her shirt to reveal a small scar, just below her breast)* And that's how I got this scar. This is my bowling trophy, my funny little cripple battle scar. And now I love my bowling trophy. I take it with me everywhere I go. I'm proud of my bowling trophy. No one ever got a bowling trophy the way I got this one. And no one ever will. This is one sexy bowling trophy.

(Brief silence before Barnes steps onstage sobbing. His sobbing gradually turns into hysterical, derisive laughter as he exits. Lou sits in the chair. Chuck pulls up next to her slowly, cautiously, but she looks away and doesn't acknowledge him.)

CHUCK: But you know what would really suck? Having a stomach tube. There was a Bowling Buddy kid with a stomach tube. That would suck so bad. You could never taste food again. No more lasagna, no more beer. Torture!

(Pause. No response from Lou.)

Man, that would suck. But then, you know, maybe after you got through all that cold turkey there would be, like, this great inner peace, like a Buddhist. Food is a big distraction. So maybe getting a stomach tube is really liberating.

(Pause. Still no response from Lou.)

Yeah, sometimes I wonder what I would've accomplished if I'd have had a stomach tube. I might be a completely different guy. I might've written a bunch of operas and stuff. Oh well, so what. I think I'm gonna drop out anyway.

LOU: You can't do that.

CHUCK: Why not?

LOU: You've got to finish your degree!

CHUCK: Oh yeah, that's real important. "Look out world, here comes another fucking English major."

(Pause.)

But what would suck worst of all would be to have a stomach tube and be on death row. Because when you're on death row, the one thing you have to look forward to is that last meal. But if you've got a stomach tube, you're screwed.

LOU: That's dumb.

CHUCK: Why?

LOU: Because you're going to die anyway, so just forget about the tube and go ahead and eat. So what if you get sick and die.

CHUCK: Yeah, but what if the governor calls?

LOU: The governor never calls. That only happens in the movies.

CHUCK: Well, just my luck, he'd call.

LOU: I don't want to talk about stomach tubes.

(Pause.)

And see, if you drop out, all you'll do is go back to that attic. And you'll spend all day thinking about stupid shit like stomach tubes.

CHUCK: Hey, that ain't such a bad life.

(Pause.)

So when's the next freight train?

LOU: How should I know?

CHUCK: I thought you'd have the train schedule tattooed on the back of your eyelids.

LOU: Well, maybe I'll stick around. Maybe I'll go to grad school.

CHUCK: Maybe I won't drop out. Maybe I'll major in PE.

END OF PLAY

Besides *The History of Bowling*, Chicago playwright MIKE ERVIN also wrote *The Plucky and Spunky Show* (with Susan Nussbaum). It was originally produced at Remains Theatre in Chicago in 1990, and later at Perseverance Theatre in Juneau, Cyrano's Off Center Playhouse in Anchorage, and The Magic Theater in Omaha. Mr. Ervin also contributed to *Activities of Daily Living*, which was produced at Blue Rider Theater in Chicago in 1994. His short story "Coitus Interruptus" appears in *Staring Back: The Disability Experience from the Inside Out*.

As a journalist, Mr. Ervin has published more than one thousand articles and essays—mostly on disability topics and jazz—in more than forty newspapers and magazines, including the *Chicago Tribune*, *Los Angeles Times*, *Progressive* and *Downbeat*. A longtime member of the direct action disability rights group ADAPT, he is proud to have been arrested more than a dozen times protesting for accessibility.

GRETTY
GOOD TIME

John Belluso

Gretty (Ann Stocking, left) and McCloud (Pamela Gordon) in the Falcon Theatre production, Burbank, California, 1999. Photo by Wesley Horton.

Author's Statement

Gretty Good Time was written out of a curiosity about the history of people with disabilities. While studying playwriting at NYU's Tisch School of the Arts, I began to investigate the realities of life for people who lived their lives in wheelchairs, as I do, but in other historical moments. I sought out the work of great playwrights as a model—writers who tell stories set in the meaningful epochs of history, but tell them from the perspective of a minority community, which stands against the oppressive traits of dominant culture, all in the hope of revealing and interrogating the traits of our own contemporary dominant culture.

Although too young to have participated in it, I think of myself as a writer who is born of the contemporary disability civil rights movement of the mid- to late 1970s. I've always felt that it was the creators of that movement who paved the way for the life I live now. Without the civil rights laws they struggled so hard to force into passage, I doubt I would have been afforded the opportunity to seek out training and create a life for myself in the theater arts. I hope there is an element of that activist spirit in the character of Gretty in this play. She is an individual who is adamant in her right to autonomy over her body, determined to express the sexuality society denies her, and unflinching in expressing her anger at the sociopolitical forces which shape her life. And, like so many disabled people, both past and present, she is determined to escape from a life of poverty and isolation.

I envision the future of my work as a continued attempt to represent disability onstage, and to represent it not as a simple biological experience, a medical condition or a "rough card drawn by the hand of fate." Like so many of my peers in the community of disabled theater artists, I instead posit the experience as a multifaceted social network that is informed by historical context. I seek to dramatize disability in a way which reveals something deeper than a simplistic illness narrative, all in an effort to create new stories, new myths, new ways of revealing the disabled body onstage.

Production History

Gretty Good Time was workshopped at Mark Taper Forum's New Work Festival (Center Theatre Group, Los Angeles) in November 1997. The production was directed by Shirley Jo Finney and the dramaturg was Pier Carlo Talenti. The cast was as follows:

GRETTY	Ann Stocking
HIDEKO	Kerri Higuchi
MCCLOUD/CAPTAIN LEWIS	Patricia Fraser
DR. CAPLAN/ANNOUNCER	John P. Connolly
MR. RALPH EDWARDS/DR. HENRY/PUPPY	Paul Mercier

Gretty Good Time received its world premiere in New York with Youngblood in association with the Ensemble Studio Theatre in January 1999. The production was directed by Susann Brinkley. The cast was as follows:

GRETTY	Fiona Gallagher
HIDEKO	Anna Li
MCCLOUD	Salty Loeb
DR. CAPLAN	Baxter Harris
DR. HENRY/PUPPY	Richard Joseph Paul
MR. RALPH EDWARDS	Ted Neustadt

Gretty Good Time was produced at the Falcon Theatre in Burbank, California, in April 2003. The production was directed by Joe Regalbuto. The cast was as follows:

GRETTY	Ann Stocking
HIDEKO/MR. RALPH EDWARDS	Jennifer Chu
MCCLOUD	Pamela Gordon
DR. CAPLAN/CAPTAIN LEWIS/PUPPY	Kip Gilman
DR. HENRY	Jay Underwood

Characters

GRETTY—lives in a nursing home. She has post-polio paralysis. Her body is paralyzed, but she has limited movement in her right arm. She is thirty-two years old and she speaks with a German accent.

HIDEKO—a young Japanese woman whose face and arms were badly disfigured by the atomic bomb, eighteen years old.

MCCLOUD—a friend of Gretty's who also lives in the nursing home, sixty-four years old.

DR. CAPLAN—director of the nursing home, forty-two years old.

DR. HENRY—a nervous young doctor, twenty-nine years old.

MR. RALPH EDWARDS—the host of the television show *This Is Your Life*.

CAPTAIN ROBERT LEWIS—one of the pilots who dropped an atomic bomb on Hiroshima.

PUPPY—Gretty's dead brother (played by the actor playing Dr. Henry).

Setting

The action takes place in two different areas of the nursing home: Gretty's room, lit by harsh lights; and a small garden in the courtyard of the nursing home, lit by sunlight.

Time

May 1955.

Author's Note

The *This Is Your Life* scenes are based on an actual episode of the television show, which aired on May 11, 1955. The character of Hideko is a composite character based on the stories of a number of young women who were brought over to the United States for plastic surgery in 1955 as part of the "Hiroshima Maidens Project."

Prologue

Soft moonlight comes through Gretty's window. Gretty is lying on the floor near her bed, her eyes open. Also near the bed is her overturned wheelchair. Hideko is standing at the foot of the bed, her back to the audience. A pause, then:

HIDEKO: I remember hearing the following from a schoolteacher: "Even though your features are not lovely, have a pure and loving heart, and your life will be full." I tried to apply this, and follow those words as they were meant. But on the day I left the classroom and went into the world, I understood how these words were false. And I could not help but conceal my face and cry.

GRETTY *(Softly)*: Yes. And now, you're leaving?

HIDEKO: Yes.

GRETTY: I am, too.

HIDEKO: So then together, we'll go?

(Gretty slowly nods. Hideko bends down and takes Gretty's foot in her hand.)

On a backwards wind . . . we'll go.

(Hideko turns, and we see her disfigured face. She leans over and kisses Gretty on the cheek. Gretty closes her eyes. Hideko disappears. Dr. Caplan enters and stands in the doorway. He enters Gretty's room. She opens her eyes.)

GRETTY *(Seeing Dr. Caplan)*: I have . . . taken a fall.

DR. CAPLAN *(Standing over her)*: Yes. You have.

GRETTY: You will help me up now.

DR. CAPLAN *(Smiling)*: Were you trying to leave us?

GRETTY *(Staring him in the eye)*: Yes. I was.

DR. CAPLAN *(Kneeling down near her head)*: And how were you to leave us? You are paralyzed, you do not have the strength.

GRETTY *(Looking away from him)*: I have a friend, who will come back for me. A backwards wind will sweep us up, into the air. And we'll go together. *(Looking at Dr. Caplan)* I will go.

(Dr. Caplan stands back up, looks down at her with a dark disgust.)

DR. CAPLAN: Then go, and I will leave you here, with your dreams. Good night.

(He exits the room. Gretty stares upward.)

GRETTY: I will go.

Act One

THE SHIT BODY

Scene 1

Lights up on Gretty and McCloud, sitting in the courtyard. Gretty is in her wheelchair.

GRETTY: She returned. *(Beat. Softly touches the spot on her cheek where Hideko kissed her)* The skin on her cheek, like raisins it felt. Dark red-colored, bumpy. A burn, terrible one.

MCCLOUD: And she came back to you last night? Another dream?

GRETTY: Yes. We'll go together. She returned. And she will return to me, again.

MCCLOUD: Why don't you dream about normal things, Gretty? Why not dream about Gregory Peck? *(Staring outward, deadly serious)* I'd kill my own dog for a date with Gregory Peck.

GRETTY: That much, huh?

MCCLOUD: That much.

GRETTY: Well, she ain't Gregory Peck. Her name's Hideko.

MCCLOUD: A Jap, huh?

GRETTY: Yes. She is.

MCCLOUD: And she's going to "fly you away"?

GRETTY: Yes.

MCCLOUD: To where?

GRETTY: Anywhere but here.

MCCLOUD: Anywhere but here. *(Whispering)* I think you're just afraid, because I'm planning *my* escape from this place. *(Beat)* Don't be afraid. *(Beat)* Don't be afraid, Gretty.

GRETTY: I ain't afraid.

MCCLOUD: You'll be fine without me.

GRETTY: I know that. *(Smiling at her)* You ain't so powerful.

MCCLOUD *(Her hands shaking with fury):* I am *so* powerful! I am too! I'll get up from this bench and kill you! I'll do whatever it takes! I'm a killer!

GRETTY: You are a needlepointer. You do needlepoint pictures of smiling kittens with butterflies on their noses. That is your only talent. *(Beat)* No talent for murder. *(Beat)* Gimme the peach.

(McCloud picks a peach up off the table and holds it in front of Gretty's face. Gretty pauses, then takes a fierce bite.)

MCCLOUD: Soooo good?

GRETTY *(Juice dripping, mouth full)*: Yes.

MCCLOUD: You could hold the peach yourself, in your right hand. You can move your right hand—

GRETTY: I want you to hold it.

(Beat.)

MCCLOUD *(Wiping Gretty's mouth)*: Fine.

GRETTY *(Smiling like a little girl)*: Besides, my shoulder is sore, McCloud.

MCCLOUD: And why is your shoulder sore?

GRETTY: I fell from my bed last night. I slept on the floor all night.

MCCLOUD: No one came in to help you back up?

GRETTY: Dr. Caplan came in, but he left me there, on the floor.

MCCLOUD *(Standing, clenching her fist)*: Oh, I tell you, Gretty, one of these days I'm gonna kill that man! I'm gonna slash his ugly chicken-skin throat!

GRETTY: With what? Your needlepoint needles? Sit down, old woman.

MCCLOUD: Hey! I'm a good friend to you, Gretty. I'm your left hand.

GRETTY: Yes you are.

MCCLOUD: Then you should help me with my escape plan. It won't be as hard as it sounds. The guards play gin rummy on Thursday nights. If you distract the nurses, no one will see me go.

GRETTY: I don't wanna help you. I don't fake no death on Thursday night.

MCCLOUD: I ain't asking you to fake your death. Just a distraction, that's all. *(Getting up)* You with your dream stories. That's where you live. In your dream stories. *(Beat)* This nursing home ain't a place for me. Death's here. *(Sniffs)* It's all over this place.

GRETTY: I'm not afraid of my dying.

MCCLOUD: I know you're not. *(Beat)* But I ain't ready. I gotta go.

GRETTY: Where will you go?

MCCLOUD *(Smiling brightly)*: Scotland!

GRETTY: Scotland?

MCCLOUD: Oh yes!

GRETTY: You have some rich family there?

MCCLOUD: Nope. All my family's here. But I don't need no stinking family! I'm a killer! I'll carve out a new life there! I'll live in a world where there is no family! No connections! *(Does a little dance)* There will be only cool winds over Loch Ness! A singing breeze blowing through my Dinah Shore hair!

GRETTY: You ain't got Dinah Shore hair!

MCCLOUD *(Stroking her hair)*: Quiet. The Scottish sun will make it soft with honey-gold highlights. And I'll watch the hairy men serenading me with bagpipes, delicate curly locks peeeking out from their kilts, but I will not speak to them! No connections!

GRETTY: No family there.

MCCLOUD *(Sitting back down)*: Exactly. *(Beat)* But Dr. Caplan knows I want to leave, Gretty. He's expecting me to try again. I won't get away with it, unless you distract the nurses.

GRETTY: I do not think . . . *(Beat)* I do not want you to go.

MCCLOUD: I'm going to go. There's rats in the showers. The nurses are cruel. And everyone's old and sick. It's grim here.

GRETTY: Fine then. Go, go to Scotland.

MCCLOUD: I'll send you a postcard.

GRETTY *(Trying to move away)*: Return to sender. It will come back. I'll be gone by then.

MCCLOUD: Don't say that.

GRETTY: You have your escape plan, and I have mine.

(Beat.)

MCCLOUD: You're just feeling sad. That's all. You're thinking about your brother, the "Puppy." You always get sad when you think about your brother.

GRETTY: I ain't sad, I'm just remembering, that's all. *(Smiling)* His big puppy eyes. Always followed me everywhere. That's why I called him the Puppy. We would walk along the beach together, and look out over the ocean. One time we saw a whale! It was swimming so close to the surface, and it turned and pointed its head . . . *(Points her head upward)* Up, up, towards the sun. *(Beat)* Then it disappeared, into the ocean.

MCCLOUD *(With great drama)*: "In vain, oh whale, dost thou seek intercedings with yon all-quickening sun, that only calls forth life, but gives it not again."

GRETTY: Yes! That's a very smart thing for you to say, McCloud!

MCCLOUD *(Proudly)*: Thank you.

(Beat.)

GRETTY: You didn't really say it, did you?

MCCLOUD: Well, no, it's from *Moby-Dick*. But the point is, you have *good* memories of your Puppy.

GRETTY: The point is, my brother is dead now. Eight years ago, it was.

MCCLOUD: And you're still sad about it. It's natural.

GRETTY *(Angry)*: I ain't sad about that. I cannot move. This is the reason. *(Squirming, trying to shift in her chair)* This. *(Beat)* More peach. *(Beat. Takes a soft bite)* You don't know what it is like, not to move right. To not have any choices. I want choices.

MCCLOUD *(Softly)*: Even if you really wanted to do it, you ain't strong enough to do it yourself, and no one's going to *help* you die. I'm certainly not going to.

GRETTY *(Smiling mischievously)*: No, I'm sure that *you* will not.

MCCLOUD: What? You got some kind of plan?

GRETTY: Well, there is a new young doctor on duty here these days . . .

MCCLOUD: Him? You're crazy, he's just a kid, and you ain't never gonna get a doctor to help you kill yourself . . .

GRETTY *(Looking away, with a slight smile)*: Yes, you're right. There's no way I could convince him to help me. I'm not powerful, like you are.

MCCLOUD: That's good! I'm glad you can acknowledge that, Gretty!

GRETTY: Yes, so I'll just, I'll stay here.

(Beat.)

MCCLOUD: You'll stay?

GRETTY: Yup.

MCCLOUD: You promise?

GRETTY: Yes.

MCCLOUD: You'll have that Jap witch to keep you company.

GRETTY: She ain't a witch.

MCCLOUD: Sounds like a witch to me, visiting you in the darkness of night!

GRETTY: Don't be foolish, McCloud! She's a good gal.

(Soft lights come up on Hideko, in the distance, breeze blowing through her hair.)

I saw her on the television once, with all those radiation burns on her face, and now she comes to me. *(Softly)* But she's only in my dreams.

MCCLOUD: She'll still be company. Even if she's only in your dreams. *(Beat. Touches her face)* Scary stuff, radiation.

GRETTY: It brings the cancers.

MCCLOUD: Yup. Terrible way to die. Slow and painful.

GRETTY: Yes. A terrible way. *(Beat)* A terrible way. *(Beat)* And yes then, I will have a fake heart attack on Thursday night. For you, McCloud. *(Beat)* For you.

Scene 2

Gretty sits in her wheelchair, staring straight ahead, watching This Is Your Life. *The theme music plays.*

ANNOUNCER *(Voice-over)*: *This Is Your Life*, America's most talked-about program, brought to you by America's most talked-about cosmetics: Hazel Bishop Long-Lasting Lipstick, Hazel Bishop Long-Lasting Nail Polish, Hazel Bishop Long-Lasting Complexion Cream. And now, Mr. *This Is Your Life* himself, Ralph Edwards!!!

(Sound of applause as Mr. Ralph Edwards enters, in spotlight. A loud ticking sound is heard in the background.)

MR. RALPH EDWARDS: Good evening, ladies and gentlemen, and welcome to our show. The ticking sound you hear in the background is a clock counting off the seconds, taking us back ten years to 8:15 A.M., August 6, 1945. This is Hiroshima, and in that fateful second a new concept of life and death was given its baptism. It was a single moment of eternity where absolute death could be chosen over absolute life. And backstage right now is a young woman whose life was forever changed in that moment. We will bring her out in just a few minutes.

(More applause sounds. Gretty looks on intently. Mr. Ralph Edwards sits on a wooden stool and picks up a large, ornately decorated book from a nearby table.)

We have been working for weeks to bring our guest to the stage tonight so we could retell the story of her life. *(Holding up the book)* The facts are between the covers of this book. Our guest will meet many people who have helped to shape her destiny, and we hope that at the end of this half hour she will have had some pleasant moments. *(Staring out into the audience)* And that *you*, ladies and gentlemen, will have a better understanding of what it is to look into the face of atomic power. To survive and die.

(Off to the side, a figure is now standing in the shadows.)

GRETTY: To survive and die.
MR. RALPH EDWARDS: And so, as all our guests wait for our show to begin, we'll take a commercial break.
GRETTY *(Staring at the figure in the shadows)*: Puppy. The time, it is coming.

Scene 3

Gretty's room. Gretty is lying in bed, eyes open, not moving. Dr. Henry leans over the headboard of the bed, staring down at her.

DR. HENRY: I see . . . I see it. It's in my sight range. I see it.
GRETTY: Don't just see it. Pull it out.

(He puts his fingers to her face, a spot on her chin, a hair.)

DR. HENRY *(Backing away)*: I don't want to hurt you.

GRETTY: You couldn't if you were trying.

DR. HENRY *(Coming closer again)*: Tough cookie.

GRETTY: I ain't a cookie. Now yank that beard hair out of its socket, boy.

(He does so.)

DR. HENRY: You didn't even flinch.

GRETTY: Nope.

DR. HENRY: You're pretty young to be getting a facial hair.

GRETTY: I ain't young.

(Dr. Henry comes around to the side of her bed, looking at her chart, smiling at her.)

DR. HENRY: You are. You're thirty-two.

GRETTY: How old are you?

DR. HENRY: Thirty.

GRETTY: And you finished medical school?

DR. HENRY *(Proudly)*: Just graduated last year. Class of 1954.

GRETTY: Jeepers creepers.

DR. HENRY *(Shaking her hand gently)*: My name is Henry.

GRETTY: Hello, Dr. Henry.

DR. HENRY: You can, just call me Henry if you, or my last name is Foster, if you would prefer, you can—

GRETTY *(Angry)*: I know what I can do.

DR. HENRY *(Backing away)*: Jeez! How can you be mad at me? We just met! What did I do?

GRETTY *(A little taken aback)*: I'm not mad at you. Don't be so sensitive, Dr. boy genius. You're doing fine. *(Showing him her chin)* You got the beard hair out, right?

DR. HENRY: Yes.

GRETTY: Then you're doing fine. I am not supposed to be holding your hand, little boy. It is the other way around.

(He takes her hand. She stares at him incredulously.)

GRETTY *(Pulling her hand away)*: Gimme back my hand! It is *mine!* My property! *Mine!*

DR. HENRY: Fine! Then . . . just . . . tell me a little bit . . .

GRETTY: I take naps at four o'clock. Do not ever wake me if I am sleeping; I have wonderful dreams. I go places there. My shows come on at one o'clock, do not disturb me then either.

DR. HENRY: Okay, you like TV shows. My wife used to watch *Search for Tomorrow*.

GRETTY: *Search for Tomorrow* is okay. *Guiding Light* and *Secret Storm*, not so good. But *This Is Your Life* with Mr. Ralph Edwards, that is the only really good show.

DR. HENRY: What's so good about that one?

(Lights come up on Mr. Ralph Edwards, slowly opening the large, ornately decorated This Is Your Life *book.)*

GRETTY: The moments that Mr. Ralph Edwards gives people are the most lovely gifts of all. They are moments where people sit down and are given their past, their history, as a gift. Beautiful, it is. *(Pretending to hand Dr. Henry a present)* "Here, it is for you. Your history. Untarnished." *(Smiling brightly)* And the people cry! So happy they are that they cry! I picture myself sitting there in their place and thinking, I am so lucky. I am surrounded by friends who I have not seen in years, but they all still love me. My past . . . is now clean.

DR. HENRY: I like that.

(Mr. Ralph Edwards slowly closes the book as lights come down on him.)

GRETTY: Don't like it too much, it's only on Wednesday nights. Once a week. It ain't exactly a . . . reason to live. *(Beat)* That is all you need to know.

DR. HENRY: Well, just, tell me where you're from, your accent sounds . . .

GRETTY: That is all you need to know.

(Beat.)

DR. HENRY *(Slowly walking out)*: Okay. Okay. Have a good day.

GRETTY: But it is Germany.

DR. HENRY: What?

GRETTY: I was born in Germany. Grew up there. My family moved here years ago. My father owned a bar.

(Beat. He smiles.)

DR. HENRY *(Flipping through the chart)*: So you're German . . .

GRETTY: Yes, I'm the "enemy."

DR. HENRY: Well, I don't really think that people should be defined by their national identity, I think people are—

GRETTY *(A little sarcastic)*: People are all the same, under the skin?

DR. HENRY: Yes. I believe that.

GRETTY: Well, how nice for you.

DR. HENRY: You disagree?

GRETTY: No, it's just I think it's a little trickier than that.

DR. HENRY: So, you're a smart cookie, as well as a tough cookie.

GRETTY: I ain't smart. I never been to college. And I ain't a cookie!

DR. HENRY *(Smiling, going back to the chart)*: Okay, okay, let's see, you said your father owned a bar, and he is . . .

GRETTY: Dead now.

DR. HENRY: Mother . . .

GRETTY: Dead now. Too.

DR. HENRY: Brothers or sisters?

(Beat.)

GRETTY: No. No sisters. Or brothers. *(Beat. Smiling like a little girl)* I'm all by myself. That's why I have to live in a nursing home, all alone.

(Beat. He goes back to the chart.)

Do you and your wife have kids?

DR. HENRY: What? Oh. *(Feeling his wedding ring)* No. No kids. I'm divorced. I just wear the ring. *(Shows her the ring)* It's a really nice ring.

GRETTY: Yes! Shiny thing!

DR. HENRY *(Staring at it)*: Yeah. It's a good ring. *(Showing it to her again)* That's a real diamond!

GRETTY: Snazzy!

DR. HENRY: Yeah.

GRETTY: A very young man to have a divorce.

DR. HENRY: Yeah. You know, how these things happen, they, happen. It's always unexpected.

GRETTY: Yes it is.

DR. HENRY *(Looking at her chart)*: And back in Germany is when the polio was contracted? When you were younger . . .

GRETTY: Fifteen or sixteen.

DR. HENRY: And you came here to America for treatment?

GRETTY: Yes. And we stayed. Things started to get bad back there. Very dark.

DR. HENRY: Yes. That was a while ago.

GRETTY: A few years.

DR. HENRY: Fifteen years. That's more than a few.

GRETTY *(Smiling at him)*: Oh good, you can count.

DR. HENRY *(Smiling back)*: Yes. I do it quite often.

GRETTY: So, you're a smart cookie, Dr.?

DR. HENRY: I hope I'm a smart doctor.

GRETTY: And a happy one too?

DR. HENRY: Yes. *(Looking out the window)* It's a good time to be a doctor. It's amazing what's going on now. With the vaccine. It's being given out in schools all over the city, right now. Dr. Salk's a hero.

GRETTY: Yeah, yeah, Dr. Jonas Salk. Jiminy Crickets, he's a hero.

DR. HENRY: It's a good thing.

GRETTY *(Staring at him)*: I know it is.

DR. HENRY: All right, is there anything else I should know about you?

(Beat.)

GRETTY: I have wishes, which I have written down.

DR. HENRY: Oh. Really?

GRETTY: Yes. Wishes, as to what should be done, if I go into a coma. Or something.

DR. HENRY *(Looking up from the chart)*: What are your wishes?

GRETTY: I should be . . . I should just die.

(Beat.)

DR. HENRY: "Just die"?

(Beat. She looks up to see his reaction.)

GRETTY: Yeah. These are my wishes.

DR. HENRY: Doctors don't do that. Doctors keep people from dying.

GRETTY: *This* is what else you should know. My wishes. *(Beat)* I heard some nurses talking. I might have to go into an iron lung.

DR. HENRY: Maybe.

GRETTY: They don't have the iron lung here in this nursing home, do they?

DR. HENRY: No.

GRETTY: I'd have to go into an institution.

DR. HENRY *(Staring at the chart, getting uncomfortable)*: I don't know. Maybe.

GRETTY: I've been in institutions. They are crummy and horrible places. Even worse than this nursing home, if that's possible. *(Beat)* I don't wanna live in an iron lung, Dr. Henry.

DR. HENRY: Drinker respirators are not that . . .

GRETTY: They weigh eight hundred pounds. Big, metal, yellow. That sound. Like the sound of a whale dying. *(Beat, softly)* Whooosh . . . whooosh . . . whooosh . . . forever whooooosh . . . whooosh . . . whooosh . . . *(Beat)* I don't wanna live. There. I would rather die.

DR. HENRY: Die.

GRETTY: Yes, but with my paralysis, it is not something . . . which I could do—

DR. HENRY: This is not, something you should be talking about, with me.

(Beat.)

GRETTY: Are you scared?

DR. HENRY: No. *(Beat)* Scared of what?

GRETTY: Of being a doctor. I would be scared. All that responsibility.

DR. HENRY: Yes. *(Beat)* I'm scared. *(Beat)* This morning, I heard a nurse call you "Gretty Good Time." What's with the nickname?

GRETTY: 'Cause when I arrive is when the good times start, you fool! Even as a little girl I'd walk into my father's bar and say, *(Little girl's voice)* "Look at these sad and lonely people! Fill up their bellies with some treats, on me!" *(Beat. Smiles brightly)* And all the customers would laugh and cheer as I sang: "Schnapps for the men, and cocoa for the laaaaadies, Schnapps for the men, and cocoa for the laaaaadies, Schnapps for the men, and cocoa for the laaaaadies. That's all you need to know!"

DR. HENRY *(Smiling)*: Wow. You're a good person to know, then, huh?

GRETTY: Yes. I am. *(Beat)* You're handsome, Dr. Henry.

DR. HENRY: Oh, well, thank you. That's nice of you to say.

GRETTY: Sure.

(Beat.)

DR. HENRY *(Exiting)*: I should be doing my rounds. *(Looking at his watch)* And you usually take a nap around this time, right?

GRETTY: Yes. I do. Yes. It's the nap time. Now. *(Beat)* Dr. Henry.

DR. HENRY *(Stops)*: Yes?

GRETTY: You have a tendon which stands out on the back of your neck, when you smile.

Scene 4

Gretty's room, lit only by moonlight coming through the window. Gretty and McCloud are lying in Gretty's bed. Both are very drunk, taking turns swigging from a bottle.

MCCLOUD: Shhhh . . . keep your voice down. *(Touching an area on Gretty's chest)* This is where it begins. It's a sensation of tightening. It's a muscle. Remember that.

GRETTY: The heart is a muscle.

MCCLOUD: Yes. And it constricts, tightens. And it hurts! You've got to remember to scream a lot.

GRETTY: Okay. I know how to scream.

MCCLOUD *(Tracing her finger down Gretty's arm)*: Good. And then a sharp pain shoots down the arm, like fire.

GRETTY: Okay.

MCCLOUD: And you have to act real scared, like you're on death's door.

GRETTY: Yes, death's door.

MCCLOUD: Very good! You're a good student!

GRETTY: I am.

MCCLOUD: They'll all believe you're having a heart attack. And maybe that cute new doctor you were talking about will come in here and give you some mouth-to-mouth, eh?

GRETTY: Dr. Henry is his name. You think he's cute?

MCCLOUD: Oh sure, but I myself prefer older men. It's a preference that's hard to fulfill at my age, but I can still prefer.

GRETTY: You've seduced many men?

MCCLOUD: It depends on what you mean by "many."

GRETTY: More than . . . five?

(Beat.)

MCCLOUD: I've seduced many men.

GRETTY: Is it better when they seduce you, or you seduce them?

MCCLOUD: I prefer to be in the driver's seat. But sometimes, once in a while, it is nice to let yourself be small, to lose yourself in a man's arms. Like I did on the night of the greatest passion I ever felt. With Scotty.

GRETTY: Scotty?

MCCLOUD: F. Scott Fitzgerald!

GRETTY: Oh jeez . . .

MCCLOUD: It's true! He and I were both expatriates living in 1920s Paris.

GRETTY: You lived in Paris?

MCCLOUD: Oh yes. I was an actress! And part-time exotic dancer. Scotty and I met at a particularly decadent little party by the River Seine. His first novel, *This Side of Paradise*, had just been published, and it instantly rocketed him to notoriety. He was the toast of the literati scene. But fame had its downsides, and I listened compassionately as he spoke of the terrible loneliness in his heart. Then, quite suddenly, he smiled at me and invited me back to his apartment. I hesitated only for a moment, and then I accepted his offer.

GRETTY *(Smiling)*: Ooohh . . .

MCCLOUD: It was a lovely little flat, tastefully decorated. I sat on the green velvet cushions of his love seat as he poured himself a whiskey. He drank whiskey by the jugful.

GRETTY: Then you two had a lot in common.

MCCLOUD *(Glares at Gretty; takes a swig from the bottle)*: Yes. We did. *(Back to her story)* And then he approached me. I reached up and touched his neck. So smooth, soft and white. The neck of a boy, it was. And I stood up, and stared at his face. His soft, warm lips. And inside of those lips, a sneaky little tongue.

GRETTY: Why do you call it "sneaky"?

MCCLOUD: For . . . various reasons.

GRETTY: And he was gentle, when he touched you?

MCCLOUD: Oh yes, very gentle. Such gentle kisses.

GRETTY: Where did he kiss you?

MCCLOUD *(Touching the left side of Gretty's chin)*: Here. *(Touching Gretty's lips)* And here. *(Touching the nape of Gretty's neck)* And here.

GRETTY *(Smiling brightly)*: And then?

MCCLOUD: And then I thought to myself, "I am about to be made love to by a man of passion, a man of words, a man of hard-liquor drinking." Everything I always wanted in a man.

GRETTY: And then what?

MCCLOUD: Then I could no longer think. All thoughts evaporated as I felt the tickle touch of his warm fingertips slowly, creeping, up, my, leg.

(They giggle, then let out a deep sigh.)

GRETTY: That's how it feels.

MCCLOUD: Yes. *(Smiling)* You'll feel it some day.

GRETTY: You think?

MCCLOUD: Oh yes. As long as you live a long enough life, you'll get your chance.

GRETTY *(Staring at the floor)*: Maybe.

MCCLOUD *(Jumping up out of the bed)*: Well, I ain't worried about leaving you behind anymore.

GRETTY: And why is that?

MCCLOUD: Because now I know you don't really want to die.

GRETTY *(Some anger)*: How do you know that?

MCCLOUD: Because someone who *really* wanted to die would never get so excited by a story of passion and life, like the one I just told you.

(Beat.)

GRETTY: You think you are so smart.

MCCLOUD: I am smart.

GRETTY: So am I.

MCCLOUD *(Looking out the window)*: The guards are gathering for their gin rummy game! *(Giggling with excitement)* It's almost time! Scotland, here I come! Now, you remember what you're going to say, what you're going to tell them it feels like?

GRETTY: Yes. The heart, it constricts, tightens. *(Beat. Stares at McCloud, who is staring out the window)* It is a muscle.

Scene 5

Late at night. Gretty is asleep in bed, dreaming. She opens her eyes and watches as Mr. Ralph Edwards creeps onto the stage.

MR. RALPH EDWARDS *(Whispering to the audience)*: And now, ladies and gentlemen, we'll take a secret peek backstage into our dressing room, as two of the guests on tonight's show impatiently wait for their television debut!

(He pulls back a curtain, revealing the backstage dressing room of This Is Your Life. *Hideko sits on a couch. Captain Robert Lewis walks into the room and stands with his back to the audience. He wears a brown pilot's bomber jacket, and aviator goggles hang from his neck. They are not aware of the fact that they are being watched. Gretty sits up in bed, watching the following exchange:)*

HIDEKO: I'm not nervous.

CAPTAIN LEWIS: That's good.

HIDEKO: This is a big studio.

CAPTAIN LEWIS: Yes. Television studios are big. Very large.

HIDEKO: A brown leather jacket.

CAPTAIN LEWIS *(Looking at his jacket)*: Yes. It's very warm. It's lined with wool.

HIDEKO: Yes. You are a pilot.

CAPTAIN LEWIS: I used to be. Now I work in a candy factory. I'm a candy maker. I'm the general manager. Of the factory. I make candy. *(Offering her a brown paper bag)* Would you like some?

HIDEKO *(Taking a piece)*: Oh, cocoa-flavored gooeys!

CAPTAIN LEWIS *(Also taking a piece)*: Yes.

HIDEKO: You smell like scotch.

CAPTAIN LEWIS: There's a bar. Across the street.

(He sits on the couch next to her. Beat. He is trying not to stare at Hideko's face. Gretty is still watching.)

HIDEKO: You must have many stories to tell from your days as a pilot. Are you a guest on *This Is Your Life*? *(He doesn't answer)* I'm a guest. We are here on a mission of mercy! To thank Americans for their compassion and generosity. Everyone here is very nice. Everywhere there are nice people in this country.

CAPTAIN LEWIS: Not everywhere.

HIDEKO *(Staring at him)*: Yes. Everywhere. You must not be a trusting man.

CAPTAIN LEWIS: I have trust. I have trusted.

HIDEKO: You must have been a star pilot, to be a guest on a TV show.

CAPTAIN LEWIS: Are you a star?

HIDEKO: I'm embarrassed to say, but YES, I AM! *(Shows him a large number of newspaper clippings)* Look, that's my picture in the

New York Times, the *New York Daily News,* the *New York Post. (Pointing)* That's me, with the other girls.

CAPTAIN LEWIS: Other girls?

HIDEKO: The other "Hiroshima Maidens." We were on all the newscasts too. *(Taking on a newscaster's voice)* "The twenty-five Jap girls who were flown here for new faces are resting comfortably in our country, where they were greeted with open arms."

CAPTAIN LEWIS *(Reading the clippings)*: "Hiroshima Maidens."

HIDEKO *(With disdain)*: Yes. That's what they call us.

CAPTAIN LEWIS: You don't like the name?

HIDEKO: No. Because I am not "Hiroshima," I am not "Japan," I am me. And I won't always be a maiden, at least I hope I won't. *(Beat. Sees him staring)* Are you staring at my face?

CAPTAIN LEWIS *(Looking away)*: No. I'm not.

HIDEKO: I'm not crying. The tear duct in my left eye is broken. It waters constantly. Sometimes I fear the rug under my feet will get wet. From all the water. *(Beat. Looking at him)* Has someone died?

CAPTAIN LEWIS: What?

HIDEKO: A friend of yours maybe? You look so sad.

CAPTAIN LEWIS: My name is Bob.

HIDEKO: I am Hideko. *(Staring at him)* I think I *have* seen your picture before. I think you *are* famous. *(He doesn't answer)* Tell me about the missions you flew. In the war.

CAPTAIN LEWIS: No.

HIDEKO: I lied before. I *am* nervous. A story would soothe me. The story of the missions you flew.

CAPTAIN LEWIS: You shouldn't be nervous.

HIDEKO: I am. I'm nervous that I will ruin this wonderful show.

CAPTAIN LEWIS *(Smiling at her)*: I'm sure that won't happen. *(Handing the newspaper clippings back)* I've already read these articles.

HIDEKO *(Taking them)*: Oh. Then you already know who I am.

CAPTAIN LEWIS: Yes. I do. You're here, for surgery, on your face.

HIDEKO: Yes. The Reverend Kiyoshi Tanimoto is my friend. He is a Christian minister from my hometown.

CAPTAIN LEWIS: Hiroshima.

HIDEKO: Yes. He gathered a group of girls who look like I do. With faces like mine. We had meetings in the basement of his church. *(A whispered aside)* He spent a lot of time telling us girls about the all-powerful Jesus Christ, but I'm a Buddhist! *(Normal voice)* We all had a great deal of fun together! We played cards and talked about movie stars!

CAPTAIN LEWIS: It sounds like fun.

HIDEKO: It was! And he arranged for us to come here.

CAPTAIN LEWIS: For the surgery.

HIDEKO *(Fear in her voice)*: Yes. The surgery.

CAPTAIN LEWIS: You're frightened?

HIDEKO: Part of me would rather not have the surgery.

CAPTAIN LEWIS: Not have the surgery? You've *got* to have the surgery.

HIDEKO: Yes, of course.

(Gretty turns away, uncomfortable. She looks at the floor.)

But, if I could fly backwards through history, on a backwards wind, and alter my past, alter that moment, so the scars never happen at all, then I would not need the surgery.

CAPTAIN LEWIS: Yes. But you can't do that . . . No one can.

HIDEKO *(With a sly smile)*: Maybe. Maybe not.

CAPTAIN LEWIS *(Coming closer, staring at her face, touching his own face)*: It hurts?

HIDEKO: There is pain. There will be even more of it too.

CAPTAIN LEWIS: You've had many surgeries before?

HIDEKO: Yes, nineteen. *(Beat)* Once, they sliced thin strips of skin from the inside of my thigh, and sewed them crisscross over the wound on my arm. But instead of healing, in three weeks the strips turned black. And fell to the floor.

CAPTAIN LEWIS: The doctors in this country are better.

HIDEKO: Are they?

CAPTAIN LEWIS: It will make you look better.

HIDEKO: Yes. It will. And it will make Americans feel better.

CAPTAIN LEWIS: Maybe.

HIDEKO: Perhaps it is a kind of duty.

CAPTAIN LEWIS: Duty.

HIDEKO: Yes. *(Beat)* I'm sorry for talking so much, Bob. I talk a great deal when I am nervous. I must sound like a silly, stupid child.

CAPTAIN LEWIS: No, you're just playful.

HIDEKO *(A hint of anger)*: I'm not playful. I'm calm.

CAPTAIN LEWIS: It's okay. But I need to go. We both need to get in our places. For the show.

HIDEKO: Yes. For the show.

(He starts to exit. Gretty sits forward.)

Bob. Your days as a pilot. The missions you flew.

(He stops.)

CAPTAIN LEWIS: What do you want to know?
HIDEKO *(Trying to find the words)*: How high did you fly?
CAPTAIN LEWIS: I flew immensely high.
HIDEKO: How high did you fly?
CAPTAIN LEWIS: I flew twelve thousand feet high.
HIDEKO: Who are you?
CAPTAIN LEWIS: I'm no one.
HIDEKO: Who are you?
CAPTAIN LEWIS: I'm Captain Robert Lewis.
HIDEKO: Have you been praised?
CAPTAIN LEWIS: I've been praised immensely.
HIDEKO: Have you been praised?
CAPTAIN LEWIS: I wasn't praised enough.

(He exits. The curtain closes. Gretty slowly lies back down, sleeps.)

Scene 6

Gretty's room, morning. She sits in bed, groggy from having been woken up. Dr. Henry paces. Dr. Caplan stands off to the left.

DR. HENRY: She's gone.
GRETTY: So? Release the sweaty bloodhounds! Alert the border guards! She's gone!
DR. HENRY *(Gesturing)*: How could you do *this*?
GRETTY *(Imitating his gesturing)*: What is *this*?
DR. HENRY: You faked a heart attack, so Mrs. McCloud could sneak away.
GRETTY: I'm almost sure I did not. Anything I said to you last night was real.
DR. HENRY: You said you had chest pains.
GRETTY: Then I did, you fool!
DR. HENRY: The tests showed no abnormal activity.
GRETTY: Everything is abnormal activity for me.
DR. CAPLAN: You've put her in danger.
DR. HENRY: We're worried about her, Gretty.
GRETTY *(To Dr. Henry)*: You are. Maybe.
DR. CAPLAN: We both are. And her family is worried.

GRETTY: They never worried much before.

DR. CAPLAN: They're worried.

GRETTY: They're a big-buck family. They got the big bucks.

DR. CAPLAN *(Slowly coming closer)*: What?

GRETTY: Her family's got the bucks, no?

DR. CAPLAN *(Brushing the hair from her eyes)*: You know I can't talk about her family's finances, pal.

GRETTY: Sure sure. Say, would you search this much if *I* ran away?

DR. HENRY: Of course we would.

GRETTY: I don't got a big-bucks son. *(To Dr. Caplan)* The state don't pay you much to take care of me. A big-bucks son could give you more money for this bed, huh?

(Beat.)

DR. HENRY: We would look for you.

GRETTY *(Rolling over and closing her eyes)*: The night *I* escape the sweaty bloodhounds can take a rest.

DR. CAPLAN: Do you know where she is? Did she tell you?

(Pause. There is a faint sound of bagpipes in the distance.)

GRETTY *(Slowly opening her eyes)*: No. She did not.

DR. CAPLAN: Yes. She told you where she was going. Didn't she?

(The bagpipes get louder as a light comes up on McCloud, dressed in a plaid cap and a kilt.)

GRETTY: No. She never told me where.

MCCLOUD *(Scottish accent)*: Aye, that's being a good lass there, Gretty.

DR. HENRY: She needs our help. She could be wandering the streets. She could be lying facedown in a ditch.

MCCLOUD: Those scallywags wish I was in a ditch. *(Beat)* That's where they think I belong.

GRETTY: She's not in a ditch.

DR. CAPLAN: You will tell us.

MCCLOUD: Don't be lettin' me down now, Gretty.

GRETTY: She's safe.

MCCLOUD: If they get me back, they'll shackle me up. *(Beat)* Pump me full of the same drugs they pump into you. *(Arms outstretched, she slowly dances to the bagpipes)* They'll make it so the only friends I have are the ones that visit me in a haaazzzze.

(Pause.)

GRETTY: She never told me. *(Beat. The bagpipes and light on McCloud fade slowly)* She never told me where.

DR. CAPLAN *(Whispering to Dr. Henry)*: She's lying.

DR. HENRY *(To Gretty)*: She was your friend. Don't you want your friend back here?

GRETTY: No. I don't.

(Lights are fully down on McCloud.)

(Staring at Dr. Caplan, a small cough) A sip of water now, please.

(Dr. Caplan pauses, then pours water into the plastic cup next to her bed. He puts a straw in the cup and holds the cup near her face. She pauses, then violently lunges her head forward, knocking the cup out of his hand. Water falls over her face and neck.)

(Staring at him) Don't call me a liar. *(Beat)* I don't know where she is.

DR. CAPLAN: They'll find her anyway.

GRETTY: Fine then. They'll find her anyway.

(Dr. Caplan exits the room. Dr. Henry approaches Gretty.)

DR. HENRY: Do . . . *(Beat)* Do you want . . . Can I dry the water off?

GRETTY *(Still staring toward the door)*: Yes. You can.

(He wipes the water off her face and neck.)

DR. HENRY: You don't blame her for leaving.

GRETTY: No. I do not.

DR. HENRY *(Softly)*: You would leave, too, if you could.

(Beat.)

GRETTY: I wanna die, boy. That's what I want.

(Beat. Dr. Henry gets up and shuts the door all the way.)

DR. HENRY: That is, not something which I, can help you with. *(Comes back to the bed, sits down)* You told me that you have wonderful dreams.

GRETTY: Not so wonderful, because when I wake up they go. And I'm trapped . . . in a shit body.

DR. HENRY: I've made suggestions. About improving the living conditions here.

GRETTY *(Softly)*: Listen to me. Things don't change here.

DR. HENRY: They can.

GRETTY: People are not good, boy. Always everywhere. *(Beat)* People gas people. Burn people. They find new ways to make people disappear. Throw them into shadows if they live. People don't learn. Then they sleep well.

(He holds her.)

DR. HENRY: I told Dr. Caplan that there needs to be more activities and he . . .

GRETTY *(Softly)*: Let go of my body.

DR. HENRY *(Not letting go)*: There are ways we can improve the quality of—

GRETTY *(A little louder)*: Let go of my body. It is my body, my property. I know what should be done with it. *(Beat)* Let go.

(He slowly does so.)

DR. HENRY: I'm sorry. *(Beat)* I know it's your body. You have rights.

GRETTY: Yes.

DR. HENRY: I believe you have rights.

GRETTY: I do. *(Beat)* I'm sorry to be so troublesome to you. *(Smiling at him)* You're a good boy.

DR. HENRY: You keep calling me boy. I'm not that much younger than you.

GRETTY: You're a good boy.

DR. HENRY: I could spend more time with you. Come hear more about your dreams.

GRETTY: They keep you busy here. Many patients, too much.

DR. HENRY: Too much. *(Beat)* Mrs. McCloud *has* to come back.

GRETTY: I *know* she is okay.

DR. HENRY *(Getting up from the bed)*: Because you dreamt about her? Just because people treat you like a child doesn't mean you have the right to act like a child.

(Beat. She's hurt by this.)

GRETTY: I worry, too. *(Beat)* But where she really is, and I don't really know where, she ain't in no shadow light. *(Beat)* I swear.

Scene 7

Back on the This Is Your Life *stage. Gretty is in her wheelchair, looking on.*

GRETTY: This is where I first saw you, Hideko.

MR. RALPH EDWARDS: Welcome back to our show. Ladies and gentlemen, this past Monday, May 8, twenty-five girls from Hiroshima arrived in New York City via U.S. Army transport. They are being treated surgically at Mount Sinai Hospital at absolutely no cost. Tonight we would like you to meet one of these girls. She has lived through the terror of an atomic bombing. She is badly disfigured.

(A very dim light comes up on Hideko, stage left, casting her into a silhouette. Mr. Ralph Edwards freezes. Beat. Gretty stares at Hideko.)

GRETTY: Staring at you, inside my TV.

MR. RALPH EDWARDS *(Addressing the audience in a hushed tone)*: To avoid causing her any embarrassment, we will not show you her face. May I present Miss Hideko Kimura, of the Hiroshima Maidens Project.

(He freezes again.)

GRETTY *(Some anger)*: But I did not understand. Mr. Ralph Edwards seems like a kind man. So why would he keep you in the dark? Keep you away from everyone else. I wondered this. *(Beat)* There, in the shadow light, you look spooky. But you're not spooky. And he kept you there, throughout the show. *(More anger)* Trapped in the spooky shadow light.

MR. RALPH EDWARDS: Miss Hideko, what message would you like to convey to our television audience?

HIDEKO *(Nervously reading her lines)*: "I-I am very happy to be in America and I thank everyone for what the United States is doing for me. People have been very—"

(She is interrupted by the sound of an airplane engine coming from overhead. She looks up to see where the sound is coming from.)

CAPTAIN LEWIS *(Voice-over)*: At zero six-hundred on the morning of August 6, 1945, I was in a B-29 flying over the Pacific. Destination: Hiroshima.

MR. RALPH EDWARDS: This is the voice of a man whose life is destined to be woven up in the threads of your own, Miss Hideko.

CAPTAIN LEWIS *(Voice-over)*: And looking down from thousands of feet over Hiroshima, all I could think was, "My God, what have we done?"

MR. RALPH EDWARDS: Now you have never met him, but he's here tonight to clasp your hand in friendship. *(Introducing him)* Ladies and gentlemen, Captain Robert Lewis, United States Air Force, who, along with Paul Tibbetts, piloted the plane from which the first atomic bomb was dropped on Hiroshima.

(Music plays and the sound of applause as Captain Lewis steps out onto the stage. He pauses, sees Hideko staring him in the eye. He returns her stare for a moment, then looks to the floor. He walks over and shakes her hand, then walks to his place next to Mr. Ralph Edwards.)

Captain Lewis, tell us about your experience.

CAPTAIN LEWIS *(Nervously reading his lines)*: "We departed the island of Tinian at two A.M. that morning, flying in our B-29. We were told that there were three prospective targets: Hiroshima, Konkura and Nagasaki. About an hour before we reached the coastline of Japan we were notified that the weather was clear in Hiroshima. Therefore, Hiroshima was our target."

(A long pause. He closes his eyes and rubs his forehead.)

(Taking a deep breath) "At 8:15 promptly, the bomb was dropped. We turned the plane to get out of the way. Shortly after, we turned back to see what happened, and in front of our eyes the city of Hiroshima had disappeared."

MR. RALPH EDWARDS: Did you write something in your log at that time?

CAPTAIN LEWIS: I wrote down the words: "My God, what have we done?"

(Applause sounds.)

MR. RALPH EDWARDS: Thank you, Robert Lewis, now a general manager at the Henry Heide Incorporated candy-making factory in New York City.

(Captain Lewis walks to the side of the stage.)

In that split second when one atom bomb exploded, one hundred thousand people were either killed or destined to die. One hundred thousand more were hurt. So many people have shown tremendous dedication in helping these survivors, and it has taken a great deal of dedication to make it possible for these twenty-five girls to come to the United States for medical aid. Now we're sure that there are many among our viewers tonight who want to share in that dedication. *(Turning to the audience)* And you can do so by sending your contribution right now, large or small, to: Maidens, Box 200, New York, 36 New York. You will be making it possible for a team of American and Japanese doctors to work together and provide necessary treatment.

(The sound of applause. Captain Lewis pulls a check out of his pocket and walks over to Mr. Ralph Edwards.)

CAPTAIN LEWIS: This . . . this donation represents my and my fellow crew members' contribution to the fund.

MR. RALPH EDWARDS: Ladies and gentlemen, fifty dollars! And a five-hundred-dollar check will be forthcoming from our show's sponsor, Hazel Bishop Long-Lasting Lipstick, Hazel Bishop Long-Lasting Nail Polish, Hazel Bishop Long-Lasting Complexion Cream—and we urge *you* to be just as generous, as it is the American way!

(Music plays, the sound of applause.)

GRETTY: Enough. No more. *(All action freezes)* Enough. Now Hideko.

HIDEKO *(Stepping out of the silhouette, walking toward Gretty)*: Yes. Now the backwards wind will take us, and we'll go, together.

GRETTY: Anywhere but here.

(Hideko hoists herself up on the back of Gretty's wheelchair. Wind begins to blow through their hair. They are soaring through darkness.)

HIDEKO: LET'S FLY!!!

(Hideko stretches out her arms. As she does this, Mr. Ralph Edwards and Captain Lewis become unfrozen.)

MR. RALPH EDWARDS *(Addressing the audience, looking up to Hideko and Gretty)*: Ladies and gentlemen, watch now as our very special guest, Miss Hideko, climbs aboard a flying wheelchair with her polio-ravaged friend, Gretty Good Time, to soar through the darkest of heavens on a backwards journey through history!

(The sound of applause.)

GRETTY *(Looking around, looking below)*: Say, how does this work, anyway?

MR. RALPH EDWARDS *(Yelling up to her)*: Well normally, history only pushes forward, like a row of dominoes toppled by the finger of man. But sometimes, if there is enough of a hurt, enough cul-de-sac, if you are an exile with nowhere else to go . . .

GRETTY: Anywhere but here.

MR. RALPH EDWARDS *(Yelling louder)*: . . . Then you *can* return. And so because of your hurt, you'll return now to clean your history once and for all, before you pay your final good-byes to this mortal coil . . .

HIDEKO *(Looking down scornfully at him)*: Enough talking, settle down, Mr. Spooky Freak.

(She snaps her fingers and lights fade on Mr. Ralph Edwards and Captain Lewis.)

GRETTY: Yes.

(Beat. The wind blows, Gretty becomes distracted.)

HIDEKO: Maybe you are afraid . . . to take this journey?

GRETTY: No. I'm not afraid. *(Beat)* It's just that tonight, I can't help thinking of my friend McCloud. *(Closes her eyes, feels the wind on her face)* She has slipped away. Off to Scotland she goes. *(Beat)* I will be alone now. No one left to feed me the peach. *(Turns back, looks to Hideko)* You cannot feed me the peach, can you?

HIDEKO: No. I cannot.

GRETTY: No. *(Beat. Smiles)* But you can keep me company during our backwards journey. *(Beat)* And that is nothing to sneeze at.

Scene 8

Dr. Henry and Dr. Caplan are having lunch in the courtyard. Dr. Caplan sits on the bench unwrapping a sandwich. Dr. Henry sits on the ground, legs crossed, slowly peeling an orange.

DR. CAPLAN: By far the most common portal through which the virus gains entrance to the body is the mouth.

DR. HENRY: Uh, yes, I—

DR. CAPLAN *(Takes a bite of his sandwich)*: In the mouth and throat (the oropharynx) it is apt to settle in the tonsils and cervical; in the lower intestines it settles in the lymphoid follicles and regional (mesenteric) lymph nodes.

DR. HENRY: Yes, the polio virus is very complicated—

DR. CAPLAN *(Swallows the bite of sandwich)*: I've always found it extraordinary that the virus apparently does no appreciable damage in the alimentary tract and its immediate and adjacent lymph nodes, where its effects seldom amount to more than a slight swelling *(Takes another bite)* of these structures.

DR. HENRY *(Impatient)*: Yes, the early symptoms are difficult to diagnose. Dr., I wanted to talk to you about Gretty Myers, she seems very, I just—

DR. CAPLAN: It is most unfortunate that the one place where the polio virus causes its most destructive and irreparable damage in the body should be in the central nervous system, particularly the gray matter of the spinal cord. For as you know, motor nerve cells, once destroyed, do not have the property of regenerating themselves as do cells of the skin, the liver, or other organs. This is why paralysis, once established, is often permanent. As with this case. *(Swallows)* This patient. *(Beat)* Her.

DR. HENRY: Gretty. Gretty Myers.

DR. CAPLAN: Did you want to talk about her?

DR. HENRY: Yes, I did, I—

DR. CAPLAN: Judging from her respiratory patterns as of late, there does appear to be some paralytic effects in the diaphragm, contrary to her original diagnoses.

DR. HENRY *(A bit taken aback)*: Oh. Really?

DR. CAPLAN: Yes. A Drinker respirator will most likely be required.

DR. HENRY: An iron lung.

DR. CAPLAN: Yes.

DR. HENRY: They weigh eight hundred pounds. They make sounds like a dying whale.

DR. CAPLAN *(Not listening to Dr. Henry)*: Yes. I've been making a number of inquiries into the appropriate facilities.

DR. HENRY: Yes. *(Beat)* Any luck?

DR. CAPLAN: There's been a certain amount of hesitancy.

DR. HENRY: Because she's on Social Security.

DR. CAPLAN: Yes. The respirator is costly to maintain. It's not unexpected.

DR. HENRY: No.

DR. CAPLAN: But I have managed to locate an institution upstate which would be willing to take her. They should have a bed available within a couple of weeks.

DR. HENRY: An institution.

DR. CAPLAN *(Taking another bite of sandwich)*: Yes. It would be better if the transfer could take place sooner rather than later, but . . .

DR. HENRY: In my observations of the patient, her respiratory system appears to be holding up okay, for the time being. *(Beat)* So maybe the transfer won't even, be necessary.

DR. CAPLAN: It is necessary. *(Beat)* This isn't the appropriate place for her.

DR. HENRY: She's unhappy.

(Beat.)

DR. CAPLAN: What?

DR. HENRY: She's unhappy, here. She'll be even more unhappy in an institution.

DR. CAPLAN: Well, yes, she's a handful.

(Beat.)

DR. HENRY: I'm not saying that she's a handful, I'm saying that she's very unhappy.

DR. CAPLAN: I think that's quite clear.

DR. HENRY: Dr. Caplan, I've been doing some research, and there's been great success, with home treatment. I read this article, Dr. Howard Rusk, and . . .

DR. CAPLAN *(Smiling slightly)*: Home treatment?

DR. HENRY: Yes, there's a new program being developed in California, it's called In-Home Supportive Services and . . .

DR. CAPLAN: She would have her own apartment?

DR. HENRY: Yes, and . . .

DR. CAPLAN: And if she fell from her wheelchair? If the apartment caught on fire?

DR. HENRY: Well, there are . . .

DR. CAPLAN: She would burn. *(Beat)* It wouldn't be possible. She wouldn't be safe.

DR. HENRY: There are attendants, they provide care . . .

DR. CAPLAN: Have you told the patient about this?

DR. HENRY: Not yet, I don't want to get her hopes up, but—

DR. CAPLAN: Dr., regardless, I'm sure this wouldn't even be an option considering her . . . medical coverage.

DR. HENRY: We could still apply, and perhaps . . .

DR. CAPLAN: The money is not there. Henry.

(Beat.)

DR. HENRY: Yes, of course. But it's, a shame . . . *(Softly)* A shame.

(Beat. Dr. Henry softly bites the orange.)

DR. CAPLAN: Yes. *(Beat)* That's a shiny ring on your finger.

DR. HENRY *(Looking at the ring)*: Oh. Thank you.

DR. CAPLAN: Real diamond?

DR. HENRY: Yes.

DR. CAPLAN: Costly?

DR. HENRY: Yes. It was.

DR. CAPLAN *(Lifting his own ring finger close to Dr. Henry's face)*: Mine's real too.

Scene 9

Gretty and Hideko, soaring through the darkness.

GRETTY: Will we pass over an ocean? I wonder.

HIDEKO: Maybe.

GRETTY: Haven't seen an ocean in quite a while. *(Beat)* You like the ocean?

HIDEKO: Yes. I do.

GRETTY: My father used to take us up to New England to visit my uncle. Those rocks were very jagged. Ocean foam. *(Beat)* I remember thinking, "I should like to climb forever on these friendly rocks." But the rocks weren't so friendly, to me. *(Smiling)* But he did climb on them, and I watched him climb.

HIDEKO: Who's "him"?

GRETTY: My brother. Little Puppy, he was. He's dead now.

HIDEKO: Oh. And you miss him.

GRETTY: Yes. The last thing I said to him was, "Shut up, little dog, little nothing."

HIDEKO: And you did not see him again?

GRETTY: No. He would try to visit me, and I would tell the nurses to send him away.

HIDEKO: And now he's gone. Maybe *this* is the reason you want to die?

GRETTY: Well, it makes people comfortable to think that there's only one reason, but there's never just *one*, is there?

HIDEKO *(Staring downward)*: No. There is not.

GRETTY: Even living in a shit body, like we both do, even then there's never just one reason. *(Beat. Staring at Hideko's scarred face)* You know.

HIDEKO: Yes.

GRETTY: What was it like for you, I wonder.

HIDEKO: What was it like?

GRETTY: After. When you became . . . when you first saw . . . those scars.

(Beat.)

HIDEKO: I awoke, after long days of sleep, in my bedroom, in my mother's house on the beach. No one else was awake, and I crawled over to the dressing table, where I picked up the mirror. *(Beat)* I looked. And saw. My face. *(Beat)* A trick was being played on me. I screamed. My chin, had moved. In a different place now, it was. *(Beat)* I found myself crawling out the door, outside, to the beach. *(Beat)* And I thought, "I will not carry this beast. I will drag it into the ocean foam, I will bury it deep within the sea, where it belongs." And I dragged my body through the pebbles and sand, towards the waves. I did not look back, but I did feel my mother's hands pulling me, restraining me, and I heard her voice, whispering, "No, Hideko. Not today. Please. You can still have many years. The beautiful work of your life can still be done." *(Beat)* And she gently touched my scars and said, "Even in your body, the way it is now, the way it always will be. Even in this body. The beautiful work of your life can still be done. So please, not today."

(Beat.)

GRETTY: Yes. I've felt that. What we feel, the suffering, it is the same.

HIDEKO *(A bit of anger)*: No. It is not. *(Beat)* We can try to imagine each other's pain, and we can recognize our similarities, but not even in your dream stories could you fully know my suffering. This dream isn't enough, you don't have the ability to capture it.

(Beat.)

GRETTY: Yes. I'm sorry. I'm sorry.

HIDEKO: Okay. *(Smiles softly, touching Gretty's cheek)* It's okay. Gentle. Gentle.

(Somewhere in the distance, a voice is heard:)

MR. RALPH EDWARDS *(Voice-over)*: Ladies and gentlemen, you are witnessing a touching moment of humanity as these two women reach over the boundaries which separate them in a gesture of empathy and—

HIDEKO *(Yelling out)*: Another word from your mouth and I will squeeze your throat till you are a dead blue shell! Yes?

MR. RALPH EDWARDS *(Voice-over)*: Sorry. I'm just trying to help.

HIDEKO: Then quiet down!

(Beat. The wind blows. Gretty notices that tears are streaming down Hideko's face.)

GRETTY: Shhh . . . the surgery will . . .

HIDEKO: I do not want the surgery. I'm tired of surgeries. I will change my past, and make these scars disappear.

GRETTY *(Leans her head onto Hideko's hand)*: Yes. And we're almost there.

(Dr. Caplan enters. Hideko backs away from Gretty. Dr. Caplan lifts Gretty from the wheelchair and puts her into the bed. She screams and struggles. He brutally straps her arm down, injects her with a sedative. He exits. Gretty drifts off to sleep. Hideko slowly exits.)

Scene 10

The next morning. The curtain is closed on both sides of Gretty's bed. Dr. Henry enters.

DR. HENRY: Morning. Shall we open this curtain?

GRETTY: No, sir.

DR. HENRY: Not even a little?

GRETTY: I'm not childish. I want it closed.

DR. HENRY: Okay. *(Beat. Sitting on her bed)* I like to go for walks. Did I ever tell you that? Sometimes I sneak away into the woods. *(Beat)* Behind the cafeteria. I like to do this by myself.

GRETTY: But now I should join you.

DR. HENRY: Yes.

GRETTY: The wheelchair will not go through the woods.

DR. HENRY: Maybe it will. *(Looking at her chart)* They've medicated you.

GRETTY: I was screaming. They're moving me, Dr. Henry. In two weeks. To an institution, upstate. They have the iron lung there.

DR. HENRY: I know.

GRETTY *(Drifting away)*: Well, I can't talk with you for very long, I am preoccupied. I have plans.

DR. HENRY: What will you be doing?

GRETTY: To the candy shoppe!

DR. HENRY *(Smiling)*: What will you buy?

GRETTY: The gooey ones. Cocoa-flavored gooeys.

DR. HENRY: Maybe I'll go with you?

GRETTY: No. I will already have company.

DR. HENRY: Someone special.

GRETTY: My Little Puppy is here.

DR. HENRY: Will he stay by your side *(Beat. Smiling)* the whole time?

GRETTY *(Beat)*: No. He won't. *(Beat)* This all will not help. You do not really want to help. You talk. That's all. *(Beat)* I can't move. *(Beat)* I gotta piss.

DR. HENRY: I'll help you.

(He puts the bedpan under her covers and positions it. She pisses.)

A catheter could . . .

GRETTY: No pipes.

(He takes the bedpan out, starts to walk away.)

I should like to see it.

(He pauses, then shows her the contents of the bedpan. She stares at it, dips her finger in, takes some on her finger.)

(Softly) Ocean foam. Pretty, it is.

(Pause.)

DR. HENRY: I told them you don't belong in an institution, but . . .

GRETTY *(Smiling)*: But there was nothing you could do. Your hands, were tied. Just like mine.

(She moves her arm. It is still strapped to the bed. He unstraps it. Beat.)

DR. HENRY *(Sitting on the edge of her bed)*: Yes. *(Beat)* My father took me fishing once with a friend of his who later killed himself. Shotgun blast. My father cried and some people said: "Coward" and: "He should have fought harder," but my father was not angry, and he still smiles . . . when I say . . . that fisherman's name.

GRETTY *(Tears coming)*: You are going to help me die?

DR. HENRY: Yes. I am. *(Beat)* My hands, are not tied.

Act Two

The Whale

Scene 1

In the courtyard, a sign hangs on a nearby wall that reads: WELCOME
HOME, MRS. MCCLOUD. *McCloud stands near a bench, a paper party
hat on her head. She is slowly waving her hands in the air, furious, trying to find the words to speak. Gretty sits in her wheelchair, also wearing
a party hat, her eyes distant. McCloud continues waving her hands for a
few beats, then finally:*

MCCLOUD: My lips, have swallowed warm human blood.

GRETTY: Oh shut up.

MCCLOUD: These hands. These hands have become the hands of
    Cain, Gretty.

GRETTY: You're drunk again.

MCCLOUD: No I'm not. *(Sitting down on the bench)* A little tipsy
    maybe.

GRETTY: Goddamn Nurse Nancy for slipping you that scotch.

MCCLOUD: She was only trying to calm me down. *(Picking up the
    Scottish accent)* She's a good lass, that Nurse Nancy.

GRETTY: Oh cut it out, you never went to Scotland! They found you
    sleeping in a toolshed on Staten Island.

MCCLOUD: No. I stowed away on a pirate ship, a Spanish galleon . . .

GRETTY: Yeah, some people call it the Staten Island ferry . . .

MCCLOUD: . . . and jumped ship near the Shetland Islands. Swam to the city of Lerwick. A boggy little port. But the Spanish pirates spotted me swimming from the ship, and they gave chase.

GRETTY: "Spanish pirates"? Shut—

MCCLOUD: Yes, Spanish pirates! They was trying to recapture Scotland to restore Spain to its former greatness as a world power! But they figured me to be a spy and hunted me through the city.

GRETTY: I have news, too, McCloud.

MCCLOUD: I eluded them. Ducked into a small tavern. Had a cup of grog while I was there. Mirth and frivolity aplenty in that place.

GRETTY: Dr. Henry is a good boy. He's going to help me.

MCCLOUD: But the tavern then fell silent. One of the pirates entered, he spotted me. Nothing more than a boy, he was. But a sharp blade in his hand.

GRETTY: He's going to help me die.

MCCLOUD: He held the blade over my head. Our eyes met. Nothing more than a boy, he was.

GRETTY: Next Thursday night. An injection. Quiet, comfortable.

MCCLOUD: We wrestled, I found strength, I pushed the blade to his throat, dug it in deep. And jerked it.

GRETTY: I'll go to sleep.

MCCLOUD: I watched the blood release, I licked my fingers, and swallowed.

GRETTY: Why are you telling me this story?

MCCLOUD: You never forget the copper taste of blood, Gretty. You never forget the kill.

GRETTY: It ain't a killing. He knows what he's doing. He's helping me do what I ain't strong enough to do.

MCCLOUD: He'll regret it. Believe me.

GRETTY: It's not true. He knows it's fair. I own my body. This is what I own. No one else.

MCCLOUD *(Back to her story)*: And once I tasted the blood of that boy I realized—

GRETTY: No more stories. Who are you to tell me these bedtime stories with morals to them? You think because I'm a cripple you need to talk to me in *stories?*

MCCLOUD: No. I, I care about you.

GRETTY: Then you should care that I have some dignity. I ain't got none now.

MCCLOUD: You do.

GRETTY: Why are you sitting so far away?

MCCLOUD: What?

GRETTY: Why are you sitting so far away from me? Come closer.

MCCLOUD: I'm comfortable here.

GRETTY *(Sniffing)*: Do you smell that?

MCCLOUD: No.

GRETTY: It's my shit. It's in my pants.

MCCLOUD: You should have told one of the nurses . . .

GRETTY: I did. She told me to wait. Now come closer.

MCCLOUD: No.

GRETTY: Come closer, McCloud.

(McCloud walks toward Gretty.)

Now do you?

MCCLOUD: Yes. I smell it.

GRETTY: Good. Now walk back to your seat.

(Beat. McCloud doesn't walk away.)

MCCLOUD: Gretty . . .

GRETTY: Walk back to your seat now. Please.

(Beat. McCloud still doesn't move.)

You think it's a cowardly act.

MCCLOUD: No. I do not. I just don't want you to go. I need you here.

GRETTY *(Staring her in the eye)*: You'll be fine without me.

(Beat.)

MCCLOUD: No. I won't.

GRETTY: This is going to happen, McCloud.

MCCLOUD: I'll tell Dr. Caplan. I will.

GRETTY: Tell him.

MCCLOUD: I will. I'm going to.

GRETTY: I wish your pirate ship sank. Taking you to the bottom of the ocean.

MCCLOUD: Not me. I don't wish that. I'd still, still rather be here.

GRETTY: Good. Now *walk*. Away.

(She does so.)

Scene 2

Lights up on a flowing river. Captain Lewis is tossing stones into the river. Mr. Ralph Edwards is lying on the ground. He slowly stands, looks around, then addresses the audience:

MR. RALPH EDWARDS *(Whispering)*: Ladies and gentlemen, we continue now with tonight's very special program. We have followed our guests as they have flown backwards through time, penetrating the tiny cracks in the skin of history, burrowing themselves deep inside the meaty muscle; the all that matters. We have just landed on the shores of the Motoyasu River, Hiroshima, Japan, where Miss Hideko will—

(Hideko comes up behind him and pushes him to the ground.)

HIDEKO: You do not belong here.

MR. RALPH EDWARDS: But we are helping to raise money for your cause, for your surgery, to give you a new start on . . . *(Beat. Sincerely)* I'm trying to help.

HIDEKO: But you do not belong *here*. Go. Now.

(Beat.)

MR. RALPH EDWARDS: Ladies and gentlemen, in respect for the raw, essential human emotion which is being tapped into, we will be cutting our visit short tonight, but first let me once again thank our sponsor, Hazel Bishop Long-Lasting Nail Polish—

HIDEKO: Go!!!

(He runs off. Hideko approaches Captain Lewis; she seems to be impatiently waiting for something.)

Thank you for the fifty dollars.

CAPTAIN LEWIS *(Startled)*: Oh. You're welcome.

HIDEKO *(Looking upward)*: A sunny morning.

CAPTAIN LEWIS: I didn't have much more money to give. I don't make much money at . . .

HIDEKO *(Still looking upward)*: I don't need much money.

CAPTAIN LEWIS: . . . the factory. Yes.

HIDEKO: Do you have the time?

CAPTAIN LEWIS: For what?

HIDEKO *(Looking at him)*: What time is it?

CAPTAIN LEWIS: Oh. Yes.

(He pulls out a silver pocket watch, but doesn't show her the time.)

You've been to this river before.

HIDEKO: Yes. As a child.

CAPTAIN LEWIS: You used to play in the water?

HIDEKO: Many times.

CAPTAIN LEWIS *(Smiling, like a father)*: It's not too deep, is it?

HIDEKO: It's deep, only in the center. *(Beat. Looking at him)* Such a sad man. I think I pity you.

(Beat.)

CAPTAIN LEWIS *(Coming in close to her)*: I want you to know that I'm . . .

HIDEKO: Step away from me. Now. And stop looking at me.

(He steps back, turns away.)

CAPTAIN LEWIS: I had a duty. Duty is a powerful force, it . . .

HIDEKO: It is nothing. Your duty was to justice. And you failed. *(Beat)* The time, please.

(He opens the pocket watch and shows her the time.)

CAPTAIN LEWIS: You're very impatient.

HIDEKO: Yes.

CAPTAIN LEWIS *(Pointing)*: There's a woman over there, in a wheelchair.

HIDEKO: That is my friend.

CAPTAIN LEWIS: A close friend?

HIDEKO: I haven't known her that long, but she's very funny, and playful.

CAPTAIN LEWIS: Like you.

HIDEKO: I'm not playful. I'm calm.

CAPTAIN LEWIS: But you seem so . . .

HIDEKO: I'm calm. *(Beat)* I'm not a child. Children are bouncy and silly. I'm calm.

CAPTAIN LEWIS: Okay. *(Beat)* I should go now.
HIDEKO: Yes.

(Hideko is looking around even more impatiently.)

CAPTAIN LEWIS: Be patient.
HIDEKO: I *am* patient.

(He starts to walk away, then moves toward her. He pulls out his watch and lays it at her feet. She pauses, indignant at this gesture, almost ready to spit at him. She pauses again, then bends down and takes the watch into her hands. He walks away. She looks at the watch, then stares up at the sky.)

Scene 3

Gretty's room. Gretty is in bed. Dr. Henry is wetting down her hair in a basin, preparing to wash it.

GRETTY: Blond, brunette, redhead?
DR. HENRY: What?
GRETTY: Which was your wife?
DR. HENRY: She had dark hair.
GRETTY: Pretty, she was?
DR. HENRY: Yes. Very.
GRETTY: I can tell, that when you sleep, that's when you see her. In your dreams still.
DR. HENRY: Yes. Sometimes. Not as much lately.
GRETTY: She's fading.
DR. HENRY: No, it's just . . .
GRETTY: Maybe you want to remember only the bad times? Easier that way?
DR. HENRY: Yes.
GRETTY: There were many bad times.
DR. HENRY: Not many. But bad, yes.
GRETTY: Were you cruel to her?

(He lathers the soap into her hair.)

DR. HENRY: I don't think I was. I spent so many hours studying, to be a doctor. Sometimes I lost my temper.

GRETTY: She felt lonely.

DR. HENRY: I tried very hard.

GRETTY: Yes.

DR. HENRY: The last thing I said to her was, "I'll call you Tuesday about those boxes."

GRETTY: You didn't call her.

DR. HENRY: She came by and picked up the boxes when I wasn't home. *(Beat. Rinsing the soap from her hair)* What about you? "Gretty Good Time" probably broke a few hearts?

GRETTY: No broken hearts. No.

DR. HENRY: No boyfriends?

GRETTY: People don't see me that way. People *decide* not to see me that way.

DR. HENRY: You think, it's a choice? People *choose* not to see you, in that way?

GRETTY: Yes. I do.

(He towel-dries her hair.)

DR. HENRY: Maybe, it's just that—

GRETTY: I don't want to debate, this morning.

DR. HENRY *(Standing up, smiling)*: Okay.

GRETTY: I'm usually washed, as well.

DR. HENRY: Oh. Okay. Should I, the nurse could . . .

GRETTY: You are a doctor, aren't you?

DR. HENRY: Yes. I am.

GRETTY *(Smiling)*: Then it's no big deal. Right?

DR. HENRY: Okay. I'll be right back.

(He exits with the basin. Beat. Some hesitation in Gretty's eyes. She tries to shift in her bed. He returns with fresh water in the basin, a towel and a fresh hospital gown.)

GRETTY: So, have you read much F. Scott Fitzgerald?

DR. HENRY *(Perplexed)*: Uh, yes. I've, read many of his books. Is he your favorite author?

GRETTY: No, I don't know any of his work.

DR. HENRY: Oh.

(Beat.)

(Dipping his finger in the water) Well, this water's nice and warm.

GRETTY *(Smiling)*: That doesn't matter much. To my body.

DR. HENRY: Gretty, you know with polio-paralysis you can still feel full sensation.

(He touches the wet face cloth to her paralyzed arm.)

You can feel this.

GRETTY: Yes. It's warm. *(He touches her arm with the palm of his hand)* And that is cold.

(He smiles and rubs his hands together to warm them up. Beat. He begins washing her face and neck.)

DR. HENRY: Is this too warm?

GRETTY: No. It's fine.

(He opens her hospital gown. She is naked. He glides the sponge over her body, softly washing her arms, her legs. A few moments pass.)

Sometimes I think of my organs, inside of my body.

DR. HENRY *(A little taken aback)*: What do you think of them?

GRETTY: How they're in me, how they sit, in me. But I've never seen them. A part of me I'll never see. *(Beat)* But you, you've seen organs.

DR. HENRY: Yes. I have.

GRETTY: Bodies split open, and you've stared, inside.

DR. HENRY: Yes.

GRETTY: You've probably seen so many, they look familiar now.

DR. HENRY: Yes. They do.

GRETTY: If you were to split me open right now *(The sponge is gliding over her stomach)* you'd see my liver. My stomach. *(It slowly glides lower)* My intestines. My kidneys. *(It slowly glides upward, toward her chest)* My lungs. *(Beat)* My heart. Beating. *(Beat)* And it would all look familiar to you.

DR. HENRY: Yes.

GRETTY: No. *(Beat)* Not all. Not the heart. You wouldn't recognize it. If you saw it.

DR. HENRY *(Rinsing the sponge)*: No?

GRETTY: No. There *is* desire in me, Dr. Henry. No one wants to see it, but it's there. Sometimes it's small, and sometimes it chokes me.

(He dries her with the towel. He puts the fresh gown on her, slowly covers her with a blanket.)

DR. HENRY: I'm sure, that it's there.

GRETTY *(Some anger)*: It is. *(Beat)* Thursday is coming.

DR. HENRY: Yes. It is.

GRETTY: You're not having second thoughts, are you?

DR. HENRY: No. Are you?

GRETTY: No. No second thoughts.

DR. HENRY: Okay.

(He starts to walk away.)

GRETTY: A perfumed soap, that was.

DR. HENRY: Yes. It was.

GRETTY: I smell, very nice now.

DR. HENRY: Yes, Gretty. *(Beat)* You do.

Scene 4

Lights up on Hideko and Gretty, sitting near the river. Hideko sits on a blanket, Gretty in her wheelchair. They are playing cards.

HIDEKO *(Looking at her new pocket watch)*: What an ugly pocket watch!

GRETTY *(Looking at it)*: It's not bad.

HIDEKO: Ugly. Ugly. Old thing. I wish it were a wristwatch! More modern!

GRETTY: That one keeps the time okay?

HIDEKO *(Looking at it one more time, then putting it away)*: I suppose. Maybe it's running a little slow. I'm tired of waiting.

GRETTY *(Looking out over the river)*: It's been a while. Are you sure this is where we're supposed to be? This is the place you needed to go to?

HIDEKO: Yes. This is the place. Soon. It will happen soon. *(Beat. Throwing her cards down)* These cards are boring. I know! We'll play *strip* poker!

GRETTY: What?!? Are you out of your mind?

HIDEKO: It's fun and sexy!

GRETTY: You wanna strip out here in the open? You're nuts.

HIDEKO: We are safe with each other. And no one will see us.

GRETTY: That man you were just talking to—

HIDEKO: He's gone now. It's just us here. Strip poker is so exciting!

GRETTY: I don't know . . . You've played it before?

HIDEKO *(Nodding)*: My friends in college.

GRETTY: Oooh. A college girl, you are?

HIDEKO *(Shuffling the deck)*: Yes. I am. Two semesters. A school taught by missionaries. I went to study violin, but I fell in love with philosophy! I wore a fuzzy black sweater and read Jean-Paul Sartre! He's so cool! Have you read him?

GRETTY: No.

HIDEKO: My friends and I would drink red wine and talk and talk about his writings!

GRETTY: Good stuff, huh?

HIDEKO: Oh yes! I remember thinking, I am tired of this nothingness which lies coiled in the heart of my being, like a worm! I am going to step forward, and become an existential man!

GRETTY: But you're not a *man* . . .

HIDEKO: I didn't think that mattered, I was going to *create my own freedom*!

GRETTY: So did you?

HIDEKO: No. Not yet.

GRETTY: Your friends sound very nice. Do you still see them?

HIDEKO: No. I had to drop out of school. Tuition's very costly. And no one would hire me. My face, not pretty. *(Beat. Smiling)* But I did have good friends there. So sweet! *(Beat)* Strip poker, Gretty! Let's play!

GRETTY: No. I don't want to.

HIDEKO *(Dealing the cards)*: You shouldn't be trapped in morality, that's just bad faith! Be free!

GRETTY: It ain't bad faith. I just don't wanna.

(Beat.)

HIDEKO: I can help you.

(Hideko takes off Gretty's slipper.)

This is how you play. You ante up.

GRETTY: Then you gotta ante up, too.

(Hideko takes off her own shoe, places it on the ground with Gretty's.)

HIDEKO: We always start with the shoes, that way it gets more and more dangerous as you go along!

GRETTY *(Smiling mischievously)*: Maybe. *(Beat)* No. Regular poker is fine. My slipper goes back on now, please.

HIDEKO *(Putting the slipper back on)*: Okay.

GRETTY *(Looks over her cards)*: Do you really believe you can do that?

HIDEKO: What?

GRETTY: "Create your own freedom."

HIDEKO: Yes. I hope. I can.

(Lights come up on Captain Lewis, sitting on a chair in a separate stage space. We hear sounds of an airplane engine.)

(Pauses, pulls out her pocket watch) It's time. *(Pointing)* That is our house, off in the distance. Do you see it?

GRETTY *(Looking)*: Yes. Pretty thing. A red roof.

HIDEKO: My mother stepped out of the house and called to me. I was playing with my friends here on the shores of the Motoyasu River. We were daring each other to get naked and jump into the water. And we were laughing. I turned, I could hear my mother's voice:

CAPTAIN LEWIS *(As Hideko's mother)*: Hideko, there are planes coming! I can hear them overhead. Come indoors with me now. Hideko, I am calling to you!

HIDEKO: But I pretended I did not hear her.

CAPTAIN LEWIS: Hideko, I am calling to you!

HIDEKO: But this time I will go inside the house. I will listen to my mother and I will bury my face in her dress, where it will not get burned.

CAPTAIN LEWIS: Hideko, there are planes overhead!

HIDEKO: But there are *always* planes overhead. There are so many that I am not frightened of them. I want to play with my friends. *(Looking toward the house)* So she returns to the house, without me. *(Beat)* Then the horrible white light, so bright that I am sure it will make God blink.

(All lights come up to full, they are drowned in light.)

And then the wind comes.

A hot wind did blow,
God's wind or the devil's wind?
And my skin was built.

(All lights come back down to normal.)

I step up from the ground, my clothing, torn, smoldering. The burning skin is immediate, swollen, very hard to move. I feel hands guiding me, pushing me back towards the river. I wade in, coooool, smoooooth. The burning is less. Then I feel more hands pushing me deeper into the river, past my neck, the water up to my chin. I hear splashing and screaming. So many have come for comfort in this cool river that people are being pushed out of the shallow ends and into the center of the river. They are drowning. My head dips under, I see faces, and bodies in the water, bodies which look like mine. *(Beat)* But I feel myself pulling, clawing. I reach the surface. I hold on, and push. I step on bodies. I step on bodies, and I reach the shore. *(Beat)* And I stood, where I stand right now. *(Beat, looking back toward the house)* I was a foolish child for not listening when my mother called me. And foolish children are ugly, they step on other people's bodies to survive. *(Beat. Touches her face)* And their faces look like their souls.

(Beat.)

GRETTY: No. You had no way of knowing this would happen.
CAPTAIN LEWIS *(Whispering)*: God's wind, or the devil's wind? God's wind, or the devil's wind?
GRETTY: You were a child, playing in a river. You don't deserve this.
HIDEKO: I enjoyed playing. Very much.
GRETTY: And you still do?
HIDEKO: Yes. I do.

(A breeze begins to blow.)

CAPTAIN LEWIS *(Faster)*: God's wind, or the devil's wind? God's wind, or the devil's wind?
GRETTY: It's time. For us to go.
HIDEKO: Yes.
CAPTAIN LEWIS: God's wind, or the devil's wind? God's wind, or the devil's wind?

(Hideko climbs onto the back of Gretty's wheelchair. She looks at her pocket watch, then sadly looks over to Captain Lewis.)

HIDEKO: Yes. There's only wreckage here.

Scene 5

Dr. Caplan and Dr. Henry sit in the courtyard, eating sandwiches. Dr. Henry is nervous, distracted.

DR. CAPLAN: Liverwurst!

DR. HENRY: What?

DR. CAPLAN *(Pointing)*: Your sandwich. It's liverwurst?

DR. HENRY: Yes. It is.

DR. CAPLAN: I haven't had a liverwurst sandwich in quite a while. It brings back many memories for me.

DR. HENRY: Oh?

DR. CAPLAN: Yes. My mother used to make liverwurst sandwiches for me as a child.

(Beat. Dr. Caplan stares at Dr. Henry's sandwich.)

DR. HENRY: Do you want a bite?

DR. CAPLAN: Yes. Thank you. *(Takes a bite)* It's very good.

DR. HENRY *(Taking back the sandwich)*: Yes. Dr. Caplan, I, I was, speaking to a nurse, and she told me that, a few months ago, Gretty—Gretta Myers—she refused to eat.

DR. CAPLAN *(Mouth full of sandwich)*: Yes. A few months ago. She refused to eat.

DR. HENRY: But she started eating again.

DR. CAPLAN *(Swallowing)*: We threatened to put a tube in.

DR. HENRY: Yes.

DR. CAPLAN: She wrestled. Squirmed. We used restraints.

DR. HENRY: Tied her down.

DR. CAPLAN: A justifiable procedure. She was uncooperative.

DR. HENRY *(Softly)*: Yes. *(Beat)* Dr. Caplan, did you consider, at all, *not* putting the tube in?

(Beat.)

DR. CAPLAN: There's real danger. Doctors have been prosecuted, they've been charged with, simply for assisting patients with . . . *(Beat)* You've heard about that New Hampshire case.

DR. HENRY: Sander. Dr. Sander. He was acquitted.

DR. CAPLAN: Some people do believe . . . *(Beat)* Autonomy over one's body is a private issue. *(Beat)* Don't you believe that to be true?

DR. HENRY: Yes. I do.

DR. CAPLAN: It's a question which makes one aware of the moral gray areas which doctors must map out for themselves. Even within the oath, one finds a great deal of ambiguity. You remember the oath? "I will follow that method of treatment . . ."

DR. HENRY: "I will follow that method of treatment which . . ."

DR. CAPLAN: ". . . according to my ability and *judgment* . . ."

DR. HENRY: ". . . I consider for the benefit of my patient and abstain from whatever is *harmful* and *mischievous.*"

DR. CAPLAN: Yes.

DR. HENRY: That's what I want to do. But—

DR. CAPLAN: I know you do. And it's very hard to know, the right way to help. But when a patient believes that their *entire life* has become "harmful" and "mischievous," it can often feel as if there really is only one way to end that harm and mischief. *(Short beat)* It's a topic which is worthy of debate. And I do think it becomes hard to justify . . . *(Beat)* There are other patients in the world, Henry. Other patients who *want* to live, who are waiting for a bed like hers, who desperately *need* a bed like hers, in a nursing home like this one.

DR. HENRY *(Staring at him)*: Patients who aren't on Social Security. Patients who can pay more for her bed than she can.

DR. CAPLAN: So she deserves your attention more than other patients do because she's poor? A very condescending attitude, Henry.

DR. HENRY: You want her out of here.

DR. CAPLAN: No, I want her to receive what I want *all* our patients to receive, and that is the treatment which she feels will best help her.

DR. HENRY: Then why don't you do it? Why don't *you* give her the injection? *(Beat. Then, calmly)* You want her gone from here, but you don't want to get your hands dirty, you—

DR. CAPLAN: I never said any such thing. I never mentioned any *injection*, did I? All I've said, is that it is a topic, which is worthy of debate.

(Dr. Caplan begins to exit.)

DR. HENRY *(Stopping him)*: You remember the last part of the oath? "If I fulfill this oath and do not violate it, may it be . . ."

DR. CAPLAN: ". . . may it be granted to me to enjoy life and art, being honored with fame among all men for all time to come . . ."

DR. HENRY: ". . . but if I swear it falsely, may the opposite of all this be my lot." *(Beat. Angry)* I remember feeling very frightened as I said those words, because this is an oath which, if broken, becomes a curse on your life.

(Beat.)

DR. CAPLAN: Thank you for the bite of your sandwich, Henry. It was very tasty.

Scene 6

Gretty and Hideko, soaring through darkness.

GRETTY: It was a nightmare. That horrible sight. Back there.
HIDEKO: I wish it had changed. *(Beat)* But it didn't.
GRETTY: You didn't change your past.
HIDEKO: Yes. I don't think that is possible, anymore.
GRETTY: So then, you will have the surgery?

(Beat.)

HIDEKO: No. I will not.
GRETTY: You will keep your face, as it is?
HIDEKO: Yes. And I will go forward. In the present.
GRETTY: Such a strong young woman, you are. *(Beat)* And I'm sorry I did not play strip poker with you. I wish I could be more playful.
HIDEKO: It's okay.
GRETTY: It wasn't bad faith. I was scared. People don't usually see my body uncovered. It frightens me. It stays covered.
HIDEKO: Why is that?
GRETTY: They'll see the twists, the bulges, the deadness. *(Beat)* It's like this journey, useless.
HIDEKO *(Her hand on Gretty's face)*: Not useless.
GRETTY: Your history is the same. It is filled with crime and injury. What good comes from seeing it?
HIDEKO: I think to move forward, we must find the balance.
GRETTY: The balance?

HIDEKO: Between remembering and forgetting, enough of both, but not too little of either. That's what we need. *(Softly stroking Gretty's face)* And it's a tricky path.

GRETTY: Yes. But maybe I don't wanna take the chance. Maybe I don't wanna see Puppy. Maybe I don't wanna remember.

HIDEKO: I'll be with you. Gentle.

GRETTY: No. Enough of this. I'm gonna wake up now. I'm gonna force myself awake. Good-bye, Hideko.

(The wind continues blowing.)

HIDEKO *(Looking downward)*: Down below, Gretty. It's New England.

Scene 7

The courtyard, evening, McCloud is lying flat on the bench, needlepointing. Dr. Caplan enters.

DR. CAPLAN: Lovely evening.

MCCLOUD: Yes.

DR. CAPLAN: The stars are very clear.

MCCLOUD: Yes. *(Looking upward)* Very eye-appealing. *(Beat)* You got a cigarette?

DR. CAPLAN: No, Mrs. McCloud, I don't smoke.

MCCLOUD: You can call me Dolores.

DR. CAPLAN: Okay, Dolores. *(Takes a few steps toward her)* What are you needlepointing?

MCCLOUD *(Rolling over, threatening him with needles)*: It's a vicious kitten! With a butterfly on its nose!

DR. CAPLAN: Just relax, Dolores. Relax.

MCCLOUD: I'm plenty relaxed.

DR. CAPLAN: Good.

(He slowly takes the needles away from her. She doesn't resist. She rolls over onto her back.)

The nurse on duty told me that you won't return to your room.

MCCLOUD: That's right. Tonight's my night out.

DR. CAPLAN: I could have the orderlies *take* you into your room.

MCCLOUD: That would be mistreatment. My son would be very angry.

DR. CAPLAN: Would he?

MCCLOUD: Yes. He would. Maybe even move me to another nursing home. You'd lose out on some bucks.

DR. CAPLAN: He's definitely worried about you. Your behavior. He and I have had many talks.

MCCLOUD *(Scottish accent)*: And not even a wee bit of truth came out in any of them, I'm sure.

DR. CAPLAN: You're son's a very well-respected man, Dolores. You think him a liar?

MCCLOUD: He is. I know it.

DR. CAPLAN: You seem to know a lot of things these days.

(Dr. Caplan sits down on the bench, McCloud's head near his lap. McCloud doesn't move.)

MCCLOUD: You smell.

DR. CAPLAN: Well, it's been a long day.

(She puts her hand on his belly.)

What are you doing?

MCCLOUD: You got a big belly. You drink a lot of beer?

DR. CAPLAN: No. I don't.

(Beat. Her hand grips his stomach violently.)

MCCLOUD: It's very important to me that you hear what I'm going to say to you.

DR. CAPLAN: Ah, I'm listening . . .

MCCLOUD: Thursday is the night that Gretta Myers is going to die.

(Beat.)

DR. CAPLAN: And how will this happen?

MCCLOUD: Dr. Henry. Is going to, help her.

DR. CAPLAN: This is a small nursing home, Mrs. McCloud. If something like this were happening here, don't you think I would know about it?

MCCLOUD: Maybe you *do* know about it.

(Beat. She takes her hand away from his belly.)

DR. CAPLAN *(Standing up)*: As I said, your son and I have had many talks about your condition. Running off, these fantasies about Scotland and pirate ships, and generally erratic behavior. He feels that you might be better off in a facility which could tend to your *psychological* needs, as well as your physical.

MCCLOUD: My son's a shit. Dumping me in this nursing home, so he can take over my money. He's a shit.

DR. CAPLAN: You need to go back to your room now, Mrs. McCloud. *(Starting to walk away)* I'll call the orderlies.

MCCLOUD: Does he know about the history?

DR. CAPLAN: What?

MCCLOUD *(Sitting up)*: Dr. Henry. Does he know about the history, of suicide in Gretty's family? Her brother killed himself. Her grandfather, too.

DR. CAPLAN: This is a private matter, and a personal one. It is up to the individual patient to determine—

MCCLOUD: You need to tell Dr. Henry about the history of suicide in her family, he'll listen to you . . . And if you don't tell him I will.

(Beat.)

DR. CAPLAN: You are getting overexcited. It's very important that you calm down. And rest. This is the exact type of hysterical behavior I've been talking to your son about *(Beat)* I'll be meeting with him again tomorrow to discuss the appropriate facilities for—

MCCLOUD: No. *(Beat)* I don't wanna go to a mental institution, Dr. Caplan. Please.

DR. CAPLAN: Well, we could hold off on looking into other facilities for now. There is a chance that these erratic outbursts will . . . *(Beat)* work themselves out.

MCCLOUD: Yes. They will. *(Beat)* I could kill you. I'm a killer.

DR. CAPLAN: You're not a killer. You're a frightened old woman. And there's no shame in that.

Scene 8

Lights up on the courtyard, the next morning. Dr. Henry is pushing Gretty in her wheelchair. He parks her near the bench. He carries a plastic cup with a straw in it. He sits on the bench. Gretty clearly doesn't want to be there.

GRETTY: My tongue is dry.

DR. HENRY: Have some juice.

GRETTY: No. It's always dry.

DR. HENRY *(Looking around)*: It's nice out here.

GRETTY: Sticky May day.

DR. HENRY: They're going to plant flowers.

GRETTY *(Uninterested)*: Really?

DR. HENRY: Yes. *(Points)* Right there. And there. *(Beat)* Y'know, you could have your own garden, your own flowers.

GRETTY: What are you talking about?

DR. HENRY: The in-home treatment program I've been telling you about—if you lived in your own home, you could plant flowers.

GRETTY *(Smiling slightly)*: A garden. *(Beat. With some anger)* And how would I water them, Dr.? Wouldn't they dry up and die? You are putting foolish ideas into my head.

DR. HENRY: There are attendants which are part of the program, they are people who—

GRETTY: It is not possible for me to live on my own. But thank you. I will have some of the juice, now.

(He holds the cup to her face, she sips. Their eyes are close. Dr. Henry looks into Gretty's eyes, smiles at her.)

DR. HENRY: Now your tongue is moist.

GRETTY *(Smiling back)*: Yes. It is. *(Pulling away)* No. *(Beat)* Don't talk about my tongue.

DR. HENRY: Okay. I'm sorry I said that.

GRETTY: My tongue is not sick. So you don't need to talk about it, Dr.

DR. HENRY: I'm glad it's not sick.

GRETTY: Are you? Why? What use do you have for it?

DR. HENRY: Use?

GRETTY: Do you have plans for my healthy tongue?

DR. HENRY: Don't speak to me this way.

GRETTY *(Her anger building)*: Do you plan to take it from me? And dissect it, maybe. Dig into the plump juicy red tissue, look deep inside it and see the bacteria and organisms growing all over it. You will measure it, and weigh it. And then, when no one is looking, you will secretly take it in your hands and give it a squeeze, just to feel the texture in your fingers.

DR. HENRY *(Shaking his head)*: No. You're not . . .

GRETTY: Do you realize where that would leave me? *(Beat)* Do you realize where that would leave me?

(He leans over and kisses her, deeply and passionately. He then pulls away and takes a few steps back. Beat.)

(Calm, a glowing smile, speaking to herself) Oh. This is how it feels.

(Beat.)

DR. HENRY: I kissed you.
GRETTY: Yes. Why did you?
DR. HENRY: It's what you wanted.

(Beat. She leans over and releases the saliva from her mouth. It drips down onto the ground. She spits the rest out.)

GRETTY: A pity kiss, it was. *(She spits again)* Take it back.
DR. HENRY: It wasn't pity.
GRETTY: Then why?
DR. HENRY: Maybe, maybe it's what I wanted to do.
GRETTY: No.
DR. HENRY: You have desire *in* you. Why can't you believe someone might have desire *for* you?

(Beat.)

GRETTY *(Terrified)*: Do you?
DR. HENRY: Yes, I do . . . You, I think you're beautiful . . .

(Beat. She stares at him.)

But I can't, I mean, I'm . . .
GRETTY: A doctor.
DR. HENRY: Yes. It's not . . .
GRETTY *(Lying)*: I don't have desire for you. *(Staring him in the eye)* I don't.
DR. HENRY: Oh, I thought . . .
GRETTY: No. *(Beat)* Yes. Yes, I do.
DR. HENRY: You liked that kiss.
GRETTY: Yes. I did.
DR. HENRY: That's what life feels like, Gretty. You have to live.

GRETTY *(Firmly)*: No. I don't. *(Beat)* I've never made a decision. I've never had control over my life. I want to have this decision as my own. *(Beat)* You've changed your mind. That's why you brought me out here. That's why you're talking about gardens and home treatment. You won't help me.

DR. HENRY: I'm scared.

GRETTY: I'm not.

DR. HENRY: You're not confused? Not even a little bit?

GRETTY: Do you care about me?

DR. HENRY: Yes. I do.

GRETTY: Then why would you make me ask you again? *(Beat)* I don't want to have to ask you again. *(Beat)* Tomorrow night. Thursday. It will be all right. You'll make it look like a natural death.

DR. HENRY: Yes.

GRETTY: The questions will be over. The confusion will be over.

DR. HENRY: I will. I will do it. I will.

GRETTY: Your life will be calm by Sunday.

Scene 9

A rocky New England shore. Gretty sits in her wheelchair, which is perched in the beach sand. Hideko sits near her. Over to the left of them, in a separate stage space, a white doctor's coat is stretched out on the stage. Over to the right of them is Puppy, in shadow.

GRETTY: That's him, over there, wading in the chilly water.

HIDEKO: He's handsome!

GRETTY: Nah, he's just a puppy.

HIDEKO: He does have big eyes. Some tears in them.

GRETTY *(Looking away)*: Crying little baby.

HIDEKO: He's sad.

GRETTY: Always sad, he was. I got sick of seeing it.

HIDEKO: That's not very kind.

GRETTY: I don't care.

HIDEKO: He cared for you.

GRETTY: Yes. He did.

HIDEKO: He was sad when the polio came, when you were sick.

GRETTY: Separated for a long time, we were.

HIDEKO: It must have been a long time in the hospital.

GRETTY: Yes. But when I was out of danger, they let me come home, while they decided what to do with me. They had to decide whether they should care for me at home, or whether I should be somewhere else.

HIDEKO *(Looking out over the ocean)*: Somewhere else.

GRETTY: Yes. The doctor said I should be put in an institution, with other polio kids. But Puppy said that was a bad idea. He said I should be treated like I was normal, even though I was a cripple now. He even convinced my parents to send me up here to New England for a weekend visit. He wanted to take me here to the beach, to show me how beautiful the ocean was. But Uncle said no, too dangerous.

HIDEKO: Dangerous? Damn the torpedoes! Full speed ahead!

GRETTY: Yes, full speed ahead. We sneaked away. He pushed my wheelchair a mile down the road. He worked up a sweat. He pushed the chair through the beach sand, to the rocks. Quiet for a while, we were.

HIDEKO: Listening to the seagull sounds, staring at the ocean foam.

(Beat. Puppy moves out of the shadows to the side of Gretty's wheelchair. He leans against it, his back to the audience.)

GRETTY: And then he stared up at me and said:

PUPPY *(Softly)*: Don't let them put you in an institution. You'll never get out. Your life will have been wasted. You can live on your own, in your own home, I know you can. But you'll die inside the ugly walls of an institution. You'll die if you have to live there.

(Beat.)

HIDEKO: What did you say to him?

GRETTY *(To Puppy)*: Shut up little dog. Little nothing. You don't know. You're a liar. *(Furious)* You lie to me and say I could live like I was normal. You should be dead for this.

(Puppy moves away from Gretty, into the shadows behind them. He slowly moves toward the doctor's coat.)

HIDEKO: And you went into the institution, and you wouldn't let him visit you, even though he needed you.

GRETTY: Yes. Three years had gone by, three years in the same institution. And then that evening came. The evening they told me what happened to him.

(Puppy picks the doctor's coat up off the floor and puts it on, becoming Dr. Henry. He prepares a syringe over the following:)

That evening. In the ugly walls.

> The ugly walls large with blue and white tile
> The nurse touched my arm and said we must talk
> She stared downward and held back a small smile
> Death on her mind, her skin was poison chalk
>
> "He's dead," and I felt a shift from inside
> My mouth filled with stones, no scream or no shout
> My belly was all swelled, my neck, my side
> A creature's movement, pushing its way out
>
> Such pressure from within, horrendous might
> The pain began to move up from my hips
> Huge my head was, and my skin stretched so tight
> Eyes with dark fear and opening my lips

(Softly singing:)

> Out spit pieces of coal, slivers of shale
> Then mouth stretched further, and out slipped, a whale.

HIDEKO: A whale.

GRETTY: Yes. Giant sea creature, whale, from my mouth, now on the floor in front of me, pointing its head up towards the sun, it was crying, horrible sounds, its body began flailing, breaking the chairs, crushing the floorboards. Stinking. And I thought, This doesn't belong here. It's too big. It's too much. The weight, the weight of this creature's body will crush everything, it will crush everyone I love. Like it crushed my Puppy. It doesn't belong here.

(Gretty uses her arm to push her body out of the wheelchair. She falls to the ground. Dr. Henry finishes preparing the syringe and needle, the injection to end Gretty's life.)

It doesn't belong here. *(Uses her arm to drag her body through the sand, toward the waves)* And I thought, I will not carry this beast. I will drag it through the pebbles and sand. I will drag it into the ocean foam. I will bury it deep within the sea, where it belongs.

(Hideko restrains her.)

HIDEKO: No, Gretty. No. Not today, Gretty. You can leave your brother to your memories. You can still have many years. The beautiful work of your life can still be done. *(Softly, gently touching Gretty's face and body. Gretty's eyes close)* Even in your body, the way it is now, the way it always will be. Even in this body. The beautiful work of your life can still be done.

(Dr. Henry slowly puts the prepared needle in his pocket. He walks toward Gretty. As he moves into the scene, Hideko pulls away, stepping back. Gretty's eyes are still closed, as if she were sleeping on the floor.)

DR. HENRY: You fell from your chair. You slept all night on the floor?
GRETTY *(Slowing opening her eyes)*: Yes. I was dreaming.

(He gently lifts her off the floor, placing her back in the wheelchair. He brushes the hair away from her face, looks into her eyes.)

DR. HENRY: I'm ready now. *(Slowly pulling the needle from his pocket)* Give me your arm.

(A short beat. She smiles lovingly at him. Hideko steps back, watching.)

GRETTY: No. Not now. *No.* Not today. *(Beat)* Not today.

(Lights fade.)

Epilogue

A split scene of Gretty and Hideko soaring through clouds, and Gretty in her room.

HIDEKO: The wind, is blowing forward.

GRETTY *(Smiling)*: Yes.

MR. RALPH EDWARDS *(Stepping forward)*: Ladies and gentlemen, our very special story is now winding down to its heartwarming ending. But first let's listen in as Miss Gretty Good Time, who has just shown amazing courage by choosing life over death, must now deal with the material realties of her life. Will she realize now that her consciousness has just been a reflection of her material experience? Will she see that she could never be happy living in a nursing home, living in chains? Will she—

HIDEKO *(Going after him)*: Will you ever shut up, Mr. Spooky Freak?!? *(Chases him off the stage, then returns to Gretty. Looking downward)* What will be waiting for you there in your room?

GRETTY: Trouble.

(Dr. Caplan and Dr. Henry enter.)

(To Dr. Henry) Good morning.

DR. CAPLAN: Dr. Henry has a piece of paper he would like me to sign.

GRETTY: Yes.

DR. HENRY: It's an application, for the In-Home Supportive Services Program. In California. It's the program I was telling you about.

DR. CAPLAN: Yes. I remember. So this program provides, home care.

DR. HENRY: Yes. There's a long waiting list. *(Looking at Gretty)* Gretty knows that. But it would still be worth a try.

DR. CAPLAN: And you need my signature.

DR. HENRY: Yes. *(Beat)* I'm sure you see, the possible benefits of home care, she would be, it could be a different life for her . . . it costs less than nursing home care, and with the psychological advantages, I really think . . .

HIDEKO: Sign it, you silly fool!

GRETTY: He will sign it.

DR. CAPLAN *(Taking a few steps toward the bed)*: You seem pretty sure of yourself, my friend.

GRETTY: Come any closer to me and I'll bite your skin.

(He stops.)

Sign it and there's a chance I could be gone. Like you wanted.

DR. CAPLAN: I never wanted you gone.

GRETTY: You're a liar. You have a hole inside of you. *(Beat)* And I know you will sign this application because the institution upstate that you were trying to dump me in has rejected the transfer.

(Beat.)

DR. CAPLAN: Yes. They have. They seem to think my diagnosis was wrong, that your respirtory patterns are not irregular enough to warrant a Drinker respirator. *(Looking to Dr. Henry)* I wonder what made them doubt my diagnosis?

DR. HENRY: I don't know. Maybe another doctor gave them . . . a second opinion.

DR. CAPLAN: Yes. Perhaps.

GRETTY *(Calmly)*: So, therefore, Dr. Caplan, I think you will sign the application because if you do not, I will continue to live, here. I will live a long life, and I promise I will scream as loud as I can, every day. And when my voice runs out, I will flail my arm wildly, every day. And when you come close to me to strap my arm down, that is when I will spit in your mouth and in your eyes. Every day I will do this. *(Beat)* So you should be *praying* that I go into home care, because I ain't gonna die in these ugly walls.

(Beat. He signs the application.)

DR. CAPLAN: Best wishes.

(Dr. Caplan exits. Hideko applauds excitedly, but then sees that Gretty is nervous.)

HIDEKO: It is a scary thing, to choose to live and move forward in this world.

MCCLOUD *(Bursting into the room, with great drama)*: Yes, but! "It is very unhappy, but too late to be helped, the discovery we have made, that we *exist*!"

GRETTY: Who said that, F. Scott Fitzgerald?

MCCLOUD: No, Ralph Waldo Emerson.

GRETTY: Did you seduce him, too?

MCCLOUD: If only I had! I'll bet he would've been a real transcendentalist tiger in bed. *(Sighs)* Too bad he was just a *little* before my time. *(Smiles, kisses Gretty on the cheek)* I'm glad you're here, Gretty.

GRETTY: Me, too.

(McCloud exits, but she inexplicably shoots Dr. Henry a look of violence as she goes.)

DR. HENRY *(Looking after McCloud)*: She's so loony.

GRETTY *(Smiling)*: I know.

DR. HENRY: Okay, I'll send the application out today. It probably will be at least a few months before we hear whether or not it gets approved. But in the meantime we are *not* gonna get our hopes up!

GRETTY *(Looking away)*: Yes.

DR. HENRY *(Noticing that something is wrong)*: You're still frightened, the prospect of living on your own, it . . .

GRETTY: What if I fall, onto the floor?

HIDEKO: Someone will pick you up!

GRETTY: What if my apartment catches on fire?

DR. HENRY: You would find a way to escape. I'm not trying to push you into this, Gretty. But I know you could live a different life out there.

GRETTY: I could live a different life here, too. Maybe.

DR. HENRY: Yes. Maybe you could. *(Beat. Smiling)* I would think of you. You'd think of me?

GRETTY: A little, I would.

HIDEKO: A little? A lot! He's so cute!

DR. HENRY: You'd think about our kiss.

GRETTY: Yes.

DR. HENRY: I was thinking, Gretty, maybe it was the wrong thing to do, I mean, to kiss you, to feel . . . I mean, I am . . .

GRETTY: A doctor.

DR. HENRY: Yes. Maybe I owe you an apology.

GRETTY: You ain't *that* bad of a kisser. *(Smiling)* No apology necessary.

DR. HENRY: You are very different now.

GRETTY: And you think it's because of your magic kiss? You "woke me up" or something? Dream on, boy!

DR. HENRY: That's not what I mean, it's just, it was a nice kiss. I enjoyed it.

GRETTY: Yes. I did, too, Dr. *(Beat)* Henry.

(Beat. Dr. Henry touches her face. He exits.
Sounds of wind. Gretty and Hideko are now soaring through the clouds together.)

Will I still see you, even if I move to California?

HIDEKO: Maybe. What would you do in California? Suntans and musclemen, maybe?!?

GRETTY *(Smiling)*: Yes, maybe, and I thought that maybe I could find a way to go back to school, to be a college girl like you, and—

HIDEKO: You will study Jean-Paul Sartre!

GRETTY: And study some history facts. I don't think I know enough history facts.

(The wind slows.)

HIDEKO: I remember another schoolteacher who once told me that history is not really about facts, but about relations.

GRETTY: Relations.

HIDEKO: To imagine your own history, you must also imagine the history of others.

GRETTY: Yes, and you must find the balance.

HIDEKO: Between remembering and forgetting.

GRETTY *(A bright smile)*: It's a tricky, tricky path.

HIDEKO: And we'll go on it together. *(Beat)* Together, we'll go.

(Lights fade.)

END OF PLAY

JOHN BELLUSO's plays include *The Body of Bourne* (Center Theatre Group/Mark Taper Forum), *Henry Flamethrowa* (Trinity Repertory Company, Victory Gardens Theater, ASK Theatre Projects), *Pyretown* (Geva Theatre Center, developed at The Public Theater's New Work Now Festival), *Body Songs*, created with legendary theater director Joseph Chaikin (Eugene O'Neill Theater Center's National Playwright's Conference, workshopped at The Public Theater) and *Voice Properties* (a short play commissioned and produced by the Actors Theatre of Louisville's 2002 Humana Festival). Mr. Belluso was a 2003 NEA/TCG playwright-in-residence at the Atlantic Theater Company in New York. In addition, he was the Director of Mark Taper's Other Voices Project, a professional developmental lab for theater artists with disabilities. He was a member of New Dramatists and Ensemble Studio Theatre. Mr. Belluso received his Bachelors and Masters degrees from NYU's Tisch School of the Arts dramatic writing program, where he studied with Tony Kushner, John Guare, Tina Howe and Eve Ensler, among others. He was born in Warwick, Rhode Island, and resided in Los Angeles up to his death in February 2006.

A Summer
Evening in
Des Moines

Charles L. Mee, Jr.

A Summer Evening in Des Moines *has never been produced. Shown here is a photo of the world premiere of* Summertime *by Charles L. Mee, Jr., from the Magic Theatre production, San Francisco, California, 2000. Celia Shuman (left) and David Roche (right). David Roche is a well-known disabled solo artist, who was with the production from the original workshop through the premiere. Roche's inclusion is an example of the nontraditional casting Mee calls for in his Author's Statement. Photo by David M. Allen.*

I am an old, crippled, white guy in love with a young Japanese-Canadian-American woman. And we talk about race and age and polio and disability, but race and disability do not consume our lives. Most of our lives are taken up with love and children and mortality and politics and literature—just like anyone else.

My plays don't take race and disability as their subject matter. Other plays do, and I think that is a good and necessary thing, and I hope many plays will be written and produced that deal directly with these issues. But I want my plays to be the way my own life is: race and disability exist. They are not denied. And, for example, white parents do not have biological black children. But issues of race and disability do not always consume the lives of people of color or people in wheelchairs. In my plays, as in life itself, the female romantic lead can be played by a woman in a wheelchair. The male romantic lead can be played by an Indian man. And that is not the subject of the play. There is not a single role in any one of my plays that must be played by a physically intact white person. And directors should go very far out of their way to avoid creating the bizarre, artificial world of all intact white people—a world that no longer exists where I live—in casting my plays.

I've said a couple of other things in the past about my writing that people like to quote back to me, and so I will repeat them here: I find, when I write, that I really don't want to write well-made scenes, narratives that flow, structures that have a sense of wholeness and balance, plays that feel intact. Intact people should write intact plays with sound narratives built of sound scenes that unfold with a sense of dependable cause and effect; solid structures you can rely on. That is not my experience of the world. I like a play that feels as if a crystal goblet has been thrown on the floor and shattered, so that its pieces, when they are picked up and arranged on a table, still describe a whole glass, but the glass itself is in shards. To me, scenes should veer and smash up, careen out of control, get underway and find themselves unable to stop, switch directions suddenly and irrevocably, break off, come to a sighing inconclusiveness. If a writer's writings constitute a "body of work," then my body of work, to feel true to me, must feel fragmented. And then, too, if you find it hard to walk down the sidewalk, you like, in the freedom of your mind, to make a scene that leaps and sings and dances now and then before it comes to a sudden, unexpected stop.

I like plays that are not too neat, too finished, too presentable. My plays are broken, jagged, filled with sharp edges, filled with things that take sudden turns, careen into each other, smash up, veer off in sickening turns. That feels good to me. It feels like my life. It feels like the world.

And then I like to put this (with some sense of struggle remaining) into a classical form, a Greek form, or a beautiful dance-theater piece, or some other effort at civilization.

Outdoors on a summer evening.
The sound of crickets.
Distant music.

As a spotlight slowly comes up on him,
Benny is lost, turning around and around.

His clothes are disheveled; his hair is deranged.
He drove all night to get here.
He looks lost and bewildered and frazzled—but cheerful and expectant.

The Ticket

In a few moments,
a Ticket Seller's kiosk appears.

The music is a little louder now.

TICKET SELLER
Hey!

BENNY
Oh, hello. Is this where I get a ticket?

TICKET SELLER
What do you want?

BENNY
I'd like to buy a ticket.

TICKET SELLER
Right—what do you want?

BENNY
I want to get in.

TICKET SELLER
You want to get in.

BENNY
To the amusement park.

TICKET SELLER
Listen to me carefully: what do you want?

BENNY
What do I want?
Well,
I guess I want to escape from my daily life, you know,
from the abyss of total meaninglessness
that I know lies just beneath my feet at every moment,
so that I feel nothing so much as unbearable hopelessness and despair
all the time
at some unconscious level,
if I don't distract myself with something.

TICKET SELLER
Right. What I mean is
do you want the family pass or the individual?

BENNY
Oh, just the individual.

TICKET SELLER
Ten bucks.

BENNY
Thanks.

TICKET SELLER
Hey! No problem.

(Deafening music.

Benny is engulfed by a projection of the amusement park's midway
and, at the same moment,
a boat enters.)

The Ship of Fools

On board are hundreds of people with telescopes,
looking for the horizon.

Here is a motley crew:
Puppets and false figures add to the population of seven live actors,
along with some three-dimensional dummies,
some two-dimensional cardboard cutouts,
a rubber/vinyl blow-up doll,
some giant puppets, some tiny puppets,
some big stuffed animals,
a Balinese shadow puppet.
These are travelers from all over the world,
tourists, natives of "exotic" lands,
moms and dads and kids and cool guys and wookiees
and people from long-gone historical eras,
explorers and visionaries and holy men.

Among the others on board are
Ella, Jorge,
and Edgar, the ventriloquist,
who has two dummies with him: Charlie and Mortimer.

Three of the people on board the boat are wearing giant fish heads
like Arcimboldo heads.
And these fish heads—Mom, Dad and their daughter, Darling—
like most of the others on board the boat,

are looking through telescopes.
The captain of the ship is a mouse named Vikram.
That is, a young man in a mouse suit
carrying his mouse head in his arm like a helmet,
with a sword strapped around his waist.
And he calls out to Benny through a megaphone
as the music fades:

VIKRAM, THE MOUSE CAPTAIN
Hello there!

BENNY
Hello!

DARLING, A SIXTEEN-YEAR-OLD GIRL
Stranger! Stranger on the port side!

VIKRAM
Put down the gangplank if you please
and let this young fellow come on board!

(And, while Darling starts to put the gangplank in place,
with the help of Mom and Dad,
the Captain and Benny continue to speak to one another.)

Going our way?

BENNY
Well, I don't know.
Which way are you going?

VIKRAM
That's just the thing.
We're not quite sure.
We seem to be a little lost.

BENNY *(Smiling)*
Lost!
Well. Never mind.
I have a map.
(Taking out his map)
There must be a place that says YOU ARE HERE.

CHARLIE, THE VENTRILOQUIST'S DUMMY
Now here's a young fellow
who seems to have sawdust for a brain.

EDGAR, THE VENTRILOQUIST
Really?
Why do you say that?

CHARLIE
Well, he seems incapable of engaging in any form of ratiocination.

EDGAR
Ratiocination.
There's a big word.

CHARLIE
Yes, it is.

EDGAR
Wherever did you hear a word like that?

CHARLIE
Well, I don't know.

EDGAR
No.

CHARLIE
I don't think I ever heard it before.

EDGAR
I see.

CHARLIE
I just opened my mouth and out it popped.

EDGAR
It just came out.

CHARLIE
Just popped right out.

Charles L. Mee, Jr.*

EDGAR
I wonder where it came from.

CHARLIE
So do I.

EDGAR
And yet you think *he* is the fellow with sawdust for a brain.

CHARLIE
Yes, I do.
And I can prove it.

EDGAR
Indeed?

CHARLIE
Watch this.
Excuse me,
but, where are you now?

(Benny looks around.)

BENNY
Well, I don't know . . .
I may be a little bit
disoriented.

CHARLIE *(To Edgar)*
Well, there you are.

VIKRAM *(Politely to Benny)*
We've all got maps and charts and compasses and sextants.
We still don't know quite where we are.

MORTON, DARLING'S DAD
I think it's pretty goddamn clear
they've planned it here so you get lost.

NANCY, DARLING'S MOM
Oh, Morton!

MORTON
You can "Oh, Morton" me all you like,
nonetheless, it seems to me
the way they have things arranged,
it's like a roach motel.

DARLING
Hello!
Are we letting down the gangplank or not?

VIKRAM
Sorry. Sorry.
Let down the gangplank.

MORTON
Forget the gangplank.
What good is he to us?
He doesn't know which way he's going, either!

DARLING
Pull up the gangplank!

NANCY
Cast off amidships!

MORTON
Hoist the mainsail!

ELLA
Wait! Stop!

(Silence.)

Let him come aboard!
Let down the gangplank.
Hi, stranger. Can I give you a hand?

BENNY
Oh . . . Well . . .
Now that you mention it . . .

*(Ella comes down the gangplank,
one hand outstretched toward him.)*

Hello.

ELLA
Hi.

BENNY
Oh.
I guess,
I guess
you must be from the Midwest, too.

ELLA
Why do you say that?

BENNY
Because of the way you say,
"Hi."

ELLA
Oh, well, yes. Yes, I am.
From Iowa.

BENNY
Iowa.
I've been to Iowa.
I really liked it—
all the
space.

ELLA
Right.

BENNY
And all the
landscape.

ELLA
Right.
The line of the distant horizon.

BENNY
Right.
And so you came here . . .

ELLA
On vacation.

BENNY
On vacation. Yes.
Yes. So did I.
What brought you here?

ELLA
I thought I'd come for a weekend
because it sounded like fun
and I like a little escape from my routine like anyone else.

BENNY
When did you get here?

ELLA
Two weeks ago.

BENNY
Two weeks! What a great escape!

JORGE
I've been here two months.

VIKRAM
I've been here three years and forty-seven days.

BENNY
Three years and forty-seven days!
That must be a record.

NANCY
We've been here ten years, three months and two days.

BENNY
Ten years, three months and two days!

NANCY
We brought Darling when she was just a little girl
and now, as you can see,
she's almost a grown-up.

BENNY
What?

DARLING
I like it here.

BENNY
Ten years?

MORTON
Okay, shall we be moving along?

VIKRAM
All right, people,
if you will just settle down on the boat
we can be on our way.

MORTON
So you keep saying
and yet you have no idea which way you're going.

NANCY
Seems to me he's going the wrong way.

MORTON
Well, I think that's obvious.

NANCY
That's exactly why I'm saying it.

DARLING
I like it here.

VIKRAM
Is everyone ready to go?
People?

NANCY
The thing is
I think we should go back to where we were
because, if you think about it,
the thing is, right now, we are in the present,
and before we were in the present,
we were in the past,
so if we want to get oriented
we should go back to the past!

MORTON
Or, if you don't want to be here,
but you want to go someplace else,
we should go into the future.

NANCY
What?

MORTON
Because where we are, we are in the present,
and if we want to get past where we are,
that would be the future.

VIKRAM
Are we ready, people?
Here we go.

(And, as they start out,
everyone is arguing about where to go.)

NANCY
Futureworld.
What you're saying is
we could go to Futureworld.

MORTON
Exactly.

JORGE
Or,
just any civilized place at all would be just fine

if we could just get out of this place
because this is like
nowhere.

CHARLIE
This is like
Limboland.

JORGE
And it wouldn't hurt just to get back to civilization.

MORTON
Where you can sit down at a dinner table and watch TV.

NANCY
Like Civilizationworld.

CHARLIE
I say we should go to Londonland in Englandland,
that's what I would call The Civilized World.

Cotton Candy

As the others all sail away on the boat,
Darling, who got off when we weren't noticing,
is left standing behind
eating cotton candy.

We hear a banjo playing furiously,
as projections behind Darling show a medley
of ten thousand amusement park rides and adventures
that whirl through at great speed:
shooting galleries and ferris wheels,
and villages and cowboy sets, western towns and posses,
and small town pharmacies and soda fountains and barbershops,
and outer space and paddle-wheel steamers and Las Vegas,
and cotton candy and ice cream and hot dogs and baseball—

while Darling does a performance piece with cotton candy.

The Roller Coaster

While Darling continues with the cotton candy,
Nancy enters as
a film of a roller coaster is projected.

Nancy stands in front of the roller coaster film,
her arms in the air above her head,
and screams over and over again.

Balloon Head

Morton comes out with a plain wooden chair.
He sits in the chair and
opens his mouth.

A country western song.

Nancy squirts a steady stream of water into his mouth
with a power squirt gun.
A balloon inflates out of the top of Morton's head
until it explodes.

Then Morton and Nancy dance.

The Open Air

A projection of the Grand Canyon
fills the back and side walls.

Edgar enters with Mortimer and Charlie.

MORTIMER, THE VENTRILOQUIST'S OTHER DUMMY
Well, tsk, I have to say,
here we are in the very middle of the natural world itself.

EDGAR
Yes.

MORTIMER
And yet, to tell the truth, this doesn't seem like Mother Nature to me.

EDGAR
Well, I expect this is a new attraction.

MORTIMER
A new attraction, I see.

EDGAR
Because it's not enough these days to have ferris wheels
and tilt-a-whirls and dart games.

MORTIMER
No.

EDGAR
No. These days people want all sorts of new and different things.

MORTIMER
Well, it's a rich country.

EDGAR
Yes, it is.

MORTIMER
In the olden days, I expect, folks had to make do
with getting drunk on Saturday night
and going to church on Sunday.

EDGAR
Yes.

MORTIMER
Or running amok and shooting the chickens.

EDGAR
Yes, indeed.

MORTIMER
Now people want more.

EDGAR
Among other things, it seems, they want to get back to nature.

MORTIMER
The great outdoors.

EDGAR
The open air.

MORTIMER
The earth itself.

EDGAR
Well, it's a lovely place.

CHARLIE
Lovely. You call this lovely.
This is a total no-man's-land.

EDGAR
Well, yes, it is.
But, you see,
here you have the open air,
the companionship of the animals in their natural homes,
the pleasure of being unencumbered by the fashions of the world,
free to follow your own thoughts and impulses,
not buffeted by all the demands for compromise
that wear away at you constantly in society.
Here you have the pleasures of the hermit in his cave,
the monk in the monastery,
the pleasures of the cloister,
the cloister garden.

CHARLIE
Right.
Whereas back home you would have made do with
a little nap in a soft bed.

EDGAR
Still, there is nothing quite like the wilds,
where you have the pleasure of letting in the universe to your soul,
the pleasure of being answerable to no other force but nature.

CHARLIE
Whereas
back home
you would have to settle
for a glass of sherry in front of the fire.

EDGAR
And yet
even for a person like yourself
who likes a little civilized comfort,
here you have
the meteors in the night sky,
the wild quince,
the fresh pomegranate,
pebbles,
moss,
hail,
hummingbirds and their nests,
the sighing of the night wind,
the scent of the violet.

CHARLIE
Frankly, I wouldn't mind going back
to some of the other places we went on our last trip.

EDGAR
Is that right?

CHARLIE
I myself found nothing wrong with Teatimeland
and their little crumpets and marmalade pots and whatnot,
that was not a bad place to be.

MORTIMER
Or Trigger's Happy Trails.

CHARLIE
Or Tuscanyworld
where the fountains brimmed with Chianti
and one could lie back
and hear the locals reciting Dante over lunch
and singing their arias from Verdi in the late afternoon.

MORTIMER
Or Tom Sawyer's Swap Shop.

CHARLIE
Or the beach party in Hamptonland
where one could simply escape into a world of celebrities
hobnobbing with Oprah and Calvin
and feeling, after all, a little special oneself
transcending the life of democratic anonymity.

MORTIMER
Or Hansel and Gretel's House of Cookies.

CHARLIE
Or Trader's Paradise
where one could hedge and arbitrage,
send the Thai baht into freefall
and have some sense of the powers and possibilities
that come from completely unlimited
and irresponsible Wealth.
That's what I call a real escape.

MORTIMER
Or Rip Van Winkle's Napping Nook.

CHARLIE
I get a little tired of Rip Van Winkle
if you want to know the truth.
There comes a time
when that sort of thing rings a bit false, if you ask me.

EDGAR
A bit false?

CHARLIE
One is not entirely insensitive, you know,
to the fact that some of these fantasies
deny the brutal forces of the real world:
the politics and economics,
the sheer muck and filth of life,
the seething animal nature of the human species itself,

the very things that have made these fantasies possible,
the substructure, if you will, that sustains these dreams—
that these fantasies finally cease to satisfy
because one cannot escape the feeling
that something really immense is missing from the picture,
which is to say the underpinning of human suffering
and power politics.
And once one cannot escape the feeling of the falseness,
the fantasy loses its power to please.

EDGAR
Indeed.
And yet this never happens to you in Hamptonland.

CHARLIE
Well, no, it doesn't.

EDGAR
Isn't that odd?

CHARLIE
Well, it may seem odd to you.

EDGAR
Yes, in fact, it does.

CHARLIE
Whereas, to those who were born to it,
it seems quite natural.

EDGAR
I see.

CHARLIE
To one who is accustomed to these sorts of things,
it feels completely comfortable.
Hamptonland, you see, is civilization.
And civilization is, by its very nature,
unhinged.

EDGAR
Indeed.

CHARLIE
Whereas,
here in Wildernessland
or Cherry Groveworld
or wherever this godforsaken place is,
one can't escape the feeling finally
that what is going on is a certain faux Nature.
A deceitful, lying sort of thing.
Totally bogus and ersatz.
Which makes me feel even more intensely
that I'm going to miss
my afternoon cup of
apricot tea
or, it may be, this would be the afternoon for mango tea,
or black mint, or raspberry,
not to mention the odd sweet
in the fading afternoon light near the hearth.

EDGAR
Well, I tell you what.
Why don't you come with me
and we will find some sticks to rub together
to make a fire here on God's own hearth.

CHARLIE
God's own hearth,
will you listen to him,
and not a bit of Irish blood in him either.

EDGAR
Come along, Charlie.
I think you're going to like this.

(As they leave . . .)

CHARLIE
Do I have a choice?

EDGAR
I think you're going to find this to your taste.

CHARLIE
Do I have a free will here?
Help!
I'm a prisoner in someone else's imagination!

EDGAR
That's enough now.

CHARLIE
Help!
Help!

EDGAR
That's enough, Charlie.

Esther Williams

A bar slides into place,
Vikram, still in his mouse suit, at one end,
Jorge at the other.

While they speak, in the glass wall behind them
Esther Williams does an underwater ballet.

JORGE
I thought,
I'm from Arkansas
and things are pretty normal in Arkansas.

VIKRAM
Right.

JORGE
And so I thought I'd just go to New York
because all the people there are, you know,
different.

VIKRAM
Yes.

JORGE
And on the way, I stopped off here for a visit
and I thought, Well,
this is special.

VIKRAM
For sure.

JORGE
All the people here—
it seems to me they're just
unique.

VIKRAM
Unique. Yes.

JORGE
Although, it turns out,
even *they* are not so welcoming
to someone *they* think is odd.

VIKRAM
No.

JORGE
And odd.
Have you noticed what they think is *not* odd?
Like Donald Duck.

VIKRAM
Like the Swiss Family Robinson.

JORGE
You think: Vacation.
And then you think: Oh! Postcards!
I miss postcards.
You know.

VIKRAM
Postcards.

JORGE
Postcards are unique.
And no one sends them anymore.
And I often wonder: Why not?
Has someone taken a moral position?

VIKRAM
I know what you mean.

JORGE
What I like about a postcard is,
with a postcard
you never can tell
which is the front
and which is the back.

VIKRAM
No.

JORGE
With a novel or a book
you always come to the end,
but you can just keep reading or writing one postcard after another
and never come to the end.

VIKRAM
Right.

JORGE
Each one unique—and never an end.

VIKRAM
Right.

JORGE
This is a kind of pleasure we don't know anymore.
And when I read a book
—which is a more sort of sustained adventure—
I get very involved in the words, but I don't know what's going on.

VIKRAM
Unh-hunh.

JORGE

You'll notice how—when you begin a sentence—
all the words depend on each other.
It's like when you move your arms.
(Watching the gesture as he makes it)
You can't get from here to there without going in between.

VIKRAM

No.

JORGE

And you might take away one word,
and then everything you say is nonsense.
This is linguistics in our time,
and everything depends on it.
You define something in a certain way
and poof, there you are.
And I always think,
Is that entirely necessary?

VIKRAM

Exactly.

JORGE

The first time I went into this house of the nieces of Louis XVI in
    Paris, there
were eight of us for lunch.
And we sat in that dining room with the silver,
all from Catherine the Great,
and we had a footman behind each chair.
And in the salon I saw,
embroidered on the brocade of the Louis XVI chairs,
these initials: MA;
and I said, "Oh, why do they say M-A?"
And this guy Arturo was so happy I'd asked
because then he could tell me that it was Marie Antoinette's crest.
So I was a great favorite with everyone immediately—
not because I was so naive
but just because I'd say whatever came into my mind.

VIKRAM
Yes.
I know just what you mean.

The Photo Booth

Nancy and Darling enter.

Nancy wears a swim suit,
carries a towel,
maybe has on a bathrobe.

She goes to the hot dog stand.

While Nancy talks, she makes herself a hot dog
with all the trimmings.

Darling sits in a photo booth,
taking pictures of herself.
As the flash goes off for each one,
her picture is projected on the back wall,
morphed so that her portrait appears in famous American photographs,
celebrity scenes and wacky scenes (a young blond in a bed filled with owls,
bobcats, butterflies, falcons, puppies), the bodies of female bodybuilders, a
party on Oscar night, and other American scenes.

NANCY
We think we've given Darling a pretty good life here,
although we're not sure she's getting the best education.

(Flash: Darling morphed.)

We always thought it was best for Darling,
bringing her here to take her mind off her big sister Dee Dee,
which we had to do
because, frankly . . .

(Flash: Darling morphed.)

Dee Dee was a sweet child and all,
and we truly loved her,

but when she just walked right out of
the Hospital for Hopeless Psychiatric Cases
and showed up back home on the doorstep with her suitcase,
well, as Morton said, we just didn't have a choice.

(Flash: Darling morphed.)

Like Morton says,
frankly, there is a thing called normal.
I didn't make it up.
I might not like to be normal myself
but I *have* to be normal, like it or not.

(Flash: Darling morphed.)

So he told Dee Dee to march right back there.
And I think he was right to put her on the train by herself
and let her get back to the hospital on her own
because I think that's how people eventually learn
to have a little self-reliance.

(Flash: Darling morphed.)

Or not.

(Flash: Darling morphed.)

Or not.
If she couldn't find her way
then, you know,
we're going to die one day ourselves.
We can't take care of her forever.
Someday she's going to have to make it on her own
and it may as well be sooner as later,
which is why we brought Darling here,
because the whole thing upset her a little bit.

(Flash: Darling morphed.)

And now we see we made the sort of mistake
a person never recovers from.

The sort of thing that's unforgivable.
And where we're living now,
it's a bottomless pit.

(Flash: Darling morphed.
Nancy splurts ketchup all down her front.)

Fred's Polynesian Dive Shop

Vikram, still in his mouse suit, stands in front of the dive shop,
towels in one hand, snorkels in the other.

VIKRAM
Me, I wasn't coming for a holiday.
What I meant to escape was poverty.
So I got this job as a guide
because people,
it seems, they don't know how to make their own way anywhere,
needing someone always to be running things for them,
telling them what to do next, where to go, how to like it, what to think,
when to eat, when to laugh,
but now this has gotten to be too much for me.
Everyone saying: Let's go here, let's go there, I don't like this,
let's go back, where are we now?
I'm asking for a modest retirement package, that's all.
Let someone else do the daily polling, the market testing,
the focus groups.
I could live my own life!
It's no pleasure for me, frankly,
not allowed ever to take this mouse costume off,
so that if I want to go to the bathroom
I just have to shit in my pants and wear them all day.
And this is not a good time for me!

Civilization

A video is projected of fashion models
coming smartly down the runway toward the audience.

MORTIMER
I don't like the story about the fellow who is pooping in his pants.

EDGAR
No. Well, I don't blame you.
That's quite a business.

MORTIMER
Yes, it is.

EDGAR
Normally, you would think,
people are trying to escape feces.

MORTIMER
Yes.

EDGAR
Not store them up in their trousers.

MORTIMER
No.

EDGAR
Trying to escape the whole animal way of life
because, I suppose, if we are reminded that we, too, are animals,
really real animals that perform natural acts—

MORTIMER
Like pooping.

EDGAR
Well, yes, like pooping, for example.
Then we are reminded that *we* are mortal creatures, too,
just like a monkey.

MORTIMER
Or a dog.

EDGAR
Right.

MORTIMER
Or a moose.

EDGAR ,
Right.

MORTIMER
Or a horny toad.

EDGAR
All right. That's enough.

MORTIMER
I didn't start it.

EDGAR
No.

MORTIMER
All this talk about feces . . .

EDGAR
Yes.

MORTIMER
I find it just a smidge embarrassing myself.

EDGAR
Well, it may be you find it embarrassing
because you feel the need to distance yourself from it.

MORTIMER
Yup, well, I think I do.

EDGAR
Which is to say probably you feel the need to deny mortality,
to deny death itself.

(Silence.)

I say, to deny death itself.

MORTIMER
Yup. Well . . . that could be it.

EDGAR
And the fear that goes with that,
that, after death, there is nothing.

MORTIMER
Oh my, well, that's a shame.

EDGAR
You know, some people think there is no heaven.

MORTIMER
My goodness.

EDGAR
They think
that heaven might be just a story people make up
so they can avoid facing the terrible truth.

MORTIMER
Yes, indeed.

EDGAR
That the truth is
the dead are like bats fluttering in a cave
or even worse.

MORTIMER
Oh my.

EDGAR
That after life, we don't even fall into hell.
We fall into nothing.

MORTIMER
Oh dear.

EDGAR
And that is why human beings are the only animals
that are always trying to escape their natural condition

because it is unbearable.
And everything we do,
all the stories we tell one another,
all the buildings we build,
all the clothes we wear,
all of civilization
is just a single great effort to escape.

(Silence.)

Probably that's what you think yourself.

MORTIMER
Well. Yup. Probably I do.
But I don't like it.

EDGAR
No.

MORTIMER
No.

EDGAR
What are you going to do about it?

MORTIMER
All this questioning is a bit of a trial, you know.

EDGAR
I'm sorry.

MORTIMER
A person doesn't like to be grilled.

EDGAR
No.

MORTIMER
A person would rather be fried or poached.

EDGAR
I see.

MORTIMER
Or boiled.
If you happened to have a little something to drink.

EDGAR
We could look for something to drink.

MORTIMER
That's very thoughtful of you.

EDGAR
Not at all.

(As they leave . . .)

MORTIMER
No, it's very kind.

EDGAR
I'm happy to do it.

MORTIMER
Exceptionally considerate of you.

EDGAR
Thank you for saying so.

The Dance Hall

Ella enters dancing to wild, exuberant music.

Benny enters and tries, in vain, to keep up with her.

Darling enters and joins Ella dancing
and does keep up with her
and they enjoy a kind of flirtation
or mutual joy in the dance.

Benny dances like a white man.

Jorge enters, takes off his shirt,
laces his feet into moon boots
and does a wild swaying back and forth
or some similar Dionysian performance event,
if the actor has his own specialty.

Vikram enters and tries to dance with Ella.
She dances with him for a time and then blows him off.

Nancy enters and dances with Vikram.

Morton enters and watches Nancy dance with Vikram
and then throws beer bottles against the wall
over and over and over.

Now, different bystanders try to enter the dance with various partners,
are thrown out of the dance,
try to get back in, etc.

Everyone leaves
until only Nancy is left dancing,
and Morton is left throwing beer bottles.

Nancy stops,
looks around.

NANCY
Morton.
Morton.

(He stops throwing beer bottles.)

Where is Darling?

(He looks around.)

MORTON
She was with you.

NANCY
No. She was with you.

MORTON
She doesn't like to be with me.
I thought she was with you.

NANCY
Are you saying
you can't keep track of her for a minute while I do something?

MORTON
I didn't see her go.

NANCY
Were you watching?
Were you paying the least attention?

MORTON
I didn't see her . . .

NANCY
Are you saying now you've lost another daughter?

MORTON
She's sixteen, you know.

NANCY
Well,
yes!

Okay, Morton.
You go that way.
I'll go this way.

(She leaves one way.
After a moment, he goes out the other way.)

The Woods

Ella and Benny are in the woods.

ELLA
Whose woods are these?

BENNY
I don't know.
So.
I guess we're lost in the woods together.

ELLA
I've never been lost in the woods.

BENNY
Neither have I.

ELLA
I'm glad I'm not alone.

BENNY
So am I.
I like nature,
but I'm a little bit afraid of it.

ELLA
Well, sure.

BENNY
Of the dark parts especially.
I'd like nature better if it were better lit.
I think everyone is, you know,
basically afraid of the dark.
Even amoebas.
I mean, every life-form,
you take them out of the light
and they begin to feel some anxiety.
I do.

ELLA
I do.

BENNY
Light, basically, is how you orient yourself,
and a person without a sense of orientation,
I mean, if you don't know where you are
and where you're going
and about where you are on the line of the place where you are

and the destination where you're going,
a person begins to freak out.
I think that's why
in jazz
they always play the melody at the top
and then,
once you know the tune,
you think: Right, let them riff
because I know where I am
and I know that, in the end,
they're going to come back to the melody.
You know what I mean?

ELLA
Well.
Sure.

BENNY
It's like
a love story.
You can just get lost in a love story because
we know
whatever happens along the way
we might get confused or we might get lost
or it's on-again, off-again
and it goes down some blind alley,
but that's how real life is,
that's how it really is to be in love.
Sometimes you never know,
sometimes it seems like it is just drifting
or it becomes hopeless,
but it doesn't matter
because in the end
with a love story
you know
either they are going to get together
or they're not.

ELLA
Right.

(Silence.)

Do you think
you could ever live in the woods?

BENNY
You mean, forever?

ELLA
Well, for a long time.
Say, like, five years.

(Silence.)

BENNY
Five years.

(Silence.)

With you?

(Silence.)

ELLA
Oh.
Oh.
Okay.
With me.

(Silence.)

BENNY
Yes.

(Silence.)

ELLA
Oh.

BENNY
I've thought about it before,
living in the country,
because that would be beautiful

and I've always found it frightening,
cut off from the world,
as it seems to me,
all alone
and
with nothing to do
but wait to get to be eighty years old
or ninety
and die.
You know, you might have thought you were going to be a doctor
or go to the moon
or just have a nice civil service job,
a career and all the ordinary stuff of life,
not throw it away on a great sort of romantic gamble
like you think,
Oh,
I'd like to go to the country for the weekend,
but to just fling myself out into the universe
and drift among the stars
and have this be my destiny.
Take the gamble that this would be a meaningful life
and one you would really like forever,
the only life you have.
I mean, not that I'm a morbid person
but, you know, it seems to me,
if you're out there alone
maybe with a farm and fields and trees
and the night sky, the stars,
you start to think pretty quickly
how you're all alone
and you just have your life on earth
and then it's over
and it hasn't been much more than a wink
in the life of the stars
and you haven't done anything
that you think is worth an entire life on earth,
so I've always felt a lot safer living in the city
where you can't see the stars at night.

ELLA
Unh-hunh.

BENNY
There you have your friends and things to do.
You get all caught up
and it's fun.
I'm not against having fun,
what I mean is
going to movies, having dinner, hanging out
you can forget entirely that you're a mortal person.
It seems: this could go on forever
until, I suppose, you meet someone, and you think . . .

(Silence.)

I could live with you forever in the woods.
And that would be a life.

(Silence.
Ella starts to back away from him.)

Or not, you know. Or not.

I didn't mean to come on so strong.

I just start talking, and I don't know when to stop.

ELLA
Stop.

BENNY
Right.

ELLA
Good.
Maybe we could just take a walk in the woods.

BENNY
Right. Good.
Good idea.
Let's do that.

ELLA
Shh.

BENNY
Right.
Quiet
like deer.

(They turn and walk into the woods.
Morton crosses.)

MORTON
Darling! Darling!

(He does the old vaudeville bit
of tripping over his own feet,

returning to see what he tripped over,

setting out again,
again tripping,

returning to see what tripped him,
seeing something on the ground,
tracking it, as though it were a string—
maybe this is the plotline?!—
to the wings,
and there getting his foot stuck in the wings,
so that he is gradually sucked offstage feetfirst.)

The Beach

A beautiful beach:
blue sky, endless sand,
lots of bright beach umbrellas.

Jorge enters
wearing a frilly shirt, lace cuffs, silk knee breeches
and a powdered white wig, carrying a suitcase.

JORGE
Damn!
Oh,

damn!
Look what you've done, you ox!

(He puts down his suitcase
as he checks his stocking.

Darling enters from the opposite side.
She is dressed in black leather
or whatever is the latest boots-and-chains fashion.)

DARLING
Excuse me.

JORGE
I've gotten a run in my stocking.
Goddamnit.
These were brand-new stockings
and I don't know where I'll ever get another pair.

DARLING
I'm sorry.

JORGE
They're from Londonland.

DARLING
Oh.
God, I'd like to go to Londonland.
I just had a makeover, but I've never been to Londonland.

JORGE
Oh, yes. Well.
And the countryside is nice, too.
I've just spent the weekend with the Duchess of Devonshire.

DARLING
You have?
Oh, God, I love Devonshire.
I've never been to Devonshire.

JORGE
It's a great attraction, you know.
If you want a real getaway,

Devonshire is the place!
In Devonshire, the silverware is gold!

DARLING
I've never been to Aspen even
or even to Aruba.

JORGE
In Devonshire, in the mornings,
everyone would get up
at eleven o'clock or noon
and they would lie around in their boudoirs
drinking Mexican chocolate or Egyptian coffee
or hot chocolate with crushed carnations.

Because, what they always said was,
they liked to drink their hot drinks
in enclosed places
at private moments.

DARLING
Oh.

JORGE
On some days they would eat nothing but vegetables,
on other days nothing but fruit,
on others nothing but sweet dishes made with honey,
and sometimes dishes all made from milk.

DARLING
Milk and honey.

JORGE
Right.
And for ordinary days,
they would dine on
peacocks and armadillos,
and slowly plumped-up quail,
and eggs fried in the fat of garden warblers.

DARLING
Oh.

JORGE
And dolphins' brains
which, it seemed to me, are the very best of all possible brains,
cooked with vanilla
and served with
tulips and jasmines
and swallows' nests from India.

DARLING
Oh.

JORGE
And every dish was served with flowers in season,
with ice and white jam and white jellies,
with citrus-flavored chocolate and colored pastilles . . .

DARLING
Dear God.

JORGE
With powders and biscuits, petits fours and compotes,
rose and violet royal conserves,
icings and frostings and candied fruit,
with glacé sugar, almond paste . . .

DARLING
Not almond paste, too,
oh God, don't say that.
I have such a problem cutting down on sweets.

JORGE
and sugared almonds too,
and mousses and meringues,
pignoccate, iced buns, iced and pearled ring-shaped cakes . . .

DARLING
Oh no, God, no.

JORGE
Snow-white milk drinks flavored with violets,
candied flowers, iced hyacinths and daffodils
with daffodil crushed-ice drinks . . .

DARLING
Oh.

JORGE
Chocolate sorbet
embellished with vanilla, orange zest and drops of distilled jasmine,
transformed into a holy and noble elixir of sweet life
as it slipped down one's throat . . .

DARLING
Oh yes.

JORGE
Or snow-chilled wine.
Oh blessed and drinkable eternity.

DARLING
Yes.

JORGE
And, after dinner, lying about recuperating,
they would blow hot tobacco smoke into their anuses by means of a tube.
It was the very pinnacle of civilization!

DARLING
Oh God, I would so love
to go to Devonshire.

Square Dance

A simple, white American church is projected.

MORTON *(As a square dance caller, steps out and sings:)*
    Four ladies to the center and back to the bar
    Four gents center with a right-hand star
    Opposite ladies for an allemande thar
    Back up boys, but not too far
    Throw in the clutch, put 'er in low
    It's twice around that ring you go
    On to the next for a do pass-o

And bring her on home as fast as you go
Down in Arkansas on my knees
I thought I heard a chicken sneeze
I looked around, here's what I saw
A bald-headed maid with a pretty little taw
Too old, too old
I'm too old to cut the mustard anymore . . .

*(He claps his hands in rhythm to the music,
and the music cuts into ecstatic mode.
He continues to sing
as square dancers,
Jorge and Darling,
Benny and Ella,
Vikram and Nancy,
and Edgar and Charlie and Mortimer,
come out and do flat-out clog-stomping
so that they seem to float in the air
and only occasionally, it seems, the heel of a boot stomps the floor
as they float in ecstasy.*

Couple by couple, they dance out.

Nancy and Morton are left behind.)

NANCY
So, did you see Darling?

MORTON
Darling?

NANCY
You didn't see she was here?

MORTON
You know, I was busy calling the square dance.

NANCY
So you didn't speak to her?

MORTON
No.

NANCY
You just let her go off again on her own?

MORTON
Are you saying you saw her?

NANCY
Of course I saw her!

MORTON
And you didn't speak to her?

NANCY
What do you mean?

MORTON
You actually saw her and you didn't speak to her?

NANCY
I thought she was with you.

MORTON *(Suddenly yelling at the top of his lungs:)*
SHE WASN'T WITH ME.

NANCY
It's all right.
Calm down, Morton.
It's all right.

Le Bistrot

Jorge, as the perfect French waiter,
wheels out a table with white linen tablecloth and
arranges the crystal wine glasses and silverware on the table
as two others bring out French café chairs.

Nancy and Morton
enter the restaurant.
Nancy a few steps ahead of Morton.

Morton starts to help Nancy with her chair
and she pushes him out of the way.

He throws her to the ground.
She gets up.

Jorge stands back at attention.

Morton throws Nancy to the ground again.
She gets up.

He throws her to the ground again.
She gets up—and jumps on him and knocks him to the ground.

As we hear a soprano sing an operatic aria,
Nancy and Morton continue to knock and throw one another to the ground,
finally throwing one another to the ground on their way out.

Jorge suavely removes the table.
Two others remove the chairs.

Starry Night

A projection of outer space, a sky full of stars.
Ella enters briskly, followed by Benny.

ELLA
It's too late for that, Benny.
The point is, you came on way too strong.
That's not the sort of thing you can take back now.
The damage has been done.
That's why people, when people play bridge,
they lead with the three of clubs,
they feel it out
and then they can build from there.
But when you throw down the ace of spades,
what is it?
You're going for a grand slam or what?

BENNY
I apologize, Ella.
I know I came on too strong,

but that's not the sort of person I am really.
I'm really a kind of laid-back sensitive kind of guy
who really believes in giving other people their space
and respecting their thing,
but don't forget
you're the one who said
did I ever think I could live in the woods
and I said with you
and you said yes
which sort of inflamed me.

(Silence.)

ELLA
I've been thinking of us being together
and what I thought was,
the mental picture that came to mind was,
I walked into Dean & Deluca
and I saw that the man in front of me was sweating and
twitching
and just then all of the automatic doors slid shut
and the lights started blinking.
The man was shooting at the produce
and screaming instructions in Arabic which no one understood.
So I started interpreting for him
because I could tell what he must have meant.
And everyone got down on the floor on their stomachs
and crawled toward the corners.

They were sleeping in the stairwells and the hallways and
on the bathroom floors.
People started to get sick.
Each night ten or fifteen of the sick, old men
were taken to the spare bedroom
and told to lie down in a clump.
The men with machine guns said
that they would fire one bullet per person into the clump
and if anyone managed to live they could live.
But when they opened fire
they just kept on shooting until everyone was hit.
Then the clumps of gold diaphanous fabric on the floor

started moving
and the hookers came out from underneath.
They were all dressed in pink silk genie outfits
and wore long, brown wigs and pink eye makeup
and black eyeliner.
They all started to sing
and they had to keep singing
until all of the old men died
and then the men with machine guns shot them, too.

You came in and led me to the bathroom.
You sat me down on the toilet and gave me ten punch lines
and told me to come up with the jokes that went with them.
I matched them up correctly
and then you added in some homeopathic remedies
where you said the herb
and I had to say what it cured.

I ran through the back wall into the garden
where all of my theater friends were having a lingerie dinner party.

Everyone was dressed in long silk gowns.

The tables were covered with silk pajamas and robes sewn together.

They were using silk panties as napkins.

And then it started raining
and everyone ran around grabbing the silk and disappearing.
So, Tessa and I ran for the elevator,
but when the doors closed we saw the elevator rolling away
and we were on an Amish school bus.
All of the kids and teachers were smiling at us and clapping.

The driver let me off at the elephant trainer's
and he said he would take me back on his elephant.

He went into the tree house and came out with a plate of three sausages.
He said that while he meditated over the sausages,
one had curled up,
which meant there was violence in my life.

I told him about Dean & Deluca.
He said that was probably it, but he still couldn't take me.

So, the elephant said he would take me on his own,
without the trainer.
So I climbed up on his back
and he started walking
and just a few steps down the road
he turned his head around and wrapped his trunk around my waist
and said that he had fallen in love with me
and he wouldn't ever let go.

What do you think that means?

(Silence;

after a moment, she turns and runs out.)

The Beach House

In the living room of a Hamptons beach house,
all white furniture.

JORGE
Do you drink champagne?

DARLING
Champagne?
Oh yes, champagne, yes I do.

(Jorge opens his suitcase out into a little folding table
with a white linen tablecloth,
a bottle and a glass and a folded napkin,
as they continue to talk.)

JORGE
Let me give you a little something
that was given to me by the Duchess of Devonshire,
who sat to my left at dinner one evening
and said to me . . .

(As he opens the bottle)
If you want to have some idea of love,
look at the sparrows in your garden,
contemplate the bull when he is presented to your heifer,
look at this proud horse,
whom two of his grooms lead to the peaceful mare
who awaits him and who turns aside her tail to receive him . . .

DARLING
She said this to you?

(Jorge pours a glass of champagne.)

JORGE
See his eyes sparkle,
listen to his neighing,
contemplate these erect ears,
this mouth that opens with little convulsions . . .

(As he pours the champagne,
he decides he needs the napkin lying on the table;
he lets go of the glass with his left hand to reach for the napkins—
and the glass remains suspended in midair as he pours the wine.)

DARLING
Oh! Oh! Watch out!

JORGE *(Calmly)*
What's that?

DARLING
Oh . . . I thought . . .
I thought you were going to drop the glass.

JORGE *(Casually)*
Oh.
This is the way they pour wine in Englandland.

DARLING
They do?

(Jorge hands the glass to Darling.)

JORGE
So, the Duchess of Devonshire said . . .
(Interrupting himself)
Would you like an omelet?

DARLING
She asked if you would like an omelet?

JORGE
No, I'm asking you: Would you like an omelet?

DARLING
Oh, yes. Yes, I would.

(Jorge takes out a chafing dish, and puts eggs, butter and flour into it as he continues to speak.)

JORGE
So, the Duchess said,
Notice this fiery breath of your stallion,
the imperious movement with which he springs
onto the object which his nature has destined for him,
but do not be envious.

DARLING
No.

JORGE
And reflect on the advantages enjoyed by the human species
who rise above nature in every way.

DARLING
Yes.

JORGE
Not only, unlike the stallion,
is your entire body sensitive.
Not only, unlike the stallion,
do your lips enjoy a voluptuousness that never grows weary.
Not only are you able, unlike the other animals,
to have sexual intercourse at all times . . .

DARLING
Right.

JORGE
But the very idea of love explodes in your mind
like champagne on your palate,
so that you make love not only with your whole body
but also with your imagination.

(Jorge takes out of the chafing dish a bouquet of flowers,
or two doves,
and hands them to Darling.)

Oh, it's not an omelet.
I don't know what went wrong.

Perhaps there's not enough light here in the jungle.

(He takes a large handkerchief,
waves it through the air,
puts his hand up inside it,
and takes out a fully lit chandelier.)

DARLING
Good grief. I've never seen anything like it.

JORGE
No.
This is how it is all the time in Englandland.

DARLING
God, I'd love to go to Englandland.

JORGE
Well.
Sure.

(He leaves, chandelier in hand.)

Ella's Dream

Ella comes in and takes the lotus position.
Darling enters and gets into a complete pretzel position.

DARLING
I guess you like that Benny guy.

ELLA
Oh.
In a way.
He's kind of a twerp.

DARLING
Right.
Funny how sometimes a person doesn't even care.

ELLA
Although, I was telling him what I thought
when I thought of us being together . . .

DARLING
Right.

ELLA
How I had this vision of all these bad things happening,
people getting shot,
horrible things.
But I didn't even tell him the worst part,
about how
in the mornings
all of the bodies of the men who had been shot would be gone,
but the spare bedroom would be filled
with piles and piles of feces and rotting intestines
that you could smell all through the house.
One of the sick people would volunteer to clean it all up,
which was a way of not being killed.
That was Benny's idea.
He said that as long as it was all cleaned up
before the children got home from school, no one would be killed.
But each night more people were taken to the spare bedroom.

All of the women had their clothing taken away and their jewelry.
Everyone wore sweat suits and sat outside during the days
eating potato chips.
Benny sent word

that he wanted me to join him at the ball
because he knew I still had my mink coat
and I would look rich and beautiful.
I snuck down to the ballroom without anyone seeing me.
When I got to the ball
there were only men with machine guns
walking around smoking.
One woman who used to be a rich snob ran by
holding a white paper tablecloth around her.
She stopped and asked me how I still had my coat.
And that's when I knew I had to run.

DARLING
Are you crazy?

ELLA
No.

DARLING
Is this the kind of thing you think
when you're just thinking?

ELLA
Well. Sure.

DARLING
And you're not afraid you're, like, really psychotic or something?

ELLA
This is the kind of thing everybody thinks about.

DARLING
They do?

ELLA
Sure.

DARLING
Do you think I have these thoughts, too?

ELLA
Sure.

DARLING
It makes it sort of scary in a way to live with someone else.

ELLA
Right.

DARLING
Or really even to live alone.

ELLA
Right.

The Prom Dress

Nancy is standing in the middle of an RV campground
wearing her prom dress.

NANCY
I think, really, if I could just get a job
that would be in some way useful,
like, for example, if I worked for a fan magazine,
say, an entertainment magazine
about movie stars and soap opera actors
and it made a profit of, say, $400 million a year
and gave maybe $80 million of that to charity
I would think: This is a useful life to live,
whereas the way it is I think I'm a completely useless person.

I'm not the sort of person who blurts things out.

In fact, just the opposite,
so much so that
when I went to the emergency room
because I thought I was having a heart attack,
the doctor said you're just panicking
from stress
and you could have a stress heart attack
if you don't just let things out a little more and relax.

Sometimes I think nothing is chance,
everything is fate,
and then other times I think everything is chance.

I wish I'd have been more, I don't know,
stable.
Which I haven't so much been.
And I could have settled down and taken care of Darling
and it wouldn't have seemed
as it seems to me now,
that my life has just gone by like a stampede
and left me in the dust.

And then when we were going through the Grand Canyon
and this little boy was vomiting pizza on Morton's feet
which just freaked Morton out,
so he stood up in the boat,
we all went into the water.
I don't know what happened to the little boy.
As far as I know he never got back up again to the surface.
But partly, I was glad I'd lost you, Morton.
I mean, I hoped in a way that you hadn't drowned,
but I used to be in love with a man
who didn't love me as much as I loved him
and now I don't love you as much as you love me
and even though I can't bear to leave you
because I know how much that hurts,
still, I wasn't hoping you would exactly drown
but, Jesus, Morton,
like everyone else,
sometimes I wish my husband were dead.

And Darling,
we took her to see *Cats* twenty-three times
and we took her to see *Phantom of the Opera* seventeen times,
but even so,
you don't know how much you love your children until they're gone.

Boxes

*Jorge enters, steps to a mike and sings a great Spanish ballad
or a great Cuban song like those of Ibrahim Ferrer.*

great Cuban ballad lyrics
great Cuban ballad lyrics

great Cuban ballad lyrics
great Cuban ballad lyrics
great Cuban ballad lyrics
great Cuban ballad lyrics
great Cuban ballad lyrics
great Cuban ballad lyrics
great Cuban ballad lyrics
great Cuban ballad lyrics
great Cuban ballad lyrics.

While Jorge sings, Morton enters and starts to dance.

Nancy enters with a large cardboard box and throws it at Morton, knocking him to the ground.

She turns and leaves.

Morton gets up and resumes dancing.

Nancy enters with a large cardboard box and throws it at Morton, knocking him to the ground.

She turns and leaves.

Morton gets up and resumes dancing.

Nancy enters with a large cardboard box and throws it at Morton, knocking him to the ground.

She turns and leaves.

Morton gets up and resumes dancing.

This continues until Morton and Nancy are exhausted.

Cheerleaders

Vikram comes out with a couple of metal stanchions
and a rope
to set up a maze-line of the sort used at banks and airports.

Other cast members join him in a line.

A voice speaks to them from a loudspeaker:

VOICE-OVER
What would you say are the official qualifications for a good cheerleader?

(Vikram looks around to see where the voice is coming from.

Finally, he answers:)

VIKRAM
I would say
a pleasing personality.

(Silence, and then, finally:)

VOICE-OVER
Okay. Good.

(Silence as everyone thinks.
Vikram turns to the others for help.)

NANCY
A good personal appearance.

VOICE-OVER
Right.

(Silence as everyone thinks.)

VIKRAM
Imagination and resourcefulness.

VOICE-OVER
Yes.

MORTON
Organizing ability and leadership.

VOICE-OVER
Okay.

JORGE
Ability and control of the body.

VOICE-OVER
And?

ELLA
A commanding voice with volume.

VOICE-OVER
Good.

MORTIMER
The desire to cheer for the team, not for personal glory.

VOICE-OVER
Anything else?

BENNY
At least average ability, scholastically.

VOICE-OVER
Right.

DARLING
Willingness to devote time to further the squad.

VOICE-OVER
One more.

VIKRAM
Character which reflects well upon the school.

VOICE-OVER
Right. Good.

(Silence.)

VIKRAM
Okay.
If I might add,

suppose Socrates was wrong,
suppose that the modern philosophers are right,
that we have never seen the truth,
and so,
if we ever do happen to see the truth,
we won't recognize it.

And if that's the case,
then, when someone violates the innocent,
when along comes a Hitler,
there's nothing anyone can say along the lines of,
this violates some fundamental human nature,
this betrays something deep within us.
If we don't know what is deep within us,
what is fixed and eternal,
what is not contingent on today,
then all we have left to say is
whatever may have been true in the past or not, we don't know,
but this is true today . . .

We need a little kindness to survive.
If nothing else,
only that,
modest enough,
no big deal,
something more than that?
No problem.
That, too, would be nice,
icing on the cake.

*(No response;
the cast disperses.)*

The Fruitcake Toss

A big red barn is projected.

*Jorge pushes a catapult onstage
and proceeds to catapult fruitcakes into the wings.*

MORTON
What is this?

JORGE
This.
This is the fruitcake toss.

MORTON
What is that?

JORGE
You see how far you can throw a fruitcake.

MORTON
I can do that.

JORGE
Go ahead.

(The men take turns catapulting fruitcakes into the wings.)

MORTON
It used to be
a man got some respect
in his own home if nowhere else.

JORGE
And other places too.

MORTON
And other places too.
Now, you don't know.
You can put a foot wrong without even knowing it.

JORGE
You can't smoke anywhere.

MORTON
You can't even say good morning to a woman
without the possibility of lawsuit.

JORGE
Or to a man either sometimes.

(While they continue to talk and toss fruitcakes,
they are joined by Benny and then by Vikram,
who join them in the fruitcake toss and in the conversation.)

MORTON
Finally, there might be too many laws in this country.

JORGE
Way too many.

VIKRAM
Too many laws.

BENNY
Except for the laws that try to help create social justice.

JORGE
Oh, social justice.

VIKRAM
That's different.
Social justice.

MORTON
Social justice, that's okay,
but regulations, those are something else again.

JORGE
Don't talk to me about regulations.

BENNY
Except for some things.

MORTON, JORGE AND VIKRAM *(Together, on top of one another:)*
Sure, sure. Clean air. Clean water.
The FDA.
You want to know what drugs you're getting.
Certain regulations . . .

MORTON
Otherwise, you want to be free.

VIKRAM
A free man.

JORGE
A free person.

MORTON, VIKRAM AND JORGE *(Together:)*
Otherwise, what is the point?
This is America.
What? This is not America?

VIKRAM
A man wants to be all he can be.

BENNY
And a woman, too.

JORGE
And a woman, too.

MORTON
Be all she can be.

VIKRAM
Otherwise, why did I come here?

MORTON AND JORGE
Why does anyone come here?
This is why a person would want to be an American!

MORTON
What happened to the American dream?

VIKRAM
The American dream is alive and well!

BENNY
Too much. Too much.
All over the world, it's too much.

JORGE
Too much, he's right.

VIKRAM
Or not enough.

MORTON
Or not enough.

JORGE
It's too much and not enough!

VIKRAM
Utopia!

JORGE
Utopia!

MORTON, BENNY, JORGE AND VIKRAM *(Shouting together,
talking on top of one another in a big jumble of words,
sometimes taking different lines, sometimes all saying
the same line but not in sync, repeating some lines,
each actor picking out what he wants to say but jumping in,
not waiting his turn, a big tumult:)*
I had a dream
I had a dream of a better life
you think: You work for it
you pay your dues
you make your sacrifices
did I hear they changed the rules?
you work like a dog
you're doing the right thing
the thing you think is the right thing
and all of a sudden nobody appreciates it
no one likes it
no one likes *you* anymore
they think you're a bad person
even evil
and all that time you thought this was America
where a man could feel good about himself
where you can make your own way
I don't say I'm entitled to anything
I'm not talking about being entitled
you give a little, you get a little

everyone is a winner
everyone's a winner
we are all winners
winners.

(Exhausted,
they all fall silent.)

Pizza

A projection of a beautiful, slow-motion film
of wild horses running in Montana.

Bob—a new character we've not seen before,
played by Edgar, doubling unrecognizably—
enters with a pizza box in his hand.

BOB
And yet, I think, nonetheless,
forgiveness is possible.

MORTON
You do.

BOB
Well, sure.
Really under any circumstances.
Uh, primarily, uh, uh, the, uh, the . . .
Primarily the question is,
does man have the power to forgive himself?
And he does.
That's essentially it.
I mean, if you forgive yourself,
and you absolve yourself of all, uh,
of all wrongdoing in an incident,
then you're forgiven.
Who cares what other people think, because, uh . . .

MORTON
Was this a process you had to go through over a period of time?
Did you have to think about it?

BOB
Well, no.
Not until I was reading the Aquarian Gospel did I,
did I strike upon . . .
You know, I had almost had ends meet because I had certain,
uh, you know,
to-be-or-not-to-be reflections about, of course, what I did.
And uh . . .

BENNY
I'm sorry, what was that?

BOB
Triple murder.
Sister, husband. Sister, husband,
and a nephew, my nephew.
And uh, you know, uh, manic-depressive.

JORGE
Do you mind my asking what instruments did you use?
What were the instruments?

BOB
It was a knife.
It was a knife.

JORGE
A knife?

BOB
Yes.

BENNY
So then, the three of them were all . . .

BOB
Ssssss . . .
(Makes the motion of slitting his throat)
like that.

JORGE
So, uh,
do you think that as time goes by,

this episode will just become part of your past,
or has it already . . .

BOB
It has already become part of my past.

JORGE
. . . Has already become part of your past.
No sleepless nights? No . . .

BOB
Oh, no. In the first three or four years there was a couple of nights
where I would stay up thinking about how I did it, you know. And
what they said . . . they told me later there were so many stab wounds
in my sister, and I said no, that's not true at all, you know. So I think
I had a little blackout during the murders, but uh . . .

(He sits,
making himself at home.)

Well, uh, they said there was something like thirty stab wounds in
my sister, and I remember distinctly I just cut her throat once. That
was all, you know, and I don't know where the thirty stab wounds
came from. So that might have been some kind of blackout thing.
You know, I was trying to re- re- re- uh, re- uh, uh, resurrect the uh,
the crime—my initial steps, etcetera. You know, and uh, and uh,
I took, as a matter of fact, it came right out of the, I was starting the
New Testament at the time, matter of fact I'm about the only person
you'll ever meet that went to, to do a triple murder with a Bible in
his, in his pocket, and, and, listening to a radio. I had delusions of
grandeur with the radio. Uh, I had a red shirt on that was symbolic
of, of some lines in Revelation, in the, in the New Testament. Uh,
I had a red motor . . . as a matter of fact, I think it was chapter six
something, verses three, four or five, or something where, uh, it was
a man, it was a man. On a red horse. And, and, a man on a red horse
came out, and uh, and uh uh, and he was given a knife, and unto
him was given the power to kill and destroy. And I actually thought
I was this person. And I thought that my red horse was this red
Harley Davidson I had. And I wore . . . it was just, you know, it was
kind of a symbolic type of thing. And, and, and uh, you know, uh,
after the murders I thought the nephew was, was the, was a new devil

or something, you know. This, this is pretty bizarre now that I think back on it. I thought he was a new devil and uh, uh. I mean basically I love my sister, there's no question about that. But at times my sister hadn't come through, uh, for me. You know and I was in another one of these manic attacks. And uh, and uh, uh, uh, you know, uh, I was just uh, I was just you know, I mean I was fed up with all this, you know, one day they treat me good and then they tell all these other people that I was a maniac and watch out for me and etcetera and like that. And uh, uh, so I went to them that night to tell them I was all in trouble again, you know, and could they put me up for the night, you know, and they told me to take a hike and uh, so uh, believing that I had the power to kill, uh, you know, that was that for them. You know. I mean when family turns you out, that's a real blow. You know. But uh, back to the original subject of forgiveness. If I forgive myself, I'm forgiven. You know, that's essentially the answer. I'm the captain of my own ship. I run my own ship. Nobody can crawl in my ship unless they get permission. I just *(Nods)* "over there." You know. "I'm forgiven." You know. Ha ha. You know. *(Laughs)* It's as simple as that. You know. You're your own priest, you're your own leader, you're your own captain. You know. You run your own show, a lot of people know that.

Who ordered a pizza?

BENNY
Oh.

MORTON
A pizza.

BENNY
I don't think anyone here ordered a pizza.

BOB
Someone ordered a pizza.
I don't go around delivering pizzas
if nobody ordered one.

VIKRAM
I think there's been some mistake.

BOB
I think you are the one who is making a mistake
if you think nobody
is going to pay me for the fucking pizza.
You know: pizza
is not returnable.

JORGE
Right.
I'll pay you for the pizza.

BOB
Plain cheese.

JORGE
Right.
Here.
Keep the change.

BOB *(Checking the money:)*
Right.
Thanks.
Appreciate it.
Which way did I come in?

(The others all look at one another.)

JORGE
Over there.
Right out that way.

BOB
Right.
Thanks again.

Dairy Queen

Jorge and Darling are having an ice cream at a Dairy Queen.

DARLING
Once I went shopping with my dad.
I just went wild.

I thought,
Oh God,
he's brought me here,
this is like a wonderland.
He'd never done anything like that for me before
and I just loved everything.
This was when I was seven or eight
and I picked out a dress,
all sort of like a flower that twirled out when I spun around
and gloves and a purse with little white beads all over it
like tiny pearls
and patent leather shoes, of course,
that shone like dark mirrors.
I was so happy
and my father looked at me
and he said,
Do you think you can afford all this?

I said, What?

He said, Can you afford all this with the allowance that you have?

I didn't understand.

With all my savings I had, I remember,
exactly sixty-two cents.

So that I had to put everything back
where it had come from.

Because my father was teaching me
the value of money.

JORGE
When I was a kid,
one night after my parents took me to see the movie *Cleopatra*,
I got together with some of my friends.
We were nine years old.
We all wore towels wrapped around our heads.
The kids in the neighborhood were all the slaves and I,
of course, was Cleopatra.

We erected statues in the living room
and I draped myself in the chiffon curtains as an outfit.
And then, when I was in the fifth grade,
I was looking at all the fashion magazines.
I would tweeze my eyebrows,
and dye my hair,
but I couldn't do it right, so it was dyed in spots.
I always was who I was and did what I did.
And also in high school,
the collegiate look was in
and I tried to work that look,
but instead I just looked like a lesbian
trying to be collegiate.

DARLING
I bet you were so cute.

JORGE
No.

DARLING
I bet you were.

JORGE
No, no, no.

DARLING
You're cute to me,
right now.
With your frilly shirt
and your satin trousers
and your little pumps and stockings
and your, probably, I don't know,
your silk underthings
all sort of frothy and windswept.
I mean if you were to take off your trousers
and your, probably, shirttails would, I don't know,
come down to your knees.
I think that would be so
(She can't breathe for a moment)
cute.

JORGE
Oh,
you know,
I . . .

DARLING
When I was growing up,
when everyone else had boyfriends
I never did
and I thought I was just ugly, you know, and worthless,
so
feeling this connection with you,
it's really special to me
and important.

JORGE
Oh God,
well . . .
It's special to me, too, Darling.
I'm, you know, probably a little old for you.

DARLING
I'm not an ageist.

JORGE
What?

DARLING
I don't think age matters.
People are always looking for what keeps them apart,
they forget to look for what draws them together.

JORGE
Right.

DARLING
I'm drawn to you.

JORGE
Yes. You are.
And, I'm drawn to you, too.

Although at the moment I'm a little distracted
because I think I dropped something back,
you know . . .

DARLING
I'll help you find it.

JORGE
No, no, don't.
Just,
you know,
I'll meet you later,
at the malt shop.

(He disappears.)

DARLING
I'm coming with you!

(She disappears after him.)

The Ball Game

*A succession of still pictures of a baseball game is projected
in the background.*

Ella is alone, eating Cracker Jack.

*Benny comes in, also with Cracker Jack,
sidles over to sit next to Ella.*

BENNY
Okay, what's your problem?

ELLA
What's my problem?

BENNY
Basically, you're not giving me the time of day.
You came on to me at first . . .

ELLA
Came on to you?

BENNY
Invited me to come on board the boat . . .

ELLA
That was not coming on to you,
that was being polite.

BENNY
Oh.

ELLA
Everyone was being so unfriendly.

BENNY
Oh, there's where I went wrong.
See, I thought you kind of liked me
and then, I don't know,
you turned into some kind of prick teaser or something.

ELLA
Prick teaser?

BENNY
Or, I don't know,
you didn't trust me for,
as far as I could see,
no reason at all.

ELLA
No reason at all?
Where should I begin?

BENNY
Suddenly you're having nightmares.
I think I was being moderately okay,
just making conversation
that could have led just to a cup of coffee or something,
although I have to admit I was hoping it might lead beyond that.

I don't know
because, frankly, I fell for you.

ELLA
You fell for me?
You fell for my what?
You don't know me.
You don't know anything about me.
I'm a total stranger.
You know how I look, that's it.
This is how you fall for women?
You fell for my what?

BENNY
I fell for your kindness.

ELLA
Oh.

BENNY
And then I thought you got scared.

ELLA
Oh.

BENNY
But I see now that I was wrong.

(Silence.)

ELLA
You're a stranger to me.

BENNY
Sure. I know.
I thought
it used to be in the olden days,
I don't know,
people would meet at church socials
or some harmless place, I don't know,
where they could talk without anyone feeling frightened

and now you have to, what,
meet through a personals ad
or walk up to someone in a bar.
How would I ever meet you
even when I'd really like to meet you
and have a chance to get past
just going by appearances or first impressions.
Get to know each other and maybe,
I don't know,
fall in love.
I don't mean to say,
like, I don't mean to come on too fast all over again,
but I did feel that first moment
when you were so kind,
I mean, I felt that was your total person
all at once,
your whole thing revealed in a millisecond
and sometimes you can tell that about a person at first glance,
but I take it back,
I take it back
because I don't want to, like,
make you uncomfortable.

ELLA
Where I come from
I couldn't trust anyone.
Especially men.
Because they would always come on to me.

BENNY
That's the problem for beautiful women.

(Silence.)

ELLA
Maybe.
Anyhow, that's what they did.
So, you come on to me
like some kind of moron
and I find it hard to get past that,
even to see if you might not be a total fool

through and through,
you know what I'm saying?

BENNY
Yes.
So you're saying
a cup of coffee would be out of the question.

ELLA
If you were just a little less pushy
I might do it.
But,
this is how you are.
You are so not cool,
do you know that about yourself?

BENNY
Still, the thing you do know about me
is I respond well to kindness,
which would seem to indicate that I, too,
like you, have some good instincts.
And a person might think, well,
there's a place to start,
there's the groundwork,
maybe it's worth seeing what could be built up from there.

(Silence.)

I guess there used to be a time
if a guy would see someone like you
there might be the circumstances that would be appropriate
and acceptable
where he could come up to you
and ask,
Do you want to dance?

(She leaves.

He watches her go, and then he goes out in the opposite direction.)

The Front Porch

Edgar sits on the front porch swing with Charlie and Mortimer.
From time to time, we hear a screen door slamming
as it does on a summer evening.

MORTIMER
This is not what I had in mind for a vacation.

EDGAR
It isn't.

MORTIMER
No.

EDGAR
What did you have in mind?

MORTIMER
Well, I wouldn't have complained about a little romance
or even true love.

EDGAR
I see, find the right girl and settle down.

MORTIMER
Yup. Or the right boy.

EDGAR
I see. And don't you think that's just another form of escapism itself?

MORTIMER
What's that?

EDGAR
Love.

MORTIMER
Oh. Yup. Yup, I do.

EDGAR

Indeed, probably you would say love is even the ultimate escape
and that is the reason for our obsession with it.

MORTIMER

Uh, yup, I probably would.

EDGAR

Although, paradoxically, probably you would say
at the same time this ultimate escape
is necessary for the survival of species
and not just this kind of love that results in procreation
but also love that does not result in bearing children
but in caring for our children,
and as far as that goes,
caring for our neighbors and their neighbors,
for society as a whole, really.
You don't mean to talk about lust or sex
but rather about deep and enduring and unselfish love
and friendship,
mutual regard and respect,
the mutual love within society as a whole,
that we call social love,
that is an essential glue to hold society together
and to allow society to survive,
to allow life itself to continue.

MORTIMER

Yup, well . . . uh . . . no doubt.

EDGAR

So, you would probably say
we come full circle to escape as the means for the species to survive
so that in fact love is not just the ultimate escape,
but also the ultimate reality.

(Silence.)

And probably you think,
if Aristotle was right
that human beings are social animals,

that we create ourselves in our relationships to others,
then, because the theater
is the art form that deals above all others in human relationships,
then theater is the art, par excellence,
in which we discover what it is to be human
and what is possible for humans to be.

(Silence.)

I say, you probably think
that theater, properly conceived, is not an escape either
but a flight to reality, a rehearsal for life itself,
a rehearsal of these human relationships of which the most essential,
the relationship that defines most vividly who we are
and that makes our lives possible,
is love.

CHARLIE
Sometimes I think you're a little slow.

EDGAR
You do?

CHARLIE
I do.
Sometimes when I talk I can see your lips moving.

EDGAR
Oh, you can?

CHARLIE
Yes, I can.
Do you move your lips when you read, too?

EDGAR
Well, I don't know.

CHARLIE
Why don't I watch you?

EDGAR
Okay.

CHARLIE
Read my mind.

EDGAR
Okay.

(He does.)

CHARLIE
Your lips aren't moving now.

EDGAR
Well, your mind is a blank.

CHARLIE
That's not true at all.
I think you can't read.

EDGAR
Maybe not.

CHARLIE
No maybe about it.
I think we've just proven it.
You seem to be some kind of an idiot.

EDGAR
I don't think so.

CHARLIE
How can you tell?

EDGAR
Read my mind.

CHARLIE
Okay.

(He does.)

EDGAR
Go ahead.

CHARLIE
Well, there's a tabula rasa if I ever saw one.
You have a mind as clean as the driven snow.

EDGAR
I'm thinking about nature.

CHARLIE
You should think a little harder.
So far all you've got is the wind whistling through the trees.

The Nuclear Family

A projection of a New Jersey highway:
XXX video stores, cheap diners, a cheap bar,
a string of parking lots and strip clubs.

Everyone is onstage eating cotton candy.

MORTON
You think
when you start out,
all you want to do is get a job,
support your family.
You think you're doing the best you can taking care of them;
the next thing you know
you've been sucked into a whole world
that seems entirely alien to you.
This was never what you had in mind at all,
but it's too late,
you made your choice.
It was inevitable from the first step you took
you were going to end up here,
inside the belly of the beast
and no way out.
This is how your life will end,
the only life you had on earth.
You're lost.
Lost.

NANCY
Or you think
you'll have children,
you'll make a home,
you'll give up all those things you thought you might do with your life
or, maybe not.
At first you think,
I can do both
because everything is possible these days
and then you find out everything isn't possible
because the family just sucks you in.
Your first child is born,
you never sleep,
you become delirious,
sleepwalking from day to day
as though you live underwater,
and just as you think you see a glimmer of the surface
you have another baby
and you go under again
as though you yourself were suspended in the amniotic fluid
and from then on forever your life has no direction and no shape,
no boundaries and no light,
suspended forever in the present moment
always two days behind or more.
You can't drown and you can't get back up to the surface
and you're hurtling forward toward the end of your life
with no control of anything anymore
and you think: How did I let this happen to me?

DARLING
Or you grow up thinking,
How can I ever get out of here?
I am suffocating with this family!
I am gagging and choking
and I say to them,
I am gagging and choking
and then they try to help,
which is like pushing your head farther underwater.
It's not that teenagers commit suicide so much
as that they are murdered by their own hands
and this is if they have ideal parents

whereas most parents, let's face it, are not even a little bit ideal.
They are hopeless,
consumed with their own lives,
their precious fucking mistakes,
their awesome misgivings,
their regrets for what they did to you when you were three
so that they are killing you now out of remorse
and you are thinking, Yes, yes, kill me,
I wish I were dead,
I can't go on living with you,
you make me crazy.

MORTON
I'm sorry, Darling,
and I suppose in some way
it is because of all that
that you wind up in love with a pervert.

JORGE
I beg your pardon?

DARLING
Dad, you crazy bigot!
You racist shit!

MORTON
What?

NANCY
Morton, can't you keep your mouth shut for a minute?

DARLING
And now you're attacking him.

NANCY
Who?

DARLING
My father.
If you had ever just left him alone
he might have been a wonderful person

but no, you hounded him into the dirt
because you are such an innate bitch.

MORTON
Now, now, Darling,
this is no way to speak to your mother.

NANCY
As though you have ever cared, Morton!

MORTON
What? You think I never cared?

NANCY
Your family this. Your family that!
You never thought for a minute of your family.

MORTON
I've thought of nothing else!

NANCY
What was the name of Darling's best friend in third grade?

(Silence.)

Who was that sadistic math teacher in fourth grade?

(Silence.)

Who was her orthodontist?
What vaccinations has she had?
Childhood illnesses?
Can you even fill out a form for summer camp?
What did she always want more than anything?
Who is her favorite music group?
Does she think spike heels are cool or despicable?
And now she finds a friend
and all you can think to do is call him a pervert?
Look at him.

*(Everyone looks at Jorge in his angel outfit;
a moment's silence.)*

This is a *good* person.
This is practically a saint!

MORTON
Women!
They never marry because they love you.
They always marry you for a reason.
For your money, or your job
or how easy you are to push around,
to get their way with raising the children,
and they take you down off the shelf
interchangeable with all the others,
no better, they think, not too much worse,
this one will do, they think.
I can make do with him,
fix him up a little.
Whereas a man might really be looking for true love,
not all men,
not all men,
I am not talking about all men.
All men might be contemptible shits
but there might be one man out of all of them
who just wanted someone to love
and someone to love him
and he was doing his best
maybe he didn't know any better
but fuck him if he doesn't measure up.
Women!
Women can have a thousand flaws
and expect to be forgiven all of them
and they are,
they often are,
not always, but sometimes by some men
under some circumstances
unless they get really pissed off
and even then
a man figures human beings are not perfect
and he doesn't hold it against them,
but a woman marries a man
and then hates him for the rest of his life
and this is not easy to live with.

Sometimes it will push him to make a mistake.
He will get desperate and frantic.
He will be blinded by anguish
and he will lash out and do something stupid
he regrets for the rest of his life.

NANCY
Men!
I give up.
It used to be I thought all they wanted was a sex object.
But now it seems they don't even want that anymore.
They can make do with a picture on the internet,
that's as close as a man wants to get to a woman nowadays.
Between abuse and complete indifference
there used to be some middle ground,
but now a man would rather live with some lingerie from Victoria's
    Secret
and a closet to keep it in
where he can go from time to time
and not come out for hours.
This is what he thinks it is to have an intimate relationship.

MORTON
This is what you think about men,
but is this what you think about me?

NANCY
I'm sorry, Morton.
I didn't want to tell you like this.

DARLING
How can you humiliate a person like this in public?

MORTON
Maybe I haven't been the best person.

NANCY
Really.

MORTON
But I'm more or less as good as people get,
give or take a little bit around the edges.

JORGE
You are a human shit pile, Morton.
You are a garbage dump.
You are a bottomless pit of snot.

DARLING
Hey! This is my dad!

JORGE
This is the creature who just attacked you—
and me—
I'm doing nothing but defending you.

DARLING
Well, don't!

MORTON
Now, Darling . . .

DARLING
Are you going to spring to his defense?
Men!
The way you stick together!

JORGE
Excuse me, I am not sticking with him.

MORTON
I don't think I am sticking with him.

DARLING
Except in the way that you both hate women!

MORTON AND JORGE
Hate women!
Not at all!
That's not true.
That's not even partly true.

EDGAR
How could anyone hate women, really?

NANCY
I knew it! I knew it!
From the first moment I met him,
I knew the only man
I've ever known
who was truly considerate and compassionate
and gentle,
who speaks with such thoughtfulness
and tries in every way to think of the other person's
needs and preferences
and I would even say—
someone who is even sexy—
is Edgar.

JORGE
Edgar!

VIKRAM
Edgar!
So you've been carrying on with a married woman behind my back?

EDGAR
Behind your back?

NANCY
And what does he have to do with you?

EDGAR
Nothing.

VIKRAM
Nothing?!

EDGAR
Well, almost nothing.
That is to say, we are good friends.

VIKRAM
Good friends!
Is that how you think of me?
After the late night conversations we have had?

The stroll along the duck pond?
The time together in the Tunnel of Love?

NANCY
And how about us?
How do you think about us?

DARLING
Mother!

MORTON
What the hell has been going on here?

NANCY
I don't care!
I don't care!
All my life I've wanted a man I could just rip into
and now that I've found him
I don't care who knows it.

VIKRAM
Edgar, did you ever tell me about her?

EDGAR
Certainly not!

VIKRAM
And you let me follow you everywhere!

CHARLIE
You seem to be some sort of helpless flirt!

EDGAR
I beg your pardon?

MORTIMER
I think he has a point there.

EDGAR
Oh, you do?

MORTIMER
Yes, I do.

EDGAR
Haven't you been with me at every waking moment?
In fact, aren't you my witness to all my behavior?

MORTIMER
Yes, I am.
And here is this sweet young fellow
who loves you,
and you've never said
forget it.
This is out of the question.
No.
You led him on.

EDGAR
I did not.

MORTIMER
I think you did.
A fellow doesn't like to be led on, you know.
He puts his heart on the line.
He can have his feelings crushed.

VIKRAM
Exactly.

MORTIMER
A person's feelings are a delicate, fragile thing.
You don't want to be putting your big, muddy boots
all over a person's feelings.
They can be damaged forever.

VIKRAM
Exactly.

MORTIMER
Inside, where a person lives,
they are a small child forever.

VIKRAM
That is so true.

MORTIMER
A ten-year-old child
who feels very vulnerable
and afraid
and sometimes very lonely
and their heart can be crushed forever.

VIKRAM
This is all I was trying to say.

MORTON
Sometimes I myself feel like a ten-year-old child.

NANCY
You are a ten-year-old child, Morton.

DARLING
There they go again.
Why can't you two be even just civil to one another?
Never mind love.
Never mind even being nice.
Just even polite would feel so good.

MORTON
Maybe you don't know how hard it is
getting from day to day,
you've lived such a comfortable life.

DARLING
I've had comforts.
I have never been comfortable.

CHARLIE *(To Edgar:)*
I think Mortimer is right.
Let's face it, the kind of person you are,
you're not interested in another person unless you can keep that person
like a toy or a pet, a plaything—

MORTIMER
A puppet!

CHARLIE
Happy if you can do whatever you like with your significant other,
but the moment that person,
say I, myself,
want my own life,
then no!
It's over.
You love me if I am an extension of yourself,
of your interests, your passions, your ideas,
your idiosyncrasies, your, frankly, eccentric tastes,
but you don't love me for myself.

You are, if you want to know the truth,
you are aloof.

EDGAR
Aloof?

CHARLIE
Aloof.

VIKRAM
Aloof.

EDGAR
I am aloof?

VIKRAM
And distant and cool.

CHARLIE
Standoffish.

VIKRAM
Reserved.

EDGAR
I am reserved?

MORTIMER
It's true you are not the sort of person who plunges in.

VIKRAM
Really, you are a typical uptight WASP.
I thought, behind the facade,
behind all the defenses,
this house of mirrors,
all these personae,
was a vulnerable human being,
even especially more vulnerable than others,
and that that was why you had to put up such defenses.
But, it turns out after all,
you have a relationship with no one except your,
who shall I say,
your friends here.
It seems to be who you are.
You are not a multiple personality.
You are not a personality at all!

CHARLIE
It seems you could be a complete lunatic!

MORTIMER *(To Charlie:)*
That seems unfair to me, Charlie.
To me, Edgar has always been a considerate person.

CHARLIE
That's because you don't even know what it is
to have a real grown-up relationship.

MORTIMER
Oh, well, I think I do.

CHARLIE
You're nothing but a mouthpiece.

MORTIMER
A mouthpiece?
How can you say that to me?
I have a heart, too, you know, Charlie.

CHARLIE
I doubt it.
You have a space where a heart should be, Mortimer,
you are an empty suit.

MORTIMER
An empty suit.

CHARLIE
A stiff.

MORTIMER
A stiff.

CHARLIE
A blockhead.

MORTIMER
A blockhead.

CHARLIE
A rag and a board.

EDGAR
Here. Here, that's enough of that.

CHARLIE
A dolt.

EDGAR
That's enough.

CHARLIE
A dummy.

EDGAR
That will do, Charlie.

MORTIMER
I think he's a little irritable today.

EDGAR
That may be.

Charles L. Mee, Jr.

MORTIMER
Maybe he has a splinter up his butt.

EDGAR
Now, now.

MORTIMER
He'll be sorry when I'm dead.

CHARLIE
You're not going to die, Mortimer.

MORTIMER
After a person is dead, you know,
then you live a life of regret
thinking of the chances you missed,
the love you had and treated not so well,
and then you feel stupid.

MORTON
I feel stupid already.

MORTIMER
I may be stupid, but
I have a sensitive soul
and I'm just trying to do my best.

VIKRAM
And, to me,
you are doing very well.
Very well.

MORTIMER
Tsk. Gosh. Thank you.

VIKRAM
To me, you are a model human being.

MORTIMER
Thank you very much.

VIKRAM
Perhaps we could start here
to build some sort of friendship.

MORTIMER
Tsk. Well. Perhaps we could.

VIKRAM
I'm going to start by making friends with you.

MORTIMER
Good idea.

Earth Angel

Hundreds of colorful hot air balloons rise in slow motion
as Darling steps up to a mike.
While Jorge dances,
she sings the song:

Earth Angel
Earth Angel
Earth Angel
Earth Angel
Earth Angel
Earth Angel
Earth Angel
Earth Angel
Earth Angel
Earth Angel
Earth Angel
Earth Angel . . .

Edgar, Charlie, Mortimer, Benny and Morton
all join Darling to sing backup.

Road Trip

Darling and Morton
are riding in an antique car
with the American landscape projected behind them.

DARLING
What do you think?
First thing: he took me into the woods.
He said,
We all have the same mother.
Every species that you see now
drawing the breath of life
has the earth as its mother.
At the appointed season,
the earth gave birth to every beast that runs wild among the hills.

Who wouldn't be a sucker for sweet talk like that?

MORTON
Right.

DARLING
He said . . .

When you think
how we used to live in the ocean
in the salt water,
you think,
We don't live there anymore.
But really, in fact, we just took the ocean with us when we came on land.
The womb is an ocean really,
babies begin in an ocean,
and human blood has the same concentration of salt
as seawater.
And no matter where we are,
on top of a mountain
or in the middle of a desert,
when we cry or sweat,
we cry or sweat seawater.

MORTON
Right.

DARLING
He said . . .

There are things that are both near and distant at the same time.
Like the course of a boat across a lake.
Like the relations between a man and a woman.
Like paradise.

So of course I fell for him.

Then he said to me: He meant nothing personal.

But, I think, if you say things like that to a woman,
she's going to take it personally.

MORTON
I think that's true.

DARLING
He said . . .

I sometimes wonder
what would it be like
to have an exquisite sense of things?

You would say, for instance,
there are elegant things—
duck eggs,
wisteria blossoms,
the Pride of China tree,
the sweet-scented Marvel of Peru.

I fell for him.

MORTON
Naturally.

DARLING
Then I was the one who said let's go to Outer Spaceworld
because I thought he'd like it
and I was just trying to think what he would like,
which of course he didn't because
he's not into techno things all that much,
which is fine,

so when he suggested, Let's just keep on going,
let's go to heaven,
I said sure. Let's go. I've always wanted to go to heaven.
And we did, we did.

MORTON
I'm just happy you're okay!

DARLING
But what I'm telling you is I'm not.
The point is: he took me to heaven.

MORTON
Frankly, Darling, I don't know
what the hell you were thinking anyway
to run off with some guy in a dress.

DARLING
He's been an angel, Daddy.

MORTON
I thought he was sweet on the fellow in the mouse outfit.

DARLING
Vikram?

MORTON
Is that his name?

DARLING
Vikram?

MORTON
Yes.

DARLING
Well, Vikram is sweet on Mortimer.

MORTON
Mortimer?

DARLING
You know, Charlie and Mortimer and Edgar?

MORTON
Mortimer the dummy?

DARLING
Daddy, you shouldn't just be always, like, name-calling.

MORTON
I'm sorry, but I thought Mortimer was, in fact,
a dummy.

DARLING
What if he is?
Vikram likes him.

MORTON
How can that be?
What is it Vikram sees in Mortimer exactly?

DARLING
I don't know.
Daddy, don't you get, like, anything that's going on?

MORTON
I guess not.

DARLING
Do you understand even what it is about Jorge?
How he's such an angel
and then he ignores me
and then he's an angel again.
It's like he can just play with me forever,
Hot, cold, hot, cold.
I just love him like crazy.

MORTON
Well, I guess that's okay then.

The Dolphin Show

We see a film of beautiful underwater aquarium life-forms,
as though from outer space—
for example, the Desmonema glaciale—
fantastic, beautiful, heartbreaking life-forms
rising up through the ocean water.

We watch the film for a while.

MORTON
Sometimes you get all caught up in things, whatever they may be,
even your career
because you think that's the thing you should pay attention to in
        your life,
providing for the things your children need
or even more than they might need, but things they want,
so that you forget to pay attention to the children themselves.

We always thought it was best for Darling,
bringing her here to take her mind off her big sister Dee Dee,
which we had to do
because, frankly,
Dee Dee was a sweet child and all,
and we truly loved her,
but when she just walked right out of
the Hospital for Hopeless Psychiatric Cases
and showed up back home on the doorstep with her suitcase,
well, I didn't have a choice.

Frankly, there is a thing called normal.
I didn't make it up.
I might not like to be normal myself
but I *have* to be normal, like it or not.

So I told Dee Dee to march right back there.

And I think I was right to put her on the train by herself
and let her get back to the hospital on her own
because I think that's how people eventually learn
to have a little self-reliance.

Or not.

Or not.
If she couldn't find her way
then, you know,
I'm going to die one day myself.
I can't take care of her forever.
Someday she's going to have to make it on her own
and it may as well be sooner as later,
which is why we brought Darling here,
because the whole thing upset her a little bit.
But now I see, with Dee Dee,
I was completely wrong.

(We watch the underwater film for a while longer.)

The Prom

Music.
Big band.
Guy Lombardo or Benny Goodman.

Summer night.

Stars in the sky.

Nancy enters in her prom dress and dances solo,
or whirls slowly like a dervish.

After a little while,
Jorge enters in his prom dress and dances solo.

After a little while,
Vikram enters in his prom dress and dances solo.

After a little while,
Darling enters in her prom dress and dances solo.

After a little while,
Ella enters in her prom dress and dances solo.

After a little while,
Benny enters in his prom dress and dances solo.

After a little while,
Edgar enters in his prom dress and dances with Charlie and Mortimer.

Finally,
Morton enters in his prom dress and dances solo.

In time everyone is dancing or whirling alone,

and then, gradually, Jorge joins Darling and they dance together.

After a while, Benny joins Ella, and they dance together.

Nancy joins Morton, and they dance together.

Edgar joins Vikram, and they dance together

as we hear over the music:

ELLA'S VOICE-OVER *(Coming from a loudspeaker)*
In my dream
we drove Bets's red station wagon like it was a convertible.
All of the windows were down
and people were lying across the backseat and
in the back bed with their feet hanging out the windows.
Music was blaring.
Your pager went off
and you said you had to go in for the lead role in *The Fantasticks*.
You were the understudy for all of the male roles
in all of the shows in New York.
It was playing on Christopher Street,
so we pulled the car up
and you convinced them to do the show out on the balcony
so we could see you perform from the car.
When it was over you took us to the largest,
oldest hotel in New York.
It had been abandoned,
gutted,
and then refurbished in a 1970s Vegas style,

but the grand, spiral staircase was still there leading all the way from the
lobby up to the twentieth floor.
We took a room up on the roof
and went out onto the boardwalk
to the A.M./P.M. mini-mart
to buy matches.
They said they wouldn't sell them to you unless you bought cigarettes.
There was a red convertible in the store that was being raffled off.
We signed up and then noticed the thing by the door.
It was Andrei's body in pieces,
shrink-wrapped into the kind of package that a yo-yo would come in.
There was the head
and torso
and just one leg.
I saw a scratch on the side of his face
and remembered that I had seen a scratch on Andrei's face earlier
    that day.
We called the police
and told them that we were sure that Andrei was the killer
because
the body was definitely his.
Just then
he came running out of the back room
and straight out the front door.
He was on his cell phone
and he disappeared
down the beach.

(Silence.)

BENNY'S VOICE-OVER
Well,
it has a happy ending.

*(While Ella was speaking,
the couples danced out together, couple by couple:*

Jorge and Darling

Morton and Nancy

Edgar and Vikram.

And, gradually, as the music fades into the distance,
we hear the sound of crickets.

A summer evening.
A starry sky.
And then,
as Benny and Ella go on dancing,
a slow fade to dark.)

END OF PLAY

CHARLES L. MEE, JR.'s play *Wintertime*, directed by Les Waters, was presented at La Jolla Playhouse and Long Wharf Theatre in the fall of 2002, and in other recent productions at ACT, the Guthrie Theater and elsewhere. *Big Love* has been performed at Actors Theatre of Louisville's Humana Festival, Berkeley Repertory Theatre, Long Wharf Theatre, The Goodman Theatre, ACT, the Next Wave Festival at Brooklyn Academy of Music and elsewhere. *True Love* was presented at the Zipper Theatre in New York and at the Holland Festival, as well as in Brussels and Berlin. *First Love* has been performed at New York Theatre Workshop and at the Magic Theatre. Among his other recent plays are *bobrauschenbergamerica, Limonade Tous Les Jour* and *Vienna Lusthaus (Revisited)*. His work is made possible by the support of Jeanne Donovan Fisher and Richard B. Fisher.

His complete works are available on the internet at www.charlesmee.org.

NO ONE
AS NASTY

Susan Nussbaum

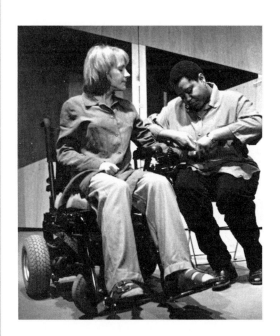

Janet 2 (Janelle Snow, left) and Lois (Patricia Pierre-Antoine) in the Victory Gardens Theater production, Chicago, Illinois, 2000. Photo by Liz Lauren.

I became disabled at age twenty-four. Up until that point, my intention was to be an actress. That would no longer be a practical career choice, not that it ever had been. But, some years later, after joining the Disability Rights Movement, and experiencing an awakening of pride and sense of self as a disabled person, I became restless to find some way to communicate my experience to others. I was stunned to find myself actually pleased to be a part of this awkward, scary, mysterious minority group. I recognized that I had, rather painfully, fallen into a world with dramatic potential that had gone completely untapped. I was anxious to exploit my advantage as an insider. I decided to write. And plays were the natural format for me.

I don't like writing very much. It requires too much discipline and provides too much opportunity for self-castigation. Consequently, I don't write as much as I should. *No One as Nasty* was an attempt to look at the class and race dynamic between a disabled white woman and her black personal assistant. It took forever to write, and wound up being more about the disabled white woman and her various anxieties than about the relationship between the two women. I tried to fix it in numerous rewrites, but the play resisted being about the thing I wanted it to be about. I wasn't a good enough writer. When it was finally produced in 2000 by Victory Gardens Theater in Chicago, I resigned myself to accepting the piece for its strengths, and hoping to do better next time.

There have been times when I've been urged to "stretch" and write about something other than disability. I have no interest in writing about anything other than disability, however. What could be more interesting than disability? And who better to write about it than me? Just when one thinks one has seen everything onstage, and heard from all segments of society, along comes this new and utterly unheard-from minority, peopled with every kind of social outcast. It's just too good to be true for any writer. The downside, of course, is that no theater wants to produce anything about disability. Everything that makes us interesting to write about also makes us qualified to be discriminated against. I suppose that someday, maybe soon, a disabled playwright or two will come along and break through, be the voice of our fledgling minority, in the way that August Wilson and Tony Kushner did. I just hope I'm not around when it happens, because I'll wish it were me.

Production History

No One as Nasty was first developed in Mark Taper Forum's Other Voices Summer Chautauqua Writer's Workshop in 1994 (Center Theatre Group, Los Angeles). In 1995 the play received a workshop production, directed by Lisa Peterson, in Other Voices' May Days and Chautauqua Nights series. The cast was as follows:

JANET	Susan Nussbaum
JANET 2	Amy Aquino
LOIS	Ella Joyce
YOUNG MAN	Armando Molina
LEADING LADY	Rhonda Aldrich
YOUNG WOMAN	Maria Canals
THERAPIST	Lois Foraker
CHARACTER MAN	Bill Applebaum

No One as Nasty premiered June 2, 2000, at Victory Gardens Theater in Chicago. The production was directed by Susan V. Booth. The cast was as follows:

JANET	Lusia Strus
JANET 2	Janelle Snow
LOIS	Patricia Pierre-Antoine
KEN	Phil Ridarelli
ACTRESS 1	Penelope Walker
ACTRESS 2	Kerry Cox
MALE ACTOR	Jesse Weaver

Characters

JANET—a woman in her thirties or forties, uses a power wheelchair.

JANET 2—sometimes in a wheelchair, Janet's dream self.

LOIS—Janet's personal assistant, African American.

BOYFRIEND—a dream character.

KEN—Janet's driver, young white guy.

MYSTERY WOMAN—a dream character, played by the actor who plays Janet 2.

EDWIN THE DOORMAN—a dream character.

JOANNA—Janet's girlfriend.

LUCY—Janet's other personal assistant, Jamaican.

MAN WITH PANTS—a dream character.

LOIS'S FRIEND

BENNY—Janet's friend.

CHRISTOPHER REEVE

BUSTER—Lois's cat, a dream character, played by a human actor.

JANET'S FRIEND

CLARK GABLE

WHEELCHAIR PUSHER—a dream character.

VARIOUS PERSONAL ASSISTANTS (PA)

Author's Note

The various locations in the play are indicated by lighting, set pieces (which can be moved on and off the stage by actors), and props, signs or costume pieces. None of the locations are realistically defined. Some problems, such as the shower, can be indicated by sound effects and a prop or two. The car can be as simple as a chair for the driver, and can appear in a fixed place onstage when needed. In my imagination, I hoped for something that could really be driven around the stage, but it's not necessary. When the actor treats it as a real car, and sound effects are added, it's better than real. Janet's dreams can be introduced by subtle sound and/or light effects as well. The actors have frequent and often lightning-speed entrances and exits, and the more doors, curtains, screens, etc., that they can appear from, or disappear into, the better.

Technical assistance from people with experience is necessary to learn how Lois transfers Janet 2 from wheelchair to bed. Janet never leaves her wheelchair until the very end, when she's lifted into her bed. Her disability is a real part of her. Janet 2 can become conveniently nondisabled when Janet needs her to be. She's the self Janet has invented to help tell her story—to make it "accessible," in a way.

Janet, in a wheelchair, addresses the audience. Janet 2, also in a wheel-chair, dials a phone, over and over.

JANET: You meet someone or not, it's an accident. Either it happens or it doesn't, it's strictly a matter of coincidence. I don't think we draw people to us when we are "ready." And the Hiroshima maidens got burned and disfigured—there's a word: "disfig-ured"—because of, why? Because. They were in Hiroshima. They were too close to avoid the fire, too far to be consumed. If I was five seconds earlier or later I wouldn't be this crip now. My life would be on some different time line. It was an *accident*; it had nothing to do with whether I was a good or a bad person. We don't live in an ordered universe where there are reasons and "it's for the best" or this happened so I and others "*could learn.*" No. It was an accident like the whole human race is an accident. Like the dinosaurs got blown away by a meteor.

(Janet 2 slams the phone down.)

JANET 2 *(Pacing in wheelchair)*: Goddamn her to the pits of everlast-ing hell. Fuck her to death. *(Dials again; talking into a machine)* Lois, it's one o'clock in the morning. Are you there? Lois? You were supposed to be here an hour and a half ago, Lois, and I mean, this is really unfair. I really, I am exhausted and you—

JANET *(Telling Janet 2 what to say)*: It's not like I don't pay her enough—

JANET 2: Do I not pay you enough, is that it? Is it? Are the demands of the job so—so— Am I an animal? Am I a member of some subspecies, Lois?

JANET: Good.

JANET 2: This is just deeply fucked on your part. This is just manipulative bullshit, Lois. Good-bye. *(Hangs up; paces in wheelchair. Like a chant or a song)* Fuck her, fuck her, fuck her fuck her fuckherfuckherfuckher.

(Lois enters. She hurries to take her coat and boots off.)

(Cheery, poisonous) No problem! Fuck me, right?

(Lois continues scurrying around trying to get ready while Janet 2 follows her.)

No problem if you're two hours late, I'm not going anywhere. That's pretty funny, isn't it, Lois? I'm a funny person. You are torturing me. This is passive-aggressive torture on your part, Lois. *(Pause)* There were no phones of any kind, I suppose? *(Pause)* Oh, really? Yes, absolutely, no phones. No phones. No phones? That's correct. *None.*

LOIS: Are you ready?

JANET 2: Am I ready? Am I ready?

(Lois helps Janet 2 into the bed. Janet 2 jerks back from Lois in disgust.)

LOIS: You're hurting my wrist.

JANET 2: You're handling me incorrectly.

(Lois stands there. Terrible tension.)

Just get me in bed.

(Lois transfers Janet 2 into the bed. She begins undressing her.)

I don't understand what I must do to convey to you how fucking tired I am.

(Lois continues undressing Janet 2.)

I can't take it. I can't.

(Lois remains silent, but continues taking off Janet 2's socks, etc. Janet falls silent, too. Then—)

Lois? I'm sorry. I'm tired and I'm sorry, I—I'm sorry. Could you say something? I mean, I am apologizing. And I'm the one who—I'm the cripple, I'm the one—look, please, just— What? What do I—will you *talk*? Will you make words come out . . . of . . . your . . . mouth? Okay? Lois?

LOIS *(Finally boiling over)*: What do you want me to say? I'm sorry. I'm *sorry*. Okay? I am goddamn, fucking, SORRY!

JANET 2: You're not sorry.

LOIS: Please, don't give me credit for giving a shit by going out of my way to fuck you up. You're so fucked up already it's beneath me to fuck you up any further.

JANET 2: What?

LOIS: I had a flat tire, okay? Okay? *Okay?!* Jesus, you are such a *bitch!* I have been trying to get here! You *know* I have been trying to get here! Have I ever—ever—ever— Am I gonna leave you stranded? Am I? What? *Can-you-make-words-now?!!!*

JANET 2 *(Bloodied, but unbowed)*: You know what? That is not the point. No, you're not going to leave me stranded, but I don't— you have almost left me stranded so often. I was stranded tonight! Is that what this is about? Do I have to be stranded to— to—

LOIS: I am here, okay? What else can I do?! I am here! That is going to have to be sufficient.

JANET 2: It does not suffice.

LOIS: I am not going to leave you stranded, as much as I would sometimes like to. I am sorry I was late, I am sorry for all the times I have ever been late, I am sorry you feel that I am not sorry. But I am trying to help your ass, so shut the fuck up or I will walk out that door! God*damn!*

(Pause. Janet 2 sees that Lois has the power. Lois continues her tasks, finally holding water for Janet 2 to drink.)

Do you want it?

JANET 2: No.

LOIS: Okay.

(Lois sets the water down, gets her things, and exits.)

JANET *(To Janet 2)*: Watch this dream.

(Boyfriend enters. Janet 2 gets up from the bed.)

BOYFRIEND: Strafengaloshkinograwformicht. Nogorwy.
JANET 2: What?
BOYFRIEND: Fermigchdiron.
JANET *(To Janet 2)*: It's a dream.

(Boyfriend and Janet 2 stand together.)

JANET 2: Look how easy everything is.
BOYFRIEND: It's hensher.
JANET 2: Yes, I understand. But something's wrong here.
BOYFRIEND: Is it your feet?
JANET 2: Yes, my feet. Where are they? *(She looks down at her feet, which seem to her to have disappeared)* I should have feet here.

(The Boyfriend kisses Janet 2.)

But what about my feet?
BOYFRIEND: Not important.
JANET 2: I'm so sorry. I'm so sorry.
BOYFRIEND: The important thing is whether you have a coherent program to lead the working class.
JANET 2: Yes.

(Boyfriend and Janet 2 begin to kiss, to get lost in each other, and they move to a shower. The Boyfriend kneels down and we see only Janet 2, holding on just barely, turning, turning, lowering herself until she is sitting, her Boyfriend gone, replaced by her Personal Assistant, PA, helping her in the shower. Janet looks on.)

(Through clenched teeth, furious) Just put the shampoo in my hand, is that too big a concept for you? Do you think you could manage to put the fucking shampoo in my hand or do I need to send you an engraved invitation? *(PA hands her the soap)* Hurry up! Hurry the fuck *up*! *(To herself)* This is all an illusion and I will be somewhere else now, I will be on a warm beach, feeling

the sun beat down on me, feeling a ladybug land on my ankle. *(To PA)* Idiot!

PA: Janet, I don't think it's right to talk to me that way.

JANET 2: What way? What fucking way? I'm not talking to *you*, I am simply talking, get it? I am saying fuck and shit and goddamn motherfucking cocksucking shit cunt world. It has nothing to do with you. You have absolutely no meaning here except to hand the soap to my dead body, get it? It's nothing *personal*.

PA *(To Janet)*: You never talk to Lois this way.

JANET: What way?

PA *(Back to Janet 2)*: I can't take this anymore.

JANET 2: Take what? Please tell me what it is, just what terrible thing it is that *you* cannot take anymore. Get out. Just get the *fuck* out, I'll send you your money.

PA: No one will know that you're here.

JANET 2 *(Screaming)*: Get out! Goddamn you to hell! Get your stupid ass out of my worthless sight! But before you go, understand this—you are *not* the asshole here, *I* am the asshole, *I* am the worthless piece of shit in this bathroom, now GET OUT OF HERE!!!!

(Ken, Janet's driver, drives on. The car radio is on loudly, drowning out Janet 2, who is screaming with rage. The PA leaves as Ken picks up Janet.)

JANET *(To Ken)*: I dreamed I was driving my van home.

KEN: You were driving?

JANET: Yes, but I was having trouble. The windshield wipers were broken and it was snowing and I couldn't see . . .

(Janet begins to live the dream. She inspects the windshields. Janet 2 plays Mystery Woman.)

Where is this, what street? I saw it was some shopping area, and I looked in the windows to kill time. This shop has cards and novelties. It's owned by a beautiful and mysterious woman.

MYSTERY WOMAN: The time is right to go on a ritual killing spree.

(Mystery Woman, followed by Janet, hits the streets.)

JANET: I am invisible. She is stunningly beautiful and all the men watch her as she passes. She is aware of her power.

MYSTERY WOMAN *(To Janet)*: I have your credit card . . .

JANET: Which she must've stolen . . .

(Mystery Woman approaches Ken.)

Ken, do not let her entrance you!

KEN: Wow.

(Ken is entranced.)

MYSTERY WOMAN *(To Ken)*: Janet said to tell you to just drop me at her apartment.

KEN: Yes, I will do what you say.

JANET: In the driveway, she kisses him. He is seduced . . . but instead of having sex with him, she sucks the strength out of his body and kills him with her last kiss.

(Ken dies. Mystery Woman enters the building. She sees Edwin, the Doorman.)

There is Edwin the Doorman.

MYSTERY WOMAN *(To Edwin)*: Janet said I could stay at her place.

EDWIN THE DOORMAN: Here is the key to Janet's apartment.

JANET: Even though she is strong enough to rip the doorknob out by the root.

EDWIN THE DOORMAN: We have a guest policy. You can order food and anything else you want and charge it to Janet.

JANET: No!

MYSTERY WOMAN *(To Edwin)*: Come with me.

JANET: In my apartment, she kisses him, sucks out his power, and kills him. She leaves his body in the tub to rot. Look, the room is filled with dead bodies. I am overwhelmed by the stench of death. Wait. One of her victims wasn't killed . . .

VICTIM: Just winded. I can identify the killer!

JANET: But the last I see her, she has dressed up and taken to the streets again, out on another spree.

(Dream ends. All exit but Ken, who drives out of the dream and picks up Janet.)

(To Ken) The driver guy wasn't really you. In the dream. He was some other—a dream device. So don't feel—

KEN: No, I get it. So what does it mean?

JANET: I don't know . . . power . . . she has the power I wish I had, or, oh, physical beauty is power, or, um . . .

KEN: Who does she kill first?

JANET: The driver. You.

KEN: You were hit by a car.

JANET: What's your point?

KEN: She drained him of power.

JANET: Well, yeah . . . but no.

KEN: You close off any discussion that gets too close.

JANET: No. Is that some "thing"? Some, "Oh, the combination has clicked into place"? The thing I don't get is, how do you not close off? No, really, I understand that openness is good. I'm open, considering how people are. I'm already way, way—and if I "open up, really open up," what's gonna be in there? Some memory? Some feeling or color or name—no—nothing will be in there that's so surprising. There is no *thing* at the center, there is no knot unraveling. No big, "Ahh yes, I see" moment of recognition.

(Pause.)

KEN: I'm reading Sartre.

JANET: Which one?

KEN: *Nausea.* Is it true he confessed on his deathbed?

JANET: No, that's impossible. That's a sick rumor started by the Pope. *(Begins to panic)* Watch that guy—that guy! Sorry. I thought he was opening his car door into us. Sorry. Backseat driver.

KEN: That's okay. But don't you think it's possible that a man searches for meaning his whole life and then suddenly embraces a supernatural belief at the end? A last grasp at emotional comfort?

JANET: Sartre would never, ever, ever sink to those depths. A person doesn't blow his life's work off just because he's dying.

KEN: What if he had—like you said—a moment of recognition?

JANET: Oh my God, you are such a romantic! He was Sartre. Terrible things happen. You don't go around having a personal relationship with God. You hafta be a fucking mercenary to do that. God is nothing more than a crooked businessman, making everybody offers they can't refuse.

KEN *(Laughing, nothing threatens him)*: I don't know. I think God's a pretty cool guy.

JANET: Yeah, uh-huh.

KEN: No, but—religion's a lesson plan—it gives some order to the chaos. I even pray sometimes.

JANET: What? You light incense. That's not religion.

KEN: You believe in what? Nothing? Nothing is inexplicably beautiful or mysterious to you? I don't believe that. I believe it's possible that there is a higher power—I'm not saying it's this guy up there with a big white beard—

JANET: Well, what color beard does he have? *(Suddenly panic-stricken)* Red light! Red light! *(Ken stops the car)* Sorry. I'm so neurotic.

KEN: So you believe in nothing.

JANET: I do not believe in divine intervention, in fateful lightning.

KEN: We're here.

(They are at Janet's. Janet 2 is there.)

JANET: Hey, thanks for the ride. *(Hands him some money)*

KEN: Any time. Take it easy.

(Janet gets out of the car. She starts to say something, then thinks better of it.)

JANET: Oh, blah blah. Yeah, you take it easy, too.

(Ken drives off. Janet joins Janet 2, who sits in the wheelchair.)

Is Lois still here?

JANET 2 *(Shrugs)*: She's hanging around.

JANET: Is that one of her hairpins? *(She points to a pink hairpin on the floor)* Goddamnit!

JANET 2 *(Rolls over for a closer look)*: Yep.

JANET: I hate when she leaves her hairpins around.

(Janet 2 stands from her wheelchair and picks up the hairpin.)

JANET 2: Should I give it back to her?

JANET: No. Throw it out. She has five thousand of those things. Let's look around. They're probably all over the place.

(The two Janets begin searching for hairpins.)

I don't know why she stays here so long. She has her own apartment for chrissake. I feel like I'm being invaded . . . by thousands of little pink hairpins. Oh God, look at this! It's a desiccated banana string!

JANET 2: What?

JANET: The stringy thing from a banana. She leaves these everywhere. And I look petty if I say something.

(Lois enters.)

JANET 2 *(To Lois)*: Lois, would you clip my fingernails?

(Lois begins clipping Janet 2's nails. The Janets, sitting on either side of Lois, say the following lines in unison:)

JANET AND JANET 2: Just try not to get the skin, okay? *(Lois continues clipping)* Because sometimes you get the clipper edge on my skin under my nail and not my nail itself, okay? *(Lois continues clipping)* Okay? *(Pause)* Ow! See like you almost got the skin that time. Just try to—am I bleeding? *(Janet 2 examines her nails)* Well, it's okay. Just really make sure you only clip just the nails, okay? *(Lois continues clipping)* Lois? *(Pause)* Okay?

LOIS: Okay. *(Continues clipping)*

JANET AND JANET 2: I wasn't sure if you heard me. Because you didn't respond, so . . . in fact, I think that's the first thing you've said all morning. *(Lois continues clipping)* Are you pissed off at me or something?

LOIS: I'm just caught up in my own thoughts.

JANET AND JANET 2: Right.

LOIS: I can go for a very long time without the need to speak. It's nothing personal.

JANET AND JANET 2 *(Not believing)*: Okay . . . if you say so—ow! You got the skin! Wait, let me . . . well, it's okay. It's not really bleeding.

JANET *(To audience)*: God, I hate this. This is so absurd . . .

(The nail job is done.)

JANET AND JANET 2: Let me look . . . *(Janet 2 examines her nails)* Okay, thanks a lot, Lois.

(No response.)

JANET 2 *(To Janet)*: She keeps her own counsel.

JANET *(To audience)*: I never keep my own counsel. Before Lois, there was this parade of assistants—just raw meat, so fuck them and fuck me. But Lois and me were like two prisoners with adjoining cells on death row. We were there for each other.

(Lois is putting Janet's shoes on.)

LOIS: You know Turnip?

JANET: The guy you're tutoring? Don't you feel guilty calling him Turnip?

(Lois continues working on the shoes.)

LOIS: Yes I do, but I can't help it. Every time I start thinking he's not totally inert, he does something to annoy the shit out of me. Like he'll be talking about, "My close, pers'nal friend, Denzel, y'unnerstan' . . ." And I'm thinking, "Yeah, right, motherfucker, now back to the business at hand—*See Spot Run*—and I'm sorry, but the man, and I *do* use that term loosely, turns into a turnip before my eyes. You could take that man's brain, blow it up a gnat's ass with a straw, and there would still be room for it to bounce around in there.

JANET *(Laughing)*: I'm glad you're out there making a difference, Lo.

LOIS: Anyway, I'm not calling him Turnip anymore. I gave him a new name: Bob.

JANET: Why Bob?

LOIS: Box of bricks.

JANET *(Laughing)*: Poor Bob.

LOIS: He has no idea, though. He's such a blockhead.

(Joanna, Janet's girlfriend, enters from the bathroom. She kisses Janet, grabs her coat, and heads toward the door.)

JOANNA: Hi, Lo. Bye, Lo. *(Exits)*

JANET: Yeah. So, I think I like this woman.

LOIS: You *think* you like her?

(Lois finishes with the shoes and the two women just sit talking.)

JANET: God, I don't know. I like how much she likes me, though.

LOIS: Um-hmm.

JANET: And she's attractive. Don't you think?

LOIS *(Laughing)*: You're the one better find her attractive. I like my "mens."

JANET: No, but come on. Really. She's attractive, don't you think? And she's smart. And, you know, she's . . . interesting. I'm—no, I realize—I absolutely think she's incredibly attractive. She calls me a lot. Which—I'm not a phone person, so—but I find I look forward to her phone calls. To the call itself. And the talking.

LOIS: Hey, you wanna go to the movies?

JANET: Oh, yeah. I am having sex with that idea.

LOIS: Well, shit, then don't sit next to me.

(Janet and Lois begin to cross to the movies.)

JANET *(To audience)*: When Lucy started working for me on Lois's days off, I had this whole plan about how I was going to have this mutually respectful relationship with her.

(Lucy enters, and starts pulling up Janet 2's pants. Lois and Janet sit like they are at the movies. They munch popcorn and watch the following scene. Lucy speaks with a Jamaican accent.)

JANET 2: So, how old is your oldest kid?

LUCY: My oldest, he eighteen.

JANET 2: Okay, so now just pull them up as far as you can, okay?

LUCY: Okay, then.

JANET 2: Uh-huh. And your youngest?

LUCY: My youngest, she six, Jan.

JANET 2: Wow. Okay, so now you just flip me onto my side and pull them up in back.

(Lucy does so, handling Janet 2 like a sack of potatoes.)

Ow! Hey, okay, not so—try and be a little more gentle if you can.

LUCY: I'm sorry, Jan.

JANET 2: So how many kids do you have altogether?

LUCY: Altogether I got seven, Jan.

JANET 2: Boy, that's a—you got a real handful there.

LUCY: It's a lot, Jan.

(Lucy pulls Janet 2 back like she's flipping pancakes.)

JANET 2: Ow! Okay, just—just let me know and I'll turn back on my own, okay Lucy? You're really strong.
LUCY: Okay then, Jan.
JANET 2: You don't know your own strength!
LUCY: Huh?
JANET 2: Just—you're really strong.
LUCY: Okay, Jan.

(Lucy transfers Janet 2 into wheelchair.)

JANET 2: So what are their names? All your kids?
LUCY: There's Horace, and Keneeta, and Kiara, and Patrice and Henry and Taleisha and Kameli. But we call Kameli "Fatty." That her nickname, Jan, because her so fat!
JANET 2: Oh. Wow. Okay.

(Janet and Lois turn their attention to the movie.)

JANET: These movie quiz things . . . look at this: "What sci-fi super-hero hailed from the planet Krypton?" Like I'm some kind of idiot who's never read a comic book in my life.
LOIS: Yeah. You're the kind of idiot who's read hundreds of comic books.
JANET: I'm not attracted to the immediate future. I'd prefer to wake up in the year 38000. I can't stand that my little speck-of-dust life trapped in this pitiful century will one day be looked back on with horror by advanced cultures.

(They munch popcorn. Janet 2 and Lucy exit.)

LOIS: I try to live in the present. I try to appreciate what I have and where I am because it'll all be over in the flash of a gnat's fart.
JANET: You mean like, "Today is the first day of the rest of my life"? Too much pressure.
LOIS: Okay, so you prefer to ignore the present?
JANET: Yes.
LOIS: Then you're not really alive.
JANET: Whatever.
LOIS: We walk along the edge every day. That's what we do. All of life takes place on "the edge," and everybody knows if you're on "the

edge," you can't look over. You look over, you lose your balance

edge," you can't look over. You look over, you lose your balance and fall in. You got to be able to walk along the edge without looking over.

JANET: I have to look.

LOIS: You don't. Just keep on walking . . . look over that way . . . okay, that's good . . . look behind you . . . uh-huh, still okay. Here I am . . . I'm walking . . . walking along . . . having a good time . . . I'm on the edge, but I'm cool. Hmm, maybe I'll just take myself a quick look . . . I think I will, seein' how good it all is . . . just a peek over the edge, just a—shhiiiit!!! Don't look over the edge.

You just have to learn to relax a little more.

JANET: Lois, I'm sorry, but—I don't see you as a particularly relaxed person.

LOIS: I'm very relaxed, but aware. I stay on my guard, so the rest of me is free to go to the movies and have fun.

JANET: How can you relax if you're on guard?

LOIS: I just can. It's a skill you pick up in Colored School, USA.

(Looking at the screen) "What film Everyman starred in *Apollo 13*?" Tom Hanks.

JANET: Please. Hollywood's tribute to "Triumph of the Will."

You know, I worry about . . . sometimes, how I—I say the wrong thing.

LOIS *(Laughing)*: But that's your specialty. Don't worry about it.

JANET: Just don't say anything at all. That's your strategy. *(Lois laughs, small and cynical)* Lois?

LOIS: What?

JANET: Have you ever had a moment when—like the times people in the streets have, you know, like that time you told me, like the time that woman spit on you? Doesn't the possibility tease at your mind that all white people are just an inch away from that?

LOIS: No. So far as I can see, stupidity doesn't have a color.

JANET: I'll be in the streets sometimes, though, and someone will do some awful crip thing on me, like some fucking nonentity stranger, just come right up to me and say some stupid—"Hey! Good to see you out and about!"—or some such nonsense or you go into the hospital, right, for a broken wrist and they want to sign you up for their new Nazi eugenics program and I think, Kill 'em all.

LOIS: I was taught, I suppose you could say I was raised—well, shit, I didn't know any white people. But everybody said they hated us. That they thought they were so much smarter. When I was bused, I went to school with almost all white kids, and they treated the black kids like they were just so much better than us, like that was just the way things were. I remember sitting there and listening to them talk in class, and I'd think, Hmm, I'm smarter than that one, and that one, and that one . . .

JANET: Yeah, that must've been . . . Did you make friends with any white kids?

LOIS: Yeah, sort of.

JANET: But you ate at the black table in the cafeteria.

LOIS: Oh, yeah.

JANET: We had a couple tables like that at my school.

LOIS: Yep.

JANET: 'Course if I had been a crip then, I would've been—God knows what table I would've been relegated to. I probably would've just had a bowl on the floor under somebody else's table.

LOIS: You could've sat at the colored table.

JANET: Really? No, it woulda been—no, but did you have any crips at your school?

LOIS: We had a couple. We had a dwarf.

JANET: Whoa.

LOIS: He was popular. He was into all the clubs, everyone liked him . . . and then there was this guy who had one leg shorter than the other. He was a racist.

JANET: You mean, unusually so?

LOIS: He was a stone-cold racist. I remember him very well. And you couldn't even beat him up.

JANET: What do you mean, 'cause he was a crip? He could get away without a beating 'cause he was a crip? Oh God, that's—that's something. But, so, what'd he—did he say racist stuff or what?

LOIS: The usual, ever-so-creative "niggah." Sometimes he'd get really inspired: "Your mother's a niggah," or something.

JANET: Uh-oh.

LOIS: Yeah. Don't wanna bring mama into it.

(Janet 2 is heard yelling from off.)

JANET 2 *(Offstage)*: Lois!

JANET: But you didn't beat him up? The gimpy racist?

LOIS: It just wasn't done. Otherwise, I would've had him up against the wall.

(Lights reveal Janet 2 in a shower.)

JANET 2: Lois!

LOIS: My mother used to tell us to watch out for the white kids: "Be careful around white people's chirren."

(Janet and Lois laugh.)

JANET 2 *(Really impatient)*: Lois!!

JANET: Lois.

(Lois gets up and crosses to Janet 2. She helps her in the shower, which continues under the following:)

(To audience) I've been sorta obsessed—although that's not the word, but—preoccupied with this thing about Christopher Reeve . . . you know, Superman, breaking his neck.

I think about him lying there, real aware of every second that passes. Each second is a year that you experience fully and you think how, when enough seconds pass, billions of seconds accumulate, something will be different. Or, maybe not. It scares the shit outta me, remembering how it was . . . You can't move, you can't *move*. And you never, ever, ever sleep . . . you just experience this passage of time as if it's a *thing*, like time has *weight* and *density*. Oh God, I don't know, but I feel . . . sorry for him, but sometimes I make jokes about him, like, "What's black and sits at the top of the stairs? Christopher Reeve after a fire." —Which is just this twisted-up way of—of—of *coping*, but I just thought I'd mention it. Anyway . . . after I heard about it, I didn't leave my house for three whole days and nights. I just stayed inside. Do you think that means I'm depressed?

(Focus shifts to Lois and Janet 2 in the shower stall.)

JANET 2: It's a little too hot. *(Pause)* Still a little tiny bit too hot. *(Pause)* It's an eensy hair too hot, barely a breath. *(Pause)* Okay. I think. Wait. It's still just the teeny teeny *tini*est smidgen of a breath too hot . . . barely move it at all—yeah, 'kay, that's it. But you should've seen it, Lo: "Loving wife feeds her crippled hubby." Like the whole thing is about her now, the wife. What a rock Christopher Reeve's wife is. How selfless, to be actually staying with him now that he's just this huge, pathetic crip.

LOIS: I didn't know you were reading the *Enquirer* now.

JANET 2: There's this whole thing about how spouses of disabled people are, you know, like they've been given this "cross to bear." I mean, fuck you! And because of this twisted, Aryan obsession in the national consciousness, nobody, in general, wants to fuck us.

LOIS: "In general," you wouldn't wanna fuck most people, though, because they act stupid or they can't be trusted.

JANET 2: Well, yes, I realize that . . . but I've been with people who were cool with the crip thing at first, then it got to them, you know? Like they didn't get that they had signed on for not just the relationship, but also the *stigma*. Or maybe I just got to them. Lo, the water's a bit too cold. It just got really cold all of a sudden. It's just, goddamn! It's really, really co— Wait! It's too hot now!

LOIS: How's that?

JANET 2: That is wonderful, oh God, that is—yeah.

LOIS: Look at it this way. At least you belong to a minority where famous stars can suddenly be members and join your movement. It's not like Christopher Reeve is gonna fall off a horse and be black.

JANET 2: Although I bet Chris sure wishes he could choose, you know? Between being treated with hatred or pity.

LOIS: What would you choose?

JANET 2: Hatred.

LOIS: Shows what you know.

JANET 2: Yeah, it shows what I know.

But this is the pièce de résistance. He tells the media, he says, "Why focus on ramps? I'll walk again." What the hell is that supposed to mean?

LOIS: It means—

JANET 2: I know very well what it means. It means my people now have a spokesperson that was like, invented by the able-bodied world for their own dark purpose. —Aaagghh, the water's cold! Too cold! Cold! Lois!!!!

LOIS: Better?

JANET 2: It's too hhooot!!!!

JANET *(To audience)*: I will always *pay* for a shower. And no matter how deeply I understand that there is nothing wrong with that, that I am surviving, I will always feel somehow that it's shameful. I am shamed. And in a few years there'll be a cure and there will be no people like me ever again and whatever I learn will leave no legacy. It will be irrelevant.

LOIS *(To Janet, while still showering Janet 2)*: What's the shameful part?

JANET *(To Lois)*: The needing.

(Janet 2 gets up from the wheelchair and crosses to Janet.)

JANET 2: Look, I think I'm pretty much done with the shower scenes. I think you've accomplished what you needed to, I really don't see that there's much else to accomplish at this point, really. I feel . . . it's cold.

JANET: Damn right, it's cold! They never tell you how cold it gets. When you're a crip you get fucking cold. Unless you're one of those crips who's hot all the time. That's why you can't have a whole bunch of crips all together in one place, because people are turning up the thermostat and opening the windows at the same time.

(Janet 2 returns to the wheelchair. Lois helps her into bed.)

JANET 2: Lois, watch the foot! The foot!

JANET *(To Janet 2)*: Oh, come on, has she ever dropped the foot? *(To audience)* "The foot." Listen to how alienated I am from my own body.

(Lois covers Janet 2 with a blanket.)

JANET 2: Why are you defending her?

JANET: She's not even listening.

JANET 2: I think she hears you.

JANET: I don't care. She pretends not to listen to irritate me.

LOIS: I'm getting the laundry.

(Lois exits.)

JANET *(To Janet 2)*: Shhh! Watch!

(Janet 2 dreams. A man appears holding a pair of pants.)

JANET 2 *(Dreaming)*: Wait. These pants are back from the cleaners. They are in a special cleaning bag. I can tell by looking at them that if I just put on these pants, very, very carefully . . . *(Begins to stand cautiously)* . . . and if I get up very, very slowly . . . I can walk in these special pants. If only I'd known all along how simple it is! It's the pants! It's been the pants all the time. Walk slowly. Walk very slowly in these special pants.

(The man with the pants disappears as the dream dissolves. Joanna joins Janet 2 in bed. Janet 2 is awake.)

JOANNA *(Laughing)*: Do you think Lois is bothered by me? I mean, when she comes in the morning and I'm lying next to you naked?

JANET 2 *(Laughing)*: Oh God, I really don't think she gives a shit.

JOANNA: She's so enigmatic. Do you think she talks about us to her friends?

JANET 2: I think she sees us from an amused distance. I assume she talks to her friends. I don't know.

JOANNA: She talks to you, though, right? You're her friend. You're confidantes.

JANET 2: We talk. We've developed a real respect for each other but, you know, it's delicate. After all these years.

JOANNA *(Laughing)*: Uh-oh, what does that mean?

JANET 2: No, we're friends. It's just a weird relationship, though.

JOANNA: Yeah. I've never been in this situation before.

JANET 2: I know.

JOANNA: Is it okay that I said that?

JANET 2: Well, yeah. I hope you don't have to watch what you say. I mean, is there something you need to talk about, though? Is the whole Lois thing a problem?

JOANNA: Well, I kinda feel like I don't get you without getting her too.

JANET 2: I—I don't think that's true.

JOANNA: That's just how I feel sometimes.

JANET 2: Okay, well . . . I'm kinda—you know, it's one of the things I deal with in my life. I mean, I don't have a life without someone who, you know, without a little help . . .

JOANNA: No, I know. I don't care. I mean, I love you. I just feel that way sometimes, but I'll work it out. It's just weird getting used to it.

JANET 2: Yeah.

JOANNA: Are you okay?

JANET 2: Sure. Yeah.

JOANNA *(Flirty)*: Do you love me?

JANET 2: You know I do.

JOANNA: Well, you know, it's nice to hear it sometimes.

JANET 2: No, I love you. I love you.

(Joanna kisses Janet 2 and exits. Lucy enters and starts putting Janet 2's shoes on.)

Okay, shoes.

JANET *(To audience)*: Lois is off. When Lois is off, I always think, I just have to survive till she's back.

(Lucy handles Janet 2's foot roughly.)

JANET 2: Ow! Lucy, you're hurting me.

LUCY: I don't like to hear you say that, Jan.

(Lois joins Janet.)

JANET *(To Lois)*: That sounded kinda funny. Kinda ambiguous. Did she mean she didn't like me to say, "Ow," 'cause she felt bad that she hurt me, or that next time I said, "Ow," she'd hafta slug me?

LOIS: What do you think?

JANET: I don't know. That's why I'm asking you. If I have this creepy instinctual feeling, I don't know. I don't know the warning signs. I've never been—attacked like that.

LOIS: It sounded like "pop goes the weasel" to me.

JANET: What? Like, oh, like—"pop"? One day, just "pop"?

LOIS: Pop goes the weasel.

(Lucy transfers Janet 2 into her wheelchair.)

JANET: Nah, you think? Lucy's so easy in some ways, so nice. And she actually shows up and does the job. And I hate breaking in a new person, I hate that.

LOIS: Then don't fire her.

JANET: She's really strong.

LOIS: Mm-hm.

(Lucy begins making the bed.)

JANET 2: Luce, could you just pull the cover down more on this side? A little more. A tiny bit more.

JANET *(To Lois)*: Remember that quad that time, moves into his own place . . . turns out the personal assistant has been making this quad give him blow jobs every day. This kinda thing—I don't know, you know?

LUCY: Okay then, Jan, I'm going. You take care now.

JANET 2: Thanks. You, too. Thanks a lot. Stay warm.

JANET: "Stay warm." I'm sitting here worrying about rape and saying, "Stay warm." So I have to wonder, what is *she* thinking?

LOIS *(As Lucy's thoughts)*: You take care now, 'cause when we seize state power, it's your ass.

JANET 2: Could you just fix my pants more, Lucy? Just pull the cuff down . . .

JANET *(As Janet 2's thoughts)*: Mammy, ah just won't eat a bite off that tray till you cinch up mah corset!

LUCY: Okay, Jan, that better?

LOIS: Miz Scarlett, you gwine eat them there hotcakes lahk yo' blessed mama tol' you!

JANET 2: No, they need to be the same length.

JANET: Ah won't do any such thing. Now pull!

LUCY: Is that okay, Jan?

LOIS: Ah knows jus' what you fixin' on doin'. You gon' dig yo' claws into Mistah Ashley Wilkes wit' yo' fahn airs.

JANET 2: The left leg is still a little shorter.

JANET: Oh, fiddle dee dee!

LUCY: Is that okay?

JANET 2: Yeah, thanks, that's great. Thanks.

JANET: It's a shit job. It's the contemporary version of picking cotton. We come from different worlds, but here we are, acting out the end result of society's racist drama.

LOIS: You act like you invented slavery. Why don't you just concentrate on being a human being? Maybe everything's not about race.

JANET: You don't think there's a racial dynamic here?

LOIS: Yeah, if you put it there.

JANET: Wait, I don't put it there, it's *there*. It's been there for hundreds of years, and it's here now, in my life, in my head. I'm trying to deal with it.

LOIS: But you make everything into a racial thing.

JANET: That's not true. There's also class, sexism, homophobia and ableism. Together with race, those are my Big Five.

LOIS: You need to listen. You talk too much and you don't listen.

LUCY: I took the garbage out, Jan, so I'll be going now.

JANET 2: Cool, thanks. See you next time, Luce. Hey, it's way too cold out there to wait for a bus. Just hop a cab home.

JANET *(To audience)*: It's gonna cost me a fortune.

LUCY: I don't mind the bus, Jan.

JANET 2: No, take a cab. It's too cold.

LUCY: Okay, then. Thanks, Jan. Bye, now.

(Lucy and Lois exit. Janet looks over at Janet 2, who is now relaxing out of her wheelchair: lying on her back, knees bent, one leg crossed over the other, bouncing up and down. Pause.)

JANET *(To audience)*: I wish I could get, like, one week off my disability per year when I wouldn't have to deal with this shit. Just a week off. One week a year, I could be completely free. Look at that position. I miss that.

Anyway.

(Janet 2 gets back into the wheelchair.)

(Demonstrating on Janet 2) Look at this. The one pant leg is higher than the other. That's the whole story of crip life. You will always have this pant leg problem, plus your crack shows in back 'cause the pants don't come up high enough—

JANET 2: Look at your pant legs. They look fine.

JANET: Yeah, fine for a cripple. You know what you are? You are an actress playing a part.

JANET 2: I understand your hostility.

JANET: Oh, really?

JANET 2: Plus you're upset because Lois is on vacation for two weeks.

JANET: You know nothing.

(The two Janets continue this discussion as Janet 2 gets into bed.)

JANET 2: You'll miss her because she's your companion, right?

JANET: Oh, for chrissakes, I'm used to her. She's not my companion. Don't do that.

JANET 2: What?

JANET: That thing of "her companion." I don't need a companion. I need my pants pulled up. I am not the old white lady being wheeled down the street by a black woman in a uniform. I am

Janet and Lois is Lois. I bet Helen Keller hated Annie Sullivan's guts.

JANET 2: Well, what should I call her?

JANET: I do not know. There is no name for it. She is who she is and I am who I—

JANET 2: Who are you?

JANET: Oh, shut up!

(Personal Assistant 1 enters and starts pulling up Janet 2's pants. New PAs enter continuously, each trying to pull up the pants. As new PAs take over, the previous ones stay and observe.)

PA 1 *(Grunting with effort)*: Okay, they're up.

JANET 2: No, I think you gotta pull 'em up in back still.

PA 1: No, they're up.

JANET 2: Just try pulling 'em up in back a little more.

*(PA 1 continues pulling, grunting.
PA 2 takes PA 1's place.)*

'Cause if you don't get 'em up in back now, they just are too low all day.

PA 2: How's that?

JANET 2: Umm, that's good. That's better. But a little more.

(PA 3 takes over for PA 2.)

PA 3: How's that?

JANET 2: Um, a little more over on this side. It's gotta be, the zipper hasta be in the middle.

PA 3: How's that?

JANET 2: Pretty good. Okay, now just pull my pant legs down, my pant cuffs, so they're exactly even with each other.

PA 3: Okay.

JANET 2: Are they even?

(PA 4 takes over.)

PA 4: Yeah.

JANET 2: Actually, just a little more. See, no, just move it so the seam is . . . yeah, a little more . . . yeah, great. Okay, great. I'll get into my chair then.

(PA 4 wheels the chair over to the bed. She drags Janet 2 onto the chair.)

PA 1 *(To PA 4)*: She's really heavy.

PA 4: Tell me about it. She should go on a diet, if she's gonna have people lifting her all the time.

PA 1: It's selfish, in a way, that she is so heavy, because we risk our backs . . .

PA 4: She could eat less. Half the time I take out the garbage there's carry-out bags in there. She eats that Chinese food every second . . .

PA 1: That is so fattening.

JANET 2: Pull me up some.

(PA 1 pulls her up.)

A little to the right. See, my hips are uneven. I'm all smooshed on this side and this side is too much—it's not enough—I'm crooked and I need to be straight, I—

PA 3: Can you believe those pants she wears?

PA 1: Oh my God, I know!

PA 3: I lose five pounds every time I have to drag 'em up over her butt.

PA 1: They're like, why don't we just get out the spray paint, you know—

JANET 2: You know what, that's just a tiny bit too much. Just move me a smidgen to the center, okay? If you want something cold to drink, just help yourself.

(The PAs get drinks.)

JANET *(To audience)*: See how I always offer people something to drink? I always do that.

(The PAs are drinking and chatting.)

PA 2: Food must be her substitute for . . . everything.

JANET 2: Could you just pull my pant legs down here? So they're more even?

PA 3: Yes, Your Highness, allow me—

PA 4: Oh no, let me!

PA 1: What is with this thing with the pants? She is so neurotic! You can spend twenty minutes just fucking with her pant legs.

Susan Nussbaum

PA 3 *(Mimicking)*: "The left leg's too short! Get down there and fix it right now, fool!"

PA 2: I saw this show where they have monkeys helping people like her. Little monkeys. You can train them to do all sorts of things.

(The PAs exit talking.)

PA 3: Yeah, get her monkey to pull her pant legs down.

(Joanna enters, walking fast, carrying a bag as if she has just packed some things and is leaving after a bad fight. Janet rushes after her.)

JANET: Will you wait? What are you saying? Are you saying . . . we . . . what? What are you saying?

JOANNA: It's really too late. It's been too late for a while.

JANET: Stop! Stop and wait! Tell me how this happened. I don't believe this is happening. You're saying you don't—I don't understand what you are feeling and all I know is I feel—

JOANNA: I don't know why it happened. I—my feelings changed. There is no reason.

JANET: But my feelings have not changed. What is it?

JOANNA: I don't know what happened. Don't make me the bad guy.

JANET: You suddenly woke up and . . .

JOANNA: It's been gradual.

JANET: And you don't want me physically anymore, you—sexually you—

JOANNA: This has nothing to do with your disability.

JANET: I didn't say it did.

JOANNA: Because you know that's not it.

JANET: I'm trying to— If it was my disability, would you tell me?

JOANNA: You know, Janet, I don't know. But this is not about that.

JANET: If it's my disability, I need to know. I am asking you to simply tell me how you feel.

JOANNA: No, it's not your disability.

JANET: Because let's face it. The disability's hard on me, of course it's gonna affect you, too. Needing help, places I can't get in, people staring . . .

JOANNA: People don't stare.

JANET: They don't? People don't stare?

JOANNA: They stare because we're two women.

JANET: You mean they do stare?

374

JOANNA: Look, fuck them and you know that's how I feel. I am not leaving you because of your disability. I'm leaving you because I just need to get out. Tell Lois good-bye.

JANET: Lois?

JOANNA: Your protector.

JANET: What?

JOANNA: Your—bodyguard.

(Lois is showering Janet 2.)

JANET 2: Lois, I am really spazzy today, okay? I am incred— *(One of her legs shoots out)* Ahh God, I am spazzing! I am spazzing! Lois! Fix my leg! Fix my leg! No! No! Lois! God. Fuck. Don't—just don't—do not hold the water on me like that because it makes me spaz. *(Spazzes out again)* No! Fuck, Lois, hang on to me! Don't let go! Don't let go! I'm spazzing! You're letting go! I'm gonna fall! Shit, I'm gonna crash! Hold me! Don't let go! God. Oh God oh God. Okay. Okay. All right. Okay. Damn. I'm sorry. I'm sorry. This is bad. This is so hard. Lois. I'm sorry. I'm just having a major spaz attack. You have no idea. I'm really—I'm—

(Lois sneezes.)

Oh God! I can't believe—God, go blow your—wash your—that was all over me! Jesus! Just go wash. Goddamn. Wait! I'm spazzing! I'm spazzing!

(Lois crosses to meet her Friend, who has just entered. Janet watches.)

LOIS: She talks to me like I am an idiot! *(Mimicking Janet)* "Lois, answer the phone. Now say hello." What'm I gonna do? Say good-*bye*? She is such a fucking bitch!

FRIEND *(Laughing)*: You have *got* to get away from that woman.

JANET *(To audience)*: This is how she probably talks about me. I'm sure she totally trashes me to her friends.

LOIS: Hey, money is honey . . . the best is she thinks she's so street-smart! She wouldn't last five minutes on the street. If that. But, of course, she's sure she knows everything and everyone else knows nothing.

FRIEND: I don't know how you do it. I'd kill her.

LOIS: I just turn her off. Switch to another station. I swear, I'm not even aware she's talking sometimes. And she's been rattling on . . . *(They laugh)* I told her I'm very quiet. *(They laugh)* So now she thinks it's my personality and she leaves me alone. *(They crack up laughing)*

FRIEND: One of these days someone's gonna haul off and belt her and then she'll be sorry. You can't just boss people around like that, I'm sorry.

LOIS: Someone's gonna kick Miss Muffet off her tuffet.

FRIEND: I'd pay money to see that.

JANET *(To audience)*: If I wasn't disabled none of this would be happening to me.

LOIS: I call her Nan.

FRIEND: Nan? Why Nan?

LOIS: No one as nasty.

FRIEND *(Laughing)*: You got that right.

JANET *(To audience)*: She always tells me she feels so close to me, yet I feel sure she puts me down to other people.

(Lois comes out of her scene and enters Janet's scene.)

LOIS *(To Janet)*: Fuck you! How would you know what, if anything, I say about you to my friends?

JANET: I sense that's how you talk about me. And I don't think it's any of your business. You don't have to be in on every single thought I ever have!

LOIS: It's my business when what you say is about me and it's stupid!

JANET: And you go around—I don't know what you're—

LOIS: Yes?

JANET: We have to establish some boundaries.

(Lois and Janet begin making their way to a restaurant.)

(To audience) And now we're meeting a friend of mine at a restaurant! It's this friend from out of town who Lois knows because she was with me when I went to see him, and I felt like I couldn't not ask Lois along because—it's a long story, but—I'm making the best of it. Lois is my friend and I love her.

(Lois and Janet sit in the restaurant with Benny. Janet 2 sits at another table with Christopher Reeve.)

(To Benny) The thing about Cornel West is he carved out some kind of niche for himself—

BENNY: I was blown away by West's position. Sometimes he really sounds like a nationalist. He's on the *New York Times* best-seller list, for chr—

JANET: You know, he's got all these intellectual credentials, but with the white community, not the black community as much—

LOIS: A lotta blacks really respect—

BENNY: Well, he doesn't really put himself over like, say, Sharpton—

LOIS: Well, I never trusted him.

BENNY: Oh Sharpton's, like, this whole transformational—he reinvented himself as a statesman—

JANET: Yeah, Sharpton's really mobilized people. Did you read the bell hooks stuff, though? She was great. She was really hilarious—

LOIS: She has a new book out—

JANET: She was saying something about the role of women, I wish I could remember her words . . .

LOIS: She was saying how men—

JANET: Oh yeah! That thing about men and dick size? She went right for the jugular! I can't remember, it was great, though.

LOIS: I thought Baraka's comment was interesting. About going to war—

JANET: Yeah, Baraka was good. He's not afraid of criticism. *(Beat)* I mean, so what did you think, Lois?

(Pause. Lois glares at Janet.)

BENNY: Yeah, the deal on Baraka is—

LOIS: She already knows all about Baraka.

BENNY: Huh?

(Tense pause.)

JANET: Whatever. Hey, are you still going to the Philippines in the fall?

BENNY: Still debating between the Philippines and Spain.

JANET: Yeah, of course. *(Notices Janet 2 with Christopher Reeve)* Hey, isn't that—?

BENNY: I think it'll be Spain. Or maybe Brazil. *(Laughing, hugging Janet good-bye)* So Lois and I're going to the record store. See you later.

JANET *(Surprised)*: What? Oh. Have a good time.

(Lois and Benny exit. Janet watches them, paranoid, hurt, then crosses to Janet 2. She is having cocktails with Christopher Reeve. Ken drives in and serves Christopher Reeve a martini through a straw.)

JANET 2: I didn't get my shoulders back for like, six weeks. Before that I was completely paralyzed, so you never know. Not that it matters one way or another. Even if you're really crippy, it's still okay, life is still definitely worth living, so don't worry, Chris. It's an adventure!

CHRISTOPHER REEVE: What about not being able to take care of yourself?

JANET 2: No problem!

KEN *(To Janet)*: What are you doing?

JANET: I'm dreaming that I'm drinking martinis with Christopher Reeve.

KEN: Are you trying to give him hope?

JANET 2 *(To Christopher Reeve)*: No, really, you might not believe this now, but all this stuff is really funny! Sometimes I laugh so hard! Well, you know what I mean, right?

CHRISTOPHER REEVE: What about getting dressed?

JANET 2: Well, phone booths are out. Maybe Lois can help you.

JANET *(To Janet 2)*: Lois?

JANET 2: Lois Lane. And people in the streets won't look at you funny.

KEN *(To Janet 2)*: You said they panic when they look at you.

JANET 2 *(To Ken)*: Shut up!

JANET *(To Ken)*: Sorry.

CHRISTOPHER REEVE: Could you help me with that olive?

JANET 2: People won't even notice, they'll think you're just the same old Chris you ever were. You will be found attractive, everyone will look at you—no, wait, I mean, they *won't* look at you. But people are idiots, Chris, even if they looked they wouldn't see, but they won't look, you are invisible now and you can just tell *People* magazine to *fuck off*, Chris, tell everyone to fucking *fuck off*—

JANET: It was such a nice dream at first.

(Ken and Janet drive off.)

KEN: I think therapists are a useful tool. Anyone who grows up in America without getting seriously depressed oughta have their head examined.

JANET: Yes, but the point of the documentary was the therapists, some of them, exploit this whole phenomenon of recalled abuse. Like this one woman goes into some trance thing, right, and suddenly remembers that when she was a fetus, she got stuck in her mother's fallopian tube— *(Panics)* Watch out! *(Cringes with fear as she thinks the car nearly crashes. Her paranoia grows throughout)* Sorry. But I mean, people are paying money for some therapist to sit there and strip-mine their personality. How can you trust them?

KEN: Look, you're having trouble adjusting: see someone. That's sensible. Don't fight the idea.

JANET: I think people should go to some . . . political theorist . . . or social activist instead. My problem is not personal, it's— *(Cringes again as the car almost, but not really, runs two people over)* —Oh God, these people are *nuts*, look at them, they've got a *death* wish. Jesus. But I'm saying, I have a problem accepting help, like it's shameful. And that's a mind-set fostered by a sick society that champions the rugged individual over all others.

KEN: True, but it's more than the accepting help thing because I know plenty of disabled people who are really happy, whereas you are completely fucked up.

JANET: Therapists are a *thing* that we do in America 'cause we have achieved this state of so-called advancement where we sit around worrying how we're not happy enough, and then we go pay someone to listen to us so our problems take on some kind of importance or legitimacy. People fighting guerrilla wars don't have time to go to therapists and worry about how happy they are.

KEN: But when the war is over, soldiers often go to therapy. You just give up, like life is supposed to be painful and difficult, and any shred of happiness is a first-world luxury.

JANET: You're right. Okay. But it's not like I don't feel happy lots of times, because I enjoy plenty of— Those fucking rollerbladers! Look at that idiot! Those people are a menace! I'd like to just take those rollerbladers and—I'm serious, I really believe they should be killed.

KEN: Relax, we're almost there.

JANET: I *loathe* rollerbladers. But anyway, I don't get how you know when you can trust someone. Maybe trust is beside the point, asking too much.

KEN: You gotta trust people. Everything is trust.

JANET: Yeah. But, see, what if you really *need*? You're just dead meat then.

*(Janet and Ken drive off.
Janet 2 is with Lois.)*

LOIS: By the way, I saw your ex.

JANET 2: What?

LOIS: We had lunch.

JANET 2: What'd she, did she call you?

LOIS: No, I called her. Thought I'd see what the old blowhard was up to.

JANET 2: Oh. I'm surprised.

LOIS: Why?

JANET 2: I thought you didn't like her.

LOIS: I never said that. I just didn't like her for you. You broke up with her. Not me.

(Pause.)

Is there a problem?

JANET 2: No. You have your own—I don't care.

(Pause.)

LOIS: Christopher Reeve is back in the papers.

JANET 2: What is with him? "I will walk again." He gives being a cripple a bad name.

LOIS: The journalists like him.

JANET 2: Yeah, the "journalists"—

LOIS: Just say there was a cure. Would you take it?

JANET 2: Oh, et tu, Lois? All this "to walk is to live" shit is just more puke under the bridge. Christopher Reeve is just the latest poster boy.

LOIS: Oh, uh-huh. It's that simple.

JANET 2: Christopher Reeve did not grow up with the expectation that he would spend the better part of his adult life waiting around for some total stranger to haul him on and off the toilet. No. He expected, he *expected*, to be Superman. He expected to play the *part* of a cripple in a movie. With *points*.

LOIS: And what did *you* expect, Wonder Woman?

JANET 2 *(Sarcastic)*: Oh, that's deep, Lois. You see me so well. Hey, I admit I had a slightly different plan for myself. But I've adjusted.

(Pause.)

What?

LOIS: Nothing.

JANET 2: It doesn't feel like nothing.

LOIS: Just a lot on my mind.

JANET 2: Lo, why do you do this silence thing all the time? I have to say, I think it's a bit manipulative.

LOIS: Think what you want. Free country.

(Pause.)

JANET 2: Yes, that's true. It's a great, great land.

LOIS: If you're not ready to play, you better get out of the playground right now.

JANET 2: This is not a game to me. I know you're trying to intimidate me—

LOIS: I don't have to *try*—

JANET 2: That's right. You don't even have to try. We both know I can't stand up to bullies—

LOIS: I don't bully. I give tit for tat.

JANET 2: Are you angry about a specific thing or is this just one of those times you let me know how deep you are and how shallow I am?

LOIS: Oh, I'm angry.

JANET 2: Oh. Well.

LOIS: There's something I've wanted to bring up for a long time.

JANET 2: Okay . . .

LOIS: Why do you talk to me like I'm stupid? Do you find that I am mentally deficient or is it just that you're so brilliant? I don't exist for you except for you to step up on my neck to make yourself look taller.

JANET 2: *What?*

LOIS: I think you heard me.

JANET 2: I *step* on your—

LOIS: And I am sick of it. There have got to be some changes made.

JANET 2: What are you talking about? When have I ever— Look, if I thought you were stupid— Look—

LOIS: You look.

JANET 2: I don't talk to you like— If I thought you were stupid, why would I include you with my friends, include you in everything— because I am proud to count you as a friend, what are you *talking* about—I don't need to look "taller"—you are completely—I mean, when? *When* have I done this? Give me an example.

LOIS: It's something that happens all the time, it happens *all the time*. And if it didn't, you wouldn't be so defensive about it.

JANET 2: When accused, a person can choose to defend oneself without being called defensive. If this terrible thing I do happens all the time, and I am completely unaware of it, which I am, then it would be very helpful if you could give me one, just *one* example of when you have felt this to happen. Not that I'm saying I haven't behaved very badly, very very badly, but the disability works on me and I vent it on you, which I know is—but I don't do that to people anymore, I don't vent—

LOIS: You don't do it to anyone but me! You don't talk to Lucy that way. But for some reason you seem to believe I will forgive you for anything. Or I have no feelings, which must be because in your eyes I am an idiot, although I don't think you would talk to a pile of dog shit the way you talk to—

JANET 2: *What way?*

LOIS (*Dead-on mimicry*): "Lois, put the groceries away. In the refrigerator. So they won't rot." "Lois, I have told you a thousand times how to put my pants on right. Look at me! Look at me! I'm sitting crooked!" "Lois, answer the phone. Say hello!"

JANET 2: That's because I want you to say hello before you press the buzzer thing!

LOIS: Shut up!!

JANET 2: Okay, okay, I know!

LOIS: I don't need to be spoken to like I am less than a worm!

JANET 2 (*Heartsick*): I hate that I sound that way. It's not you, I mean, it's not that I don't respect you, it's just that I am this angry, abusive . . . shithead, and the words come out of my mouth and—not that I don't want to take responsibility for what I say, although, you know, I probably am bad about that too, but we are together all the time, for years you have been doing this job, and we're friends, it's such a—maybe being together so much, maybe I'm paranoid because you know how—

LOIS: How what?

JANET 2: How much I—intimate details about my life—things that are—private things—

LOIS: So in your mind, I'm going around giving away your precious secrets? What do you think people see when they look at you? They see what they wanna see. They see what they're trained to see. I got nothin' to do with it. (*Janet 2 is speechless*) I think you know I'm not a blab.

JANET 2: No, I don't. I know what I know. What you choose to have known. You know everything about me—more than I *choose* to have known.

LOIS: Well, that's how it is.

JANET 2: What is that supposed to mean? If things are just—the way they are, why are we having a discussion here at all? What's the point of trying to work anything out? Maybe there is no point.

LOIS: I am telling you how I feel, you can deal with that or not.

JANET 2: I'm trying to deal with it, I'm trying but it's just not *working*.

LOIS: Try harder.

JANET 2: Do you think I'm not trying? Jesus! God! Do you think I enjoy sitting here getting criticized?

LOIS: You don't even hear yourself!

JANET 2: I *do*—

LOIS: If I talked to you the way you talk to me—and I have *been* there for you, all the times I have—

JANET 2: I have always been incredibly supportive of all your interests, and appreciative of your—friendship, your—being there—

LOIS: And I get sick and you could give a rat's ass about how I'm doing, all you care about is when I'm back at work—

JANET 2: That's not true.

LOIS: Oh, let's not even *try* to twist this. I'm standing too close to you if there's lightning.

JANET 2: But it's not true!

LOIS: Have you heard what I'm saying to you? Or are you just gonna keep coming up with reasons and excuses?

(Pause.)

JANET 2: Are you saying I'm a racist?

LOIS: This is not about racism! Although if it makes you happy, yes! Yes, you are a racist, but so is *everybody* a racist! You're no more than most.

JANET 2: It's in there, though. Racism's in there. It's everywhere. I don't know what the right thing is to say. I'm sorry. I'll try to pay closer attention to your needs. I'll try not to step on your neck.

LOIS: Mm-hmm.

JANET 2: I feel really *bad*.

LOIS: Whose fault is that?

JANET 2: Look. Look.

LOIS: *Look.* Look at *what?*

JANET 2: I have tried to be your friend as well as . . . your employer. I don't— There's no manual for this— I try to—

LOIS: *Bull*shit.

JANET 2: Then why don't you quit? I mean, I really wonder that. I don't want you to, but I don't know why you stick around if it's such a bad deal. And it is a bad deal, right? It's like marriage with none of the benefits. Half the time I'm apologizing to you for . . . stuff— I don't even know why it's happening, and I feel bad . . . that you're so . . . angry. I'm sorry. It's like I get so—so—so—but it's not you, it's that I—I just got thrown when you said about my "stepping on your neck." That's a really sickening image . . . Maybe—maybe we need to step back, I mean, maybe we need to think about—or we both—we should think—about your leaving. Because I feel—I'm this person with problems and I don't want to hurt you anymore. I don't know.

(Pause.)

LOIS: Oh. Uh-huh.

JANET 2: I don't know. Maybe it would be good. It could be—liberating for us.

LOIS: Uh-huh.

JANET 2: I mean, it's for the best. To hold onto our friendship.

LOIS: Mm-hmm. All right then.

(Lois exits.)

JANET *(To Janet 2)*: Do you think she got it?

JANET 2: Yeah. I think so.

(Lucy showers both Janets simultaneously. No one speaks.
Janet 2 gets up from her wheelchair and has a dream. People enter ice-skating. One skater carries a flag that reads ANOTHER DREAM.)

Everyone's going ice-skating.

(She joins the skaters.)

I never really cared much for ice-skating, but here I am. It's cold out. I'm wearing thin socks under these skates. How will I know if my feet are cold? I should've worn heavier socks.

(She bends down and touches her feet.)

There's Lucy. Hi Lucy!

(Lucy skates by.)

LUCY: Hi, Jan!

JANET 2: How will I know if my feet are cold if I can't feel them? If I get frostbite on my feet, will you be here to help me?

LUCY: We call my daughter Fatty, Jan, because her so fat!

JANET 2: They don't have ice-skating in Jamaica, do they, Lucy? Isn't it fun? I'll just skate a little bit longer. No one gets frostbite from such a little bit of skating.

JANET *(To audience)*: I'm not saying this to make the situation be, "It's for the best," but Lois leaving is for the best. She's too much in my life. I need to get free of her. *(Pause)* Plus, I don't have a choice anymore.

(The skaters exit.)

LUCY *(Skating by as she exits)*: You don't got no choice, Jan.

JANET *(To Lucy)*: What? Wait! *(To audience)* Don't make this be about my disability, even though it is, it also isn't. It's true: I'm something, I'm this other thing, in another world, but it's wrong to say, "You don't have choices." I have the same choices as anyone. I have the same. How many do any of us have? See, 'cause I love my disability, in this insane way, it's the only thing that's given me any choices at all—I mean, not to romanticize, not at all—but it took me down a different path, set me down in another place, made me a part of this secret society. We all live in the context of something, right? We operate within the guidelines. Choice is—I don't even know that word. Fuck that word.

(Janet 2 crosses to Janet.)

JANET 2: I'm trying to understand, based on what you've said . . .

JANET: Lois is leaving and she's always been there and now my life will be filled with strangers coming into my house and pulling up my pants. And I will deal with it—

JANET 2: And you've said how much you hate that—

JANET: Because I *have* to because everyone deals with what they have to in order to stay alive. The thing is, I don't want these people

in my house, I don't want their hands on me, I don't want them
making their private judgments, I don't want them to see me
angry or happy or in bed alone or with someone. I just hate all
of their guts, particularly Lois.

JANET 2: Wait, no—wait—

JANET: My life is this fragile thing that depends on someone else
answering an ad and doing a job. I am someone's job. That's
who I am. I am someone's job. The only thing that's worse is
when I turn into someone's friend, because then things just get
too fucking smothering for words.

JANET 2: All of us depend on each other, in a sense, to do our jobs.

JANET: Please. There's a dividing line drawn by able-bodied people,
and on one side of the divide is what's okay and on the other is
what's bad.

JANET 2: No one says it's bad. You get so much positive feedback
from people. But you insist on dwelling on the negative.

JANET: Wrong. It's okay to build stairs to get to places, but too
expensive and ugly to build ramps.

JANET 2: There are ramps everywhere!

JANET: Well, thanks for the favor! I'm a grateful cripple now!

JANET 2: What do you want? Do you want everyone to run out and
get disabled so you won't be misunderstood?

JANET: Yes. I want everyone to be disabled. I want everyone to be
really, really disabled. Then no one will be disabled, 'cause disabled will be normal, and there will be a small minority of able-
bodied people who will comprise a slave underclass.

JANET 2: That's the kind of attitude that really turns people off. I have
been trying my best to do this play, and I think I have been sensitive and hardworking, but maybe I'm not cutting it. Maybe
you should find another actress. Although, I mean, I don't know
if you saw my résumé, but—

JANET: I always said you were doing a terrific job. You're very believable.

JANET 2: You think so? Because what I'm getting from you is very
different.

JANET: I love what you're doing with the hands.

JANET 2: You do?

JANET: Yes.

JANET 2: Are we being honest here?

JANET: Yes.

JANET 2: I feel . . . guilty for being relieved I'm not really you.

JANET: Well . . . I'm glad I'm not you.

JANET 2: Wow.

JANET: Really.

(The Janets sit and listen to answering machine messages together.)

MESSAGE 1 *(Woman's voice)*: Hello. I'm calling about the ad. To take care of the invalid. Call me back. Thank you.

MESSAGE 2 *(Woman's voice)*: Hi! I'm calling about the job? My name is Michelle Bean? I was really excited to see the ad because it's my dream to work in a people-caring environment? So please call me back, I'd really love to hear from you. Thanks lots! Bye-bye.

MESSAGE 3 *(Man's voice)*: Yeah, calling about the ad. My name's John Beekman. 877-4437. I'd appreciate a call back.

MESSAGE 4 *(Warm, cheerful, older black woman)*: God bless you today! Please call me about the job that I read about in the ad. Leave a message at the tone of the beep!

MESSAGE 5 *(Woman's voice)*: Hello. *(Pause)* Are you there? *(Pause)* I'm calling about the job. Please pick up. Pick up the phone, please. I know someone's there. *(Pause)* Hello? I'm getting tired of holdi— *(Machine cuts off)*

MESSAGE 6 *(John Beekman again, angry)*: Yeah. I called about the job and no one called me back. The least you could do is return my call. Call me back.

(Lucy enters.)

JANET 2: Lucy, thanks a lot. I mean, really a lot.

LUCY: You're welcome, Jan.

JANET 2: No, I mean, I don't know what I'd do without you. It's not just a job, you know? It's my life.

LUCY: Jan, you know what? I had a dream that you stood up out of your wheelchair and walked. And your mama was so proud, Jan. Her so proud of you. And then you wore a beautiful dress, and you got married, Jan. And everybody was at your wedding. Everybody was there. And we had a good time, Jan. Everybody had such a good time at your wedding, and you was dancing, Jan.

JANET 2: Well, thanks, Luce.

LUCY: You're welcome, Jan.

(Lucy exits. Janet 2 pulls Janet into a dream.)

JANET 2: We were in an apartment, and there was a knock on the door. I'll get it!

(Lois is at the door, with her cat, Buster.)

LOIS: Here is my cat, named Buster.
JANET 2: Buster isn't a cat.
JANET: What?
LOIS: Keep my cat for me. *(Exits)*
JANET 2 *(Studying Buster)*: She's more like a tiny ratlike creature, cute but strange-shaped . . .
JANET: Unlike anything I've seen.
BUSTER: Nice place.
JANET AND JANET 2: She can talk.

(Janet 2 lies on floor next to Buster.)

BUSTER: I prefer nonfiction to fiction. That is, if you believe there is such a thing as nonfiction.
JANET 2: She's very bright, sensitive, and unaware of her predicament. Which is her terrible strangeness.
JANET: She is very vulnerable. Anyone could mistake her for a lesser creature . . . a rat . . . and kill her. *(To Janet 2)* All the times Lois told me Buster talked to her, she didn't mean she meowed . . .
JANET 2: But actually talked.
JANET: I wonder how many other things Lois told me that I misinterpreted.
BUSTER: I don't even have fur, really. Just a fine smooth hair on my skin. Is that wrong?
JANET 2: No, it's right. Wait, I must record this event in my diary. *(Writing)* Lois thinks Buster's a cat . . .

(Dream ends.
Janet speaks to the audience:)

JANET: After Lois left, I felt guilty, but I was really glad I didn't have to see her anymore, and struggle to figure out our relationship. I didn't want to think about it. I'd still find her hairpins, behind cushions, all over the place, for months and months, until finally, I stopped finding them. I figured after some time passed, I'd miss her, and I really wanted to miss her, but I didn't. But even though we didn't see each other, she still kept in touch with a lot of my friends, who were now also her friends.

(Janet 2 and her Friend have a phone conversation.)

FRIEND: I had dinner with Lois the other night.

JANET 2: Oh, really?

FRIEND: Boy, is she pissed at you.

JANET 2: What? Why?

FRIEND: I don't know. I guess she just doesn't understand why you fired her.

JANET 2: What?!

FRIEND: She'll get over it. She's just a little raw from it still.

JANET 2: I didn't fire her! It was a mutual—I absolutely did not fire her.

FRIEND: Whatever.

JANET 2: No, wait—I mean, is that what she's saying? I can't believe she's going around saying that. That is the most unfair—because I did not—this is unbelievable. God. I feel—this is—I gave her a severance check the size of a—! Not that that matters, but still, I hope you see that she is a little—delusional here. I mean, she basically quit! What else did she say?

FRIEND: She said you were a bitch, and that she hated you, but I'm sure it was just a passing thing. She's just angry. Don't worry about it. I mean, you guys were so close.

JANET 2: She said she hates me?

FRIEND: Well, yeah, but she was just working through some stuff.

(Janet 2 and Friend exit.)

JANET *(To audience)*: I did fire Lois. Then why do I always feel like she quit? You make these bargains with people. Lois helping me get dressed made me independent, and my paying her made her independent. But after a while, I felt like she was keeping me dependent, and she felt like I had her on a short leash. So you start hating the person who rules your world, and the only way to really get free of them is to get rid of them. It's the same for whole societies, really. Like Cuba and the U.S. You know, except between me and Lois, sometimes we were both Cuba, and sometimes we were both the U.S. Or like Puerto Rico. Maybe statehood has some advantages, if you don't mind selling your soul to the devil. Not that I am the devil. Or Lois. But anyway, I bumped into Lois one day. I was walking down the street . . .

(Lois runs onstage shouting:)

LOIS *(Breathless)*: Janet! Janet!

JANET: Oh, hey, hi Lois. Hi, I didn't see you.

LOIS: I've been chasing you for a while.

JANET: Really? I didn't—

LOIS: So how are you?

JANET: I'm fine. I'm good. I was just on my way to—you know, doing errands. You look great. I like your hair. I really like your pants. How are you?

LOIS: Oh, fine, fine. Still crazy.

JANET: Oh God, I was sorry to hear about Buster. I was really sorry—

LOIS: Yeah. I miss her.

JANET: She was a cool cat. Are you thinking of getting another one or—?

LOIS: Naw, I'm still in mourning, you know how it is. I don't think I'll be looking for any other cat for a while.

JANET: Yeah. No.

LOIS: Well, I'm glad I caught up to you.

JANET: You and me both.

LOIS: You take care.

JANET: No, I will. You, too, Lois.

(An awkward moment. Should they hug? Janet backs away a bit.)

(To audience) That was the last time I saw her.

(We see Lois for a moment in her own light. Then she exits. Ken and Janet 2 drive onstage. Janet gets in the car with them.)

(To Ken) I had a dream about a labyrinth again. I was coming from the movies, and I was driving all these people home.

(Clark Gable and Wheelchair Pusher enter.)

JANET 2: Clark Gable is here.

CLARK GABLE: I just received an award, but I feel depressed, undeserving.

JANET 2: Clark, don't feel sad. I'll cheer you up. I'm a very funny and nice person. Let me give you a ride home.

(Everyone gets in the car. They act out the events as Janet describes them.)

Hey, Clark, you doing okay back there?

CLARK GABLE: I'm hanging in there!

JANET: We got lost and drove around for hours in this maze underground, up flights of stairs, people had to get out and push the car over tracks, through mud.

JANET 2: Everyone is being so helpful. This will all work out fine. Don't worry, everyone will get home all right.

CLARK GABLE: The car is ruined from pushing it through rough terrain. We must get out and push you in your wheelchair now.

JANET 2: Okay. Are you sure this is safe, pushing me up and down all these subterranean stairs?

WHEELCHAIR PUSHER: You are very safe with us.

JANET 2: Yes, I believe you. It's so late. Everyone must stay at my place tonight. I live on Clark Street.

JANET: Clark again. I don't live on Clark in real life. And we finally got to my place, after retracing our steps and getting lost a bunch more times.

JANET 2: You can sleep there, and you guys can sleep there, and Clark, you can sleep with me. *(Stands and poses as if in bed. Clark Gable stands behind her, spooning her)* Okay, now I am in bed. Clark is spooning me.

CLARK GABLE: Don't worry. I can't see your hemorrhoids.

JANET 2: Hey, and you don't worry about that award, Clark.

(The dream ends.
Ken turns to Janet.)

KEN: Clark. Clark Kent. Superman.

JANET: Oh. Yeah.

KEN: What is the labyrinth?

JANET: The never-ending struggle.

(All, including Janet 2, help Janet into bed. Then everyone exits, leaving Janet alone in bed.)

This one woman comes just at night to put me in bed. I think she's been eating stuff out of my refrigerator afterwards, before she leaves. Which is okay with me, but strangely irritating. Why should it be irritating? If she asked, I'd just say, "Help yourself." But anyway, the reason I think she's been eating stuff is because the lid of the pickle jar was on really tight, and I never screw lids on tightly. Now I sound petty, and it is petty, I suppose, sitting around thinking about the pickle jar and how to broach the subject with this woman. If at all.

She has a weight problem. She's fat. I could let the whole thing go, just spare her the embarrassment. That'd be taking the high road. Or I could say, "It's okay if you want to eat stuff but just don't screw the lid on tightly." Then she'd know I know. She might deny it. But she'd still know *I know.*

I hate myself for even having this discussion. Maybe I'll just forget about the whole thing. Ha ha. No, but maybe I'll let it pass. Unless it gets out of hand. I can't get anything open. It's sad, really, that I'm thinking about this at all. The fact that I am just proves how far I have—slid.

Plus, she has a serious personal hygiene problem. She smells unbelievably bad. Not sweaty, but something else. Something else. And that puts me in a bad mood. I can't stand it that every night she comes over and every night she smells. Sometimes I'm slightly rude to her. Like she'll say, "Can you believe this weather?" and I'll say, "Yes." Then I immediately want to yell at myself and just calm down and act like a human being. I was really sure that after Lois left, I would be on my best behavior for the rest of my crippled life. Didn't I learn? I have to redouble my efforts. I'm committed to that.

(Pause.)

I could be dead wrong about the pickles.

(Fade to black.)

END OF PLAY

Susan Nussbaum is a Chicago-based playwright, director and actress. She has had seven plays produced, including *No One as Nasty*; *Parade*, winner of the Illinois Arts Council 2000 Literary Award; *Happy Birthday from Ho Chi Minh*, produced by Blue Rider Theater, Chicago, 1995; *Telethon,* produced at Live Bait Theater, Chicago, and Blue Line Theater, Los Angeles, 1994; *The Plucky and Spunky Show*, produced by Remains Theatre, Chicago, 1990; *Mishuganismo*, produced by Remains Theatre, 1991; *Staring Back,* produced at Second City e.t.c. and Organic Theater, 1983–1984. Her most recent commission from Mark Taper Forum's Other Voices Project, *Crippled Sisters,* has not yet been produced. *Staring Back* and *The Plucky and Spunky Show* have also been produced at theaters throughout the U.S., including The Group Theater in Seattle, Firehouse Theatre in Portland, The Magic Theater in Omaha and Perseverance Theatre in Juneau, Alaska.

As an actress, Ms. Nussbaum has appeared at The Goodman Theatre, Steppenwolf Theatre Company, Second City e.t.c., among many others. She is the recipient of the Carol Gill Disability Culture Award and the Award of Excellence from Superfest XXI, a San Francisco disability-themed film festival. Her play *Mishuganismo* was published in the anthology *Staring Back: The Disability Experience from the Inside Out* (Plume/Penguin, New York, 1997).

Afterword: The Casting Question

By Victoria Ann Lewis

When William Butler Yeats and Lady Gregory set out to create an Irish/Celtic literary theater that would "reveal the true nature of Ireland," they drew the line at casting Irish actors. Instead, Yeats and Gregory traveled to England where they cast and rehearsed their revolutionary plays with English actors. Not surprisingly, few Irish actors of the day could make a living on the stage relegated as they were to playing the Irish drunk in melodramas.

The casting situation for disabled actors in the twentieth century reflects this same discriminatory model. With rare exceptions, such as the employment of deaf actors in Mark Medoff's *Children of a Lesser God,* the standard practice has been for nondisabled actors to play the big disabled roles like Shakespeare's Richard III, Laura Wingfield in *The Glass Menagerie,* Helen Keller in *The Miracle Worker,* Kenneth Talley, Jr. in *Fifth of July* or Ken Harrison in *Whose Life Is It Anyway?* Robert David Hall, currently starring as coroner Dr. Albert Robbins on the television forensic drama *CSI: Crime Scene Investigation* and a double amputee, remembers reluctantly turning down a nonspeaking role early in his acting career. He was asked to play the victim of a shark attack who drags himself, bloody stumps and all, out of the ocean.

In the 1980s, disabled, deaf and hard-of-hearing performers in the three major performing unions—Actors' Equity Association (AEA), Screen Actors Guild (SAG) and American Federation of Television and Radio Artists (AFTRA)—joined together in Los Angeles and

New York City to advocate for nondiscrimination and equal employment provisions in the performing unions' contracts with producers. Arguing along with women, ethnic minorities and actors over forty that in order for "the American scene" to be "portrayed realistically" television and film producers must encourage the employment of actors from these underrepresented groups, disabled actors fought for contractual language protecting performers with disabilities from discrimination. The Interguild Committee of Performers with Disabilities won the SAG negotiations and soon AEA and AFTRA followed with comparable affirmative action provisions for disabled artists. In 1986 the Non-Traditional Casting Project (NTCP) was founded to seek solutions to the problem of racism and exclusion in theater, film and television. From its inception, NTCP has included performers with disabilities as part of their mission. But still today the choice disabled roles go to nondisabled actors, such as Tom Cruise in *Born on the Fourth of July,* playing disabled Vietnam vet Ron Kovic; Daniel Day-Lewis in *My Left Foot,* playing Christy Brown, the Irish writer with cerebral palsy; or Tom Hanks, playing developmentally disabled Forrest Gump. Particularly galling for disabled actors is the fanfare and award giving that often accompanies these "star turns."

It is not always easy to find disabled talent, as Mike Ervin (*The History of Bowling*) discovered when he set out to cast the role of quadriplegic Chuck for *Bowling*'s premiere at Chicago's Victory Gardens Theater. Aspiring disabled actors are routinely discouraged from pursuing professional training in the arts, which leaves them at a disadvantage in the highly competitive world of the legitimate theater. In the end Ervin did find a talented if inexperienced disabled actor, Robert Ness, who received critical acclaim for his performance as Chuck. Ervin learned from this experience that:

> there is no substitute for casting actors with disabilities. That doesn't mean that you'll always be able to find one. You may be forced to punt and go with a walkie-talkie. But if you do, something will always be missing. I thought it was important to hire one of our own for symbolic and solidarity reasons. If we don't give them a break, who the hell else ever will? Also, their conspicuous absence would make the statement that there just aren't any of us who are good enough to cut it. Before we found Bob, I never realized the artistic importance of casting our own.

John Belluso struggled to convince producers and directors to cast disabled actors on similar aesthetic grounds, arguing that disability is a social identity with a long history, not a biological medical condition to be mimicked. Belluso pointed to many hours of rehearsal time spent trying to familiarize nondisabled actors with the "given circumstances" of life lived with a disability.

Disabled casting is pivotal to the artistic integrity of many of the plays in this anthology. Writing in 1970, David Freeman did not mandate the casting of disabled actors in his play *Creeps*, but he took a firm line on the depth of research he asked of actors cast as one of the young men with cerebral palsy in the play: "There can be no substitute for the first-hand observation of these physical problems, and one might even suggest that the play not be attempted if such opportunities for such first-hand observation are not available." Doris Baizley and I stipulated in the cast list for *P.H. *reaks: The Hidden History of People with Disabilities* that the four disabled roles "must be played by actors with disabilities." We took as our model Mark Medoff's casting policy for his groundbreaking play *Children of a Lesser God.*

Medoff's licensing contract for union productions of *Children* required that the roles of Sarah, Orin and Lydia had to be played by deaf or hard-of-hearing actors or rights would not be granted. Arguably the legal provision alone might not have been successful if there had not been a pool of trained and experienced deaf and hard-of-hearing actors ready to take advantage of this opportunity. But there were. In 1967 the National Theatre of the Deaf established a Professional Training School which was funded by the United States Office of Education. Thus one play—and more importantly a clear and uncompromised commitment to equal opportunity—can revolutionize the artistic development of an entire generation of actors. The importance of both artistic leadership and artist advocacy in democratizing the American stage cannot be overemphasized. Think of the profound contribution Joe Papp made to the American theater when he insisted on multicultural casting for any play produced in his theaters. His mandate for diversity benefited not only the actors cast at The Public Theater, but future generations of actors who saw evidence on Papp's stages that careers in the theater were possible for people of color. Similarly, protests by Asian American actors over the casting of white performers in *Miss Saigon* brought the inequities of casting for ethnic actors to the attention of casting directors and producers, challenging them to look beyond their customary talent pools.

Discrimination is not limited to casting but extends even to playwriting. Many of the playwrights in this collection confronted economic and attitudinal barriers in their pursuit of a career in the arts. After he was blinded, Lynn Manning (*Shoot!*) was denied funds from the Department of Rehabilitation to obtain a B.A. in English, and offered in its place training as a vendor. Why would he want to pursue a job teaching English, his rehab counselor queried, when he could run his own newspaper stand? Only one playwright in this collection, John Belluso, obtained an M.F.A. in Playwriting—the calling card of choice for a professional career in the theater. Belluso earned this degree because of his talent and hard work. But the chance to compete for such recognition was only available, as he graciously acknowledged in his Author's Statement, because a generation of disabled advocates before him had fought for legislative and cultural change.

There are significant barriers that prevent young people with disabilities from even dreaming about a career in the theater: low expectations, discouragement from adults, lack of support from vocational counselors, lack of art programs that accommodate students with disabilities, and the absence of role models, to name just a few. If a disabled person does emerge from childhood with a desire to pursue a career in the arts, further obstacles lie ahead, particularly if one is economically disadvantaged and dependent on public support. Chuck Close, the world-renowned visual artist who became disabled mid-career, has a remarkably clear grasp of the economic injustice that disabled people encounter in the arts:

> I could afford to get back to work. I made a lot of money with my art, so I could build a wheelchair-accessible studio and hire assistance. I have excellent medical insurance, for which I pay an arm and a leg. Even so, I have about $50,000 a year in unreimbursed medical expenses. If I didn't make that $50,000, plus enough to live on, I'd have to go on Medicaid and become a ward of the state. So another artist, equally committed, equally determined to return to painting, but without the income, might not have been able to do so.

Disabled artists without independent means are blocked in their pursuit of a career in the arts by the so-called "work disincentives" built into our social service support systems that penalize disabled people who earn money. The Chairman of the National Endowment for the Arts under President Clinton, William Ivey, encountered this catch-22 in his days as a folklorist. Older American storytellers who received grants in honor of their status as "living legacies" found themselves stripped of their Social Security benefits for life because they had exceeded the allowable income for someone on state assistance. According to Ivey, these older artists had to fight "for months, even years" to have their benefits reinstated. A similar fate awaits the disabled actor or writer dependent on Social Security who gets a break and lands a union acting role or receives a play commission or sells a screenplay. Ambition and success are health-endangering.

In addition to the financial barriers there is the problem of casting. More than half the writers in this book are also performers who were fed up with the stereotypical roles they were offered—victims or villains—and out of necessity turned to writing. Most would recognize themselves in the observation of Shari Weiser, a professional actress of small stature: "On stage I'm always asked to be this diminished person shaped by other people's ideas . . . [I am] always playing people who need someone to tell them what to do. No one has asked me to play anyone remotely like me." Even Charles Dullin, one of the great French actors and experimental directors of the early twentieth century, who had a severe spinal deformity and progressive rheumatoid arthritis, commented at the end of a brilliant career: "The drama of my life lies in my round back . . . I cannot play roles in which one looks up to heaven." Like many actors with a disability, he played the so-called "third roles" in conventional dramas—the misfit, drug addict, madman or old men. When Shari Weiser was cast as Little Princess Angie in *P.H. *reaks*, it was the first time in her ten-year career that she had played a woman, and only the second time depicting a human being (Hoggle in Jim Henson's film *Labyrinth*). As Cornerstone Theater Company's Lynn Jeffries, who designed *P.H. *reaks*, remarked: "I've heard any number of horror stories about race, gender and age-based casting and type-casting since I've lived in Los Angeles, but I've never heard one anywhere near as startling as Shari's. Everyone else was at least envisioned as a *human being*."

The excerpt on page 398 is from: Kaminker, Laura. "Chuck Close and the Salvation of Work." *New Mobility*, December 1998: 31–39.

Select Bibliography

This bibliography does not, for the most part, cover memoir, fiction or poetry, due to the comparatively large number of published works in these forms (compared, that is, to drama) and the editor's reluctance to prioritize this rich body of work. This bibliography guides the reader to discussions of disability history and culture that will hopefully inform further explorations of other disabled writers and artists.

Plays

Byron, Lord George. *The Deformed Transformed.* Whitefish, MT: Kessinger Publishing, 2004 (also as an e-book).

Neuhof, Katinka. *Blue Baby,* in Kenny Fries, ed, *Staring Back: The Disability Experience from the Inside Out.* New York: Plume/Penguin, 1997.

Nussbaum, Susan. *Mishuganismo,* in Kenny Fries, ed, *Staring Back: The Disability Experience from the Inside Out.* New York: Plume/ Penguin, 1997.

Sealey, Jenny, ed. *Graeae Plays 1: New Plays Redefining Disability.* London: Aurora Metro Press, 2002.

Books and Articles

PERFORMANCE, DANCE, THEATER AND MEDIA

Albright, Ann Cooper. *Choreographing Difference: The Body and Identity in Contemporary Dance.* Hanover, NH: Wesleyan University Press, 1997.

Auslander, Philip and Carrie Sandahl, eds. *Bodies in Commotion: Disability in Performance*. Ann Arbor: University of Michigan Press, 2005.

Bogdan, Robert. *Freak Show: Presenting Human Oddities for Amusement and Profit*. Chicago: University of Chicago Press, 1988.

Crutchfield, Susan and Marcy Epstein, eds. *Points of Contact: Disability, Art, and Culture*. Ann Arbor: University of Michigan Press, 2000.

Fahy, Thomas and Kimball King. *Peering Behind the Curtain: Disability, Illness, and the Extraordinary Body in Contemporary Theater*. London: Routledge, 2002.

Fries, Kenny, ed. *Staring Back: The Disability Experience from the Inside Out*. New York: Plume/Penguin, 1997.

Gill, Carol J. "Developmental Obstacles to Careers in the Arts for Young Persons with Disabilities." (See "National Forum on Careers in the Arts for People with Disabilities" in the Websites section.)

Hevey, David. *The Creatures Time Forgot: Photography and Disability Imagery*. London: Routledge, 1992.

Klobas, Lauri E. *Disability Drama in Television and Film*. Jefferson, NC: McFarland, 1988.

Kuppers, Petra. *Disability and Contemporary Performance: Bodies on Edge*. London: Routledge, 2003.

Norden, Martin F. *The Cinema of Isolation: A History of Physical Disability in the Movies*. New Brunswick, NJ: Rutgers University Press, 1994.

Pointon, Ann with Chris Davies, eds. *Framed: Interrogating Disability in the Media*. London: British Film Institute, 1997.

Thomson, Rosemarie Garland, ed. *Freakery: Cultural Spectacles of the Extraordinary Body*. New York: New York University Press, 1996.

Walker, Pamela Kay. *Moving Over the Edge, Artists with Disabilities Take the Leap*. Davis, CA: Michael Horton Media, 2005.

Disability Civil Rights

Charlton, James I. *Nothing about Us without Us: Disability Oppression and Empowerment*. Berkeley, CA: University of California Press, 2000.

Fleischer, Doris Zames and Frieda Zames. *The Disability Rights Movement: From Charity to Confrontation*. Philadelphia: Temple University Press, 2000.

Hockenberry, John. *Moving Violations: War Zones, Wheelchairs, and Declarations of Independence.* New York: Hyperion, 1995.

O'Brien, Ruth. *Voices from the Edge: Narratives about the Americans with Disabilities Act.* New York: Oxford University Press, 2004.

Russell, Marta. *Beyond Ramps: Disability at the End of the Social Contract.* Monroe, ME: Common Courage Press, 1998.

Shapiro, Joseph P. *No Pity: People with Disabilities Forging a New Civil Rights Movement.* New York: Three Rivers Press/Random House, 1994.

DISABILITY STUDIES

Davis, Lennard J. *Bending Over Backwards: Disability, Dismodernism, & Other Difficult Positions.* New York: New York University Press, 2002.

_____. *Enforcing Normalcy: Disability, Deafness and the Body.* London: Verso, 1995.

_____, ed. *The Disability Studies Reader.* New York: Routledge, 1997.

Deutsch, Helen and Felicity Nussbaum, eds. *"defects": Engendering the Modern Body.* Ann Arbor: University of Michigan Press, 2000.

Fiedler, Leslie A. *Freaks: Myths and Images of the Secret Self.* New York: Simon & Schuster, 1979.

Fine, Michelle and Adrienne Asch, eds. *Women with Disabilities: Essays in Psychology, Culture, and Politics.* Philadelphia: Temple University Press, 1988.

Finger, Anne. *Elegy for a Disease: A Personal and Cultural History of Polio.* New York: St. Martin's Press, 2006.

Gallagher, Hugh Gregory. *FDR's Splendid Deception.* St. Petersburg, FL: Vandamere Press, 1999. (third ed)

Goffman, Erving. *Stigma: Notes on the Management of Spoiled Identity.* Englewood Cliffs, NJ: Prentice-Hall, 1963.

Linton, Simi. *Claiming Disability: Knowledge and Identity.* New York: New York University Press, 1998.

Longmore, Paul K. *Why I Burned My Book and Other Essays on Disability.* Philadelphia: Temple University Press, 2003.

_____ and Lauri Umansky, eds. *The New Disability History: American Perspectives.* New York: New York University Press, 2001.

Meade, Teresa and David Serlin, special issue eds. "Disability and History," *Radical History Review*, Volume 94, Winter 2006. Durham, NC: Duke University Press, 2006.

Mitchell, David T. and Sharon L. Snyder. *Narrative Prosthesis: Disability and the Dependencies of Discourse.* Ann Arbor: University of Michigan Press, 2001.

_____, eds. *The Body and Physical Difference: Discourses of Disability.* Ann Arbor: University of Michigan Press, 1997.

Proctor, Robert N. *Racial Hygiene: Medicine Under the Nazis.* Cambridge, MA: Harvard University Press, 1988.

Stiker, Henri-Jacques. *A History of Disability.* Ann Arbor: University of Michigan Press, 2000.

Thomson, Rosemarie Garland. *Extraordinary Bodies: Figuring Physical Disability in American Culture and Literature.* New York: Columbia University Press, 1996.

Zola, Irving Kenneth. *Missing Pieces: A Chronicle of Living with a Disability.* Philadelphia: Temple University Press, 1982.

DEAF AND HARD-OF-HEARING HISTORY AND THEATER

Baldwin, Stephen Charles. *Pictures in the Air: The Story of the National Theatre of the Deaf.* Washington, DC: Gallaudet University Press, 1994.

Bragg, Lois, ed. *Deaf World: A Historical Reader and Primary Sourcebook.* New York: New York University Press, 2001.

Burch, Susan. *Signs of Resistance: American Deaf Cultural History, 1900 to World War II.* New York: New York University Press, 2004.

Groce, Nora Ellen. *Everyone Here Spoke Sign Language: Hereditary Deafness on Martha's Vineyard.* Cambridge, MA: Harvard University Press, 1985.

Winefield, Richard. *Never the Twain Shall Meet: Bell, Gallaudet and the Communications Debate.* Washington, DC: Gallaudet University Press, 1987.

Magazines

Disability Studies Quarterly: the first journal in disability studies. Available at: http://www.dsq-sds.org

Kaleidoscope: examines the experiences of disability through literature and the fine arts, and challenges stereotypical and patronizing attitudes about disability. Available at: http://www.udsakron.org/kaleidoscope.htm

Mainstream: for more than twenty-five years, this magazine produced by, for and about people with disabilities has been an advocate for disability rights, and covers news and current affairs, new products and technology, profiles of movers and shakers, education, employment, sexuality and relationships, housing, transportation, travel and recreation. Print version suspended in 1999. Available at: http://www.mainstream-mag.com/

Mouth: a bimonthly disability rights magazine whose readers' "only special needs are for human rights and straight talk." Available at: http://www.mouthmag.com/

New Mobility: written by and for wheelchair users, this magazine is dedicated to disability culture and lifestyle, and provides a forum for sharing life experience. Available at: http://www.newmobility.com/

Ragged Edge: a successor to the *Disability Rag*, an international magazine focusing on disability issues from a civil rights perspective, this magazine covers disability rights culture, ideas, revolution and humor. Available at: http://www.ragged-edge-mag.com/

Websites

Disability Social History Project: a community history project inviting participation and submissions from people with disabilities. Site includes a history time line, bibliographies on women, gays and lesbians and links. Available at: http://www.disabilityhistory.org/

Disability Studies in the Humanities Listserv: a moderated forum for discussion and a bulletin board for those interested and involved in disability studies across the broad range of humanities scholarship. Available at: http://www.mith2.umd.edu:8080/disc/resources/ index.jsp#listserv

Media Access Office of the California Governor's Committee on Employment of People with Disabilities: functions as a liaison between the disability community and the entertainment industry, promoting the accurate portrayal of persons with disabilities and a recognition of disability as part of diversity initiatives in the performing arts. Projects include a casting clearinghouse for union and non-union disabled talent, acting workshops and the annual Media Access Awards. Available at: http://www.disabilityemployment.org/

National Arts and Disability Center: great resource for national (and international) listings of disabled artists and performing arts companies. Organized around categories of performing and visual arts. Good place to begin a search. Pointers on how to make programs accessible. Available at: http://nadc.ucla.edu

National Endowment for the Arts Office for Accessibility: established in 1976 as the advocacy-technical assistance arm of the Arts Endowment for people with disabilities, older adults, veterans and people living in institutions. Leadership initiatives include: Universal Design and Careers in the Arts for People with Disabilities. Available at: http://www.nea.gov/resources/accessibility/brochure.html

National Forum on Careers in the Arts for People with Disabilities: dedicated to removing the barriers of discrimination and prejudice that prevent people with disabilities from pursuing careers in the visual and performing arts. Includes Carol J. Gill's "Developmental Obstacles to Careers in the Arts for Young Persons with Disabilities." Concept paper for National Forum on Careers in the Arts for People with Disabilities (Kennedy Center, 1998). Available at: http://artsedge.kennedy-center.org/forum/papers/gill.html

Non-Traditional Casting Project: works to eliminate discrimination and increase participation of artists of color, female artists and artists with disabilities in theater, film and television. Programs include a national online talent bank, consulting and information services, roundtables and forums, and a resource guide. Available at: http://www.ntcp.org

"Ouch! That Site for Disabled People": funny, hip cultural site from Britain, kind of like *People* magazine, covering television and radio for disabled artists. Available at: http://www.bbc.co.uk/ouch/tvradio/wsa/

University of California Berkeley, Regional Oral History Office, Disability Rights and Independent Living Movement: ongoing project documenting the Independent Living Movement. Available at: http://bancroft.berkeley.edu/ROHO/

World Institute on Disability: a not-for-profit research, training and public policy center promoting civil rights and the full societal inclusion of people with disabilities. Site includes educational and employment resources as well as national and international research programs and initiatives. Available at: http://www.wid.org

As founding director of Mark Taper Forum's Other Voices Project, VICTORIA ANN LEWIS created and directed a series of documentary, community-based plays with a variety of communities, including two television specials for Norman Lear, *Tell Them I'm a Mermaid* in 1983 and *Who Parks in Those Spaces?* in 1985; as well as the stage plays *The Greatest Story Never Told* in 1987 for the AFL-CIO, and *Teenage Ninja Mothers* in 1991, with African American and Latina teen mothers. Ms. Lewis's critical writing has been published in *American Theatre, Radical History Review, Michigan Quarterly Review* and various collections and anthologies. Ms. Lewis's credits as an actress include The Old Globe, Center Theatre Group/Mark Taper Forum, the Los Angeles Theatre Center, the Eugene O'Neill Theater Center and Ensemble Studio Theatre. She was an ensemble member of San Francisco's Lilith Theater, and Family Circus Theater in Portland, Oregon. In 2000, Ms. Lewis received a Ph.D. in theater from UCLA, and she is now an associate professor of theater at the University of Redlands.